HOUSES
of the National Trust

HOUSES
of the National Trust

Lydia Greeves

First published in the United Kingdom in 2008

This revised and updated fourth edition published in 2021 by

National Trust Books,
43 Great Ormond Street
London, WC1N 3HZ

An imprint of Pavilion Books Ltd

ISBN: 9781911657118

A CIP catalogue record for this book is available from the British Library.

10 9 8 7 6 5 4 3 2 1

Reproduction by Rival Colour Ltd, UK
Printed and bound by 1010 Printing International Ltd, China

This book can be ordered direct from the publisher at the website www.pavilionbooks.com, or try your local bookshop. Also available from National Trust shops and www.nationaltrust.org.uk/shop

Lydia Greeves is very grateful to all those in the properties of the National Trust who helped her with this new edition. She would also like to acknowledge 'Joseph Rose and Company' by Ashleigh Murray, from the *Georgian Group Journal* (Vol. XX), as the source of information on the company and their work at Nostell.

Page 2: At The Homewood, one of two modernist houses in the care of the Trust, the living area was designed as a flexible space, which could be turned into one huge room.

Contents

Introduction

The National Trust cares for a large and wonderfully diverse collection of buildings. Of those covered in this book, most are houses, but there is also a good representation of other types of building, from ruined castles and former monasteries, inns, chapels and follies, to the watermills, windmills, tithe barns and market halls that once played such an important part in the rural economy. Between them, they span almost a thousand years of history, from the time of William the Conqueror to the present day. Among the earliest is the remarkable one-storey Norman hall at Horton Court, deep in the Cotswolds, which was built for the prebendaries who were responsible for the church across the road. Dating from the same period is Corfe Castle, now a dramatic ruin standing high on the Purbeck Hills, but once an impregnable stronghold, one of the many built by William the Conqueror in the years after his victory at Hastings to consolidate his hold on his new kingdom. The most recent buildings include the terraced house on a post-war Liverpool estate where Paul McCartney and John Lennon, then in their teens, worked out their first songs and developed the individual sound that would come to define the Beatles, and two examples of modernist domestic architecture: 2 Willow Road, looking over London's Hampstead Heath, and The Homewood, in leafy Surrey.

Although the preservation of buildings and their contents is now seen as a core aspect of the Trust's work, this has not always been so. For the first 40 or so years of its existence, from its establishment in 1895 until the 1930s, the Trust was primarily concerned with the acquisition and protection of the countryside, a focus which partly reflects the principal aims of its founders, Octavia Hill, Robert Hunter and Canon Hardwicke Rawnsley. This determined trio had backgrounds in the Commons Society and the Lake District Defence Society and were only too aware that the beauty of England was being eroded by uncontrolled development. For them, the National Trust was primarily a vehicle for educating public opinion and for acquiring and

LEFT Twisted finials and chimneys ornament the south front of Elizabethan Barrington Court.

safeguarding threatened landscapes that were worthy of protection. Among the first properties to come to the Trust were a stretch of coastline in Wales, part of Wicken Fen in Cambridgeshire, Brandelhow on the west side of Derwentwater in the Lake District, and the shingle spit of Blakeney Point in Norfolk.

The Trust's remit to preserve places of historic interest as well as natural beauty was at first interpreted as applying to small, ancient buildings, as typified by the two properties the Trust acquired in its initial ten years of existence. The first, bought in 1896 for £10, was Alfriston Clergy House, an exquisite, half-timbered building dating from c. 1400 that was in an advanced state of dilapidation. A few years later, in 1903, the Trust bought the tiny medieval manor known as the Old Post Office in the centre of Tintagel, which was threatened by redevelopment for the tourist trade. To be strictly accurate, the Old Post Office was the third building to be acquired by the Trust as, in 1900, Robert Hunter had negotiated the gift of the semi-ruinous Kanturk Castle, a fortified Jacobean manor in Co. Cork. When Ireland was divided in 1921, Kanturk lay in what is now known as the Irish Republic and in 1951 the Trust gave it to An Taisce, the National Trust for Ireland, on a thousand-year lease.

Significantly, these buildings came to the Trust without any contents and this was also true of Barrington Court, the Trust's first substantial property, which was bought in 1907. The purchase price and bill for initial repairs together came to the then massive sum of £11,500. Built of golden Ham Hill stone and with a roofline display of twisted finials, Barrington is a great Elizabethan mansion with an exterior that is as dramatic as that of Montacute, which lies only a few miles away. When bought, though, the house was a shell in an advanced state of dilapidation and without many of its fittings, which had been taken out and sold. Maintaining this property, which was a constant drain on the Trust's slender resources, proved to be a salutary lesson in the pressures and difficulties involved in caring for houses of this size and the need for endowments to cover ongoing expenditure. But anyone who has wandered through Barrington's atmospheric rooms or sat in the beautiful compartmental gardens with their Jekyll-inspired planting will know the Trust's decision was the right one.

Fortunately, in the years before the Second World War, just at the time when owners of great country houses were being faced with ruinous increases in taxation, death duties and running costs, a change in the Trust's status in 1937, which enabled the Trust to hold land and investments to provide for property upkeep, and the introduction of the Country Houses scheme in 1940, by which owners could transfer their houses to the Trust, together with a suitable tax-free endowment, while continuing to live there, paved the way for a number of the finest properties, together with their contents, to be gifted. Blickling was given to the Trust in 1940, Wallington was acquired in 1941, Cliveden in 1942, West Wycombe in 1943, Polesden Lacey and Lacock Abbey in 1944. Many more followed after 1946, when the government decided to accept houses and land in lieu of death duties and to hand suitable properties over to the Trust.

These grand houses, and many smaller acquisitions, offer a unique record of changing tastes and fashions in architecture and decoration and house an unrivalled collection of precious and beautiful things. Moreover, unlike most museums and galleries, where what is on show has no connection with the building in question, the paintings, furniture, books and other contents in Trust properties are often intimately connected with the history of the house and of the family, or families, who have lived there and, in many cases, continue to live there. Bess of Hardwick herself probably worked on some of the Elizabethan embroideries and other hangings which are a unique feature of Hardwick Hall; luminous landscapes by Turner at Petworth reflect the artist's friendship with the 3rd Earl of

Egremont, who arranged for Turner to have a studio in the house; and a shoal of tiny, glittering fish displayed at Ickworth, each a beautifully crafted silver scent bottle or vinaigrette, was acquired by the 3rd Marchioness of Bristol, whose husband was the great-grandson of the eccentric Frederick Hervey, the Earl-Bishop, who was responsible for building this most extraordinary of houses. Gifts and loans of furniture and paintings, such as the Rembrandt self-portrait which was given to Buckland Abbey, with other Dutch works, in 2010, and the donation of particular collections, such as the display of delicate English drinking glasses at Mompesson House, have further enriched what is on offer.

But grandeur is only one side of the story. At many houses, as well as being conducted through the finely decorated show rooms, visitors are also able to see the extensive quarters, often grouped round a courtyard of their own, where an army of servants kept the establishment going, cooking meals of many courses for the dining room, cleaning clothes and linen, brewing beer and making butter, cream and cheese from milk brought in from the home farm. Some 40 servants were employed at Penrhyn Castle in the late nineteenth century, among them the men who tended to the 36 horses in the stables and the French chef who presided over the gastronomic dinners served to the Prince of Wales and his entourage during their visit to the house in 1894. A property may have a prettily tiled dairy, and at Ham House, the great brick palace set beside the Thames just upstream of Richmond, there is even a late seventeenth-century still house, where soaps, sweet-scented waters and ointments were prepared. At Llanerchaeron, in the depths of rural Wales, there are original cheese presses and cream pans made of slate in the buildings grouped round the late eighteenth-century service courtyard. These rare survivals are typical examples of the Trust's extensive collection of the kind of practical objects that were once seen everywhere but are now uncommon, among them such things as leather fire buckets, double-handled creamware pottery jugs used for carrying milk from the dairy to the house, spits and other equipment for roasting meat over an open fire, and a range of carts, carriages and other conveyances. Particularly memorable is the large collection of early bicycles, one of them with a wooden frame as well as wooden wheels, that now hangs in one of the attics at Snowshill, the modest Cotswold manor which Charles Wade, that most individual of collectors, stuffed with a mix of household objects and more precious things.

As Snowshill shows, smaller properties can be just as fascinating as the grander and more imposing places. In many cases, too, more modest buildings enjoy magnificent settings, or take the intrepid visitor on excursions to remote corners of the countryside that would otherwise remain unseen. Anyone who has visited the gentrified farmhouse known as Plas-yn-Rhiw, set in a far corner of the long Llŷn peninsula, will remember the views over the sea towards the mountains of Wales, the tang of salt in the air, and the sense of being somewhere very remote, as much as the little granite-walled house itself, filled with the possessions of the indomitable Keating sisters. Similarly, a visit to Lindisfarne Castle, built on a dolerite crag at the southern end of Holy Island off the Northumberland coast, has all the ingredients of an adventure, not least because this intriguing place, created out of what was once a small Tudor fort, can only be approached over a causeway that is under several feet of water at high tide. And across country to the south, the Tudor hunting lodge of Newark Park, perched high on a spur of the Cotswolds, enjoys panoramic views over wooded slopes plunging to the Severn valley.

Many smaller places have connections to people of note. A little stone cottage set high above the Tyne, and originally thatched with heather from the hills, was the birthplace of the engraver and naturalist Thomas Bewick; Compton Castle, a walled and towered medieval manor hidden in a fold

ABOVE This imposing marble-floored hall at Petworth was created for the proud 6th Duke of Somerset, who remodelled the house in the late seventeenth century.

of the soft south Devon countryside just inland from the sea, is the seat of the Gilbert family, whose Elizabethan forebears include the adventurer Sir Humphrey Gilbert, who claimed Newfoundland for Elizabeth I in 1583; and the half-timbered farmhouse at one end of the little Kentish village of Smallhythe was lived in by the actress Ellen Terry from 1899 until her death in 1928 and is full of mementoes of her life and work. Most recently, in 2017, the Trust acquired the little brick cottage looking out towards the Malvern Hills where Edward Elgar, that most English of composers, was born in 1857.

Most numerous are the properties connected with writers, among them the little cob and thatch cottage where the poet and novelist Thomas Hardy was born in 1840, and which he immortalised in *Under the Greenwood Tree*; the elegant Georgian house on the banks of the Derwent in the little Cumbrian town of Cockermouth where William Wordsworth was born; weather-boarded Monk's House in the village of Rodmell, which Leonard and Virginia Woolf bought as a country retreat in 1919 and where she wrote in a shed at the far end of the garden; and Bateman's, buried in a deep Wealden valley, where Rudyard Kipling produced some of his most celebrated work. In 2000, the Trust was gifted the Greenway estate on the banks of the Dart, where an atmospheric woodland garden plunging steeply to the river surrounds the plain Georgian house which Agatha Christie, one of the best-selling authors of all time, and her husband bought in 1938 as a holiday home.

This book covers both the Trust's grandest places, such as Knole and Petworth, and the many lesser houses and other buildings that are open to visitors. All are worth seeing, but those described in the separate section at the back of the book are, on the whole, the kind of properties that would not detain you long, are not regularly open, or only to be seen by appointment, and do not justify a lengthy detour or a day out. This end section is rich in windmills and watermills, barns and dovecotes, monuments and follies and other small and mostly vernacular buildings, many of them, such as Wilderhope Manor in the remote wooded countryside of Shropshire, or Sticklebarn Tavern in the Lake District, in beautiful surroundings.

Today the Trust is huge, but the philosophy and principles on which it rests remain unchanged. Most importantly, as its founders recognised, it is completely independent of government subsidy, relying for its income on the generosity of the public together with support from bodies such as the Heritage Lottery Fund, Historic Buildings Council and the National Heritage Memorial Fund, which may recommend a grant to make up an endowment or help meet the cost of a major acquisition. Increasingly, too, local authorities have provided financial assistance. Nevertheless, although rich in terms of what it holds, the Trust is always short of money. When Tyntesfield, a major example of Victorian gothic architecture, was due to be sold by public auction in 2001, the necessary funds were only secured by a whirlwind appeal. The sum of over £20 million that was raised included a vital contribution from the National Heritage Memorial Fund. In 2009 the Trust had to dig deep into its own resources to come up with an adequate endowment for Seaton Delaval, John Vanbrugh's theatrical baroque house on the coast of Northumberland.

Secondly, as a result of an Act of 1907, which also gave the infant charity statutory authority, the Trust has the unique power to declare its properties and land inalienable, which means they cannot be sold or mortgaged. This is a priceless asset, which effectively means that anything gifted will be safeguarded for ever.

Thirdly, and again this has been a principle since its early days, the Trust exists to conserve historic buildings and places of natural beauty for everyone to enjoy. Over the years, though, the way in which the history of a place is presented has changed and developed. The contribution of women, people of different ethnic backgrounds and other groups which have been neglected in the past is now being recognised, as is the fact that many estates were acquired, and houses built and furnished, with wealth obtained through slave trading and from plantations worked by slave labour or some other form of exploitation. These troubling histories are now seen as integral to the appreciation of many of the Trust's properties.

Today, tourism, and the visiting of historic properties, is a major activity. But this is nothing new. As Jane Austen shows so clearly in *Pride and Prejudice*, when Elizabeth Bennet and her uncle and aunt go to visit Pemberley, Mr Darcy's grand country house, it was understood that people would turn up at these places and ask to be shown round. Elizabeth and the Gardiners are attended to by the housekeeper, 'a respectable-looking elderly woman', and it was part of a housekeeper's duties to act in this way when the owners were absent, a task that usually brought them a generous tip. Jane Austen was describing the world she knew, of the late eighteenth and early nineteenth centuries, but interest in country seats goes back at least another hundred years. When the pioneer travel writer Celia Fiennes journeyed round England on horseback in the late seventeenth century, visiting the houses of the great was part of her itinerary. By the later eighteenth century, among the educated and leisured, it was commonplace. As Boswell recorded in his journal, he and Dr Johnson were taken round Kedleston in 1777 by the elderly Mrs Garnett, who was housekeeper there for over 30 years and whose portrait by Thomas Barber hangs in the house. When talking to visitors, she presumably referred to the printed catalogue of pictures and statues which she is shown holding in her hands. Some 250 years later, the Trust's guidebooks are the descendants of such catalogues.

OPPOSITE Cragside, set on a steep Northumbrian hillside, is a picturesque array of gables, mullioned windows and soaring chimneys.

A la Ronde

Devon
2 miles (3.2 kilometres) north of
Exmouth on the A376

On the northern fringes of Exmouth, with views across the Exe estuary, is a delightfully uninhibited, late eighteenth-century *cottage ornée*. Looking rather like a dovecote for humans, A la Ronde is a small, sixteen-sided, three-storey house, with rough limestone walls and a steeply pitched conical roof – now tiled but originally thatched – topped off with tall brick chimneys. Dating from a time when Exmouth was a fashionable resort, it was built in *c.* 1795, almost certainly to designs by the Bath architect John Lowder, for two resourceful spinsters: Jane Parminter, daughter of a Barnstaple wine merchant, and her younger cousin Mary. They had both recently returned from an extensive Grand Tour which had occupied them, intermittently, for several years. The design of the house, with wedge-shaped main rooms divided by triangular lobbies, and curious diamond-shaped windows on the exterior angles, is unusual enough; even more so are the decorative schemes initiated by the Parminters.

These are rare survivals of the kind of time-consuming, intricate techniques involving paint and paper, shell and feathers, sand and seaweed, which were much indulged in by Regency ladies but which, due to their fragility, have mostly been lost. The interior of the property stands out, too, for the skilful use of awkward angles and corners. The main rooms are arranged around a central octagon. The eight doors off have marbled yellow and green architraves, ingenious seats fold down over the openings and there are unique painted chairs with octagonal seats. The west-facing drawing room has its eighteenth-century tub chairs and sofa, the original marbled skirting and painted pelmet and the contemporary feather frieze, with a delicate pattern of downy concentric circles that is still largely intact.

Pictures here include a large silhouette group of the Parminter family in 1783 and landscapes of paper, sand and seaweed, with feathery trees stretching out microscopic branches. A chimney board with shellwork surrounding a watercolour of St Michael's Mount (*see* p.292) is a prelude to the gallery at the top of the house. Alas, so fragile that it can only be viewed on video, this is a *tour de force* of feather-, shell- and quillwork, with shell-encrusted recesses and a zigzag frieze setting off feathery bird portraits resting on moss and twigs.

Jane died in 1811, Mary in 1849. Partly due to Mary's will, which aimed to keep the house as it was and to allow only unmarried kinswomen to inherit, A la Ronde had a succession of sympathetic owners who, while adding to the collections and furniture and moving or re-using some of the decorative schemes, preserved the unique character of the place. The most drastic changes were made by A la Ronde's only male owner, the Rev. Oswald Reichel, who lived here from 1886 to 1923. Reichel added the third-storey dormer windows and roofline catwalk, introduced six rectangular windows to light the ground floor and was responsible for a dark Victorian note in some of the rooms. Sadly, his changes also resulted in the loss of the original thatch and of a weather-vane shaped like a dove. After his death, the family struggled to keep the property intact until increasing difficulties brought it to the National Trust in 1991.

OPPOSITE A la Ronde: this whimsical sixteen-sided house on the outskirts of Exmouth was built in the 1790s for Jane and Mary Parminter, who were cousins, and originally had dovecotes hanging from the eaves.
ABOVE LEFT The intricate decoration of the Shell Gallery took years of work to complete.

Alfriston Clergy House

East Sussex
4 miles (6.4 kilometres) north-east of Seaford, between the A27 and the A259, in Alfriston village

Looking over the village green towards Alfriston's fine fourteenth-century church is a small, timber-framed building with a thatched roof. Dating from *c.* 1400, shortly after the parish was taken over by nearby Michelham Priory, it was probably designed for a newly appointed priest. Although much altered, it still has the form of a typical Wealden hall house, with a central hall rising to the rafters flanked by two-storey blocks to either side. Ogee-headed doorways in the hall, which is simply furnished with seventeenth-century pieces, lead to what was once the service wing. A floor that had been inserted over the hall, subdividing the space, was removed by the Trust, who were also responsible for reinstating the original rammed chalk floor, the lumps of chalk being laid and sealed with sour milk.

Bought in 1896 for only £10, when it was virtually derelict, the Clergy House was the first building to come to the National Trust. It is surrounded by a small cottage garden with views of the Cuckmere valley.

BELOW The Clergy House, with its attractive timber framing and thatched roof, is one of a number of historic buildings in the village of Alfriston, which was recorded in Saxon times.

Anglesey Abbey and Lode Mill

Cambridgeshire
In the village of Lode, 6 miles (9.6 kilometres) north-east of Cambridge on the B1102

An interest in horse racing led Huttleston Broughton, later 1st Lord Fairhaven, and his brother Henry to purchase Anglesey Abbey in 1926. A typical stone Jacobean manor house with mullioned windows and tall chimneys, it was conveniently placed for Newmarket and the family stud near Bury St Edmunds and set in good partridge-shooting country. Apart from the vaulted monks' calefactory, or warming room, now the dining room, few traces remained of the Augustinian priory established here in the early thirteenth century from which the house takes its name.

Although his sporting interests were never neglected, over the next 40 years Lord Fairhaven transformed and extended the house, of which he was sole owner from 1932, and filled it with an exceptional and wide-ranging collection of works of art. His taste had been formed as a child in New York where his American mother, the oil heiress Cara Leyland Rogers, had furnished the family house with exquisite things, and where his parents moved in the same circles as the Fricks, Rockefellers and Vanderbilts. And there was no shortage of money. Lord Fairhaven's great wealth came not only from his mother but also from his English father, who made a fortune in American railroads and mining.

Comfortable, intimate interiors, where log fires were kept burning all day, were created with the help of the architect Sidney Parvin, who introduced panelling, antique stone fireplaces, a vaulted corridor, a stone spiral staircase and other 'period' touches. These rooms are the setting for carefully arranged groupings of fine furniture, clocks (of which 39 are on display), silver, tapestries, small bronzes and other statuary, and paintings. In the dining room, the medieval vaulting is complemented by a massive refectory table and by a sixteenth-century carved oak cabinet, but elsewhere objects of very different date and character, some of which Lord Fairhaven inherited from his mother, are set harmoniously together. In the living room, a goat modelled by the great eighteenth-century sculptor Michael Rysbrack sits on a late seventeenth-century poker-work Italian cabinet, a Regency clock devised as a pagoda stands against a French tapestry, and

BELOW The Jacobean south front of Anglesey Abbey, with square-headed mullioned and transomed windows, dates from *c*. 1600, although the period porch was added in the twentieth century.

there are eighteenth-century English landscapes on the walls, one of them a Suffolk coastal scene by Gainsborough. Also here is a medieval wooden carving of St Jerome and the lion, with the beast depicted looking up at the saint affectionately.

Lord Fairhaven's exceptional collection of books, some with very fine bindings, are housed in the spacious and airy library, doubled in size by mirrors on the end walls, that was built on by Sidney Parvin in 1937–8. The 6,000 or so volumes now here, overlooked by John Constable's panoramic riverscape showing the opening of Waterloo Bridge in 1817, include rarities such as Saxton's atlas of the English counties of 1574–9 and many spectacular illustrated books from the period 1770–1820. Intriguingly, the shelves are made of elmwood taken from Waterloo Bridge when it was demolished in 1934. Two exquisite eighteenth-century silver chandeliers in this room, each carrying a royal crown, were designed by William Kent for George II.

Lord Fairhaven had a particular liking for nudes by the fashionable Victorian painter William Etty, about 20 of which, brought from his mother's house, now hang in the abbey. He also acquired a unique collection of views of Windsor, where he lived for a time in the Great Park. Displayed in the two-storey gallery designed by Sir Albert Richardson that was built onto the house in 1955, these paintings faithfully record changes in landscape and architecture over 300 years and range in style from the toy castle depicted in an early seventeenth-century canvas to William Daniell's mistily romantic view down the Long Walk, executed in the early nineteenth century. On the lower floor hang the three paintings for which this space was primarily created, a biblical scene by Aelbert Cuyp, and two of the sublime landscapes by Claude that inspired the naturalistic gardens of the eighteenth century. In *The Landing of Aeneas*, each slave rowing the boat carrying the Trojan leader is an individual, two looking over their shoulders to see how far they are from the shore.

To set off his house, Lord Fairhaven transformed 40 acres (16 hectares) of unpromising fen into a garden on the scale of an eighteenth-century landscape. A composition in trees and grass against the backdrop of towering East Anglian skies, this is a place of long vistas punctuated by an urn, a statue or some other eye-catcher. Broad avenues and walks, such as the wide grassy ride lined by double rows of horse chestnuts which runs

for half a mile (0.8 kilometre) to the west of the house, provide a bold geometric framework, within which are some areas of very different character. Some are grand set pieces, like the curved border in the herbaceous garden, with its spectacular summer displays; others are more intimate and enclosed, such as the small sheltered lawn where William Theed's *Narcissus* contemplates his image in the still waters of a pond. Several

vistas focus on the water-mill at the junction of Quy Water and Bottisham Lode at the northernmost tip of the garden. A white weather-boarded building with a projecting lucarne (dormer window) on the fourth floor, the present structure dates from the eighteenth century, but there has probably been a mill here since the time of the Domesday Book. Today the mill is once again a working water-mill, used for grinding flour.

ABOVE Lord Fairhaven's winter drawing room, where the paintings hung against Jacobean oak panelling include a serene landscape by Claude.

Antony

Cornwall
5 miles (8 kilometres) west of
Plymouth via the Torpoint car ferry,
2 miles (3.2 kilometres) north-west
of Torpoint, north of the A374,
16 miles (25.6 kilometres)
south-east of Liskeard, 15 miles
(24 kilometres) east of Looe

Antony stands at the end of the long neck of land forming the far south-eastern corner of Cornwall, an isolated peninsula bounded by the estuaries of the rivers Tamar and Lynher to the east and north, and by the sea to the south. The best way of approaching Antony is by boat, as it has been for centuries, crossing to Cornwall by the car ferry from Plymouth to Torpoint rather than taking the much longer route by road over the Tamar Bridge. The house is beautifully set. The entrance front faces up a slight rise crowned by a wrought-iron screen, but at the back the ground falls away across terraces to a sweep of grass and woodland beyond. Attractively grouped clumps of trees frame glimpses of the Lynher and of the Forder viaduct carrying Brunel's railway west to Penzance and east to Saltash and Plymouth.

The Antony estate has been the property of the Carews, and their descendants the Pole-Carews and Carew Poles, since the early fifteenth century. The main block of the present house was built by Sir William Carew and his wife Lady Anne Coventry between 1720 and 1724. An elegant, two-storey rectangle faced with beautiful silvery-grey stone, it is ornamented only with the plainest of pediments marking the central bay and with pilasters framing the front door. The architect is as yet unknown. Red-brick colonnaded wings enclosing a courtyard on the south front, thought to have been designed by James Gibbs, were added a little later. It is a charming and entirely satisfying house, one of the best of its date in the West Country, and was built to be lived in, not as a show place: modest, oak-panelled rooms lead off the hall and upstairs there are only five principal bedrooms, the space for a sixth being taken up by the huge and elegant staircase.

Antony is exceptional for the quality of its furnishings and for the collection of family and other portraits. George I pier-glasses in the saloon, where three long windows look out towards the Lynher, and a Soho tapestry hanging in the room next door, were made for the house, and other pieces that have always been here include a set of early eighteenth-century walnut-framed settees and chairs. At the same time, each generation of the family has continued to enrich the house, a

OPPOSITE ABOVE This ship's figurehead greets visitors from one of the brick colonnades enclosing the forecourt.
OPPOSITE BELOW The elegant staircase, rising from an arched opening in the hall, is hung with family portraits.

ABOVE Antony's elegant north front looks across a sweep of grass to tree-framed vistas of the Lynher estuary.

more recent acquisition being the endearing Chinese ceramic figures from the Qing period (1644–1912) displayed over the fireplace in the tapestry room.

The portraits, including several works by Sir Joshua Reynolds, enhance every room. Most memorable is the likeness of Charles I painted at his trial that hangs in the hall. The king is shown dressed in black and wearing a large beaver hat, his sad eyes pouched with weariness. Painted by Edward Bower, this is one of the last of the portraits that record Charles's final days and only here has the famous pointed beard turned grey. John Carew, who had sat in judgement on Charles, was himself executed at the Restoration. His tragic elder brother Alexander, whose portrait hangs in the library, suffered the same fate at the hands of the Parliamentarians, dying with a troubled and divided mind, uncertain which cause was right.

No such doubts assailed the historian Richard Carew, author of the great *Survey of Cornwall*, who inherited the estate in 1564. His striking portrait, painted in 1586 when he was 32, faces Charles across the hall. Two years later he must have seen the Armada sail up the Channel along the coast for which, as deputy lieutenant of the county, he was responsible.

Antony's landscaped setting, with tree-framed lawns sweeping down to the Lynher and views across to the opposite bank, is partly due to Humphry Repton, who was consulted in 1792 and produced one of his earliest Red Books at the house. The terraces above the lawns were once planted with parterres and there is a more formal garden to the west with clipped yew hedges, espaliered fruit trees, a sheltered flower garden and a knot garden. An eighteenth-century dovecote squats by the house; some striking modern sculptures, by William Pye and others, were commissioned by Sir Richard Carew Pole, who until recently lived at Antony; and hidden in a tangle of the Antony Woodland Garden (not owned by the National Trust) beside the Lynher is a bath house of 1784, with a plunge bath that fills with the tide.

Ardress House

Co. Armagh
7 miles (11.2 kilometres) from Portadown on the B28 Moy road, 5 miles (8 kilometres) from Moy, 3 miles (4.8 kilometres) from Loughgall, intersection 13 on the M1

Ardress House is not quite what it seems: the apparently Georgian entrance front disguises what was originally a seventeenth-century farmhouse, one room deep, the roof of which still rises above the urn-studded parapet. Moreover, the long, two-storey façade with an impressive array of sash windows is partly an illusion, one end of it being nothing more than a screen wall with false openings added in the interests of symmetry. There is a pedimented portico giving dignity and importance to the front door, but it is not placed centrally between the windows on either side. Inside, the gradual evolution of the house comes through in the contrast between intimate and homely rooms, a worn flagged floor in the hall, and grander later additions.

This piecemeal gentrification was partly the work of the architect George Ensor, who married the heiress of Ardress, Sarah Clarke, in 1760 and moved here from Dublin some 20 years later. Although he doubled the size of the house, a full remodelling was beyond his means and, apart from adding the classical portico on the entrance front, he concentrated his resources on an elegant new drawing room. Ardress's finest feature, the room is dominated by delicate Adam-style plasterwork. An intricate pattern of intersecting circles and arcs round the central medallion on the ceiling, one of several showing figures and scenes from classical mythology, is picked out in muted tones of yellow, mauve and grey, with a rich blue as contrast, colours that were typically used by architects of the time. Whirls of foliage here are echoed in more extravagant loops and chains framing more medallions on the walls. Playful plaster cherubs stand along the frieze. This exceptional plaster decoration was the work of the outstanding stuccadore Michael Stapleton, who is known for the magnificent interiors he created in eighteenth-century Dublin, where Ensor's brother John was a leading architect.

LEFT Gentrification of Ardress House in the mid-eighteenth century accounts for the Georgian entrance front, which conceals an older building behind.
OPPOSITE One of the plaster medallions decorating the walls of the drawing room.

The lawyer and author George Ensor II's additions to the house in the early nineteenth century, including the extended entrance façade and curving screen walls framing the garden front, are a more mixed bag. His new wing at the back of the house contains a cavernous dining room which, since the Trust demolished an extension giving access, can only be reached from outside. An internal door would upset the Stapleton plasterwork in the drawing room next door. The dining room is now hung with seventeenth-century Dutch and Flemish paintings on loan from the collection of Earl Castle Stewart, among them a rare signed picture by the Flemish artist J. Myts. The diminutive haloed figure of Christ on the road to Emmaus is portrayed in a Northern European setting, with gentlemen in frock coats and a cluster of steep-roofed half-timbered houses marking a little town in the distance.

Fine period furniture includes a locally made oak and applewood bureau-bookcase of 1725 in the little parlour, a mahogany Irish side table with characteristic five-clawed feet and lion's mask decoration in the dining room and a pair of Neo-classical settees in the drawing room. An early nineteenth-century table which sits in the centre of the room is the one on which George V signed the Constitution of Northern Ireland when Ulster was formally separated from the rest of the country in 1921.

A cobbled yard behind the house was the focal point of the estate and is a reminder of the working farm Ardress once was. Outbuildings here include a dairy, a smithy, a cow byre, a threshing barn complete with horse-powered thresher, and a boiler house where large quantities of potatoes were cooked for the pigs. There is a formal garden and landscaped woodland near the house; beyond, the farmland, orchards and woods of the estate slope down to the Tall River.

The Argory

Co. Armagh
4 miles (6.4 kilometres) from
Moy, 3 miles (4.8 kilometres)
from the M1, exit 14

The barrister Walter McGeough Bond's decision to build on his newly inherited land at Derrycaw in the 1820s was influenced by the terms of a very curious will. He and his three sisters had been left the bulk of their father's fortune, their unfortunate elder brother inheriting only £400, but Walter was not allowed to live at Drumsill, the family house, while his sisters remained unmarried. He was wise to provide himself with an alternative establishment as two of his sisters remained at Drumsill until they died, rich and eccentric old spinsters.

Walter McGeough Bond's house was completed in 1824, but in the early 1830s he employed the brothers Arthur and John Williamson, associates of the much more famous Dublin architect Francis Johnson, to remodel and extend it. Echoes of Johnson's austere style appear in the modest two-storey stone building set on a rise overlooking the Blackwater River, its plain Neo-classical façades given added interest by the lengthened centre windows that were introduced on the west and south in the late nineteenth century.

The drawing room, fitted out with mahogany furniture, sumptuous curtains and upholstery, an abundance of cushions and *objets* and fur-draped chairs, is typical of The Argory's largely original interiors, which powerfully evoke the lifestyle of the Irish gentry during the early nineteenth century. The family traditionally entertained at tea-time and the white cloth on the dining-room table is set with china and silver as if awaiting guests. Tea was also occasionally taken at the round walnut table in the organ lobby on the first floor, where

ABOVE The Argory's atmospheric interiors evoke country-house living in nineteenth-century Ireland.

a magnificent instrument made by James Bishop of London was commissioned by Walter in 1822. Three surviving 6-foot (1.8-metre) barrels hold a selection of music chosen on the advice of Samuel Sebastian Wesley, nephew of the founder of Methodism, whose recommendations seem to have resulted in a mixture of suitably uplifting hymn tunes, such as 'See, the conquering hero comes', and excerpts from *The Magic Flute*. The instrument can also be played manually. Personal possessions in the bedrooms have a strong period feel. A wardrobe is filled with Lady Bond's early twentieth-century outfits, including fashionable narrow-waisted jackets and tiny Italian shoes. Another holds her hats.

A unique feature of The Argory is the survival of its historic interior lighting, including some fittings, such as the impressive Argand lamp chandeliers, that were installed when the house was first built. Originally powered by oil, the fittings were converted to gas in 1906 and run from the plant still seen in the stable yard, which was put in by the Sunbeam Acetylene Gas Company of Belfast at a cost of £250. Acetylene gas was viewed as a cheaper alternative to electricity and, to this day, The Argory has no electric lighting.

A little Victorian rose garden leads into the pleasure ground sloping down to meadows fringing the Blackwater River. There is a pair of garden pavilions, of the same date as the house, linked by a long curving walk, and a wide lawn is studded with two yew arbours and a handkerchief tree and framed by shrub borders.

Arlington Court

Devon
7 miles (11.2 kilometres)
north-east of Barnstaple on
the A39

The plain, grey stone façades of this classical house are no preparation for the cluttered Victorian interior, where boldly patterned and coloured wallpaper sets off mahogany furniture and display cabinets overflowing with shells, snuffboxes, model ships, pewter and precious objects. The main block of the house was built in the early 1820s for Colonel John Chichester by the Barnstaple architect Thomas Lee and still has some internal decorative schemes of 1839, designed by John Crace and installed by the decorator George Trollop. But the collections are all the work of Rosalie Chichester, the last of the Chichesters of Arlington, who lived here for 84 years until her death in 1949.

The only child of the flamboyant and extravagant Bruce Chichester, who hung his father's opulent staircase hall with yachting pictures more suited to a gentleman's club than a

BELOW The main block of Arlington Court, marked by the single-storey porch, was built in a plain Greek Revival style in 1820; the service wing to the right was added in 1865.

private house, Rosalie had been taken on two world cruises in her father's schooner *Erminia* before she reached her teens. Perhaps fired by these early experiences, she was always an enthusiastic traveller. Together with her paid companion, Chrissy Peters, who had come to Arlington in 1912, Rosalie visited Australia, New Zealand and America on tours organised by Thomas Cook. The Pacific shells and other mementoes she brought back from her travels were added to her growing collections, among them such things as model ships, tea caddies, candle snuffers and paperweights. Although her stuffed birds, Maori skirts and African clubs are no longer in the house, and the National Trust had to make the rooms less crowded before they could be shown to visitors, Arlington is still full of Rosalie's treasures, including the largest collection of pewter held by the Trust. Her favourite piece, a slightly malevolent red amber elephant from China, is prominently displayed in the Ante Room, one of three sunny rooms that interconnect along the south front. There is a thirteenth-century Flemish psalter in the drawing room next door and a mystical watercolour by William Blake that was found on top of a pantry cupboard in 1949 now hangs in the dining room.

On the first-floor landing another watercolour, of Miss Chichester's parrot Polly, reflects her passionate love of all living plants and creatures. Budgerigars and canaries were kept in brass cages in the house, Polly was allowed to fly around freely and peacocks could wander in from outside.

Shady lawns surrounding the house are planted with specimen trees, including an ash collection. Some distance away is a formal garden laid out in 1865, where a conservatory against a high brick wall looks down over three grass terraces and a fountain pool guarded by metal herons, the birds of the Chichester crest. Next to it is a kitchen garden, which the Trust has revived. To the west of the house, beyond the little parish church filled with Chichester memorials, is the colonnaded stable block remodelled by Rosalie's father. This building and a modern extension now house one of the finest carriage collections in Britain. Largely dating from the nineteenth century, and brought together after the Trust took over the house, the exhibits range from carriages made for children and a pony carriage made for Queen Victoria to a travelling chariot that was driven to Vienna.

ABOVE The boudoir, intended as a ladies' retreat, still has its original rose and gold silk wall-hangings.
OPPOSITE Rosalie Chichester, accompanied by her parrot Polly, spent much of her time in this sunny drawing room at one end of the south front.

Arlington is the centre of a thriving agricultural estate, as it has been ever since the Chichester family came here in the fourteenth century. A walk leads down to the thickly wooded valley of the River Yeo, where two great piers on the lake, half a mile (0.8 kilometre) below the house, are all that was built of the suspension bridge Rosalie's father had planned to carry a grand new drive. The lake and woods, which have been rejuvenated by the Trust, are a haven for wildlife, as Miss Rosalie intended, and the Jacob sheep in the park are descendants of those she introduced here as part of her wildlife sanctuary.

Ascott

Bedfordshire
½ mile (0.8 kilometre) east of
Wing, 2 miles (3.2 kilometres)
south-west of Leighton Buzzard,
on the south side of the A418

Entrepreneurial talent rarely passes from generation to generation, but Mayer Amschel Rothschild (1744–1812), who founded the family banking business in Frankfurt during the Napoleonic Wars, was blessed with five sons whose drive and ambition matched his own. While one inherited his father's mantle, the others went to Paris, Naples, Vienna and London to set up branches of the firm. The wealth generated by this extraordinary clan financed this rambling neo-Jacobean house overlooking the Vale of Aylesbury and the outstanding collection it contains, as well as the more flamboyant magnificence of Waddesdon Manor a few miles away (see p.360).

Ascott is the creation of Leopold de Rothschild, great-grandson of the founder of the family fortunes and son of

Baron Lionel, the first Jewish British MP. The little Jacobean farmhouse he took over in 1876 is now buried in the gabled ranges, all black-and-white half-timbering and diamond-paned windows, added by the architect George Devey and his assistant James Williams in the years that followed, transforming the house into a massively overgrown cottage. But, despite Ascott's size, the rooms are pleasingly domestic in scale. Rothschilds live here still and the atmosphere is that of a beautifully furnished private house. Leopold's son Anthony removed most of the original Victorian décor in the 1930s and recently Sir Evelyn de Rothschild, Anthony's son, has again redecorated the rooms on show.

Predominantly Dutch and English paintings include Aelbert Cuyp's panoramic *View of Dordrecht*, its wide canvas filling one wall of the low-ceilinged dining room. The town lies on the left, a low sun lighting up a row of gabled houses on the glassy river and giving a warm glow to the clouds heaped overhead. A faint mark in the centre of the picture shows where the canvas was once divided so it could be sold in two halves. A striking painting of a woman by Gainsborough, thought to be a likeness of the Duchess of Richmond, her flaming red curls set off by the silky sheen of her blue satin dress, is one of a number of fine English portraits at Ascott. There are three of Stubbs's distinctive horse studies, including the only known canvas in which he shows mares without any foals, and a major work from the Italian Renaissance, Andrea del Sarto's arresting *Madonna and Child with St John*. Elegant eighteenth-century English furniture, such as the two oval pie-crust tables and the walnut and mahogany chairs covered with tapestry and needlework in the oak-panelled library, contrast with the contemporary French pieces elsewhere.

Anthony de Rothschild added paintings and English furniture to his father's collection and also introduced the oriental ceramics that are now such a prominent feature of the house. The earliest pieces are ceramics from the Han (206BC–

OPPOSITE Ascott's gabled, half-timbered ranges date from the late nineteenth century, when an existing Jacobean farmhouse was extensively remodelled for Leopold de Rothschild.
LEFT An exceptional collection of paintings at Ascott includes this portrait of Sarah Ley, Mrs Richard Tickell, by George Romney.

AD220), Tang (618–906) and Sung (906–1280) dynasties, with the cream of the collection, in deep rich colours, from the Ming (1368–1644) and Kangxi (1662–1722) periods. These were the centuries that produced sophisticated, three-colour ware in vibrant shades of blue, purple and burnt yellow, such as the elegant vases decorated with flowing chrysanthemums.

But it is the paintings, one of the best small collections in Britain, that make a visit to Ascott so rewarding. And afterwards visitors can enjoy panoramic views to the Chilterns from the terraced lawns that fall away from the house.

Ashdown House

Berkshire
2½ miles (4 kilometres) south of
Ashbury, 3½ miles (5.6 kilometres)
north of Lambourn, on the west
side of the B4000

Set high up on the rolling, windswept Berkshire Downs, some 2½ miles (4 kilometres) from the nearest village, is this unusual and appealing seventeenth-century house. Built of a pleasing combination of creamy chalk, quarried from the downs nearby, and honey-coloured Bath stone, Ashdown is square in plan and exceptionally tall and narrow, with three main storeys rising to a hipped roof and a crowning cupola. There is something Dutch about it, as if one of the contemporary town houses that are packed tightly along the canals of Amsterdam had been suddenly uprooted and put down in this isolated spot. The architect may have been William Winde (*see* p.49), who spent his early years with exiled Royalists in Holland and would have seen similar buildings in Leiden, Amsterdam and The Hague. Ashdown would look even more out of place in its downland setting were it not for the fact that its outline is broadened and softened by detached pavilions on either side, possibly added some 20 years after the main block was built in the early 1660s.

Appropriately enough, this singular place was constructed for the eccentric and endearing William, 1st Lord Craven. Also one of the richest men of his day, the 1st Lord was devoted to Charles I's sister, Elizabeth of Bohemia, who had reigned for only one winter with her husband Frederick when the forces of the Hapsburg emperor forced them into exile in 1620. Craven met Elizabeth in The Hague, where she and Frederick had taken refuge. He gave her unstinting support, particularly during the English Civil War, and offered her his London house when she returned to England after the Restoration.

Craven intended that Ashdown would be a refuge for the queen from plague-ridden London and had the house designed as a hunting lodge from which to watch the chase, which is why it is so tall. Sadly for Lord Craven, Elizabeth never came here, dying in 1662 before the house was completed. But she left the 1st Lord all her papers and pictures, and this legacy accounts for the portraits of the Winter Queen and her family that now enrich the interior. Presented to the National Trust by the Treasury from the Craven Collection in 1968, these portraits hang in the hall and on the staircase that rises the

height of the building. Echoing the strong associations of the exterior, all except three are works by or after two Dutch artists, Michel Miereveldt and Gerard van Honthorst.

The west front of the house is now set off by a formal parterre based on a seventeenth-century engraving, such as Winde might have designed. The twists and curves of box and gravel are best seen from the roof, and from here there are also spectacular views over the woodland surrounding the house and to the Berkshire Downs beyond. Long breaks cutting through the trees mark the north–south ride that shows clearly on Kip's engraving of 1724.

OPPOSITE Delightful Ashdown House, perched high on the Berkshire Downs, was intended to serve as a grandstand for watching hunting and coursing on the open country around.
BELOW Among the portraits on show is Gerard van Honthorst's painting of Charles I's sister Elizabeth, who was Queen of Bohemia for only one winter before being forced into exile. Like the other pictures from the Craven Collection, it was presented to the National Trust by the Treasury in 1968.

Attingham Park

Shropshire
4 miles (6.4 kilometres)
south-east of Shrewsbury,
on the Telford road

Few family mottoes can be more apposite than that of Noel Hill, 1st Lord Berwick: 'Let wealth be his who knows its use.' This wily politician, who obtained his peerage through expedient loyalty to William Pitt the Younger, poured the fortune he inherited into this grandiose classical house, set, like Wallington (*see* p.362), in full view of a public road, from which it was devised to look as magnificent as possible.

Designed in 1782 by the individual Scottish architect George Steuart, and a rare survival of his work, Attingham consists of a main three-storey block linked by colonnaded corridors to pavilions on either side, with a classical portico rising the full height of the house on the entrance front. Seen from the bridge taking the road over the River Tern, the façade stretches 400 feet (122 metres) from pavilion to pavilion, while inside there are 80 rooms, an unusually large number for a house of this period. The layout of the interior is equally singular, with the rooms on the west side, including the library and dining room, making up a set of masculine apartments, and those on the east, including the drawing room, a set of feminine rooms.

On the 1st Lord's untimely death at the early age of 44, with Attingham not yet completed and furnished, the house passed successively to his two elder sons, who were responsible for the splendid Regency interiors. Acquisitions during a lengthy Grand Tour in Italy formed the basis of an extensive art collection built up by the 2nd Lord, who commissioned John Nash to add the grand picture gallery in 1805–7. One of the first to be built in a country house, this room is notable for the revolutionary use of curved cast-iron ribs to support the windows in the roof, an innovation that was to be used in the design of the Crystal Palace. Although the 2nd Lord's paintings were largely dispersed in a sale of the entire contents of the house that followed his financial ruin in 1827, a disaster that was not helped by his marriage, at the age of 41, to the 17-year-old Sophia Dubochet, who helped him spend his fortune, the mixture of Italianate landscapes and copies of Old Masters now hanging two and three deep in the gallery conjures up the splendour of the original collection. A pair of Neapolitan landscapes by Philipp Hackert (1737–1807) includes a view of Pompeii showing the small extent of the excavated area at the

end of the eighteenth century and the garlanded vines that can still be seen in this part of Italy.

Nash was also responsible for the theatrical staircase, with a mahogany handrail inlaid with satinwood and ebony, which rises confidently to a half landing. In the drum-like space available, however, there was not room for the two flights into which the stairs divide to continue elegantly to the first floor, and Nash hid his unsatisfactory solution behind jib doors.

The Regency flavour continues in the dining room. Boldly decorated in deep red and gold, with gilded mouldings framing a show of portraits, the room is dominated by George Steuart's plasterwork design on the ceiling, with its gilded wreath of lacy vine leaves, and there are more vines decorating an original set

of mahogany dining chairs. The tiny, feminine boudoir on the other side of the house, with a domed ceiling painted with frail tendrils of foliage and medallions depicting cherubs set against rose-tinted clouds, has one of the most delicate late eighteenth-century schemes to survive in England and may be one of the few rooms to have been completed before the 1st Lord's death.

The paintings and furniture now seen in the house were largely collected by the diplomatist 3rd Lord – described by Byron as the only Excellence who was really excellent – during his 25 years in Italy. He was responsible for the collection of white and gold Italian furniture in the drawing room and picture gallery, some of which may previously have belonged to Maria Theresa, Queen of Sardinia, and for the glittering silver displayed in the old wine cellars, once stocked with some 900 bottles of sherry, port and Madeira.

Parkland dotted with mature oaks, elms, beeches and pines slopes gently down to the Tern. The initial layout, of 1769–72, was by Thomas Leggett, but the planting schemes reflect the hand of Humphry Repton, who produced a Red Book for Attingham in 1797. A grove of Lebanon cedars marks the start of Leggett's Mile Walk, which loops down to the river and returns past the walled garden.

BELOW The Scottish architect George Steuart designed Attingham's grandiose entrance front, dominated by a three-storey portico.

The estate, some 3,707 acres (1,500 hectares) of farmland and woodland, stretches across the winding course of the River Severn. On the south side of the river, about 1½ miles (2.4 kilometres) south-west of the house, is Cronkhill, the individual Italianate villa that Nash built for the 2nd Lord in 1802 as an eye-catcher on a low ridge above the river. Built of brick faced in stucco, with round-headed windows and wide-eaved, low-pitched roofs, Cronkhill is delightfully asymmetrical, with a round tower at one end, an arcade enfolding two sides of the main block and a second tower, lower and square in plan, behind. A timber-framed seventeenth-century farmhouse that Nash refaced in brick forms a long south wing, balancing the composition. A pioneering example of the Picturesque style, Cronkhill's design may well have been inspired by the towered and stuccoed rural buildings, of a type seen in many parts of Italy, that often feature in Claude's idyllic landscape paintings, a couple of which were owned by Lord Berwick.

Essentially a residence for a gentleman farmer rather than anything grander, the house was built for Francis Walford, Lord Berwick's agent, who took over the running of the estate in 1804, and it is set close to a group of brick farm buildings. The main reception rooms, ornamented with simple Neo-classical mouldings and fireplaces, reflect the shape of the building: the dining room, in the round tower, being octagonal; the library, in the other tower, being square; and the drawing room, in the main block, rectangular. There is an elegantly curved cantilevered staircase and there are French windows giving access from the main rooms to the arcade, from where there are glorious vistas south over the River Severn and east to the Wrekin. One of Nash's most original buildings, both eye-catcher and viewpoint, Cronkhill marks a watershed in the design of the smaller country house and was to inspire many imitations, even if not as boldly conceived, some of them, such as the villas on the north-western edge of Regent's Park in London, in urban rather than rural settings.

LEFT The intimate boudoir designed for Anne, wife of the 1st Lord Berwick. In the interests of symmetry, it was given five doors, but only two of them give access into the room.

Avebury

Wiltshire
6 miles (9.6 kilometres)
west of Marlborough, 1 mile
(1.6 kilometres) north of the A4
Bath road, at the junction of the
A4361 and the B4003

The leafy village of Avebury is set in a shallow valley below the ridge of the Marlborough Downs. Immense stones incorporated in several buildings were taken from the prehistoric stone circle that is enmeshed with the village, like some surreal sculpture park, with grassy hollows showing where boulders were removed. In early Saxon and medieval times, when this pagan monument was feared, the village stood further west, outside the circle and its massive bank and ditch and close to the River Kennet, with the church set as a shield between the villagers and the prehistoric remains. Over time, as the stones lost their power, the village crept eastwards across the bank and into the circle, where the narrow main street is now lined with some fine eighteenth-century houses as well as earlier buildings, some of brick, some of flint or cob.

The National Trust owns most of the village and also the old manor on an originally monastic site outside the circle bank, beside the ancient St James's church. The manor's charming classical gateway is approached through what was the estate farmyard, past a thatched and weather-boarded great barn and a moss-encrusted sixteenth-century dovecote. Set back across a stretch of grass is a long, asymmetrical, many-gabled range, with tall chimneys and some stone-mullioned windows. This is the eastern and oldest wing of a rambling building set

BELOW Avebury Manor's rambling east range incorporates the oldest part of the building, dating from the mid-sixteenth century.

round three sides of a small courtyard. Incorporated within it is the modest house, one room deep, built by the upwardly mobile William Dunch in *c.* 1557 and still in evidence in the massive roof beams and low, wide Tudor doorways of the kitchen. A more regular mid-eighteenth-century frontage on the south wing, with a roofline parapet, conceals the range added by James Mervyn in *c.* 1600, although the playful classical porch, ornamented with fluted pilasters, was part of the Elizabethan façade. The spacious parlour, with an elegant ribbed plasterwork ceiling extending into the garden from the south end of the Tudor range, may also be an Elizabethan improvement, while on the western side of the house is a 1920s library in the same spirit as the old building, with a pretty flight of stone steps leading down into the garden. Interior remodelling of the south wing in the mid-eighteenth century accounts for the carved and pedimented doorways in the dining room and the deep coved ceiling in the room above, while some seventeenth-century oak panelling and other period features, such as the stone fireplace in the parlour, were introduced by Colonel and Mrs Jenner, who lived at Avebury from 1902 to 1929 and restored the house.

Acquired by the Trust in 1991 without any contents, and for many years let to a tenant, in 2011, as a result of an innovative collaboration with the BBC, the manor was refurnished to show how it might have looked at different times in its history. Nine modest rooms, two of them no more than intimate closets, were refitted in period styles taken from the sixteenth to the twentieth century in an approach that linked the house to people associated with it. Traditional skills and materials were used to make appropriate furnishings, although these are in many cases modern interpretations of period designs rather than direct reproductions.

In the parlour, the original plasterwork is now accompanied by an heraldic panel over the fireplace incorporating the coat of arms William Dunch acquired in 1550, and by specially made, Tudor-style oak furniture and rush matting. In the Georgian dining room, some pieces of armorial porcelain and hand-painted Chinese wallpaper allude to the tenure of Sir Adam Williamson, who became governor of Jamaica; motifs on the wallpaper include illustrations of the kind of English trading ships that would have called at Jamaica, and of the manor and stone circle. The bedroom above, with its eighteenth-century

coved ceiling, is fitted out with a state bed and high-back chairs as part of a suite of rooms that could well have been prepared for Queen Anne when she came to dine at the manor; while an Art Deco parlour in the Tudor part of the house reflects the interests of the archaeologist Alexander Keiller, who lived here while excavating the stone circle in the late 1930s.

Some furnishings have been bought or salvaged rather than specially made and just a few, such as the semi-circular tables which stand either side of the fireplace in the dining room, are genuine antiques. All the rooms are based on historical parallels and evidence, such as the inventory made

OPPOSITE Avebury's Georgian dining room, where the hand-painted Chinese wallpaper includes depictions of the manor and of the great stone circle which enfolds the village.
BELOW In the Tudor bedroom, decorative oak panelling introduced by the Jenners complements the original plasterwork frieze, shown here before it was brightly painted as part of the recent transformation of the manor.

on Sir Adam's death in 1798, and a sale catalogue of 1902, but a sense that this is theatre rather than historic experience is heightened by some defiantly modern interpretations of the real thing. Dunch's parlour is lined by printed hangings imitating tapestry and some specially commissioned paintings include three acrylics by Corin Sands, one of which is a take on the exotic bird paintings that were much admired in the early eighteenth century.

The manor is surrounded by a beautiful compartmental garden developed by Colonel and Mrs Jenner and laid out within an existing framework of Tudor and eighteenth-century walls in brick and stone. There is much clipped yew and box and gateways give views out into the countryside and of the pinnacled tower of the church.

Baddesley Clinton

Warwickshire
¾ mile (1.2 kilometres) west of
the A4141 Warwick–Birmingham
road, at Chadwick End, 7½ miles
(12 kilometres) north-west of
Warwick, 15 miles (24 kilometres)
south-east of central Birmingham

This exceptional medieval manor house set in an ancient park lies in a remnant of the Forest of Arden. Although only 15 miles (24 kilometres) south-east of Birmingham, the surrounding countryside, criss-crossed by a network of sunken lanes, still has an essentially medieval character, with the waves of former ridge and furrow showing in fields that are now under grass.

The present house, built round three sides of a courtyard, dates from the fifteenth century, but it is encircled by a moat that is probably much older and was dug to surround an earlier building. The only way into the manor is over the two-arched, eighteenth-century bridge that leads to the crenellated gatehouse. Grey walls punctuated with mullioned windows fall sheer to the water on either side and there are tall, red-brick Elizabethan chimneys that form splashes of colour against the roof. Despite its guarded appearance, this is not a forbidding place. Its small panelled rooms, filled with mostly seventeenth- and eighteenth-century oak furniture, are intimate and homely.

Baddesley Clinton is a remarkable survival. From the early sixteenth century until 1980, when it came to the National Trust, this romantic moated house was lived in by generation after generation of the Ferrers family who, despite financial pressures, managed to preserve the manor and the estate. In 1940, when the house was first offered for sale, the estate lands were the same as those shown on a map of 1699. Succeeding generations have left their mark on the manor. Henry Ferrers, the Elizabethan antiquary who owned the house from 1564 to 1633, did much to embellish it, rebuilding the south range and introducing oak panelling, carved heraldic overmantels and richly coloured armorial stained glass. Much of this decoration survives, although some, such as the stone chimneypiece now in the great hall, was once elsewhere. Although a Catholic, Henry seems to have avoided penalties for recusancy, despite the fact that Eleanor Brooksby, the widow to whom he let the house in the late sixteenth century, when persecution was at its height, sheltered Jesuit priests here and created hiding places for them. One of these, formed out of an old sewer and viewable through a glass panel in the kitchen floor, is where

ABOVE Henry Ferrers, the Elizabethan antiquary who remodelled Baddesley Clinton in the 1570s, was responsible for the great hall, with its oak panelling. The magnificent fireplace was made for Henry, but was originally elsewhere in the house.

eight men evaded capture in October 1591, standing motionless with their feet in water for four hours. Then, in 1604, Henry was unwittingly involved in the Gunpowder Plot when his Westminster house, which he had let to one of the plotters, was used to store the gunpowder for blowing up Parliament. Although he was never penalised for his religion, Henry died heavily in debt and the family was further impoverished by taxation and appropriations during the Civil War. But this shortage of funds is probably the reason why Baddesley survived unchanged.

At the end of the nineteenth century, the manor's medieval character was further enhanced by an artistic quartet. In 1867 Marmion Edward Ferrers had married Rebecca Dulcibella Orpen, whose romanticised portraits of her friends and life at Baddesley are now a feature of the house. Two years later the couple were joined by Rebecca's aunt, Lady Chatterton, a romantic novelist, and her husband Edward Dering, who devoted his fortune to the house and estate. All four revelled in the antiquity of the place, added further stained glass and other embellishments and created the Catholic chapel,

sumptuously fitted out with leather hangings decorated with flowers and birds in gold, pink and blue. Both Lady Chatterton and Rebecca liked to paint in the great parlour on the first floor of the gatehouse, lit by a great mullioned and transomed window inserted in the 1630s. Today, the high barrel ceiling, sparse furnishings and rippling reflections from the moat create a sense of airy spaciousness that contrasts with the dark intimacy of the rest of the house.

ABOVE Baddesley Clinton, one of the most romantic of medieval houses, is surrounded by a moat that was probably dug to protect an even older building.

Barrington Court

Somerset
2 miles (3.2 kilometres) north
of the A303 between Ilchester
and Ilminster, at the east end of
Barrington village, ½ mile
(0.8 kilometre) east of the B3168

Twisted finials and chimneys reaching skywards from every gable and angle transform Barrington's roofline into a forest of stone fingers. Pre-dating Montacute, which lies some 10 miles (16 kilometres) or so to the east (*see* p.224), by about 40 years, this fine mid-sixteenth-century house has the same indefinable charm, a blend of romance, fantasy and age. Completed by 1559, it is an early example of the characteristic Elizabethan E-plan, with long wings projecting either side of the original entrance court on the south front. Honey-coloured façades of Ham Hill stone with generous mullioned windows and buttressed gables are typical of the best architecture of the day.

But, unlike Montacute, Barrington was not designed for a high-flying politician. Although Henry Daubeney, the ambitious Tudor courtier who owned the estate in the early sixteenth century, may have planned a grand country seat here after he was created Earl of Bridgwater in 1538, he died bankrupt ten years later. Barrington was built by William Clifton, a prosperous London merchant, who bought the property in 1552. William Strode, whose father had acquired Barrington in 1625, was responsible for the fine late seventeenth-century stable block in the style of Wren which sits beside the house.

From the outside, Barrington belongs to the Elizabethan age and the plan of the house is still essentially sixteenth century. But almost everything else about it, including its setting, is the result of restoration and remodelling in the 1920s. During a long period of decline in the nineteenth century, most of the original decorative features were torn out and sold and the court became a farmhouse, ultimately being used to store cider and keep chickens. When the National Trust bought the house, in 1907, it was an empty, derelict shell, with 'attics full of owls'. It was rescued by Colonel A. Lyle, who took a long lease on the place in 1920, restored the court and filled it with his collection of period woodwork rescued from other derelict houses. Deceptively authentic oak panelling, such as that lining the magnificent gallery that runs the length of the house on the top floor, and other decoration,

including a honeycomb of wooden ribs covering the ceiling of the small dining room, was brought here by Lyle. Lacking a staircase to replace the one that had been lost, he had a replacement made in oak and then sandblasted to look old.

Colonel Lyle was much helped by his friend, the architect J. Edwin Forbes, who prepared a master plan for remodelling both court and stables and for redesigning the surrounding landscape. The present entrance on the north side of the house, approached down an avenue of mature chestnuts and across a spacious grassy forecourt, was all part of Forbes's vision, as was the row of cottages in Arts and Crafts style beside the drive. Forbes converted the stables into additional accommodation for the Lyles, adding the tall chimneys that are now such a distinctive feature of the place, and he designed new farm buildings.

Strode House, as the old stable block is called, is now a shop and restaurant. The court is shown as a sequence of atmospheric, unfurnished rooms. The library in the east wing, lit by windows on three sides, is painted a soft sea-green as the Lyles had it and the great hall, with a gallery at one end and a sprung floor for dancing, is where the Lyles held

ABOVE A great display of twisted finials and chimneys marks the roofline of the early Elizabethan Barrington Court, which was the first country house to be acquired by the Trust.
LEFT In the 1920s, Colonel Lyle enriched the house with period woodwork salvaged from elsewhere, such as these seventeenth-century oak doors.

a ball in 1925 to celebrate the restoration. Upstairs rooms interconnect as they would have done in Tudor times, there are some period bathrooms, and a few original features include a painted overmantel bearing the Strode arms in the former Great Chamber.

Barrington is approached from the west through an enchanting formal garden, the only part of Forbes's scheme for an Elizabethan-style layout round the house to be fully realised. Laid out in brick-walled compartments, it was originally planted with advice from Gertrude Jekyll and is enclosed on two sides by the moat Forbes created to evoke Barrington's Tudor origins.

Basildon Park

Berkshire
Between Pangbourne and Streatley, 7 miles (11.2 kilometres) north-west of Reading, on the west side of the A329

This classical mansion standing high above the River Thames, with views to wooded slopes rising to the Chilterns across the valley, was built between 1776 and 1783 by the Yorkshire architect John Carr. One of Carr's best works and his only house in the south of England, it was commissioned by another Yorkshireman, Francis Sykes, who had bought the Basildon property in 1771. Sykes was one of the self-made men who made vast fortunes in the service of the East India Company. He was also politically ambitious and managed to obtain a Parliamentary seat, for Shaftesbury, in 1768, the year he returned from India. Being close to London, Basildon was an ideal choice for someone with political aspirations and several other men who had made themselves rich in India lived in the tranquil countryside

BELOW A dramatic portico, with massive columns standing out against the shadowy recess behind, dominates Basildon's entrance front.

round about, among them his friend Warren Hastings. Sykes lost his Parliamentary seat in 1773, when there was an enquiry into the activities of the Company and he was charged with corruption, but he re-established himself in the 1780s, was made a baronet and became a Member of Parliament again, for Wallingford, in 1784.

John Carr's Palladian villa, built of beautiful honey-coloured Bath stone, is both restrained and suitably grand. A pedimented portico, its massive columns standing out against a deep shadowy recess behind, dominates the three-storey entrance front looking over the park. To either side, linked to the main house by screen walls that hide service courtyards, are two-storey pavilions, their pedimented façades echoing the design of the central block. Originally, all three parts of the house were linked internally but this is no longer so, the windows and doors on the screen walls being only dummies.

Carr's classical decoration in the hall, with its delicate plasterwork ceiling subtly coloured in pink, lilac, green and stone, survives unaltered. His magnificent staircase, lit from above by graceful lunettes and with an elegant wrought-iron balustrade that curves gently upwards, is also little changed. But other interiors were never completed by Carr, probably because Sykes was distracted by financial and family concerns. He was devastated by the death of his son John at sea, and his heir, Francis William, amassed large gambling debts and was involved in an expensive trial for adultery. Sir Francis lost money on his investments too. In 1838 the decline in the family fortunes forced his grandson to sell to the Liberal MP James Morrison, a similarly self-made man whose upward path in life had been eased by marriage to his employer's daughter, Anne Todd. Now a merchant prince, he needed a suitably grand setting to display his considerable collection of pictures. Morrison employed his architect-friend J.B. Papworth to complete the house and he and his ten children lived here in style. This was Basildon's golden age. A fast train link with London brought many distinguished visitors, J.M.W. Turner and Bishop Samuel Wilberforce among them.

On James Morrison's death, in 1857, Basildon passed first to his son Charles and then, briefly, to his daughter Ellen, who died only seven months after her brother in 1909. Major James Archibald Morrison, Charles's and Ellen's nephew, who then inherited, had a passion for country pursuits and mainly used

Basildon for shooting parties, while also offering the house as a convalescent home for wounded officers during the First World War. But James Archibald's lavish lifestyle and three marriages seriously eroded the fortune he had inherited and he was forced to sell the estate. Its purchase by a property developer in 1929 was the start of over twenty years of decay and neglect. During these years, Basildon survived a scheme to re-erect it in America (no purchaser could be found) and plasterwork and other fittings were removed.

The house was saved by the 2nd Lord and Lady Iliffe, who bought it in 1952 and restored it with great skill, installing mahogany doors, marble chimneypieces and other fittings, such as the mouldings used to create the pedimented bookcase in the library, salvaged from another Carr house, Panton Hall in Lincolnshire, to replace what was missing. They filled Basildon with period furnishings and the kind of seventeenth- and eighteenth-century paintings Sir Francis Sykes might have acquired on a Grand Tour and which suit the house, among them, for example, the landscapes by Orizzonte and Galeotti's vast *Rebecca at the Well* which hang in the Green Drawing Room. The cream of the Iliffes' collection was hung in the adjoining Octagon Drawing Room, the grandest room in the house, with its three great windows looking over the Thames. Clustered round the doors on either side and set against red walls in accord with eighteenth-century taste are vivid portrayals of seven of the apostles and God the Father by Pompeo Batoni, whose skills as a portraitist were much sought after by visitors to Rome. Furniture in this room includes a pair of gilt pier tables of the 1780s with exquisite marquetry tops standing below finely crafted mirrors of the same date. Among other treasures in the house is a crimson state bed of *c.* 1829 with its accompanying suite of furniture that was bought at the sale of the contents of Ashburnham Place, once one of the finest houses in south-east England, in 1953. Sykes himself ordered the armorial porcelain laid out in the dining room. Dating from 1765 to 1770, this features a woman of Bengal, where Sykes had been Resident at the Nawab's Court, on the crest.

Likenesses of the Iliffes, his by Graham Sutherland, hers by Frank Salisbury, who portrays her in a simple white dress, are also in the house and what was Lady Iliffe's sitting room is now devoted to some of Sutherland's watercolour studies for his great tapestry, *Christ in Glory*, which hangs behind the altar

ABOVE Lady Iliffe covered the walls of the Octagon Drawing Room, the grandest room in the house, with red felt, which she put up herself with the help of the cook.

in Coventry Cathedral. The study for Christ's head, many times life-size, hangs above the fireplace, while his two huge hands, raised in blessing, are set over the doors to either side.

Parkland studded with carefully placed chestnuts, beeches and limes still comes right up to the entrance front, as it did in Sir Francis Sykes's day. James Morrison added the balustraded terrace walk that now frames a lawn at the back of the house, and he also introduced the pair of huge stone dogs set on plinths on the north side of the grass, which he bought on a trip to Italy in 1845–6. Lord and Lady Iliffe were responsible for most of the other garden ornaments and some of their planting, such as the white rambling rose on the terrace balustrade and the wildflower meadow near the rose garden, survives.

Bateman's

East Sussex
½ mile (0.8 kilometre) south of
Burwash on the A265; approached
by the road leading south from
the west end of the village

This modest Jacobean house lies in the richly wooded Dudwell valley, deep in the Sussex Weald. Built in about 1634, as the date over the porch records, and constructed of sandstone from a quarry just across the lane, it has traditional gabled façades, stone-mullioned windows and a massive central chimney-stack formed of six brick columns. A tradition that the house was built by a local ironmaster may reflect the fact that the Wealden iron industry was at its height in the early seventeenth century, when there were several forges on the River Dudwell.

In 1902 this peaceful and secluded place was bought by the 36-year-old Rudyard Kipling, then at the height of his fame as a writer, and his wife Carrie. This is where they lived for the rest of their lives, he dying in 1936, she three years later. Kipling broods over the stairs in a painting by John Collier, his dark three-piece suit slightly too big for him, the eyes behind the glasses tinged green and blue. In tune with Edwardian appreciation of seventeenth-century furniture and design, he and his wife created interiors that perfectly complement the building and which are still as the Kiplings left them. At the top of the stairs is the book-lined study where Kipling wrote, flinging himself down on the day-bed to smoke and review what he had done, or when inspiration deserted him. The room is still much as he had it, although much tidier. The long, early seventeenth-century walnut refectory table under the window where he worked still has his array of 'writing tools' and 'essentials', among them a canoe-shaped pen tray, boxes of clips and pins flanking the blotter and a fur seal he used as a paperweight. The large Algerian wastepaper basket beside the desk was where he threw discarded drafts of the stories and poems that he wrote and rewrote, honing what are now classics of the English language.

Kipling produced some of his greatest works here, including *Puck of Pook's Hill*, called after the hill visible from the house, 'If' and 'The Glory of the Garden'. For these he drew his material from the Kent and Sussex countryside, no longer looking east to the India of his childhood for inspiration. But the house also reflects his strong links with the sub-continent, with oriental rugs in many of the rooms and Kipling's large collection of Indian artefacts and works of art on display in the parlour and study. His delightful bookplate shows a diminutive figure reading on top of an elephant.

The peaceful garden running down to the River Dudwell owes much to the Kiplings, who laid out paths and hedges, planted the rose garden and created the pond, paying for the work out of the £7,700 he received for the Nobel Prize in 1907. Kipling's sundial is engraved with the words 'It is later than you think'. As might be expected from the author of *Kim*, the pond was designed with young people in mind, shallow enough for his children and their friends to use for boating and bathing. It is immortalised in the visitors' book, where the initials FIP stand for 'fell in pond'. There are two eighteenth-century oast-houses near the house and beyond, in a garage beside the potting sheds, is the Rolls-Royce Kipling bought in 1928. On the river, where the garden becomes half-wild, with trees and bulbs in long grass, is an eighteenth-century water-mill. Kipling converted it to produce electricity when he first came to Bateman's, but it has now been restored for grinding flour.

ABOVE The study at Bateman's is where Kipling worked, sitting at the table by the window and writing on pads of blue paper that were specially made for him.

ABOVE Bateman's, where Rudyard Kipling lived for over 30 years, lies deep in a
wooded valley of the Sussex Weald.

Bath Assembly Rooms

North Somerset
In Bennett Street, north of
Milsom Street, east of the Circus

Although Bath had been known as a spa since Roman times, it was only under the influence of Richard 'Beau' Nash, the leader of fashion in eighteenth-century Britain, that what had been a provincial watering place became an international resort. Visionary town planning and elegant architecture by John Wood and his son was transforming the city, turning it into a suitable setting for fashionable society. By 1769, when work started on the Assembly Rooms – the third set to appear in the town – John Wood the Elder had died, leaving Queen Square and the partially finished Circus as his showpieces. John Wood the Younger carried on his father's work, completing the Circus and designing beautifully proportioned streets, terraces and public buildings to realise his father's vision, a scheme that would be crowned by Wood the Younger's Royal Crescent, completed in 1775.

His elegant Assembly Rooms, just east of his father's Circus, were completed in 1771 and were described in the *Bath Guide* for 1772 as 'the most noble and elegant of any in the kingdom'. Straight from the world of Jane Austen, they were a place where the company could amuse themselves with dancing or playing cards, strolling from one pursuit to another as the fancy took them and refreshing themselves with ices and claret cup or by drinking tea. Built in the Palladian style, the Rooms are set across a wide pavement, with two austere classical façades to either side of the central pedimented entrance. This plain exterior gives no hint of the splendours within. The magnificent 100-foot (30-metre) ballroom rises through two floors to a high coved ceiling, with Corinthian columns picked out in white against blue flanking windows at the level of the second floor and lining the interior wall. The largest eighteenth-century room in Bath, it would have been filled with 800 to 1,200 people on ball nights. The five great candlelit chandeliers illuminated the glittering company and an orchestra set on a stage at one end provided music for the dancing. Those who came here were expected to conform to certain standards of dress and behaviour, as laid down by the Master of Ceremonies. Captain William Wade, the Rooms' convivial and decorative host from their opening in 1771 until 1777, still scrutinises visitors from Gainsborough's full-length portrait. His published rules included instructions on where to sit, as well as exhortations on dress such as 'no Lady dance country-dances in a hoop of any kind'.

The tea room, with a double screen of columns at one end, is similarly splendid. Completing the original suite was the Octagon, or card room, where an organ was provided for entertainment when card-playing was banned on Sundays, but in 1777 another card room was added to cope with the numbers who flocked here. During the Regency, Bath lost its status as *the* fashionable resort as seaside towns such as Brighton became increasingly popular. Concerts graced by such celebrities as Johann Strauss and Franz Liszt continued to draw people in, but the Rooms became primarily a venue for lectures, notable speakers who appeared here included William Wilberforce and Charles Dickens, and were increasingly poorly attended. They closed at the start of the First World War, although they were briefly turned into a cinema in the 1920s. They were restored by the City of Bath after they had been presented to the National Trust in 1931, only to be severely damaged by bombs in 1942. Reconstruction began in 1946, initially under the close supervision of Sir Albert Richardson, whose determination ensured the accurate reproduction of original features. Subsequent redecoration, and major restoration in the late 1980s, has been based on original colour samples found in the City Archives, thus re-creating the complete eighteenth-century scheme.

ABOVE LEFT After incendiary bombs gutted the Bath Assembly Rooms in 1942, every detail of the plasterwork and other decoration was re-created.
OPPOSITE The magnificent ballroom was filled with dancers on ball nights. Spectators looked on from settees arranged in tiers along the walls and an orchestra set on a stage at one end provided music for the dancing.

The Beatles' Childhood Homes

Woolton and Allerton
Liverpool

The distinctive musical voice of the Beatles, the sound of the '60s, was born in two unremarkable houses in the suburbs of Liverpool. Set less than a mile (1.6 kilometres) apart on either side of Allerton Park, but in different leagues socially, are the childhood homes of John Lennon and Paul McCartney, whose song-writing partnership was the engine behind the Beatles' success. No. 20 Forthlin Road, where the McCartney family moved in 1955, when Paul was 13 and his brother Michael 12, is part of the Mather Avenue estate, built between 1949 and 1952 by Liverpool Council.

A two-storey, brick-built house with three rooms on each floor, there is nothing special about No. 20, although the city architect, Sir Lancelot Keay, planned the estate well, specifying good materials and such modern conveniences as an inside toilet, which the McCartneys' previous house had not had.

Where Forthlin Road is part of a terrace, Mendips in Menlove Avenue, where John came to live in 1945 at the age of 5, is a 1930s, pebble-dashed semi designed to appeal to the aspiring middle-classes who would value its bay windows, leaded panes, Art Nouveau-style stained glass and other tasteful features, such as Art Deco fireplaces. At Mendips, John was brought up by his mother's sister, Aunt Mimi, and her husband George, who, childless themselves, gave John the stable and loving home he needed after his parents' marriage had fallen apart. After George's sudden death in 1955, it was the rock-like Mimi who kept John's teenage rebelliousness within bounds. Early experiences and interests fed through into John's later writing, among them his love of nonsense

ABOVE LEFT The houses are full of period details.
BELOW The living room at Forthlin Road has been re-created as the McCartneys had it, with protective coverings on the arms of the suite and runners sewn together covering the floor.

verse, which was a continuation of his childhood enthusiasm for the fantasy world of Lewis Carroll, and his use of lyrics inspired by newspaper headlines, which was rooted in the fact that Uncle George used the *Liverpool Echo* to teach John to read. The teenage Lennon would sit writing poetry and songs in the front room, encouraging Mimi to keep what he threw aside because he 'would be famous one day'. And he practised the guitar which he had badgered his mother into getting him until his fingers were raw.

Paul had the advantage of being part of a musical household. His father Jim, who brought up the boys after their mother died not long after the move to Forthlin Road, played show tunes on the upright piano which dominated the living room; he rigged up extensions from the radio so the boys could listen to Elvis, Fats Domino and other idols while they were in bed; and, inspired by seeing Lonnie Donegan at the Liverpool Empire in 1956, Paul bought an acoustic guitar on which, like John, he practised for hours.

When Paul was 15 and John 17, the boys met at a church fête in Woolton where John was performing with his skiffle group. Paul joined the band and he and John started to compose songs at Mendips, among them 'Please Please Me'. But, although Mimi warmed to John's new friend, the noise they made did not go down well. They tried taking refuge in the glazed porch, which has an ideal bathroom acoustic, but then retreated to Forthlin Road. Paul was still at school, John at art college, but they would both play truant in the afternoons and practise undisturbed while Jim was out at work. 'Love Me Do' and 'I Saw Her Standing There' both came out of these afternoon sessions, and the lyrics they scribbled down in a school exercise book immortalised places in the neighbourhood, such as Penny Lane and Strawberry Field.

Paul's friend George Harrison, whom he had got to know on the bus to school, joined them in 1958 and in 1960, with Pete Best playing the drums, they began to call themselves the Beatles and got their first big break, in Hamburg. A year later they had their debut at Liverpool's Cavern Club and their new manager, Brian Epstein, whose father had sold Jim his upright, had got them an EMI recording contract; in 1962 Ringo Starr replaced Pete, and in 1963 the boys took off, with concerts all over the country, recording sessions and television and radio appearances.

ABOVE The kitchen at Mendips, where John's Aunt Mimi would cook his favourite meal of egg and chips.

At Forthlin Road, Jim and Michael were increasingly besieged by fans and in 1964 Paul bought his father a new house 5 miles (8 kilometres) from Liverpool. No. 20 was sold to the Jones family, who lived here for 30 years and made a number of changes, such as replacing the sash windows. The National Trust acquired the property in 1995 and has returned it to what it would have looked like when the McCartneys were living in the house. The back garden still has its original coal shed and outside WC, and there are displays of Beatles memorabilia loaned by Hunter Davies and evocative photographs by Michael McCartney.

Mimi stayed on at Mendips after the Beatles became famous, but in 1965, when she retired to a bungalow that John had bought her in Dorset, the house was sold. John's second wife, Yoko Ono, generously bought the house when it subsequently came up for sale and gave it to the Trust in 2002. Now presented with a 1950s interior, it conjures up the world of Lennon's formative years with authentic touches, such as the posters in his former bedroom.

Beatrix Potter Gallery

Cumbria
In Hawkshead, next to the
Red Lion Inn

As well as Hill Top, the little farm she purchased in 1905 (*see* p.175), and the village of Near Sawrey, Beatrix Potter also captured the nearby market town of Hawkshead in several of the delicate illustrations for her children's books. A cluster of small, limewashed houses ranged round three squares and along two main streets, the town still looks very much as she knew it in the late nineteenth and early twentieth centuries. Next to the Red Lion Inn, overlooking one of the squares in the centre of town, is the low, cream-coloured building where Beatrix Potter went to consult the local solicitor, W.H. Heelis & Son, on her property purchases in the district, all of which were to come to the National Trust. William Heelis, the junior partner she saw regularly over the years, not only gave advice on her acquisitions, but also kept an eye on her property when she was away and attended sales on her behalf. In 1912 he asked her to be his wife.

William Heelis left the building to the Trust on his death in 1945, although it continued to be a solicitor's office until 1988. A gallery since then, the intimate rooms are now used for a changing exhibition of Beatrix's watercolours, including illustrations for her children's books, and of her sketches and other ephemera from the Trust's Beatrix Potter collection, with a different aspect of her life illustrated every year.

BELOW This small house in the middle of Hawkshead, now the Beatrix Potter Gallery, was once the offices of W.H. Heelis & Son, where Beatrix Potter discussed business with her future husband.

Belton House

Lincolnshire
3 miles (4.8 kilometres)
north-east of Grantham on the
A607 Grantham–Lincoln road

Belton is at peace with the world. Built in the last years of Charles II's reign to an H-shaped design by the gentleman-architect William Winde, its simple Anglo-Dutch style seems to express the confidence and optimism of Restoration England. Symmetrical honey-coloured façades look out over the tranquil, wooded park, the grandeur of the broad flight of steps leading up to the pedimented entrance front offset by domestic dormers in the steeply pitched roof and a delightful crowning cupola.

The interiors reflect Belton's long association with the Brownlow and Cust families, descendants of the ambitious and wealthy Elizabethan lawyer who bought the estate in 1609. Family portraits hang in almost every room, from Reynolds's imposing study of Sir John Cust, Speaker of the House of Commons from 1761 to 1770, which greets visitors in the marble hall, to Lord Leighton's magical portrait at the top of the stairs of the last Countess Brownlow as a young woman, the colour of the bouquet she holds against her long white dress echoed in the autumnal trees behind.

High-quality decorations and furnishings, including magnificent wall mirrors, a brilliant-blue Italian lapis lazuli cabinet and the remnants of an extensive collection of Old Masters, speak of wealth well spent. Glowing panelling lines the formal seventeenth-century saloon in the middle of the house, setting off delicate limewood carvings with minutely realised fruit and flowers that suggest the hand of Grinling Gibbons. Early eighteenth-century gilt wall mirrors between the three long windows looking onto the garden reflect a set of Charles II walnut chairs arrayed on the pink and green Aubusson carpet, their seats and backs upholstered in faded crimson velvet and a host of cherubs adorning the frames. Two more cherubs, their grumpy expressions perhaps due to their rather precarious position, perch uncomfortably on the monumental reredos in the largely unaltered north-facing chapel, where an exuberant baroque plaster ceiling by Edward Goudge contrasts with James Wyatt's Neo-classical compositions of the 1770s in other parts of the house.

Apart from the silver awarded to Speaker Cust for his service to the House of Commons, and the fine porcelain seen in almost every room, such as the massive blue-and-white Chinese Kangxi vases in the Marble Hall, some of the most prized pieces at Belton are the vast paintings by Melchior d'Hondecoeter acquired by the 3rd and last Earl. He and his wife presided over a golden age in the late nineteenth century, when Belton was sympathetically restored. The last Earl also made changes to the garden, adding a final layer to the harmonious blend of styles and periods that characterises the grounds. To the north of the house is his re-creation of a baroque Dutch layout, a formal composition of clipped yew and gravel walks punctuated

RIGHT Grinling Gibbons may have carved the limewood garland framing this portrait of 'Old' Sir John Brownlow, whose investments in sheep farming in the seventeenth century greatly increased the family's wealth.

by urns and pieces of sculpture, among them an eighteenth-century sundial clasped by Father Time. Further from the house is the more extensive sunken Italian garden dating from 1810 that was designed by Jeffry Wyatville and is overlooked by Wyatville's elegant orangery of 1820.

The last Earl's Dutch garden was based on an engraving of the original elaborate baroque layout. A lime avenue sweeping east across the park to a tall prospect tower silhouetted against the sky is a remnant of this scheme, and an unrestored picturesque wilderness to the west is also a survival of an earlier layout, as depicted in a number of eighteenth-century

paintings of the house and grounds in the breakfast room. Twentieth-century portraits hanging here include a likeness of the 6th Lord Brownlow, Lord in Waiting to Edward VIII during his brief reign and a close friend of the king. Edward VIII stayed several times at Belton, perhaps deriving strength from the serenity of his surroundings.

ABOVE A fortune made from sheep farming and the law financed the building of Belton House in 1685–8. The north front looks over nineteenth-century formal gardens.

Beningbrough Hall, Gallery and Gardens

North Yorkshire
8 miles (12.8 kilometres)
north-west of York, 2 miles
(3.2 kilometres) west of Shipton,
2 miles (3.2 kilometres)
south-east of Linton-on-Ouse

Set on a slight rise above the water meadows of the River Ouse, looking out over a tree-studded park, is this great baroque house. Built of red brick and stone, with long sash windows lighting the two principal floors and little pavilions crowned with cupolas either side of the main block, it is a product of the cultivated, secure decades of the early eighteenth century and was largely complete by 1716. Ornate stonework, including two lifelike horses struggling to escape sculptured drapery, marks the central bay, a splayed flight of steps rises to the entrance and tiny casements in the attic storey are squeezed in between the massive console brackets supporting the prominent cornice.

Beningbrough was built for John Bourchier, who inherited the estate in 1700, when he was only 16, and set out to replace an existing Elizabethan manor after returning from a four-year Grand Tour. Much of his time abroad was spent in Italy, and it seems Bourchier wanted to reproduce the drama and extravagant decoration of the great baroque palaces that he had seen in Rome in this mansion peacefully set in the English countryside. It is not known exactly who designed the house. The talented local carpenter-architect William Thornton, who oversaw construction, may have done more than just supervise the work and, given his knowledge of Italian architecture, it is probable that Bourchier himself was closely involved. Both men would have been able to consult books on architecture which illustrated baroque buildings in Rome.

The even treatment of the two principal floors is baroque in inspiration and much of the exterior detailing, such as the paired brackets supporting the cornice, is taken from Italian sources. Similarly the imposing entrance hall that rises through two storeys on the north side of the house would have reminded Bourchier of what he had seen in Italy. The strongly axial layout of the interior, with dramatic spatial effects, is also characteristic of baroque architecture. There are long vistas down the corridors running the length of the house on both floors, the lower closed by the greenery of the conservatory at one end, the upper with openings into the entrance hall.

The pine-panelled rooms are ornamented with woodcarving of exceptional quality which stands out in high relief on friezes and overmantels, decoration that was usually executed in plaster being here realised in wood. This was probably the work of French Huguenot craftsmen employed by Thornton, who was closely associated with a group that had established themselves in the north of England. Thornton and his men were also responsible for the majestic cantilevered staircase rising to the Saloon on the first floor. What appears to be delicate wrought-iron work in the banisters has again been executed in wood. Another grand architectural space, with giant fluted pilasters framing the windows and punctuating the interior walls, the Saloon runs across five bays on the garden front and would have been used for balls and other great occasions. The formality of early eighteenth-century life comes through in the apartments on the ground floor, where suites of rooms were used for receiving visitors as well as sleeping; stepped shelves over the fireplaces in the intimate closets at the corners of the house, where only the closest friends would have been admitted, would have been crowded with oriental porcelain in the fashion of the time in the eighteenth century.

The Bourchiers continued to live at Beningbrough until 1827, when Margaret Earle (née Bourchier), the last of the line, left the house to William Henry Dawnay, a close friend and distant relative by marriage of one of her two sons, both of whom had predeceased her. Major improvements made by the Dawnays at the end of the nineteenth century included installing electricity, adding on the conservatory and modernising the farms on the estate, but in 1916 the merchant banker Guy Dawnay decided to sell the house. Beningbrough was bought by a local famer, who parcelled up the 6,000-acre (2,400-hectare) estate and offered it in several lots. The house, home farm and 375-acre (152-hectare) park were acquired, for only £15,000, for Lady Chesterfield, a wealthy shipping heiress who was the wife of the 10th Earl of Chesterfield. This was a new golden age for Beningbrough. The Chesterfields filled the house with fine paintings and furniture from their Herefordshire home and redecorated, painting the Saloon peacock blue. In the early 1920s, Lady Chesterfield set up a stud farm, one of the thoroughbreds she reared here winning the St Leger in 1941, while a cobbled yard close by the house is where Lord Chesterfield bred his beloved Labradors.

LEFT Beningbrough Hall, built in the early eighteenth century, is notable for baroque spatial effects, such as the long vistas across the house, and for the quality of the panelling and other woodwork.

During the Second World War, crews from the nearby airfield at Linton-on-Ouse were billeted here, leaving burn marks from their cigarettes on the panelling of the room that they used as a bar. Lord Chesterfield had died in 1933 and Lady Chesterfield, who returned after the war, lived here until her death in 1957. Beningbrough came to the Trust the following year, after the sale of the contents. Until recently, the interior was furnished in period style with loans and bequests and with pieces and pictures that had been bought back by the Trust, and from 1979 to 2019 the house benefited from the loan of an outstanding collection of period portraits from the National Portrait Gallery. Now, not for the first time in its history, the presentation of the house is being radically rethought in a long term project that will see Beningbrough revitalised and reinvented.

A door in the wall of the cobbled yard by the Victorian laundry leads out to the garden spread round three sides of the house. With the help of the designer Andy Sturgeon, this too is being revitalised. Formal layouts with clipped hedges and a fountain pool border the house. To the east is a productive walled garden. There are magnificent herbaceous borders and a newly created pergola which will, in time, be hung with white wisteria, while the ha-ha walk has been enriched with thousands of bulbs. The view south across the park is as serene as it always has been.

Benthall Hall

Shropshire
1 mile (1.6 kilometres) north-west of Broseley on the B4375, 4 miles (6.4 kilometres) north-east of Much Wenlock, 6 miles (9.6 kilometres) south of Wellington

Although the estate lies only a couple of miles from Coalbrookdale, the traumas of the Industrial Revolution passed Benthall by, isolated as it is on a plateau above the River Severn, with precipitous wooded slopes falling to the river. Seat of the ancient Benthall family, whose origins stretch back to Anglo-Saxon times, the estate was sold away from the family in 1844 but was bought back in 1934 and Benthalls live here still. With its tall, moulded brick chimneystacks and mullioned and transomed windows, the house has changed little since it was built in the late sixteenth century. The south front that looks towards the Shropshire Hills is charmingly asymmetrical. The projecting porch is off-centre, two-storey bay windows are spaced unequally to either side, and there is a shallow wing at the west end. Nothing lines up with the gabled roofline. Five stone tablets set in a playing-card pattern above the door in the porch, perhaps alluding to the wounds of Christ, were probably advertising the family's Catholic sympathies, and these may also account for the hiding place under the floor in the little room above.

Early seventeenth-century interiors include a carved staircase of *c.* 1618, with grotesque heads adorning the massive newel posts and the leopard of the Benthall crest proudly

displayed on the panel at the turn of the stairs. In the sunny, welcoming drawing room, lit by windows facing south and west, an elaborate white plaster ceiling and frieze merge with off-white oak panelling. Lions, horses, stags, griffins and other mythical creatures look down on the room from their plaster roundels. Rococo chimneypieces of *c.* 1760 here and in the dining room were added by T.F. Pritchard, whose Iron Bridge, spanning the River Severn just to the north, is perhaps the most evocative symbol of the Industrial Revolution.

The intimate tree-shaded garden owes much to tenants who lived in the house in the nineteenth century. The terraces, rockeries, rose garden and shrub banks were established by Robert Bateman, who came to Benthall in 1890 and whose father created the individual layout at Biddulph Grange in Staffordshire (also owned by the National Trust). The distinguished botanist George Maw and his brother, who rented the house earlier in the century, were responsible for the display of autumn and spring crocuses and started a tradition of peopling the garden with unusual plants. An avenue of horse chestnuts to the south of the house follows the line of the original drive and earthworks in grassland to the north mark the site of the medieval village, which was destroyed by besieging Royalists in the Civil War.

BELOW The gabled frontage of Benthall Hall, with its tall chimneystacks and mullioned windows, is still largely as built in the late sixteenth century.

Berrington Hall

Herefordshire
3 miles (4.8 kilometres) north
of Leominster on the west side
of the A49

Berrington is the creation of Thomas Harley, the 3rd Earl of Oxford's remarkable son, who made a fortune from banking and from supplying pay and clothing to the British army during the American War of Independence. He became Lord Mayor of London in 1767 at the age of 37. The architect of his austere, three-storey house, with its domestic quarters clustered round a courtyard behind, was the young Henry Holland.

The house is set above the wide valley of a tributary of the River Lugg, with views west and south to the Black Mountains and Brecon Beacons. This was the site advised by 'Capability' Brown, whom Harley took to see the estate in 1775 shortly after he had acquired it, and who was to landscape the park, creating the lake with its artificial island (Berrington is one of the best examples of his work). Holland, who was Brown's son-in-law, started on the house three years later. In 1778 Holland was 33. He had made a name for himself in aristocratic circles by designing Brook's club in St James's in London and he was to go on to build Carlton House for the Prince Regent. He was an early advocate of the stripped-down French version of neo-classicism, which was gradually replacing the more decorative Palladianism in fashionable circles in the 1770s, and this was the style he adopted for Berrington, setting the mood with an entrance lodge in the form of an unadorned triumphal arch.

The house is a plain Neo-classical box, cased in reddish-brown sandstone. Its main feature is the massive pedimented portico on the entrance front approached by a wide flight of steps, and there is a roofline balustrade. The treatment of the interior is more lavish. Feminine plaster ceilings now decorated in muted pastel colours adorn the principal rooms. Holland is at his most fanciful in the drawing room, where painted roundels on the ceiling, thought to be by Biagio Rebecca, are set off by white plaster cherubs leading seahorses by blue ribbons over a lavender background. Biagio Rebecca probably also executed the prominent grisaille panels in the library, deep shadows in those depicting Milton, Chaucer, Shakespeare and other eminent Englishmen of letters on the ceiling giving them a three-dimensional quality, as if they were made of plaster. Pedimented bookcases divided by slender pilasters run round the room like a series of temple façades.

Holland's most original interior at Berrington is the staircase hall. Rising to a glass dome carried on delicate metal ribs, it shows an extraordinary ability to use perspective and space to dramatic effect, as in an engraving by Piranesi. The rooms are set off with a collection of French furniture, including pieces that belonged to the Comte de Flahaut, the natural son of Talleyrand, and Napoleon's stepdaughter Hortense.

In the dining room, four panoramic sea paintings, three of them by Thomas Luny, are a tribute to the distinguished Admiral Rodney. Father-in-law of Harley's daughter Anne and one of the most eminent admirals of the eighteenth century, he played a prominent role in the American War of Independence. The paintings show important incidents in the war at sea, in which Rodney was in action against the French and Spanish, who had allied themselves with the rebellious Americans. Two large pictures at either end of the room are of the Battle of the Saints on 12 April 1782, an engagement that Luny, who served as a purser, may have witnessed. One is a morning scene showing Rodney breaking the French line; the other depicts the surrender of the French flagship in the evening of the same day.

More poignant reminders of members of the Cawley family, to whom the estate was sold in 1901, hang in Lady Cawley's room. One of the photographs shows the 1st Lord Cawley and his four sons on horseback in front of the house, ready for a day's hunting. A few years later three of the young men had lost their lives in the First World War.

OPPOSITE The columns of the great portico at Berrington Hall were carefully spaced so as to allow uninterrupted views over the valley below from the windows of the hall.

ABOVE The finest of the interiors created by Henry Holland at Berrington is the staircase hall, with its screens of scagliola columns, delicate glass dome and bold spatial effects.

Birmingham Back to Backs

West Midlands
On the corner of Inge Street and Hurst Street, opposite the Hippodrome Theatre, Birmingham

When Birmingham was growing rapidly as an industrial centre in the late eighteenth and early nineteenth centuries, developers threw up street after street of brick-built, back-to-back houses, with one of each pair forming part of a terrace facing the street in front, the other looking over a courtyard behind. Three storeys high, but with just one room on each floor, and with windows only on one side, these houses were home to sizeable families, and often to their relatives and a lodger as well, all of whom had to use the communal privy and wash-house in the court. Cheap, high-density housing like this covered acres of Leeds, Liverpool and other industrial towns as well as Birmingham, but during the nineteenth century, as many became disease-ridden slums, increasing concern about public health led to controlling legislation. The 1858 Public Health Act, which allowed local councils to prohibit back-to-backs, was followed by the 1908 Housing Act, which made them illegal. Building back-to-backs was banned in Birmingham in 1876, but many existing courts survived until the slum-clearance programmes that followed the Second World War.

Court 15, Inge Street, which was lived in until 1966, is the only complete survival of a courtyard of early nineteenth-century back-to-backs. The housing forms an L-shape, with three pairs of back-to-backs on Inge Street adjoining a terrace of five blind-back houses on Hurst Street. These tenements make up the north and west sides of the inner court: on the east is a tall brick wall that was once the blind back of housing in an adjacent yard and the south side is closed by a modern brick wall. During most of the nineteenth century the court was occupied by artisans – button makers, leather workers, locksmiths and the like – some of whom worked from home, using one room in the house as a workshop. On Hurst Street, the lower floors were all converted into shops by 1900.

A tunnel entrance from Inge Street leads into the brick-paved yard, where two communal wash-houses survive, the water for them once heated in coppers over a brick hearth. Four back-to-backs have been fitted out to show what life in Inge Court and Hurst Street was like at different times

ABOVE These two houses only have a frontage onto the yard and have been given bay windows to let in more light. There were people living here until 1966.

in their history. Reconstructions have been based on what is known of the families and individuals who lived here, and provide authentic re-creations of period furnishings and lifestyles. One is based on the life of a Jewish watchmaker and his family, whose well-kept house includes artefacts such as a Seder plate for Passover and a nine-branched candlestick; another, with damp and peeling wallpaper, shabby clothes and little to be seen in the cupboards, reflects the day-to-day existence of the struggling Mitchell family, who were here during the recession and unemployment of the 1930s; while the most recent interior is based on the life of an immigrant from the Caribbean, George Saunders, who opened a tailor's shop in the court, using the upper floors of the tenement as a workroom and for storage. A water pump has been reinstated in the courtyard and washing lines, a hoop and an old pram give the place a lived-in atmosphere.

Blickling Estate

Norfolk
On the north side of the B1154,
½ mile (0.8 kilometres) north-west
of Aylsham on the A140, 15 miles
(24 kilometres) north of Norwich,
10 miles (16 kilometres) south of
Cromer

A winding road from Aylsham leads to this serene Jacobean mansion set in almost 5,000 acres (2,000 hectares) of gently undulating park and estate in a loop of the River Bure. Built of warm red brick with stone dressings, Blickling has curving Dutch gables, generous leaded windows, massive chimneystacks and corner turrets, each carrying a gilded weather vane. On the southern entrance front, long, low service wings, their lines continued by yew hedges, frame the approach. The house was designed for Sir Henry Hobart, James I's distinguished Chief Justice of the Common Pleas, by Robert Lyminge, who transformed an existing medieval and Tudor manor. In the early sixteenth century the old house had belonged to the ambitious Sir Thomas Boleyn, whose rise at court had much to do with Henry VIII's interest in his daughters, which Sir Thomas encouraged. Tradition has it that Anne, the younger of the two sisters, was born at Blickling. She married the king in 1533, only to be executed three years later. No traces of the Tudor and medieval manor can be seen, but its ghost lives on in the dry moat ringing the house, now planted with roses, hydrangeas and hostas, and in many features of the layout and dimensions of the new building, such as the double courtyard plan. Further remodelling in the eighteenth century by Thomas and William Ivory for John Hobart, the 2nd Earl of Buckinghamshire, resulted in a house that is a harmonious combination of Jacobean and Georgian, the later work, to the north and west ranges, blending beautifully with the earlier.

Rich and showy Jacobean decoration and fittings show Sir Henry spared no expense in creating interiors to match his

BELOW Blickling is one of the loveliest of country houses, with façades of warm red brick embraced by corner turrets and decorated with curving Dutch gables. Picturesque service wings frame the approach to the house.

status. The 1620s staircase, with carved figures on the newel posts, is a striking feature of the portrait-hung great hall, to which it was moved in 1767, while the south drawing room at the end of the east range, once the great chamber of the Jacobean house and the room where Charles II was entertained in 1671, still has its outstanding plasterwork ceiling by Edward Stanyon and the original ostentatious chimneypiece. An ante-room off the drawing room leads into Sir Henry's spectacular Long Gallery, running 123 feet (37.5 metres) down the east front and adorned with another intricate plaster ceiling by Stanyon. Here, his decoration intermingles heraldic motifs, including a generous display of the Hobart bull, with delightful depictions of the senses. In one panel, a stag listens entranced to a man playing the mandolin, his lady following the music for him with her finger; in another, a woman lifts a brimming glass to her lips, her lap full of luscious fruit. In about 1745 the gallery was converted into a library to accommodate the books inherited from Sir Richard Ellys, a distinguished theologian and antiquary who, with an eye for the rare, curious, old and beautiful, assembled an outstanding collection of works, recognised as such by his contemporaries in the early eighteenth century. The 12,000 volumes housed at Blickling, which form one of the most remarkable country-house libraries in England, include a very rare Eliot Indian Bible printed in Massachusetts in 1663, the most significant Bible in the Trust's care, a unique maritime atlas of the same period, spectacular books of engravings and books from the Aldine Press in Venice, several of which are in contemporary bindings. Above the bookcases, J.H. Pollen's delicately painted frieze, full of timid rabbits and other wildlife of the Norfolk countryside, is part of the Pre-Raphaelite mural decoration commissioned by the 8th Marquess of Lothian shortly after he inherited the house in 1850.

A door from the gallery leads into one of the rooms fitted out in 1778–82 to display the works of art acquired by the 2nd Earl during his congenial three-year posting as Ambassador to the court of Catherine the Great. There are only three paintings here now, but the room still displays the magnificent tapestry,

LEFT The atmospheric Jacobean Long Gallery was once used to display portraits, but now houses one of the most exceptional country-house libraries in England.

given to the 2nd Earl by the empress as a parting present, which shows Peter the Great triumphing over the defeated Swedish army at Poltava in 1709.

An RAF museum in the east wing, with displays of photographs and of equipment, clothing and other memorabilia, is a reminder of the role Blickling played in the Second World War, when aircrews from RAF Oulton, a satellite Bomber Command airfield just to the west of the estate, were billeted in the house and in Nissen huts in the grounds.

Just a few years before the outbreak of war, Philip Kerr, the 11th Marquess of Lothian, who had faced ruinous death duties on inheriting Blickling in 1930, came up with a plan by which great houses, their contents and historic estates could be left to the nation rather than gradually sold off to meet taxation. His vision, which was worked out together with James Lees-Milne, was enshrined in Parliamentary bills in 1937 and 1940. All the Trust's major houses were acquired as a result of the marquess's scheme; Blickling, which was bequested in 1940, being one of the first.

Reflecting Lothian's vision, Blickling came with its surrounding estate. A rolling wooded park landscaped in the eighteenth century stretches away to the north and west of the house, with beeches, sweet chestnuts and huge mature oaks framing a long sinuous lake, while a formal garden remodelled by Norah Lindsay in the 1930s, and flanked by formal wilderness areas with wooded walks, borders the Jacobean east front.

LEFT This eighteenth-century temple, set on a substantial terrace, closes the view down the central walk across the formal garden.

Bodiam Castle

East Sussex
3 miles (4.8 kilometres) south of Hawkhurst, 1 mile (1.6 kilometres) east of the B2244

By 1372, halfway through the Hundred Years War, England had lost control of the Channel and had begun to suffer devastating French raids. The Sussex ports of Winchelsea and Rye had both been destroyed a few years earlier; the manor of Bodiam, lying only some 10 miles (16 kilometres) from the coast and at the furthest navigable point of the River Rother, must have seemed similarly vulnerable. In 1385, Sir Edward Dalyngrigge, a veteran of the wars in France and an important figure in the defence of Sussex, asked Richard II for permission to fortify his house.

Rather than improving his manor, Dalyngrigge chose to build anew, on a site closer to the river and a strategic bridge. Work started in 1385 and the fine, four-square castle which still stares south across the Sussex marshes was completed several years later. Built just before siege artillery changed the approach to castle design, Bodiam's strength lay in the height and might of its tower-studded circuit walls, which rise sheer from a broad moat. The massive gateway, equipped with machicolations and gunports, is reached from the north bank

ABOVE These three arches connected the great hall to the kitchen range. The two outer doorways gave access to the buttery and pantry, the taller central one to a passage leading to the kitchen.
BELOW Bodiam, with a massive gatehouse protecting the entrance on the north front and a wide moat, looks everything a castle should be. The approach, over three bridges and two islands, was originally defended by drawbridges and an outlying barbican.

across three bridges and two islands. Originally, to repel any attacker, this approach involved a dog-leg to the west bank, three drawbridges and an outlying barbican, the remains of which stand on one of the islands. A ground-hugging Second World War pillbox by the path up from the car park shows how much defensive thinking has changed.

Although now in ruins, enough of the interior survives to give a vivid picture of the realities of castle life. The deep well and the remains of a pigeon loft suggest a preoccupation with being besieged, but in fact the French threat soon receded and the remnants of traceried windows and a number of fireplaces tell a different story. Like many contemporary buildings in France and England, which Dalyngrigge must surely have seen, Bodiam combines domestic comfort with the trappings of defence and it is very likely the castle was built to be a status symbol as much as a fortress. The great courtyard beyond

the gatehouse is surrounded by the outlines of domestic accommodation, including a traditional great hall with adjoining buttery, pantry and kitchen, such as would have been found in any mansion of the period, and personal chambers for Dalyngrigge and his wife, Elizabeth. Separate quarters, each suite with its own fireplaces and garderobe, were provided for his household. A chapel catered for the spiritual needs of the retinue and their lord. The emphasis on the castle as a grand residence also comes through in the recently identified remains of landscape gardens beyond the moat. Dips and hollows in the grass mark what was a series of ponds and there was a terrace on the hill above from which to admire the castle and its setting.

ABOVE Bodiam, with its massive tower-studded walls, was built at the end of the fourteenth century, just before siege artillery led to a change in castle design.

Brockhampton Estate

Worcestershire
1½ miles (2.4 kilometres) east
of Bromyard, on the north side of
the A44 Worcester road

The undulating oak-studded parkland of the Brockhampton estate falls away steeply into a deep, leafy valley. In the depths of the valley, reached by a private road that seems to descend for miles, is an enchanting timber-framed medieval manor house surrounded on three sides by a moat. A little gatehouse is set over the moat, its upper floor jettied out over the lower and the whole thing so warped and twisted that it lurches crazily. Set back 50 feet (15 metres) or so, and facing south across a grassy court, is the manor itself, an L-shaped building in which a great hall open to the rafters filling the stub of the L is attached to a two-storey wing. Red-brick chimneys rear up from the end walls and in spring, when the orchards that surround it are in flower, the house sits amongst apple and damson blossom.

When the manor was built, probably some time between 1380 and 1400, only a generation had passed since the devastations of the Black Death, which massively reduced the population of England. Crumbling walls on the fringes of the Malvern Hills to the east were typical of abandoned settlements on marginal land, and the economic depression of these years also saw the fragmentation of many great estates. But the middling landowners with modest holdings in well-endowed country were better placed to survive and prosper. John Domulton, a descendant of the Brockhampton family which was here from at least the twelfth century, may have been just such a man. His house is small and unpretentious, but it was comfortable for its day. A great chamber, for the family to distance themselves from their servants and retainers, once filled the upper floor of the wing. The moat, which originally encircled the house, may well have been necessary in the unsettled country of the Welsh Marches, but may also have been regarded as a status symbol. The gatehouse is a later addition, dating from the fifteenth century.

Massive timbers from the estate were used to build the house and there is woodwork of high quality here, particularly evident in the framework and roof of the hall. A ruined Norman chapel in the farmyard to the west of the house was probably built by the Brockhamptons in about 1180 and high in the parkland above is the mid-eighteenth-century red-brick Brockhampton Court (not open), built to replace the old manor far below. The Court was left to the National Trust, with the rest of the property, in 1946, by Colonel John Talbot Lutley, who wanted Brockhampton preserved as an example of a traditional agricultural estate.

BELOW Medieval Lower Brockhampton lies deep in a leafy valley. An enchanting gatehouse, its timbers twisted out of shape, straddles the moat.

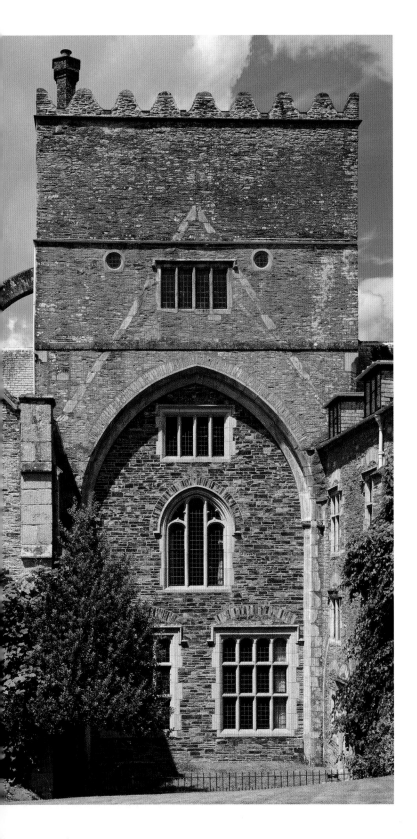

Buckland Abbey

Devon
6 miles (9.6 kilometres) south of
Tavistock, 11 miles (17.7 kilometres)
north of Plymouth

Francis Drake's tiny *Golden Hind* left Plymouth on a cold winter's day in December 1577 and did not return until nearly three years later, on 26 September 1580. This historic voyage was the first circumnavigation of the globe by an Englishman, a venture that included crossing the unknown expanses of the Pacific Ocean. A national hero on his return, Drake needed a house that reflected his newly acquired status, ironically choosing to purchase the abbey that had been so recently converted by his rival, Sir Richard Grenville. It was from here that Drake planned his assault on the Spanish Armada a few years later.

Set among sloping green lawns and exotic trees and shrubs on the edge of the sleepy Tavy valley, Buckland Abbey is rich in associations with Drake. There are many echoes, too, of the great Cistercian monastery that was founded here in 1278 and which was dissolved in 1539, passing to Sir Richard Grenville two years later. Like Lord Sandys at Mottisfont (*see* p.228), Grenville chose to convert the thirteenth-century abbey church rather than using the domestic buildings of the community. The abbey's great crossing tower, its south wall marked clearly with the roofline of a demolished transept, dominates the house; there are blocked arches and traces of monastic windows and, inside, the tracery of the chancel arch and other stonework can be seen, including a carving of a winged ox – the ox of St Luke – which ornaments a corbel protruding into a corner of the dining room. Drake lived at Buckland for only 15 years, but the abbey remained in the Drake family until 1946, when it was sold to Captain Arthur Rodd, a local landowner. Captain Rodd immediately presented the abbey to the Trust.

Shown in association with The Box, Plymouth's museum and gallery complex, which, together with some other organisations, has loaned exhibits to the abbey, the interior is a mix of museum-like displays and furnished rooms. The long gallery that runs the length of the former nave on the top floor is devoted to imaginative changing exhibitions. Drake's coat of arms over the fireplace, on which a fragile ship is guided by the divine hand of providence, heralds what can be seen on the floor below. Gorgeous banners, regularly rotated for conservation purposes, may have flown on the

Golden Hind; one shows the golden leopards of England on a red ground. There is a gold model of the ship and other cases contain Elizabeth I's commission of 5 March 1587, giving Drake command of the fleet with which he 'singed the King of Spain's beard', and Armada medals, the first ever struck to commemorate a historical event. Silverware that was at Buckland in the 1940s and 1950s illustrates a later chapter in the history of the house and a fragment of granite window tracery takes visitors back to the community that lived here for some 300 years, growing gradually richer on an income derived from tin mines in the Tavy valley as well as from the tenants on their estates. An important recent addition to what is on show in the house is the Rembrandt self-portrait that came to Buckland in 2010 as part of a group of five Dutch paintings bequeathed by Edna, Lady Samuel of Wych Cross. Only authenticated as a genuine Rembrandt in 2014, the portrait is thought to have been painted in the mid-1630s and shows the artist in a velvet cap adorned with ostrich feathers and with lovelocks falling over his left shoulder. It is the only Rembrandt owned by the Trust.

The one interior to survive unchanged from the sixteenth century is the great hall. Dating from Sir Richard Grenville's conversion of the abbey, it is warmly panelled in oak and decorated with an elaborate ceiling and a holly and box frieze adorned with carved figures. Contemporary plasterwork on the end walls symbolising Grenville's retirement to Buckland shows his shield hanging on a tree and a large pile of discarded arms. The Georgian dining room, and the elegant staircase curling up through the house, were added as part of late eighteenth-century improvements by Sir Francis Henry Drake, 5th Baronet, in the 1770s. A gate near the bottom of the staircase was to keep dogs from the upper floors.

A picturesque group of granite outbuildings with lichen-stained roofs includes an ox shed introduced by the agricultural improver William Marshall, who spent four years at Buckland in 1791–4. Close by the abbey is the huge, heavily buttressed monastic barn, built in about 1300. Almost 160 feet (49 metres) long, it is one of the largest in Britain, eloquently suggesting the wealth of the community. The cider press housed here was used to crush fruit from the orchards that once stretched down to the River Tavy. Sinuous hedges like window tracery enclose a little herb garden planted beside the barn, where it is easy to imagine white-robed figures moving silently from bed to bed collecting lovage, balm or sweet cicely. There is a re-creation of an Elizabethan garden too and the recently acquired Cider House garden. Waymarked trails lead round the working estate, where the woods are carpeted with bluebells in spring.

OPPOSITE At Buckland Abbey, Sir Richard Grenville converted the monastery church into a country house, leaving the outline of a demolished transept on what had been the church tower.
RIGHT Georgian alterations at Buckland Abbey included the insertion of this splendid staircase, which rises right through the house. A gate kept dogs from the upper floors.

Buscot Park

Oxfordshire
Between Lechlade and Faringdon,
astride the A417

This modest estate straddling the River Thames in the fertile valley above Oxford was the scene of an agricultural experiment in the nineteenth century when a rich Australian, Robert Tertius Campbell, turned Buscot into the most progressive farm of its time, largely given over to sugar beet. His grandiose schemes, which eventually overwhelmed his resources, included a distillery for converting the sugar into spirit and over 6 miles (9.6 kilometres) of railway for bringing in the crop.

In 1889, two years after Campbell died, Buscot was sold to Alexander Henderson, later 1st Lord Faringdon, politician, financier and connoisseur, who was responsible for some of the finest paintings in the important collection that is now such a feature of the house. The 1st Lord's son died before him and it was his grandson, Gavin, the 2nd Lord, who inherited the estate. A prominent socialist, he was as enthusiastic about art as his grandfather.

The house, built in 1780–3 for Edward Loveden Townsend on a rise above the flatlands of the Thames, is a plain classical composition, with a pediment marking the south-facing entrance façade and two generous bays rising the height of the building on the north front. The pavilions to either side, and the imposing flight of steps flanked by bronze centaurs leading up to the entrance, were added by Geddes Hyslop in the 1930s for the 2nd Lord, who also did much to reinstate the original character of the house, removing nineteenth-century alterations. The interiors, in particular the three interconnected rooms on the north front which look over a grassy fountain terrace to the Thames valley beyond, are both sensuous and cultivated, with extravagant chandeliers, inlaid and painted Regency and Empire furniture (including neo-Egyptian pieces by Thomas Hope), a fine collection of oriental porcelain, bronzes and other *objets*, richly coloured carpets and gleaming mahogany doors.

BELOW Buscot's south front, with a steep flight of steps, flanked by bronze centaurs, rising to the pedimented entrance bay.

The hang of the Faringdons' catholic art collection gives character to each room. An original filigree ceiling looks down on the Italian paintings in the drawing room, among them Giovanni Pace's powerful *St Jerome*, Palma Vecchio's strangely asymmetrical *Marriage of St Catherine* and a tondo by Botticelli. Here, too, is the delightful *Rest on the Flight into Egypt* attributed to Andrea Previtali, in which the Holy Family are shown enjoying a substantial picnic of bread and cheese, the food carefully set out on a white cloth on the ground. There is a fine portrait by Rembrandt of the golden-haired Pieter Six amongst a show of Dutch Old Masters, while English eighteenth-century works include portraits by Reynolds and a sketchy Gainsborough landscape. A number of canvases reflect the 1st Lord's interest in the Pre-Raphaelites, perhaps inspired by his neighbour, William Morris, whose house at Kelmscott lies close by over the fields. Works by Rossetti and Millais are overshadowed by Burne-Jones's stupendous cycle based on the story of Sleeping Beauty, the *Legend of the Briar Rose*, which runs around the walls of the saloon in richly coloured panels on a gilded ground. The knight who has come to wake the beautiful princess faces her across the room, as if he has to fight his way through the rose forest on the walls to reach her, past the sleeping knights entangled in thorny branches and the old king himself, slumbering on his throne, his grey beard reaching to his waist.

As the comfortable sofas, piles of books and family photographs suggest, Buscot is still lived in by the Henderson family and the collection continues to grow. A number of late twentieth-century paintings include an intriguing portrait of the poet and artist Ian Hamilton Finlay by Eileen Hogan and there are two arresting pieces of contemporary glass resembling still Mediterranean rock pools by Colin Reid. The extensive grounds, too, have continued to evolve. Innovations by the present Lord and Lady Faringdon, such as the inspired ornamental planting of the walled garden, have further enhanced the existing layout, with an Italianate water garden created by Harold Peto between 1904 and 1913 linking the house to the lake in the eighteenth-century parkland and radiating avenues through the flanking woodland, each focused on an urn, an Italian wellhead or some other feature.

Calke Abbey

Derbyshire
9 miles (14.4 kilometres) south of Derby, on the A514 at Ticknall between Swadlincote and Melbourne

Set some distance from any public road, Calke Abbey lies hidden in a fold of the landscape in a beautiful eighteenth-century park, insulated from the world by thousands of trees grouped in picturesque clumps and windbreaks and framing a chain of ornamental ponds. Built in 1701–4, it is an imposing three-storey baroque house set round a courtyard, its plainness relieved by corner pavilions decorated with fluted pilasters. But behind the symmetrical grey sandstone façades are substantial remains of an Elizabethan building and the abbey's low-lying position, in a hollow of the park, reveals its earlier, monastic origins, some of the fabric having probably been recycled from the priory of Austin canons that was established here in the early twelfth century. Substantial remodelling by William Wilkins the Elder between 1789 and 1810 for Sir Henry Harpur, 7th Baronet, accounts for the pedimented entrance portico, the roofline balustrade and the suite of reception rooms on the first floor, of which only the dining room, with its Neo-classical decoration, and the library, where the rolled-up maps attached to the bookshelves are among the fittings supplied in 1806–7, are as he designed them.

Like Kedleston Hall only a few miles to the north (*see* p.188), Calke has been in the hands of the same family for hundreds of years, each generation of the Harpurs and Harpur-Crewes contributing to the extraordinary individuality of the house. More remarkably, little has been changed since the mid-nineteenth century, providing a unique insight into mid-Victorian England.

William Wilkins's drawing room still has the striking gold and white wallpaper that was hung in 1841–2, and it is still as cluttered as it appears in a photograph of 1886, crowded with chairs and stools, numerous occasional tables and ornaments under glass domes. Display cases full of glistening polished stones are no preparation for the contents of the room next door, the saloon remodelled by Henry Isaac Stevens in 1841. Stevens's coffered ceiling decorated with the Harpur boar and his elegant panels hung with family portraits fade into insignificance beside the cases of stuffed birds and geological specimens, and the stag trophies mounted on the walls. A

noble head even looks down on Tilly Kettle's charming portrait of Lady Frances Harpur and her son, the future 7th Baronet, painted in *c.* 1766.

These exhibits reflect the interests of Sir Vauncey Harpur-Crewe, who inherited Calke in 1886 and filled the house with his collections. Spending much of his time at Calke, Sir Vauncey was very solicitous to his tenants and employees, but did not always get on well with his children, with whom he sometimes communicated by letter. Passionate about birds and butterflies, he forbade his tenants to cut the hedges so as to provide maximum cover for nests. Carriages now displayed in the stable yard reflect his insistence that motor vehicles should not be allowed on the estate.

The three Georgian baronets, two Sir Henrys and Sir Harry, were equally passionate about horse racing, an interest that is commemorated by paintings of racehorses by Sartorius and Sawrey Gilpin in the library, by three florid eighteenth-century racing cups and, in the case of Sir Harry, by the riding school

added to the impressive brick stable block in 1767–9. It is thought that Lady Caroline, wife of the 5th Baronet, one of the Henrys, was given the sumptuous early eighteenth-century state bed, its beautiful Chinese silk hangings, embroidered with dragons, birds, deer and other traditional motifs in rich blues, reds, greens and oranges, still as fresh as when it arrived. This exceptional survival was found in a packing case in the former linen closet, and many more treasures lay forgotten behind closed doors or languishing in outhouses, among them Victorian dolls in mint condition, books full of dried flowers, a Georgian chamber organ and a harpsichord by Burkat Shudi. Household objects that would have been thrown away long ago in other establishments, such as lamps that were in use until electricity was installed in 1962, have also survived here.

After Sir Vauncey died in 1924, apart from a brief period during the Second World War when some evacuees and, later, soldiers were billeted here, the house slowly shut down.

Declining family fortunes made it difficult to maintain and by the time of Charles Harpur-Crewe, who inherited in 1949, only a core of habitable rooms was occupied. The extensive servants' quarters were shut up, and other rooms became filled with the wreckage of unwanted things. These rooms, and the long bleak corridors connecting them, are shown much as they were found and are deeply atmospheric. Wallpaper is stained and peeling, great cracks snake across ceilings, and paintwork is chipped and flaking. Seen with the shutters largely closed, the effect is of a place turned in on itself, of abandonment as much as decay. In the bowels of the building is the old kitchen and a series of cave-like wine and beer cellars and, from the north side of the courtyard, where grass grows between the paving stones, a long, dimly lit, brick-vaulted tunnel, used by the gardeners to deliver vegetables to the house without being seen, winds far underground to emerge in the brewhouse in the stable block.

Several members of the family lie buried in the graveyard and vaults of the little church, which crowns a rise to the south of the house. Although apparently of the nineteenth century, its appearance is due to a remodelling, in 1827–9, of a simple Elizabethan building, some parts of which, such as the roof trusses, were re-used. Nearby, hidden by a screen of trees, are the late eighteenth-century walled gardens, a combination of the ornamental and the practical. Mixed borders against the walls and geometrical beds in the lawn of the flower garden echo Victorian planting schemes, and neat rows of fruit and vegetables, including some Victorian varieties, have been planted in the original physic garden. A vast grassy arena at the top of the slope with an orangery on the north side and views over Staunton Harold reservoir was once the kitchen garden.

When Charles Harpur-Crewe died in 1981, while setting mole traps in the park, his brother Henry, who inherited the estate, faced death duties of £8 million. Despite the problems involved, including interest mounting up at the rate of £1,500 a day, Henry was determined to preserve Calke and, four years later, after special grants from the National Heritage Memorial Fund and English Heritage, a successful public appeal and an anonymous donation, it was successfully transferred to the National Trust.

Canons Ashby

Northamptonshire
On the B4525 Northampton–
Banbury road

Set in the rolling, thinly populated countryside of south Northamptonshire, this ancient courtyard house reflects the bookish, conservative and never very wealthy family who lived here for 400 years, gradually altering and adding to the place but never rebuilding it. Little has changed since the early eighteenth century when the motto 'Ancient as the Druids' was inserted over the drawing room fireplace. A lime avenue from the garden leads to an unexpectedly grand church, all that remains of the Augustinian priory founded here in the twelfth century that gave Canons Ashby its name. Although reduced to a quarter of its former length, the church is still impressive, with a striking red and white arcade on the west front and a massive pinnacled tower. Bumps and furrows in the grass mark the site of the medieval village that once straggled up to the priory.

John Dryden's modest H-shaped Tudor manor, built with material from the demolished east end of the church, forms the great-hall range of the house. His squat staircase tower, like an echo of a Cumbrian pele, is now the centrepiece of the south front. The wings to the east, enclosing the cobbled internal courtyard, were added by John's son Sir Erasmus, the 1st Baronet, in the 1590s. Unlike the finished stone and brickwork of the exterior, the courtyard walls are rough and irregular, patterned with lichen and moss and set with leaded casement windows.

Painted decoration in the house was uncovered by the National Trust in the 1980s. Some of it, such as the illustration of a story from the Old Testament with a great sailing ship at anchor in front of a walled city, dates from Sir Erasmus's time and is in grey-blue monochrome, but the array of crests and devices in the servants' hall, depicted in full colour, is older,

from the time of Sir Erasmus's father. Intriguingly, some of the symbols here, such as set squares and dividers, point to a connection with early freemasonry in Scotland, over a century before it was organised in England. Sir Erasmus was also responsible for the vast chimneypiece in the drawing room, but it was his son who added the striking domed ceiling, every inch of it crowded with elaborate plasterwork featuring thistles and pomegranates on stylised curving branches. Three long sash windows lighting this room, added when Edward Dryden remodelled the south front in 1710, look out over a rare survival of a formal garden of the same date, with a vista down a flight of terraces falling away from the house to a grand baroque gateway and across the park beyond. Enclosing walls are all of a piece.

Edward Dryden was also responsible for Canons Ashby's dignified west front. This now faces onto a grassy court but for centuries, from 1550 to c. 1840, it was used as the main entrance to the house. An imposing baroque doorway dominates the façade, and Edward probably commissioned the sculptor Jan Van Nost to supply the leadwork coat of arms above the entrance and figures for the garden, of which only a statue of a shepherd boy survives. He also purchased the exquisite needlework-covered furniture in the Tapestry Room, with flowers and pastoral scenes embroidered on the seats and backs.

The present approach to the house, across the cobbled courtyard and up steps into the great hall, was arranged by Sir Henry Dryden, the much-loved Victorian squire of Canons Ashby who was known as the Antiquary. Fired by a lifelong interest in medieval architecture, Sir Henry measured and recorded all aspects of the house, down to the catches on the casement windows, and largely preserved it as it was, his only major addition being the oak bookcases in the little library where he wrote his learned articles. Leather-bound volumes now filling the shelves include the works of the three important literary figures associated with the house: the poet Edmund Spenser (1552–99), author of *The Faerie Queene*, who was a cousin of Sir Erasmus Dryden's wife, Frances; the poet laureate John Dryden, who visited the house as a very young man in the 1650s to pay court to his cousin, daughter of the 3rd Baronet; and the playwright and novelist Samuel Richardson (1689–1761), who is said to have written much of *Sir Charles Grandison*, his improbable moral tale about a virtuous paragon, at Canons Ashby.

ABOVE A huge pendant hangs from the centre of the plasterwork ceiling that was added to the drawing room in the 1630s.

The house is shown through Sir Henry's life and times and his meticulous records and period photographs have been used to re-create the Victorian planting of the terraces, with island beds and topiary yew on the grassy upper levels giving way to fruit and vegetable gardens framed by apples and pears on the lower terraces.

ABOVE Canon Ashby's south front, with its Tudor staircase tower, looks over terraced gardens where the Victorian planting schemes have been re-created.

Carlyle's House

London
24 Cheyne Row, London SW3 –
off Cheyne Walk, between
Battersea and Albert Bridges on
Chelsea Embankment

When the historian and philosopher Thomas Carlyle and his wife Jane moved to London from Scotland in 1834, they decided to rent this unpretentious, red-brick Queen Anne house in a quiet back street in Chelsea, then a much less fashionable and salubrious area than it is now. Part of a terrace of houses built in 1708, No. 24 is tall and narrow, with two rooms and a closet on each floor and a strip of a garden behind. This is where the Carlyles lived until their deaths, hers in 1866 and his 15 years later, furnishing the house with good but unremarkable pieces of the period, among them the sofa in the ground-floor sitting room, which Jane bought second hand in 1835, and a wealth of books and pictures. Still filled with the Carlyles' possessions, the walls crowded with photographs, watercolours and drawings of themselves, their families and places they loved, this otherwise modest house conveys a remarkable impression of the historian and essayist and his lively and intelligent wife.

The basement kitchen with its cast-iron range and old stone sink, originally filled by pumping water from a well beneath the floor, is very little changed. Here Carlyle retreated to smoke so as not to offend his wife, and this is where their maid slept at night. Upstairs is the book-lined drawing room which the Carlyles enlarged in 1852, inserting the Victorian fireplace. Jane decorated the screen covered with illustrations cut from books and magazines that stands in a corner, while the reading chair was a present to Carlyle on his 80th birthday. It was in this room that Carlyle wrote *The French Revolution*, the work that was to establish his reputation, painstakingly rewriting the manuscript of the first volume after it had been accidentally burned while on loan to John Stuart Mill. In the attic room filling the top of the house, which Carlyle built on in 1853 in a vain attempt to provide himself with a soundproof study, a fragment of manuscript is all that remains of the original draft. Among other mementoes on display here now is the buff dressing gown Carlyle is wearing in a poignant watercolour by Helen Allingham, painted when the writer, beard and hair both snowy white, was 84.

While Thomas Carlyle was a leading social theorist who saw the evils of industrial capitalism but also, more controversially, wrote in support of slavery, Jane Carlyle is remembered for her witty and caustic correspondence with family and friends, and for the wide circle of eminent figures she received in Cheyne Row – Dickens, Tennyson, Browning, Thackeray, Ruskin and Darwin among them. While Thomas Carlyle's reputation has dimmed over the years, Jane's observant letters are now regarded as among the best in the English language.

BELOW Carlyle's hat still hangs by the garden door in the hall of the red-brick terraced house in Chelsea where he and his wife Jane came to live in 1834 and which is filled with their belongings.

Castle Coole

Co. Fermanagh
1½ miles (2.4 kilometres)
south-east of Enniskillen on the
A32 Belfast–Enniskillen road

This austere white palace, James Wyatt's masterpiece, is one of the finest Neo-classical houses in the British Isles. Built between 1789 and 1795 for Armar Lowry Corry, Viscount and later 1st Earl of Belmore, it was designed to provide a suitably grand setting for a newly ennobled member of the peerage and also to surpass Florence Court across Lough Erne to the south, the house that had recently been embellished by Lowry Corry's brother-in-law, Lord Enniskillen (*see* p.146).

The shady path up from the car park by the stables suddenly emerges on the grass in front of the house to give an oblique view of the dazzling entrance façade faced in creamy Portland stone. A pedimented portico rising the height of the house is echoed in colonnaded wings linking the main block to pavilions on either side, a rather old-fashioned Palladian design, reminiscent of Robert Adam's Kedleston (*see* p.188), which may reflect the fact that Wyatt had to work with the foundations for a scheme of *c.* 1785 by the Irish architect Richard Johnston. This constraint clearly did not dim his enthusiasm. The quality of the interior detailing is superb: fine plaster ceilings by Joseph Rose and carved chimneypieces by Richard Westmacott are matched by similarly superior craftsmanship in the joinery of doors and floors. Unusually,

BELOW Castle Coole, built in the 1790s, is a palace of a house, whose architect, James Wyatt, never actually visited the site, sending drawings from London to be implemented, and adjusted, by the local clerk of works.
OPPOSITE The oval saloon at Castle Coole, where even the mahogany doors are curved, is fitted out with opulent Regency furnishings which act as a foil for the cool Neo-classical decoration.

a complete set of building accounts and many drawings have survived and these show that Wyatt even designed furniture and curtains. But he never visited Castle Coole, leaving his plans to be realised, and often altered, by the clerk of the works, Alexander Stewart. Rose and Westmacott too worked from afar, providing decorative features in London that were then shipped to Ireland. The Portland stone cladding of the exterior was brought by boat from Dorset to a special quay built at Ballyshannon and then taken by cart and barge up Lough Erne.

Sadly, Lord Belmore's ambitions far outstripped his purse, exhausting his funds before his new mansion was fully fitted out. Wyatt's chastely elegant interiors were furnished in an opulent Regency style between 1802 and 1825 by Belmore's son, whose relish for the job matched that of his father. The 2nd Earl spent over £26,000, more than it cost to build the house, with the fashionable Dublin upholsterer John Preston, whose fine furnishings include one of the few state beds in Ireland.

Extensively restored by the National Trust to reflect its early nineteenth-century appearance, Castle Coole is an intriguing blend of classical and Regency. The dignified entrance hall, with a screen of mock-marble columns and statues in niches, is painted a welcoming pink as it was by the 2nd Earl. In contrast, grey scagliola pilasters ringing the oval saloon beneath Joseph Rose's delicate ceiling echo the original colour scheme, while stoves set in niches and the curved doors following the line of the walls are again strongly reminiscent of designs for Kedleston.

The saloon is the centrepiece of the north front, dividing rooms of very different character. The dining room on one side, still lit only by candles, is pure Wyatt, with fan-like plaster tracery arching over the curtainless windows, slate-green walls hung with family portraits and a delicate classical frieze. The drawing room at the other end of the house is furnished with gilt couches and chairs upholstered in salmon pink and with a richly patterned nineteenth-century Aubusson carpet. The library across the hall is more comfortable, with a plentiful supply of cushions and bolsters lying casually on the red velvet of the masculine Grecian sofas. The heavy folds of the crimson curtains with their plump tassels are immortalised in white marble on Westmacott's extraordinary chimneypiece, executed while Wyatt was employed on the house but not to the

ABOVE As this view down one of the colonnades shows, Castle Coole has an austere and sculptural beauty.

architect's surviving design. Substantial servants' quarters in the basement reflect the number of staff that would have been necessary for a house of this quality.

Castle Coole looks out over a wooded park that was landscaped in the late eighteenth century and slopes gently down to Lough Coole, the site of a previous house. The double oak avenue, along which Castle Coole has been approached since about 1730, has been replanted and will reach maturity some time in the middle of this century.

Castle Drogo

Devon
4 miles (6.4 kilometres) south
of the A30 Exeter–Okehampton
road via Crockernwell; or turn off
the A382 Moretonhampstead–
Whiddon Down road at Sandy Park

When Julius Drewe, the self-made millionaire, retired from his retailing business in 1889 aged only 33, he was determined to set himself up as a country gentleman. Fired with the belief that he was descended from a Norman baron and that the family name had been given to the Dartmoor village of Drewsteignton, he resolved to build a castle on the land that he thought had once belonged to his remote ancestors. Castle Drogo, set on moorland to the west of the village and built of local granite, looks both suitably medieval and as if it is rooted in the landscape. Early drawings for the castle show a significantly larger building, but this individual country house is striking enough as it is.

As the spectacular views from the roof confirm, the site, on a spur high above the gorge of the River Teign, was well chosen. The entrance drive runs along the top of the bluff, but the castle is far more impressive if approached by the steep path leading up from the river far below, when a great mass of granite walls and towers topped by battlements and pierced by mullioned windows suddenly rears up from the bracken-covered hillside ahead. The entrance tower with twin octagonal turrets on the west front has a genuine portcullis and the heraldic Drewe lion is proudly displayed over the arch leading to the front door.

This ambitious building was commissioned in 1910 from Sir Edwin Lutyens, then at the height of his powers and with the transformation of Lindisfarne Castle already behind him (*see* p.209). The great architect's interiors combine the elemental grandeur of the castle with the comfort expected of a country house. The castle emerges most strongly in the bare granite walls, exposed plaster and unpainted woodwork of the stairs and corridors, and in the sophisticated handling of these spaces Lutyens was at his most inspired. The main corridor leading from the entrance hall is an architectural *tour de force*, with an intriguing interplay of domes and vaults, while the great staircase, framed by cliffs of granite and lit by a vast, east-facing mullioned and transomed window, descends beneath a ribbed stone vault of sculptural intensity. Lutyens ingeniously devised a second stair, for the servants, within the core of his main staircase.

The family rooms, lit by generous mullioned windows, are more intimate and welcoming, their walls covered with panelling or hung with tapestry. The main staircase links the dining room, lined with Cuban mahogany and hung with family portraits, with the airy drawing room three flights above, where panelling painted a soft green, chintz-covered sofas and windows on three sides create a restful, luxurious atmosphere. Similarly, the bathrooms, one with an elaborate shower arrangement, were designed with pleasure in mind. Exotic Spanish furniture in several of the rooms was acquired as a result of the spectacular bankruptcy of the banker Adrian de

LEFT The main staircase is walled by cliffs of granite and lit by a soaring east window. A portrait of Julius Drewe dressed as a country gentleman, by Charles Hardie, hangs at the turn of the stairs.

ABOVE Castle Drogo's entrance tower has a workable portcullis, operated by a winch in one of the turrets, arrow slits, and the heraldic Drewe lion carved in relief above the archway.

Murrieta, friend of the Prince of Wales (the future Edward VII) and extravagant social butterfly, whose vast red-brick mansion at Wadhurst in Sussex Drewe purchased in 1899.

Lutyens took as much care with the extensive servants' quarters in the bowels of the castle as he did with the rest of the house. The vaulted service corridor is another great architectural space, the unadorned granite and plaster of the walls and the absence of detailing, such as skirting boards, producing a powerful impact. In the lofty kitchen, lit only through a lantern in the roof, a rough beechwood table and other fittings, even the pastry boards, which were curved to fit the table, were made to his design, as were the oak cupboards, table and teak sinks in the substantial pantry.

Lutyens was also involved in the formal garden to the north of the house, where yew hedges are clipped in geometric shapes and granite steps lead up a flight of terraces. The layout was devised almost entirely by Lutyens and he also had ideas for the planting, but these were developed in conjunction with the garden designer George Dillistone, with contributions from the Drewe family.

Sadly, Julius Drewe died only a year after the castle was completed in 1930, but he must have been pleased with his progress in life. Whereas *Burke's Landed Gentry* ignored his similarly wealthy retailing rivals Lipton and Sainsbury, the land Drewe acquired with the fortune amassed from his Home and Colonial Stores gained his inclusion.

A major programme of building works, which has made the castle watertight for the first time in its history, was completed in 2020.

Castle Ward

Co. Down
7 miles (11.2 kilometres) north-east
of Downpatrick, 1½ miles
(2.4 kilometres) west of Strangford
village on the A25, on the south
shore of Strangford Lough,
entrance by Ballyculter Lodge

Castle Ward, crowning a gentle slope above Strangford Lough, is a very Irish house. Although built at one period, from 1762 to 1766, it is classical on the west side, with a central pediment supported by four columns, and gothick on the east, with battlements, pinnacles and ogival windows. The interior follows the same eccentric approach, with the rooms on one side of the house, the hall, dining room and library, decorated in a Palladian idiom, while those on the east, the saloon, morning room and boudoir, are in an opulent and light-hearted gothick, with pointed doors and plaster vaulting. This architectural curiosity was built by Bernard Ward, later 1st Viscount Bangor, who had inherited the estate in 1759, and his wife Lady Anne. Wanting to replace the existing house, the couple looked at buildings in both styles before deciding to combine up-to-the-minute classicism, which showed them to be people of taste, with gothick features that suggested their ancient lineage, in their new home. The versatile architect is unknown, although tradition has it that, like the stone of which the house is built, he may have come from Bath (the stone was brought from England in Lord Bangor's own ship and unloaded in Castle Bay below the house).

Sadly, despite their close collaboration on the architecture of Castle Ward, Bernard and Anne's relationship was increasingly strained. Only a few years after the house was finished, the couple separated and Anne went to live in Bath. By the time the 1st Viscount died, their eldest son, Nicholas, was insane and the estate was divided between his two younger brothers, one of whom, after moving Nicholas to Downpatrick, is thought to have removed most of the contents of the house. But the elaborate decorative schemes have survived almost unaltered. Three-dimensional plaster motifs stand out white against the green walls of the hall: here a festoon of musical instruments, including drums and tambourines, across the room a cluster of agricultural implements, a harrow, axe and billhook. A pedimented door opens into the gothick saloon, where ogival mirrors between the ecclesiastical traceried windows reflect a cluttered Victorian interior, with photographs on many surfaces, stuffed birds under a glass case, a gossip seat and family portraits hung two deep on the inside wall. The boudoir next door, transformed by the voluptuous curves of the gothick ceiling into a large, pink-walled tent, is even more exuberant. There could hardly be a greater contrast with the restrained

BELOW Castle Ward's attractive classical entrance front, with a pediment carrying the family's coat of arms above the central portico.

treatment of the elegant cantilevered staircase, lit by a Venetian window on the half-landing and ornamented with a frieze of acanthus-leaf scrolls on the side walls.

From the only addition to the house, the Victorian porch, steps lead down past an impressive array of bells to the housekeeper's room, the wine cellar and the kitchen in the basement. A long, whitewashed tunnel runs from here to the stable yard and the Victorian laundry, stables and tack room set around it, well away from the house as was the fashion in eighteenth-century Ireland.

A collection of framed watercolours in the boudoir, a scrapbook of drawings and photographs, scientific instruments and other things occasionally on display in the house celebrate the exceptional Mary Ward (1827–69), scientist and painter, whose husband Henry became the 5th Viscount on the death of his brother in 1881. It is hoped that a room devoted to her legacy will replace the Mary Ward museum that used to be in the basement.

Castle Ward has one of the most beautiful settings of any house in Ulster, with an eighteenth-century landscape park, in the English style, sloping down to the lough and views over the water framed by mature oaks and beeches. To the north of the house is the Temple Water, a serene artificial lake created in the early eighteenth century which is overlooked by a little classical temple. The formal Victorian garden near the house is different in character, with grassy terraces planted with palms and roses rising from a sunken, brightly flowering parterre to a line of Irish yews and a pinetum beyond.

Corn- and saw-mills, a drying kiln and slaughterhouse set round a yard near the Temple Water were once the centre of a thriving agricultural estate. Here, too, is the early seventeenth-century tower-house which the Wards built soon after they came to Ireland from England. Nearby is a row of slate-roofed late Victorian cottages that were provided for estate workers. It is believed that, only a few decades before, in 1852, the village of Audleystown had been flattened to improve the view from the house of Audley's Castle, a prominent tower-house dating from the fifteenth century that stands on the edge of Strangford Lough.

OPPOSITE The boudoir on the gothick side of Castle Ward has a suspended plaster ceiling which transforms the room into a billowing tent.
BELOW In contrast to Castle Ward's coolly classical entrance front, the other side of the house has a playful gothick façade.

Charlecote Park

Warwickshire
1 mile (1.6 kilometres) north-west
of Wellesbourne, 5 miles
(8 kilometres) east of
Stratford-upon-Avon, 6 miles
(9.6 kilometres) south of Warwick
on the north side of the B4086

Charlecote has been the home of the Lucy family for some 800 years. The present house, begun by Sir Thomas Lucy in the mid-sixteenth century, stands on the banks of the River Avon at the centre of an extensive wooded deer-park grazed by fallow deer and a herd of rare Jacob sheep. The estate is within easy reach of Stratford, and there is a story that Shakespeare was caught poaching here and brought before Sir Thomas Lucy, the resident magistrate, in Charlecote's great hall. The rough oak paling that still surrounds most of the park has been perpetuated since Elizabethan times.

The house is built of red brick to a pleasingly irregular E-shape. With banks of decorative chimneys arrayed across the roofline and octagonal corner turrets crowned with gilded weathervanes, Charlecote seems to sum up the very essence of Elizabethan England, especially when the brickwork is mellowed and burnished by the sun. Queen Elizabeth I visited the house in 1572, an occasion that is proudly celebrated in the display of her arms over the two-storeyed porch. With the exception of the porch, however, most of the present building is the result of 'Elizabethan' restoration in the mid-nineteenth century by George Hammond Lucy and his wife Mary Elizabeth, who not only refitted every room but also extended the house to the south and west, obscuring much genuine Elizabethan brickwork in the process. The general effect is rich and lush, reflecting advice from the designer and antiquarian Thomas Willement, who, as well as advising on neo-Elizabethan plasterwork ceilings and other period features, even produced convincing Elizabethan versions of such things as fitted bookshelves and pile carpets, unknown in the sixteenth century. The Willement touch is particularly evident in the sunny and comfortable library, where he designed the Elizabethan-style bookcases to house the Lucys' fine collection of books, which includes a late fourteenth-century *Book of Hours*, and also the carpet, the wallpaper and matching chintz covers on the furniture, and the fire grate and doorstops.

George Hammond Lucy also added Old Masters to the run of family portraits in the house and what remains of his collection, after the most valuable paintings were sold to pay debts in the later nineteenth century, hangs in the drawing room. He was responsible, too, for most of the furnishings, many of which came from the 1823 sale of the contents of William Beckford's Fonthill Abbey in Wiltshire. The most expensive purchase was the sixteenth-century Italian marble table in the great hall, which was made for the Borghese Palace in Rome. An intricate inlay of coloured marbles and semi-precious stones covering the top features brightly coloured

OPPOSITE Charlecote's entrance front dates largely from the nineteenth century, but the porch with its classical columns is an Elizabethan survival and carries the arms of Elizabeth I, who came here in 1572.
LEFT The great hall at Charlecote Park is hung with portraits of the Lucy family who have been living on this site since at least the twelfth century and who still inhabit the house.

birds and a slab of onyx like a section through a fossilised tree. Mary Elizabeth, who carried on altering and furnishing the house after George's death in 1845, modernised the drawing-room wing and purchased the gigantic, ornately carved neo-Elizabethan buffet that dominates the dining room.

Two generations earlier, in the mid-eighteenth century, George Lucy, a cultivated and much travelled bachelor, had employed 'Capability' Brown to redesign the park, sweeping away the seventeenth-century water gardens (shown in the painting above Shakespeare's bust in the great hall) and altering the course of the River Hele (now the Dene) so that it cascaded into the Avon within sight of the house. George Lucy

was also responsible for introducing the Jacob sheep, which he brought back from a trip to Portugal. The balustraded formal garden between house and river, with steps into the Avon, is a nineteenth-century addition.

Some of the earliest parts of the house are in the extensive outbuildings, where the stable block includes a brew-house that was in operation until the 1890s, a wash-house, and a coach-house displaying a collection of vehicles used at Charlecote into the first half of the twentieth century. But only the rose-pink gatehouse with its fretwork stone balustrade survives unaltered from Sir Thomas Lucy's original Tudor mansion, a tantalising taste of what has been lost.

Chartwell

Kent
2 miles (3.2 kilometres) south of
Westerham

Winston Churchill, whose home this was, once declared that he bought Chartwell 'for that view'. Set high up on the side of a little Kentish valley, the house looks over the garden that falls away steeply below to wooded slopes across the combe, and to the soft countryside leading onward to the Weald beyond. There are vistas from almost every room and, as the many doors to the garden suggest, a sense of a house linked intimately with its surroundings. This serene setting, still breathtakingly beautiful, was to provide Winston Churchill with inspiration and strength for over 40 years, from 1922 until he left Chartwell for the last time in 1964.

The appeal of this unpretentious red-brick house, with its comfortable, airy rooms created by Philip Tilden out of a gloomy Victorian mansion, lies in its powerful reflection of a gifted and complicated man, whose spirit still seems to linger on here. His bold and colourful paintings hang throughout the house, some, such as the simple study of a magnolia on an upper landing, tranquil still-lifes, others recording landscapes he loved, in France, Italy and Morocco as well as around Chartwell. A half-finished canvas stands on the easel in his garden studio, paints laid ready nearby. Finished pictures hang four and five deep on the walls round about. In the airy, flower-filled drawing room, a card-table is set for the bezique he so much enjoyed and a painting over the fireplace records one of the finest colts from his racing stable. A velvet siren suit, his characteristic wide-brimmed hats and cigar boxes also suggest a man who relished the pleasures of life.

But there are other mementoes too. In the lofty study, with its high roof open to the rafters, is the wide mahogany stand-up desk at which Churchill liked to work. His *A History of the English-Speaking Peoples* and *The Second World War* were mostly

LEFT Chartwell, the home of Winston Churchill from 1922 until 1964, looks out over terraced gardens laid out by the Churchills and the soft, wooded countryside of Kent and Sussex beyond.
OPPOSITE Seven round-headed windows looking over the garden light the dining room, where dinner, served at eight, was usually accompanied by champagne. The circular tables and the chairs were made for the Churchills by Heal's in the 1920s.

composed in this room. Here he reflected on the growing power of Germany during the 1930s, a threat that he felt was perceived by him alone. The study is still essentially as he left it, crowded with family photographs, a dispatch box on the table. A portrait of his father hangs by the fire and a drawing of his mother confirms her exceptional beauty. Elsewhere, medals, uniforms and other reminders of a life devoted to his country include Churchill's terse directive to Field Marshal Alexander, instructing him to expel the enemy from North Africa, and the field marshal's equally short reply, informing the prime minister that he had done so. Chartwell is also very much a family house. The signatures of Lloyd George, Balfour and Field Marshal Montgomery in the visitors' book are interspersed with the more tentative efforts of the four young Churchills' friends and cousins. And it was the children

who decided to mark their parents' 50th wedding anniversary by planting the borders filled with 32 varieties of golden roses that run in a long corridor down the kitchen garden, framed by beds of vegetables, soft fruit and flowers. Close by is the wall that Churchill built when he was in the political wilderness before the Second World War.

A loose framework of hedges and walls, with steps from one level to another, divides the spacious garden that falls away to the lakes in the depths of the combe. Stretches of trees and grass are complemented by planting schemes reflecting Lady Clementine Churchill's love of cool colours and simple and direct effects. Her walled rose garden lies to the east of the house and there are many butterfly-attracting plants. Most evocative is the secluded pond, where an ample garden chair marks the spot where Churchill came daily to feed his golden orfe and ponder life.

Chastleton House

Oxfordshire
At Chastleton off the A44, 4 miles
(6.4 kilometres) south-east of
Moreton-in-Marsh

On the fringes of the Cotswolds, eastwards into Oxfordshire, is an unspoilt landscape of well-wooded farmland and limestone villages. Less than a mile (1.6 kilometres) off the main road from Oxford to Evesham, a leafy, narrow lane runs steeply up through a straggle of cottages. At the top of the village, set back across a grassy court beside a stump-towered church, is a square, many-gabled Jacobean house. Of mellow local stone, with tall, three-storey ranges set round a tight internal court and mullioned windows, Chastleton is a charming and unaltered example of the kind of manor house which must have adorned a thousand English villages, lived in by families untouched by high office and national events. There are sophisticated touches, such as the arresting south front, with its show of glass and advancing bays, and some fine plaster ceilings, but much else, such as the rough and mossy dry-stone walls lining the entrance court, is rustic and ad hoc.

Until it came to the National Trust in 1991, Chastleton had been in the hands of the same family for almost 400

years. Built in *c.* 1610–12 for Walter Jones, a successful wool merchant, who bought the estate in 1602 from Robert Catesby, the future Gunpowder Plotter, it had been owned by Jones's descendants ever since, with tapestries and furniture identifiable on the inventory taken after his death in 1632. Early prosperity did not last. Although the family was staunchly royalist in the Civil War, when Arthur Jones is said to have evaded a Roundhead search party after the Battle of Worcester by hiding in a secret chamber, there were few rewards at the Restoration, and growing financial difficulties culminated in Henry Jones's imprisonment for bankruptcy in 1755. Chastleton's character comes from the slow accumulation of contents in a house that, like an old coat, was sometimes cut to fit but never drastically altered or updated.

Above a substantial basement, where the smoke-blackened kitchen ceiling, said to ensure the family's luck, remains unwhitewashed, is a sequence of parlours and chambers, some tapestry-hung and the grander with carved chimneypieces of stone or wood and decorative plasterwork. Panelling, now dark with age and dirt, is used like wallpaper, and there are pegged plank doors, undulating floors and deep windowsills. The plan is conservative, centred on a traditional great hall, with an oriel window lighting the high-table end and a carved strapwork screen, and with staircases in crenellated towers to either side of the house. The most ornate interior is the great chamber, where the overmantel, carved with the arms of Jones and his wife, still has much of its rich red, blue and gold colour scheme and the ceiling is an extravaganza of trailing vines and hanging pendants; the most glorious is the bare and airy long gallery on the third floor, with its silvery panelling and plasterwork barrel ceiling. The long refectory table in the hall, leather chests in the gallery, and the blue and red flamestitch hangings lining a little closet are among the furnishings given on the 1633 inventory; a brief burst of refurbishment after 1697, when Walter Jones married the forceful Anne Whitmore, accounts for the James II walnut chairs and exquisite Queen Anne crewelwork; and the family's poverty ensured the survival of some seventeenth-century woollen hangings that were once commonplace and are now very rare. There is also an unbroken run of family portraits, including works by Kneller and Hudson, and a leather-bound Bible in the library is said to have been used by Charles I on the scaffold. All is seen in a

ABOVE The splendid east staircase, with its carved newel posts, bears the date 1636 but in fact was built in 1830.
OPPOSITE Ornate plasterwork covers the barrel ceiling of the atmospheric long gallery at the top of the house.

shadowy half-light, brightened by shafts of sunlight through leaded casements.

It was Anne Whitmore who probably laid out the topiary garden to the east of the house, with a yew circle embracing 24 box figures. Once an impressive display of arboreal sculpture, these are now a collection of intriguingly individual amorphous shapes. To the north is a sequence of grassed terraces where a lawn laid out for croquet recalls the nineteenth-century Walter Jones Whitmore, who first codified the rules of the game.

ABOVE One of the two battlemented staircase towers at Chastleton overlooks the topiary garden to the east of the house, where the 24 box figures are being allowed to become increasingly amorphous.

In a field beyond the garden, on a sightline from the house, there is a mature oak, said to have grown from an acorn off the Boscobel tree that sheltered the fugitive Charles II, and a delicious eighteenth-century dovecote stands in the parkland rising to the summit of Chastleton Hill.

Chedworth Roman Villa

Gloucestershire
3 miles (4.8 kilometres) north-west of Fossebridge, off A429 Cirencester–Northleach road

At the top of a peaceful wooded combe in the depths of the Cotswolds, low limestone walls, the stumps of former columns, terraces cut into the hillside and bumps and hollows in the grass mark the site of what was once one of the grandest villas of Roman Britain. These remains trace out three long wings, one storey high and one room deep, which were arranged round two courtyards running down the hill. Covered galleries fronted each wing and a cross gallery divided the more prestigious upper courtyard from what lay below. At the highest point of the site, an octagonal pool filled by a spring from the hillside marks the remains of a water shrine. The villa faces east, with glorious views down the combe to the pastoral Coln valley, from which it would have been approached.

Although parts of the villa date from the late second century, when three simple buildings and a bath house were constructed here, the remains are largely from the mid-fourth century. This period was a golden age, when the Romanised British aristocracy built villas to rival those of the Mediterranean world, many of them on the fertile estates of the Gloucestershire Cotswolds. Chedworth, only a few miles from the important Roman town of Corinium Dobunnorum (Cirencester) and from the great Roman highway of the Fosse Way, running from Exeter to the Humber, was particularly well placed. Who lived here is not known, but the owner must have been a man of some consequence, one of the British elite who headed up a sizeable household which would have included people who had been enslaved as well as servants.

Although the walls are nowhere more than a foot or two above the ground, this remarkable place, which for centuries lay buried beneath soil and woodland, still has substantial remains of the lavish decoration and up-to-the-minute technology with which it was fitted out. Water from the spring at the top of the valley was fed by gravity to two sets of baths, one the equivalent of a modern sauna, where the stream filled a deep plunge pool, the other providing the steamy heat of a Turkish bath. Stone channels in the floor of the communal latrine were kept clean by running water, and the spring also fed taps in the kitchen. Pillars of brick and stone exposed in some rooms were part of the sophisticated heating system, which channelled hot air under the floors, and fragments of painted plaster suggest once-vivid colour schemes and paintwork that simulated marble. Most memorable are the villa's mosaic floors, their tesserae, in shades of white, olive, blue, grey, brown and red, mostly made of stones from local sources. The designs are predominantly geometric, using patterns seen across the Roman empire, but the impressive floor in the dining room in the west range includes Bacchic scenes, featuring drunken satyrs, and representations of the four seasons, Winter warmly clad, like an ancient Briton, in a hooded cloak, a hare dangling from one hand, wood clasped in the other.

The prosperity and political stability that underlay Chedworth did not last. The withdrawal of Roman power in AD410 was followed by the collapse of the Romanised way of life, and it seems the villa became part of a farm and was then abandoned, to be gradually absorbed by the surrounding woods. Over the years, stones were taken for use elsewhere and, in the seventeenth century, the ruins were used to feed a lime kiln, but generally the villa was forgotten. It was uncovered in 1864 by James Farrer, the uncle and guardian of the 3rd Lord Eldon, on whose land Chedworth lay. His interest sparked by a gamekeeper, who showed him fragments of mosaic picked up in the woods, Farrer dug out the remains, rebuilt parts of the walls and added protective coverings to the best rooms and mosaics. He also built the little museum displaying finds and carved stonework which stands in the middle of the site, at one end of the mock-Tudor hunting lodge added by Lord Eldon in 1866.

LEFT The ornate mosaic floor in the dining room at Chedworth includes depictions of partying satyrs and maenads.

Cherryburn

Northumberland
Off the A695 at Mickley,
11 miles (17.7 kilometres) west
of Newcastle

A roughly built sandstone cottage set high above the deep green valley of the Tyne was the birthplace of the eminent artist and naturalist Thomas Bewick (1753–1828), who is best known for his intricate engravings. At the age of fourteen, Bewick was apprenticed to a leading engraver in the nearby town of Newcastle, who, working with copper and silver, taught the boy how to produce the precise and delicate effects he was later to realise in wood. Once his apprenticeship was over, Bewick went into partnership with his old master and, in November 1785, on the day his father died, began working on the engravings for the delightful company of animals which illustrate *A General History of Quadrupeds*, the book that would bring him to the attention of a wider world. Published in 1790, the *General History* was an instant success and was followed, a few years later, by two volumes on British birds, the illustrations for which Bewick drew from life.

The cottage, originally heather-thatched but now tiled and somewhat smaller than it was in Bewick's childhood, looks over a sloping cobbled yard to the substantial farmhouse built in the late 1820s by Thomas's brother William, who took over the family smallholding and partly demolished his former home, using what remained for stabling. Although the bedroom under the roof from where Bewick watched the changing seasons did not survive William's attentions, what remains of the cottage has been reconstructed as it was in Bewick's day on the basis of detailed drawings made by his son Robert. Bewick's desk, original box blocks and other mementoes, and a splendid collection of his publications acquired with the help of the National Heritage Memorial Fund, are on display in the farmhouse, where there are also demonstrations of traditional printing methods. Bewick himself lies in the graveyard of Ovingham church, less than a mile (1.6 kilometres) away across the valley.

LEFT The life and work of the engraver Thomas Bewick are captured at Cherryburn, where the National Trust cares for both the sandstone cottage where he was born in 1753 and the family farmhouse built in the 1820s. OPPOSITE There are many rare sixteenth- and seventeenth-century books in Chirk's exceptional library.

Chirk Castle

Wrexham
½ mile (0.8 kilometre) west of
Chirk village off the A5

Chirk Castle is an elegantly appointed house within the carapace of a medieval fortress. Magnificent Baroque entrance gates, a filigree of white ironwork that once closed Chirk's forecourt and now forms a screen by the approach road, suggest a mansion of elegance and style. But the building that suddenly appears on the brow of the hill on the drive through the undulating, oak-studded park is unexpectedly menacing, with drum towers projecting from battlemented fourteenth-century walls.

A pointed archway marked with the grooves of a portcullis leads into the internal courtyard. Here the west range still has the character of the stronghold Roger Mortimer started in c. 1295 as part of Edward I's campaign to subdue the Welsh. Deep underground, reached by a spiral staircase in the thickness of the walls, is a dungeon hollowed out of the rock. Only two narrow beams of light reached those who were incarcerated here. In the courtyard outside a great shaft falls 93 feet (28.5 metres) to the castle well.

These reminders of the turbulent Middle Ages contrast with the later interiors commissioned by the Myddelton family, who came to Chirk in 1595 when the castle was sold to the merchant, financier and founding member of the East India Company, Thomas Myddelton I. In the late eighteenth century, Joseph Turner of Chester created an elegant staircase and a suite of state apartments in the fashionable Neo-classical style within the massive walls of the north range. Gothic touches by A.W.N. Pugin, who was commissioned to redecorate the castle in the 1840s, have been mostly toned down or removed, but some of the strong colour schemes and other details that he introduced remain. The sumptuous saloon, with gilded doors and dados and a red and white chimneypiece of Sicilian marble, is graced with an Adam-style coffered ceiling, coloured a brilliant blue by Pugin and his collaborator J.G. Crace and inset with Greek mythological scenes by the Irish painter George Mullins. Mortlake tapestries hang on the walls and the fine contemporary furniture includes pier tables and mirrors by Ince & Mayhew, a pair of stylish serpentine settees and the earliest signed harpsichord, of 1742, by Burkat Shudi, the intricate marquetry of the interior depicting eagles with outstretched wings. Among the seventeenth- and eighteenth-century family portraits hanging in these rooms are pictures by Francis Cotes of Richard Myddelton and his wife, who commissioned the state apartments, and two rare portraits by the Flemish landscape painter Peter Tillemans.

A door from the drawing room leads into the 100-foot (30-metre) long gallery that fills the first floor of the east range. Created in the 1670s, when Sir Thomas Myddelton IV, 2nd Baronet, repaired the extensive damage that Chirk had sustained in the Civil War, the gallery is more than twice the size of the saloon and is little changed, apart from the addition of a ribbed heraldic ceiling and fireplace tiles by Pugin. Dark oak panelling, perhaps by the gentleman-architect William Winde, is grandly conceived, with massive broken pediments crowning the doors and a bold cornice of carved acanthus leaves running above a show of early portraits. Among the few pieces of furniture, all of them probably part of the original contents, is a delicate seventeenth-century Dutch cabinet of ebony inlaid with tortoiseshell and ivory. The silver-encrusted interior is decorated with scenes from the life of Christ that were painted in the Antwerp studio of Frans Francken the Younger; one of them shows Our Lord blessing children against a backdrop of the gabled façades of a Flemish town. Declining a peerage from King Charles II, who had spent two nights at Chirk during the Civil War, Sir Thomas Myddelton II, grandfather of the 2nd Baronet, accepted this cabinet instead.

In 1820, an open colonnade beneath the gallery was transformed by the Chester architect Thomas Harrison into a suite of neo-gothic family apartments. Subsequently redecorated by Pugin, these still contain Harrison's fan-vaulted ceilings and many features made for Chirk in the 1840s, such as the delightful metalwork door plates and knobs, firebacks and gasoliers supplied by John Hardman & Co. to Pugin's designs, and Pugin's stone fireplace in the drawing room. Chirk's exceptional library is also in this range, the many rare sixteenth- and seventeenth-century books that it contains includes a copy of the first popular edition of the Welsh Bible, which was sponsored, in 1630, by Sir Thomas Myddelton, the purchaser of the estate.

These neo-gothic rooms are fitted out in a 1930s idiom to reflect the life of Thomas, 8th Lord Howard de Walden, the shy and eccentric millionaire and patron of the arts who leased Chirk from the Myddeltons from 1911 to 1946. Specially commissioned furniture reproduces that shown in period photographs and in a portrait of the family by Lavery; a gothic suit of armour commissioned from Felix Joubert, on loan from Dean Castle, reflects the 8th Lord's passion for medieval pursuits; and paintings and other works of art on loan from the family, the Tate and the National Gallery of Wales include a portrait of the 8th Lord by Augustus John, a bust by Rodin, and views of the castle and surrounding countryside by Wilson Steer.

Chirk's park was landscaped by William Emes in the late eighteenth century. The garden falls away on the east side of the castle, where the walls are softened by climbers. A show of topiary includes a massive hedge cut to resemble a battlemented wall; a sunken rose garden is centred on a sundial; and a mixed border flanking a sweep of grass was first established by Colonel and Lady Margaret Myddelton, who restored the garden after the Second World War. A lime avenue hidden in woodland is the only feature to survive from a seventeenth-century formal layout, and a little pavilion sits at one end of a long terrace, the views from here taking in a great sweep of the Welsh borders.

Clandon Park

Surrey
At West Clandon on the A247,
3 miles (4.8 kilometres) east of
Guildford on the A246

Clandon Park looks as if it would be more at home on the corner of a piazza in Venice or Florence than set down in the Surrey countryside. A massive block of a house, three storeys high above the basement, and 11 windows wide on the long garden façade, it is built in the reddest of brick with stone dressings and a central pedimented section of stone on the entrance front. There is a roofline balustrade, but nothing rises above it to relieve the clean geometry of the building. Only the heavy *porte-cochère*, added in 1876 in an attempt to make the entrance hall warmer, breaks the original lines.

This Georgian country house, built in the 1730s, was designed by the Italian architect Giacomo Leoni for Thomas, 2nd Baron Onslow, who wanted to replace the Tudor house his great-grandfather had acquired in 1641. It was built using the fortune of Thomas's wife, Elizabeth Knight, whose substantial inheritance from her uncle included a sugar plantation in Jamaica.

One of only five surviving buildings by Leoni in England, Clandon was, until recently, the most complete, with much of the original decoration still intact. Most impressive was Leoni's cool and airy Marble Hall rising through two storeys, its Palladian proportions and classical statues offset by a theatrically baroque plasterwork ceiling, with life-size male figures perched on the cornice, one leg over the edge, as if they might leap down at any moment. This all changed on 29 April 2015, when a devastating fire raged through the house. Thanks to Leoni's generous building specifications, with walls four bricks thick at basement level, and the fact that the original wooden lintels had been replaced with concrete, the shell of the house, along with the roofline parapet, withstood the fire. Some notable interior features, such as intricately carved marble chimneypieces by John Michael Rysbrack in the Marble Hall, panelling and decorative plasterwork, also survived. Showing how capricious fire can be, the dining room known as the Speakers' Parlour on the north-west corner of the house was almost untouched.

Although many of the contents were consumed by the fire, over 400 items from the collections on display here were rescued, including silver by Paul Storr, gigantic side tables

from the Marble Hall, embroidered chairs, porcelain, clocks and an extremely rare carpet of *c.* 1760 by Claude Passavant from his Exeter factory. The painstaking process of clearing the debris left by the fire has revealed hundreds more fragments of ceramic, decorative plasterwork, joinery, ornate metalwork and marble. Most importantly, the portraits of the three members of the Onslow family who served as Speakers of the House of Commons were cut from their frames and saved from the fire, as was the painting by William Hogarth and his father-in-law James Thornhill showing Arthur Onslow, who was speaker from 1727 to 1761, presiding over the House of Commons. The Onslow state bed, with priceless hangings that pre-date the building of the house, was also rescued, although its restoration presents a huge challenge.

Many of Clandon Park's original contents were sold or removed over the years and, before the fire, the Onslow family pieces were complemented by eighteenth-century English furniture, porcelain, textiles and carpets from the bequest of the connoisseur Hannah Gubbay. Remarkably, together with important pieces of furniture, some of her collection of

BELOW This little cherub decorating the chimneypiece in the saloon was among the sculptural detail which survived the devastating fire at Clandon in 2015.

seventeenth- and eighteenth-century porcelain Chinese birds and other ceramic creatures, which were such a feature of the house, survived the fire. A long-eared porcelain rabbit was discovered buried in ash in the state bedroom, having fallen through from the floor above, and a little green stoneware duck that was made in South Korea over 600 years ago and was also in a case on the first floor had a similarly lucky escape. This beautiful thing, once used by a calligrapher to hold water, having fallen out of its case and through the collapsing floor, was found, almost undamaged, amongst the debris in a doorway some 30 feet (9 metres) below. Somehow it seems

ABOVE Clandon's marble hall after the fire, showing one of the carved chimney pieces by John Michael Rysbrack that withstood the flames.

appropriate that this little duck should have been a symbol of happiness and fidelity.

The approach to rebuilding Clandon Park, which is still being worked out, will draw on a recent feasibility study and research into how the house was constructed and the materials that were used. Despite the ongoing work, the house was opened to visitors again just a few months after the fire, which was a major feat in itself.

Claydon

Buckinghamshire
In Middle Claydon, 13 miles
(20.9 kilometres) north-west
of Aylesbury, 3½ miles
(5.6 kilometres) south-west
of Winslow

A combination of ambition and gullibility led Ralph, 2nd Lord Verney, to create one of the most extraordinary houses in England. Inheriting the family estate in 1752, Verney initially contented himself with reconstructing and extending his father's old-fashioned Jacobean manor house, but some ten years later he embarked on a far more grandiose scheme for a great west front, partly, it seems, to produce a house to rival that of his much richer neighbour, Earl Temple of Stowe. The restrained classical exterior of the surviving west wing conceals extraordinary decoration by Luke Lightfoot, an eccentric and difficult genius variously described as cabinetmaker, master-builder and surveyor, but emerging at Claydon as a carver of unique talent.

Lightfoot's work in the North Hall and Chinese Room is in a class of its own. Ceilings, overmantels, doors and alcoves are encrusted with lacy white woodwork. Herons, swan-like birds and fantastic wyverns with barbed tails perch on the tracery. Necks are coiled and snaky, wings outstretched, claws extended. Tiny bells hang from the roof of the built-in pagoda-like feature in the Chinese Room, which was fitted out when the fashion for chinoiserie in eighteenth-century England was at its height. Carvings resembling oriental summer-houses, with trelliswork connecting the supporting columns, surmount the doors. Bamboo furniture made in Canton in about 1800 completes the effect.

Lightfoot's extravagance and the failure of a speculative housing project in which he had persuaded Lord Verney to invest led to his dismissal before the house was completed. Exquisite plasterwork adorning the saloon and staircase is by Joseph Rose, who was employed at Claydon after 1768. Working in plaster where Lightfoot worked in wood, Rose used conventional classical motifs but executed them with skill and ingenuity to create two of the finest Georgian interiors in England. The stairs are one of the marvels of Claydon, with

delicate ears of corn quivering in the ironwork scrolls that make up the balustrade and a jigsaw of box, mahogany, ebony and ivory forming the parquetry treads.

Growing financial difficulties, unrelieved by lawyers employed to help manage mounting debts, led to the sale of the contents of the house in 1783, and Verney's grandiose ballroom and huge rotunda by the architect-squire Sir Thomas Robinson were demolished by his niece when she succeeded to the estate. The Javanese musical instruments filling the museum room, an assortment of gongs and wood and bamboo xylophones collectively known as a gamelan, were a present to Sir Harry Verney, 2nd Baronet, who inherited the property

RIGHT This intricate doorcase in the Chinese Room at Claydon House is typical of the outstanding decoration by the brilliant Luke Lightfoot, who created in wood what others would have realised in plaster.

in 1827. Florence Nightingale would have seen this unusual gift from Sir Stamford Raffles, lieutenant governor of Java, when she came to visit her elder sister Frances Parthenope, Sir Harry's wife. The room where Florence always slept is decorated as it was in her day, her sitting room has been re-created, and there are many mementoes of this formidable woman, among them letters she wrote as a young girl, a watercolour of her pet owl, and reminders of the privations she endured in the Crimea, two photographs showing how thin and frail she looked on her return. Unfortunately there is no record of what this most Victorian of women thought of the extravagant rococo decoration of her sister's home.

BELOW Claydon House as it is today, with a handsome front overlooking the park, was once part of a much grander mansion, with a vast ballroom, much of which was demolished in the 1790s.

Clevedon Court

Somerset
1½ miles (2.4 kilometres) east of
Clevedon, on the B3130

During the nineteenth century, the seaside village of Clevedon was transformed into a fashionable resort with Italianate villas, a pier and a Royal Hotel. But the Eltons of Clevedon Court who had done so much to improve the town lived on in the remarkable medieval manor that Abraham Elton I, a Bristol merchant, had acquired in 1709.

Seen from the south, Clevedon is a picturesque assemblage of low, stone-built ranges, mullioned windows, steeply pitched roofs and tall chimneys, all set against the thick woods of Court Hill. Despite some later additions, Sir John de Clevedon's early fourteenth-century house has survived virtually unchanged, its buttressed walls and the portcullis groove on the projecting two-storey porch suggesting that he needed to build with defence in mind. A four-storey tower, with narrow loop windows, at the north-east corner of the house is probably part of this fourteenth-century work. Carved out of the hillside and rising sharply behind the house are terraced gardens, planted with tender shrubs and adorned with two summer-houses.

Finely crafted fourteenth-century arches on the right of the traditional screens passage bisecting the house were openings to the medieval buttery, kitchen and pantry. To the left is the great hall, now embellished with an eighteenth-century coved ceiling and thickly hung with a mixed bag of Elton family portraits. Sir Abraham, the 1st Baronet, dressed in his scarlet robes as Mayor of Bristol, proudly surveys the descendants who were to enrich Clevedon with literary and artistic associations. A cartoon of William Makepeace Thackeray at the top of the stairs, a shock of white hair standing out from his head and pince-nez on his nose, recalls the novelist's friendship with Sir Charles, the 6th Baronet, a gifted poet whose elegy for his two drowned sons moved his contemporaries to tears. Sir Charles's youngest daughter Jane, with whom Thackeray fell hopelessly

ABOVE LEFT The window of Clevedon Court's medieval chapel, filled with a net of stone tracery, stands out on the south front of this ancient house.
BELOW Clevedon as seen from the garden terraces cut into the hill behind, with the four-storey medieval tower on the extreme left, and the great hall range dominating the main part of the house.

in love, inspired characters in his novels and the description of Castlewood House and garden in *Henry Esmond* is based on Clevedon Court. The poet-baronet's circle also included Charles Lamb and Coleridge, and Tennyson composed his elegy 'In Memoriam' for Sir Charles's nephew Arthur Hallam, who was a close friend of Tennyson and died tragically young.

The family's artistic streak appeared again in Sir Edmund Elton, whose Eltonware pots and vases made of clay from the estate, most of them in rich, dark colours but some pieces of a striking sea-blue and all with metallic glazes, are displayed in the old kitchen and whose vivid portrait by Emmeline Deane hangs in the hall. This remarkable self-taught man began his career as a potter in about 1880, building up an international reputation for his work. Fragile glass walking sticks, some shot through with spirals and twists of colour, glass rolling pins and improbable pipes tinged rose-pink, crimson and blue are part of the collection of high-quality local Nailsea glass which is also shown in the house.

Another side of Victorian Britain emerges on the stairs, where boldly patterned wallpaper by G.F. Bodley shows off a number of prints and engravings collected by Sir Arthur Elton, 10th Baronet, illustrating triumphs of engineering in the late eighteenth and nineteenth centuries, from Abraham Darby's iron bridge at Coalbrookdale, constructed in the 1770s, to the Menai Strait, Severn and Clifton suspension bridges and a host of viaducts and aqueducts that were vital to the achievements of the age.

A tall red and green Eltonware candlestick, designed with Sir Edmund's characteristic flair, stands in the tiny first-floor chapel that was part of John de Clevedon's manor and originally consecrated in *c.* 1320. A net of stone tracery across the south wall, filled with brilliantly coloured Victorian stained glass by Clayton and Bell, not only recalls the patron saint of fishermen to whom the chapel was originally dedicated but also the Bristol Channel only a mile (1.6 kilometres) or so to the west, where the little islands of Flat Holm and Steep Holm stand out black against the sea in the light of a setting sun.

LEFT The medieval Great Hall, with Elton family portraits covering the walls, is at the heart of Clevedon Court.

Cliveden

Buckinghamshire
3 miles (4.8 kilometres) upstream
from Maidenhead, 2 miles
(3.2 kilometres) north of Taplow
and the A4

This three-storey Italianate palace floating on a chalk terrace high above the River Thames is a *tour de force* by Sir Charles Barry, who is best known for designing the Houses of Parliament. Built in 1850–1 for the Duke and Duchess of Sutherland, it replaced two earlier houses that had been destroyed by fire, the first a Restoration house by William Winde for the 2nd Duke of Buckingham, which burned down in 1795, the second a Georgian-style house designed in 1827–30 for Sir George Warrender by the Edinburgh architect William Burn, who made use of the foundations and surviving wings of the earlier building. Cliveden had just been sold to the Sutherlands when it was burned down again in 1849. The smoke from the fire alerted Queen Victoria as she came out of chapel at Windsor and she sent fire engines from the castle, which is only 5 miles (8 kilometres) away, but the house was largely gutted. An inscription running below the roofline records the seventeenth-century building, much of whose character and shape Barry preserved, as well as the construction of the present mansion. The two wings surviving from the original house, added on by Thomas Archer for the Earl of Orkney, Cliveden's new owner, in 1706 and linked to the main block by curved corridors, flank a great sweep of gravel on the entrance front, from where the drive, shaded by an avenue of limes, runs straight to an extravagant marble fountain by Thomas Waldo Story. Ornate stables on the west side of the forecourt, with a top-heavy clock-tower rising high above them, were added in the 1860s.

From the south, Cliveden is more of a piece and more imposing. Here, Barry's main block, with an urn-studded roofline parapet, rises grandly over a long arcaded terrace, 28 arches wide, which extends far beyond it on either side. A legacy of the Restoration house, this magnificent feature, its crumbling brick- and stonework now fully restored, was

BELOW Cliveden's south front looks out over a great grass terrace where the elaborate parterre was first devised in the early eighteenth century.

ABOVE The rococo panelling in Cliveden's seductive French dining room came from an eighteenth-century hunting lodge outside Paris.

embellished in the eighteenth century by a central double staircase that descends in elegant elbows of stone to a grassy platform. Immediately below the arcade, on a bank above the grass, is the mellow brick and weathered stone of an early seventeenth-century balustrade, its central opening framed by elaborate pedestals, which was brought here from the Villa Borghese in Rome in 1896.

The Borghese balustrade was introduced by William Waldorf, later 1st Viscount Astor, who bought Cliveden in 1893. Lord Astor also commissioned J.L. Pearson, then in his mid-seventies, and his son Frank to remodel the interior of the house, but some of the painted decoration introduced by the Duchess of Sutherland still survives on the staircase ceiling, where figures by the French émigré artist Auguste Hervieu depict the Sutherland's four children in the guise of the seasons. Of the three rooms shown (Cliveden is now a hotel), the most seductive is the French dining room, lined with green and gold rococo panelling and with a marble chimneypiece and painted overdoors, all of which came from a mid-eighteenth-century hunting lodge near Paris. Pearson's capacious, low-ceilinged, oak-panelled hall, with a carved stone chimneypiece of *c.* 1525 from a French château at one

end and early eighteenth-century Brussels tapestries on the walls, is dominated by Sargent's vivacious portrait of Nancy Astor, wife of the 2nd Viscount, and the first woman to sit in the House of Commons. Given the house and its contents as a wedding present by William Waldorf in 1906, Nancy and her husband made Cliveden famous as a centre of literary and political society before the First World War, entertaining Henry James, Rudyard Kipling, Curzon and Churchill here. The house parties continued between the wars, when the so-called Cliveden Set, supporting Chamberlain and appeasement, were seen as politically significant, but the guest list, which included Charlie Chaplin, was as eclectic as ever. Only a few years later, during the Second World War, Lord Astor decided to give Cliveden to the National Trust, but the family continued to live here until 1966, and it was during these years that Cliveden was caught up in a political scandal. It was here, in 1961, that John Profumo, Secretary of State for War, began his liaison with Christine Keeler, a relationship that was to end his political career and seriously undermine the government of the day when it was revealed, two years later, that Keeler was also having an affair with the Soviet naval attaché Yevgeny Ivanov.

The rustic cottage on the banks of the Thames where Christine Keeler stayed lies in the extensive wooded grounds, ornamented with garden buildings, Italian sculpture and other features, that surround the house and stretch down to the river. There are long walks and drives through the trees and magical views over the river and its still pastoral valley. Much of the landscaping dates from the early eighteenth century, when Charles Bridgeman laid out avenues and rides and created the grass amphitheatre carved into the hill for Lord Orkney. The parterre on the great grass terrace to the south of the house was also first devised, by Orkney himself, at this time. It was later developed for the Sutherlands by John Fleming, who edged the beds with clipped privet and spruce. The box hedging seen today was introduced subsequently. The 1st Viscount Astor, as well as bringing in the Borghese balustrade, was also responsible for the informal water garden, with stepping stones leading to a pagoda on an island, and for converting the Octagon Temple, one of two ornamental buildings designed by Giacomo Leoni for Lord Orkney, into a family chapel and mausoleum. The magnificent yew maze which Astor sketched out in his first year at Cliveden has recently been replanted.

Clouds Hill

Dorset
9 miles (14.4 kilometres) east of Dorchester, ½ mile (0.8 kilometre) east of Waddock crossroads on the B3390, 1 mile (1.6 kilometres) north of Bovington Camp

This little brick and tile labourer's cottage on the slopes of Clouds Hill was a haven for T.E. Lawrence, better known as Lawrence of Arabia. After the First World War, in which he had played a major role in the campaign for Arab independence in the Middle East, Lawrence needed a retreat where he could recover from his experiences and pursue an undemanding occupation. An attempt to join the RAF under an assumed name ended in exposure and dismissal and in 1923 he tried again, enlisting as a private in the Tank Corps at Bovington Camp under the name T.E. Shaw. Clouds Hill, which he first rented and then bought, was just a mile (1.6 kilometres) from the camp. Its tiny rooms with their simple, even austere furnishings are as Lawrence left them, a direct reflection of his monastic way of life and complex personality. His books have gone from the shelves lining the downstairs room, but the wind-up gramophone with a huge horn on which he used to play Mozart and Beethoven still dominates the music room in the roof and his cell-like bedroom, lit by a porthole window which came from a 1914 battle cruiser, is as it was.

Here Lawrence would come to read or write by the fire whenever he could get away from the camp, finding the peace he needed to work on his revision of *Seven Pillars of Wisdom*. Friends were served picnic meals washed down with water or Lawrence's own blend of China tea, but never with alcohol.

For Lawrence the cottage was an earthly paradise. He rejoined the RAF in 1925 but came back to Clouds Hill to live out his days on his discharge in 1935 at the age of 46. Five days later he was dead, killed in a fatal crash when returning to the cottage from Bovington Camp on his motorcycle. The shed where he kept his machine is now used for an exhibition on Clouds Hill and Lawrence's life and times.

LEFT In the downstairs room at Clouds Hill, which was once lined with his books, T.E. Lawrence used to read by the fire in the evenings, sitting in the armchair that he had designed.

Clumber Park

Nottinghamshire
4½ miles (7.2 kilometres) south-east of Worksop, 6½ miles (10.4 kilometres) south-west of Retford, 1 mile (1.6 kilometres) from the A1 and the A57, 1 mile (1.6 kilometres) from the M1, junction 30

The former seat of the dukes of Newcastle, this great landscape park was carved out of one of the wildest parts of Sherwood Forest in the late eighteenth century by the 2nd Duke. At its heart, overlooking an L-shaped serpentine lake dotted with wooded islands, stood the Palladian mansion designed by Stephen Wright, who enlarged an existing hunting lodge in the late 1760s. Wright was also responsible for the decorative lodges and gates at the park's seven entrances, the grandest of them, such as the imposing arch of Apleyhead Lodge, crowned with the greyhounds of the ducal crest, and he built the elegant balustraded bridge crossing the lake and the two porticoed classical temples overlooking the water.

When the 2nd Duke's mansion was largely destroyed by fire in 1879, the 7th Duke rebuilt the house, incorporating what had survived, to a design by Sir Charles Barry, but this replacement was largely demolished in 1938. Only the duke's study, now a café, remains; the outlines of the rest of the house are marked by paving stones in the grass. An attractive brick stable yard dating from the eighteenth century has Wright's clock tower and cupola over the entrance, and elegant late nineteenth-century glasshouses, with a central palm house projecting in a fan of glass, overlook the walled kitchen garden, one of the grandest surviving from the eighteenth century in England.

The former parsonage, a substantial red-brick building, now used for functions, in a corner of the stable yard, was for the cleric officiating in the eye-catching High Victorian chapel, crowned by a soaring 180-foot (55-metre) spire, that dominates the nineteenth-century pleasure grounds. Set on the shores of the lake and the third chapel at Clumber, it was built in 1886–9 by G.F. Bodley for the 7th Duke, whose passionate Anglo-Catholicism is reflected in the lavish treatment. The interior, lit by tall gothic windows, seems like a miniature cathedral, the vaulted roof in shadow high above the nave. Brass candlesticks stand along the elaborately carved rood screen and ornate Flemish-style chandeliers light the Rev. Ernest Geldart's walnut and cedar choir stalls, with musical angels carved out of limewood looking down from crocketed canopies. Stained glass by C.E. Kempe, rich hangings and velvet and silk altar frontals, including an early work by J.N. Comper, add to the sumptuous effect.

A house and school for the boys of the chapel choir were incorporated in the model village built by the 5th Duke in the 1850s at the east end of the lake, its gabled neo-Elizabethan houses artfully arranged to give the impression that the village had grown piecemeal. Ornamental kennels built for the 7th Duchess, who bred Clumber spaniels here, are now a microbrewery supplying pubs round about.

LEFT Clumber Chapel, as large as a parish church, was built in 1886–9 by G.F. Bodley, who re-used stone from a chapel left unfinished twenty years before.

Coleton Fishacre

Devon
2 miles (3.2 kilometres) from Kingswear; take Lower Ferry road, turn off at the tollhouse

Near the mouth of the Dart estuary, on the headlands east of the river, a deep combe runs steeply down to the wooded cliffs above Pudcombe Cove. At the top of the valley, with its back against the slope, is a long, low house, with mullioned windows, tall chimneys and steep tiled roofs. Below, filling a natural amphitheatre, is a richly planted garden. Architectural near the house, with terraces, steps and walls continuing the lines of the building, the garden becomes wilder and more jungle-like as it nears the sea. Both house and garden were created in the mid-1920s for Rupert and Lady Dorothy D'Oyly Carte, who had spotted the valley while sailing along the coast and saw its potential for a place in the country. Son of the impresario who promoted Gilbert and Sullivan, Rupert was by

BELOW Set at the head of a small Devon valley running down to the sea, Coleton Fishacre was built in the 1920s as a weekend retreat and looks out over a magical garden falling away below.

then running the company that produced their operettas and also his father's other enterprise, the Savoy Hotel. While Lady Dorothy lived at Coleton Fishacre, Rupert came down from London for weekends, often bringing distinguished guests, such as the conductor Sir Malcolm Sargent, with him. After Rupert's death, in 1948, the house was sold and the contents largely dispersed. The present furnishings have mostly been introduced by the National Trust, who have based their recreation of the rooms on an article about Coleton Fishacre that appeared in *Country Life* in May 1930.

The house, its walls now softened by climbers and shrubs, is built of Dartmouth shale quarried from the combe and roofed with Delabole slates. Begun in 1925 and finished a year later, it was designed by Oswald Milne, a former protégé of Sir Edwin Lutyens, in an Arts and Crafts idiom, with much attention to craftsmanship and materials and with a flowing roofline that unites the rather rambling layout. While his treatment of the exterior looks back to the late nineteenth century, Milne's Art Deco interiors are very much of their time. The impression is of a comfortable, unpretentious family house but also of a kind of spare modernism, relieved by strong splashes of colour, original honeycomb ceiling lights and other details.

Rooms are low ceilinged, walls are often roughly plastered, with smooth coves marking junction points, and there are deep windowsills lined with black Staffordshire tiles and much use of limed oak and pine. Long passages on both floors are bland and impersonal, but the main rooms have individuality and character.

At the west end of the house, angled out from the main building so as to give clear views over the garden, is the saloon. Entered down a theatrical flight of steps, and almost 40 feet (12 metres) long, the room is dramatically furnished in yellow and green, including original carpets made in the 1930s by the designer Marion Dorn. A little library filling the bay on the garden front is fitted out with pine shelves and is dominated by George Spencer Hoffman's delightfully rose-tinted bird's-eye view of Coleton Fishacre, setting the house and combe in an enchanting blue-green patchwork of fields and lanes bounded by the sea. The original ultramarine scagliola table top and lapis lazuli bell-push in the dining room at the east end of the house bring the sea indoors and, whenever the weather was clement enough, meals were taken in the airy, vine-hung loggia, with views deep into the valley which lies beyond.

Upstairs, where almost none of the D'Oyly Cartes' furniture survives, the rooms have been fitted out with 1930s-style oak pieces from Heal's. Lady Dorothy's bedroom has been re-created from photographs and the black-and-white floral fabric designed by Raoul Dufy that was used for the curtains, cushions and seat-covers, and the near-black carpet, have been reproduced. Original features include splashes of colour from blue-green glass tiles round the basins in every room and period bathrooms with sunken baths and pictorial tiles by the young Edward Bawden. A glitter of gold on the stairs comes from the gleaming cupolas and crosses in a painting of St Mark's, Venice by W.R. Sickert, which had belonged to Bridget D'Oyly Carte and has been loaned back by the British Council. In the substantial servants' quarters at the east end of the house, a double sink in the kitchen is supported on sections of the railway track that was used to bring stone from the garden quarry.

Even before the house was completed, Rupert and Lady Dorothy were planting shelter belts to protect the valley from the prevailing wind and together they planned every detail of the garden, capitalising on the drama of the site, with its panoramic views, and on the presence of a little stream rushing

ABOVE These playful cigarettes evoke weekend parties, when a ship's bell was rung to summon guests back from the cove for pre-dinner drinks.
OPPOSITE Art Deco alabaster light fittings, a cool green 1930s carpet by Marion Dorn, and the strong yellow cushions in the Saloon at Coleton Fishacre offset the spare modernism of walls and ceiling.

headlong to the sea. Paths contour round the sides of the combe, follow the stream, or zigzag steeply up and down, with steps linking different levels. An upper path from the lawn by the loggia leads along the north side of the valley to the vine-hung gazebo, perched high above the quarry. The lower garden is spread out below, filled with colour in spring from a display of rhododendrons, azaleas, magnolias, dogwoods, camellias and Chilean fire trees. Mature specimen trees flourish throughout the garden and always there is the sea beyond, with a gate leading from the lower garden out onto the cliffs above Pudcombe Cove.

Compton Castle

Devon
At Compton, 4 miles
(6.4 kilometres) west of Torquay,
1 mile (1.6 kilometres) north of
Marldon

A delight of towers, battlements and buttresses, this fairytale place, more fortified manor than castle, is hidden in a deep and lush south Devon valley 2 miles (3.2 kilometres) from the sea. A heavy wooden door in the high defensive wall of the north front leads into the stone-flagged courtyard round which the house sprawls on three sides. Opposite the entrance is the reconstructed great hall, rebuilt in 1955 to its original medieval form and rising two storeys to an oak-timbered roof. A stone spiral stair leads to the solar on the first floor of the west wing and this side of the court is closed by a little chapel, its great traceried window on the north front still protected by the original defensive grille. Beyond the hall, in a corner of what was a second yard behind, is the splendid kitchen, with a hearth with bread ovens at each end filling the wall. Five towers, all provided with garderobes, are incorporated in the house and a sixth, the watch-tower, is set into the south-east corner of the massive curtain wall that surrounds the castle.

This magical fortified house, one of very few to survive so unaltered, was built between the fourteenth and sixteenth centuries. The fortifications date from the reign of Henry VIII, when the Gilbert family, who had lived here from the mid-fourteenth century and had recently built a manor on the Dart (see Greenway, p.157), probably felt threatened by the French raids on Teignmouth a few miles north along the coast and on Plymouth to the west. Although the new defences did not make the manor impregnable, they would have deterred attack from a roving shore party.

Two Gilbert boys born in the mid-sixteenth century, half-brothers to Walter Raleigh, were among the small group of Westcountrymen who earned a place in the history of Elizabethan England. John, the eldest, who became Vice-Admiral of Devon, played a major part in the defences against the Armada, providing for a possible landing in Torbay. And it was he who reported to Sir Francis Walsingham that Francis Drake had captured the Spanish galleon *Nuestra Señora del Rosario*, which was brought into the estuary of the River Dart nearby.

His younger brother Humphrey was one of the brave men who crossed the Atlantic in fragile ships in a wave of colonisation

ABOVE A jumble of towers, gabled roofs and buttressed walls marks out Compton Castle, a magical fortified house buried in a lush Devon valley only a few miles from the sea.

and expansion. Armed with the first Letters Patent granted by the Crown for the 'planting' of an English colony, he claimed Newfoundland for his queen on 5 August 1583, sadly drowning when his tiny ship *Squirrel* foundered on the return voyage. His torch was picked up by his half-brother, Sir Walter Raleigh, but the settlement Raleigh's expedition established on an island off what is now North Carolina was subsequently abandoned and it was Humphrey's youngest son, Raleigh Gilbert, who in 1607 founded the first permanent English colony in North America, calling it Jamestown after the new king.

The confidence of the age, which elsewhere led to the building of prodigy houses such as Hardwick (see p.169), or Wollaton Hall in Nottinghamshire, here led men to risk their lives in a quest for new lands, preserving Compton Castle as an unaltered medieval manor. Sold by the Gilbert family in 1785, and neglected for over a century, the house was bought back in 1931 in a ruinous state and restored by Commander and Mrs Walter Raleigh Gilbert, who refurnished it as a family home and whose portraits by Denis Fildes hang in the solar. Gilberts live here still.

Corfe Castle

Dorset
On the A351 Wareham–Swanage
road

The ruins of Corfe Castle rise like jagged teeth from the summit of a steep chalk hill that guards the only natural route through the Purbeck Hills. Although now reduced to broken walls and towers, this monument to the power of medieval kings is still architecturally striking and dominates the little village huddled below. Strategically placed and the most defensible of all English castles, Corfe was eventually undone by treachery, not by the might of a besieging army.

Although there may have been a royal hunting lodge at Corfe in Saxon times and there is a tradition that the child-king Edward the Martyr was murdered here in 978, the castle was begun by William the Conqueror, whose fortifications formed part of the network of carefully placed strongholds with which he consolidated his hold on his new kingdom after 1066. These early Norman defences were gradually strengthened, with wooden features such as the original timber palisade being slowly replaced in stone. The massive keep crowning the hilltop, still rising some 70 feet (22 metres) in dramatic fingers of stone, was completed during the reign of Henry I, who imprisoned his elder brother Robert, Duke of Normandy here in 1106. The tower-studded curtain wall looping round the crest of the hill was a later addition, dating from the early years

BELOW Corfe Castle was begun by William the Conqueror, but was later strengthened and enlarged to form the great fortress whose ruins crown the Purbeck Hills.

of the reign of King John (1199–1216), when Corfe's position so close to the south coast became of considerable importance in the renewed war with France. After the loss of Normandy in 1204, the castle was in the first line of the king's defences against a French invasion.

In a time when monarchs would travel round their kingdoms administering justice and enforcing loyalty by their presence, Corfe was a centre for government and administration as well as a stronghold. Part of the huge sum of £1,400 spent on building operations at Corfe during John's reign went to construct the king's 'Gloriette', a tower-house arranged round a courtyard in the topmost inner ward. The quality of the surviving masonry shows that this was a building of distinction, a compactly planned domestic residence fit for a monarch, with a great hall, chapel and parlour, and chambers for the queen overlooking a garden.

Apart from a brief period in the mid-sixteenth century, Corfe remained in royal hands until Elizabeth I sold it to Sir Christopher Hatton. About 50 years later the castle and estate were bought by Sir John Bankes, a staunch Royalist, who also purchased the neighbouring property of Kingston Lacy (*see* p.192). Of major strategic importance to both sides in the Civil War, Corfe was twice besieged. In 1643 Mary, Lady Bankes, who must have been a woman of character, held the castle against a force of local Parliamentarians in her husband's absence, but in the winter of 1645–6 Corfe was again attacked and fell through the treachery of one of the defenders, who arranged for enemy troops, disguised as reinforcements, to enter the castle. The victorious Roundhead colonel, impressed by Lady Bankes's courage, not only allowed the garrison to depart but also permitted his spirited opponent to take the keys of the castle with her; these may be the ones that now hang in the library at Kingston Lacy. Corfe was deliberately ruined, leaving only the romantic remains that inspired one of Turner's evocative watercolours.

LEFT The ruins of Corfe Castle, standing high on the chalk ridge crossing the Isle of Purbeck, are dominated by the remains of the great twelfth-century keep at its heart.

Cornish Mines and Engines

Cornwall
On the west coast near St Just, at Pool, 2 miles (3.2 kilometres) west of Redruth on either side of the A3047, and other locations

The tall outlines of ruined engine houses standing high on windswept moorland or perched on lonely cliff-top sites are romantic reminders of the great days of the Cornish mining industry in the mid-nineteenth century. At the height of the boom, the population of the county almost doubled as newcomers flooded in to provide the manpower needed for the extraction of rich sources of tin, copper and china clay. Now only the china clay quarries remain open, but the technology refined here in Victorian times was exported all over the world, from South America to Australia.

The phenomenal growth in the Cornish mining industry in the early years of the century was partly due to the demise of the once hugely productive copper mines on Anglesey and the lack of other major sources of tin and copper until the 1830s, but another important factor was the expiry of the patent on the Boulton and Watt steam engine in 1800. This engine was more efficient than the previous generation of Newcomen engines, but mine owners had to pay a royalty to use it and the patent inhibited the development of high-pressure steam technology. The moment restrictions were removed, Cornish engineers – in particular Richard Trevithick, the first to realise the potential of high-pressure steam – set about producing more efficient engines, leading to the establishment of a number of great engine-building firms, such as Holman's of Camborne and Harvey's of Hayle. These developments gave Cornwall the lead in mining technology that it was to hold for half a century.

The National Trust owns several survivals from this great chapter in Cornish history, most of them now included in the Cornish Mining World Heritage Site. On the Penwith peninsula in the far west, a rich mining coast is centred on St Just. At the Levant mine about 2 miles (3.2 kilometres) north of the little town is the oldest surviving beam engine in Cornwall, sited in a tiny engine house right on the cliff edge. Once again being worked by steam, this machinery was designed by Francis Michell, a member of the engineering Michell family, and was built by Harvey's in 1840. Even more spectacular are the engine houses at Botallack, which cling to the rocks just out of reach of the pounding Atlantic. This whole mining coast, with Botallack and Kenidjack at its heart, has been the focus of considerable restoration and stabilisation by the National Trust in recent years and is now known as the Tin Coast.

At the East Pool and Agar mine, straddling the A3047 east of Camborne, is the largest of the great beam engines left in Cornwall, commissioned from Harvey's in 1891 and put to work pumping out water here in 1925. With a gleaming cylinder 7 feet (2 metres) in diameter and a huge beam weighing some 52 tons, this monster could lift 450 gallons (2,000 litres) of water a minute from a depth of 1,700 feet (518 metres). The 1853 engine designed by one of Trevithick's former pupils at South Crofty tin and arsenic mine about a mile (1.6 kilometres) to the south-west could operate at even greater depths, raising 340 gallons (1,500 litres) a minute from some 2,000 feet (610 metres).

A working example of the rotative engines normally used for lifting men and materials survives at the East Pool mine, where F.W. Michell's 1887 engine made by Holman's is now powered by electricity. Also at East Pool is the Industrial Discovery Centre, which gives an overview of Cornish mining and sets it in context.

There are a number of other empty engine houses in the Trust's care, some in situations as dramatic as those of Penwith. Wheal Prosper dominates the cliff above Porthcew Cove, while Towanroath engine house at Chapel Porth is perched on a ledge high above the sea. Equally romantic is Wheal Betsy, set on lonely Black Down on the western edge of Dartmoor in Devon, its tall chimney a conspicuous sight from the A386 to Okehampton. Richard Trevithick's whitewashed thatched cottage at Lower Penponds, Camborne, from where he departed for the silver mines of Peru in 1816, also belongs to the Trust.

OPPOSITE The north Cornish coast carries many reminders of the great days of tin mining in the nineteenth century, among them these engine houses at Botallack, romantically set on the edge of the cliffs just above the pounding sea.

Cotehele

Cornwall
On the west bank of the Tamar,
1 mile (1.6 kilometres) west of
Calstock by footpath (6 miles/
9.6 kilometres by road), 8 miles
(12.8 kilometres) south-west of
Tavistock

The River Tamar, dividing Devon from Cornwall, has proved one of the most effective natural boundaries in England. Until 1962, when a suspension bridge was opened at the mouth of the river to link Plymouth and Saltash, the first road crossing was 15 miles (24 kilometres) upstream as the crow flies, but almost double that distance following the twists and turns of the river. For the villages and hamlets along its banks, the Tamar was for centuries the only effective route to the outside world. So it was for this Tudor courtyard house, lying at the head of a steep valley running down to the river.

Low granite ranges set round three courtyards were based on the medieval house of the de Coteheles, which was transformed and extended between *c.* 1485 and the mid-sixteenth century by successive generations of the Edgcumbe family, in particular Sir Richard and his son, Sir Piers. The approach, past Sir Richard's massively buttressed barn and through a battlemented gateway tower, the arch of which is just wide enough to admit a loaded packhorse, signals the ancient character of the place. The rooms are small and mostly dark, reached by flights of worn stone steps and through heavy wooden doors in granite archways. Tudor windows embellished with heraldic stained glass light the great hall, with its rough lime-ash floor and whitewashed walls rising the height of the house to a decorative timber roof. A refectory table made of ash stands below the large window at the dais end and a display of arms and armour on the walls includes Elizabethan matchlocks, Civil War breastplates and lobster-tail helmets as well as some exotic pieces, such as long Indian swords.

The family chambers, with their large Tudor fireplaces and richly coloured hangings used like wallpaper, seem more inviting. On the late seventeenth-century bacchic tapestries

adorning the little Punch Room, naked figures treading huge vats of grapes as if indulging in a communal bubble bath are clearly preparing a vintage to fill the arched niches in the cupboard-like wine cellar in one corner. In the Red Room upstairs, rich crimson drapery on the huge four-poster is set off by faded seventeenth-century arras on the walls, children at play with marbles and hoops on three of the panels contrasting with the scene of nightmarish violence by the bed illustrating the death of Remus. Across the landing, steps lead up to the rooms in the three-storey battlemented tower that was added in the second half of the sixteenth century. At the top of the tower, reached by a steeply winding stair, are two bedrooms, one of them reputedly slept in by Charles I in 1644 on his march from Liskeard to Exeter, while some intriguing and unusual ebony furniture in the Old Drawing Room that fills the floor below, once thought to be Tudor, is now regarded as having come from southern India, and to have been made, in some cases, as long ago as the mid-seventeenth century.

In 1547–53, shortly before the tower was added to Cotehele, the Edgcumbes built Mount Edgcumbe, a much grander seat at the mouth of the Tamar, and this became their main residence. Improvements in the 1650s at Cotehele, such as the construction of the main staircase, were made by Colonel Piers, who returned here for about a decade in *c.* 1652. From the 1660s, however, the old house was left largely undisturbed for 200 years, although the antiquarian interest of the place was already being recognised in the eighteenth century. In 1789, George III and Queen Charlotte visited the house, the queen recording her impressions in some detail. Even when the widow of the 3rd Earl of Mount Edgcumbe, Lady Caroline, returned here in 1862, thus initiating another period of family occupation, much of the house remained unchanged. The east range was improved and updated to provide modern comforts, such as central heating, but the new work was carefully designed to blend with the old.

The remodelled range where the Dowager Countess lived looks over a luxuriant garden, sheltered by woodland, laid out

ABOVE LEFT Stained glass in the little chapel that is squeezed into a corner of the main courtyard. The chapel was licensed in 1411, but the building was remodelled at the end of the century.
OPPOSITE The Tudor hall, with its arch-braced timber roof and rough lime-ash floor, is one of Cotehele's most evocative interiors.

in a valley leading down to the Tamar. At the head of the valley, just below some stone-walled terraces, are a medieval stew pond and a domed dovecote that once provided meat and fish for the community here. Hidden in the woods and set along the river are further reminders of the way the Cotehele estate once operated and of the one-time importance of river traffic.

Cotehele Quay, described in 1819 as 'a very large and commodious quay with a most desirable situation on the river', lies a quarter of a mile (0.4 kilometre) downstream from the garden. At the end of the nineteenth century, when strawberries and other soft fruit from growers in the valley were taken over the river to Bere Alston station on the new Plymouth–Tavistock line, the quay would have been regularly visited by the sailing barges that plied the river, one of the last of which, *Shamrock*, is berthed here. Earlier in the century there had been shipments of ore from mines in the wooded Danescombe Valley upstream, the sites of which are now marked by grassy humps and some old mine buildings. These mines, at their peak in 1844–70, were just some of the many which exploited rich sources of copper and arsenic along the Tamar Valley.

The old grey-stone buildings clustered round the quay, one of which houses displays telling the story of the valley, seem too tranquil for this industrial past, but hidden in the woodland across a reedy inlet to one side are the remains of a row of huge lime kilns, now romantically shrouded in greenery but once a source of lethal fumes. A path from here leads through woodland up the tributary valley of the River Morden to another picturesque group of estate buildings, including a three-storey eighteenth-century mill powered by an overshot wheel. This is now in working order and produces stoneground wholemeal flour that is sold in the National Trust shop and elsewhere. Other buildings have been used for re-creations of a wheelwright's shop, with a lathe driven by a huge flywheel, a forge, and a saddler's shop filled with harness, lengths of chain and stirrups.

Above the house, beyond a sloping daffodil meadow, is a building of a different kind. Set in a field is a triangular tower with granite pinnacles and dummy gothic windows that gives the illusion, from only a short distance away, of being much more substantial than it is and was perhaps built to celebrate the visit of King George III and Queen Charlotte. Panoramic views from the top look west to Kit Hill and east to Dartmoor, and in the valley below are the graceful arches of the Calstock Viaduct. This beautiful structure was built to carry the new railway opened in 1908, whose advent did much to undermine the river traffic.

Coughton Court

Warwickshire
2 miles (3.2 kilometres) north
of Alcester on the east side of
the A435

Only an expanse of grass separates Coughton Court from the main Studley to Alcester road, giving passing motorists a memorable view of the great Tudor gatehouse dominating the entrance façade. Dating from the early years of Henry VIII's reign, when even in remote countryside on the southern fringes of the Forest of Arden men could at last build to please themselves rather than to protect their property, the gatehouse is a glittering glass lantern, with the stone tracery and gleaming panes of a two-storeyed oriel window stretching the width of the two upper floors. Though Sir George Throckmorton thought it prudent to surround his new house with a moat, this may also have been regarded as a status symbol rather than purely as a means of defence. Less showy Tudor ranges flank two sides of the courtyard beyond the gatehouse, their domestic gabled façades and half-timbered upper storeys a direct contrast to the stone splendour of the gatehouse and a foil for a formal garden with box-edged beds planted with white roses. Lawns framed by avenues of pollarded limes stretch away from the open east side of the court, past two sunken gardens, towards the little River Arrow and peaceful wooded countryside beyond.

The Throckmortons, whose descendants live here still, first came to Coughton Court in 1409 and much of the fascination of the house derives from its continued association with this prominent Roman Catholic family. Increasingly prosperous during the fifteenth and sixteenth centuries, they were to pay a high price for their faith during the reign of Elizabeth I and the years that followed, when Roman Catholicism was associated with treason. In 1584 Francis Throckmorton was executed for his part in a plot to depose Elizabeth and replace her with Mary, Queen of Scots. Francis's cousin, Thomas, was more circumspect. Although he lent Coughton to the conspirators in the Gunpowder Plot, he took care to be absent on the night of 5 November 1605 when a small group waited anxiously for news in one of the gatehouse rooms.

Like Baddesley Clinton only a few miles to the north-east (*see* p.36), Coughton was a refuge for recusants. Mass continued to be celebrated here and priests were concealed in ingenious hiding places, among them a compartment above the newel

ABOVE The magnificent Tudor gatehouse at Coughton Court, with a beautiful double-storeyed oriel window lighting the upper floors, is one of the finest of its kind in England.

stair in the north-east turret, discovered only in 1858, that was furnished with a bed and a folding leather altar. Another reminder of these times is the painted canvas hanging in the room above the hide that displays the arms of all the Catholic gentry who were imprisoned for recusancy during Elizabeth's reign. Other religious memorabilia include a magnificent early sixteenth-century cope of purple velvet embroidered in gold.

Staunchly Royalist during the Civil War, the Throckmortons' loyalty was tested when the house was besieged and occupied by Parliamentary troops in 1643, the rising ground where the Roundhead army placed their guns only too visible in the view west from the top of the gatehouse tower. Two generations later the entire east side of the courtyard was destroyed when Coughton was sacked by a Protestant mob running wild after the flight of James II and it was never subsequently rebuilt. A number of mementoes in the house, including a linen shift that belonged to Mary, Queen of Scots in the year she was beheaded and locks of hair from the Old and Young Pretenders, reflect the Throckmortons' allegiance to the Stuart cause.

In later years, partly as a result of prudent marriages, the family fortunes revived. The stone-built gothick wings on either side of the gatehouse were added in the 1780s by Sir Robert, 4th Baronet, who embarked on an extensive refurbishment of the house when already an old man and who probably also filled in the moat. Sir Robert, whose portrait by Largillière presides over the drawing room, was responsible for the delicate gothick entrance hall, which he created out of the ground floor of the gatehouse, and for the elegant classical staircase, which is now hung with a magnificent array of early family portraits. Like the Catholic memorabilia and other contents, many of these paintings were brought to Coughton when grander family properties elsewhere were disposed of. There is some fine furniture, including a set of late seventeenth-century, walnut-veneered Dutch chairs and a cabinet of the same date with a mirrored recess that was used to hold the Host, while the tapestry bedroom is hung with eighteenth-century pastels of the family, most of them by William Hoare of Bath.

A mid-Victorian Roman Catholic chapel close to the house was one of the family's last building ventures. House and chapel stand cheek by jowl with the ancient parish church just to the south in a group that is an enduring reminder of the divisions bred by religion.

Cragside

Northumberland
13 miles (20.9 kilometres) south-west of Alnwick on the B6341 and 16 miles (26 kilometres) north of Morpeth via the A697

When the inventor and industrialist William Armstrong visited Rothbury in 1863 as a break from the unrelenting pressures of his factory on the River Tyne, he decided to purchase what he could of the secluded Debdon Valley, a place where he had so often wandered as a boy during family holidays. Four years earlier he had seen the army adopt the new gun he had developed after the poor British performance in the Crimean War and, as a result, his prosperous engineering firm was being gradually transformed into a vast industrial concern. Once primarily concerned with hydraulic machines, by the late nineteenth century Armstrong's was an international arms manufacturer, rivalled only by Krupps of Germany.

A couple of watercolours showing tall chimneys belching smoke over factory buildings ranged along the Tyne are the only direct reminders of the works that financed the rambling house set high above a ravine on the Debdon burn, with a

ABOVE This grand drawing room, with a monumental marble chimneypiece filling the end wall, was the last addition to Cragside.

jumble of gables, soaring chimneys, mullioned windows and half-timbering framed against a wooded hillside. But there are other pointers to the inventive mind of the man who built it. This was the earliest house in the world to be lit by hydroelectricity and water was also used to power a saw-mill, a revolutionary hydraulic lift and even a kitchen spit.

Armstrong's activities are reflected too in the gradual transformation of Cragside, which was originally built, in 1864–6, as a modest weekend retreat. Shortly after the completion of this first building, Armstrong engaged the distinguished architect Richard Norman Shaw to enlarge it. Over the next 15 years, Shaw turned the house into a country mansion and enriched it with some of his most original work.

The grandest rooms were designed for important overseas clients. The King of Siam, the Shah of Persia and the Crown Prince of Afghanistan all slept in the monumental black walnut bed, with solemn owls carved on the end posts and a massive half-tester, which Shaw created for the guest chambers. No doubt they appreciated the plumbed-in washstand and the sunken bath in an alcove in the dressing room next door. A long, top-lit gallery with a wooden barrel ceiling leading from the Owl Suite was once hung with the best of Armstrong's Victorian paintings. These were mostly sold after his death, but pictures and sculpture are still set against the deep-red walls, and at the far end is Shaw's *tour de force*, the drawing room completed for a royal visit in 1884. The top-lit cavernous interior is dominated by W.R. Lethaby's Renaissance-style carved marble chimney-piece, with veining in the stone round the fireplace suggesting running water. Inglenooks with red leather settees are set on either side and white lamps hang in clusters from the ceiling like bunches of snowdrops.

The little rooms of the original lodge and Shaw's early additions for the family are quite different in character. His beautiful and unusual library with magnificent views of the glen is perhaps the most harmonious room in the house, the warm reds and browns of the furnishings setting off brilliant-blue tiles and onyx panels framing the fireplace and glowing enamelled electric lamps along the low bookcases.

Armstrong alone seems to have been responsible for Cragside's wildly romantic setting, for which the hillside was blasted to expose craggy rock formations and over 1,700 acres (688 hectares) of pleasure grounds created by planting millions of conifers, rhododendrons and alpines on what were originally bare slopes. A pinetum was established in the valley and on the steep slope below the house, like an expanse of scree above the burn, is a huge rock garden, planted with heathers, alpines and shrubs. On a south-facing slope on the other side of the valley, reached across Armstrong's steel footbridge and up a steep path from the stream, is a formal terraced garden with ferneries, a fruit house and a display of Victorian carpet bedding. An intricate network of paths snakes across the estate, with dramatic views to the Cheviots from the higher routes, and a scenic drive takes in the lakes over 340 feet (100 metres) above the house which were used to feed the hydroelectric turbine.

Croft Castle and Parkland

Herefordshire
5 miles (8 kilometres) north-west of Leominster, 9 miles (14.4 kilometres) south-west of Ludlow

This engaging house, with slender corner towers and rough stone walls, has a long history. Dating back to a time when this glorious countryside on the Welsh borders was insecure and torn by rebellion, the shell of the house is the four-square castle round a central courtyard which the Croft family, who came here from Normandy some years before the Conquest, built to defend their property. Much modified since, particularly in the seventeenth century, Croft's interiors were then substantially remodelled in the eighteenth century and features from various periods contribute to its present picturesque appearance. In the centre of the entrance front, Georgian bays with playful gothick sash windows frame a mock-Jacobean castellated porch, added in 1913. The approach is through what appears to be a medieval archway, but this too was a more recent addition, probably built in the 1790s.

ABOVE The elegant staircase hall at Croft Castle, with its delicate gothick plasterwork, was created by T.F. Pritchard in the 1760s when he remodelled the interior of the house.

The country house takes over inside. Thomas Farnolls Pritchard, the Shrewsbury architect who designed the world's first iron bridge at Coalbrookdale, was responsible for the light-hearted gothick interiors introduced in 1765, his pointed arches in white plaster against a coffee background on the stairs strongly reminiscent of a row of church windows. Even the stair balustrade looks ecclesiastical: column clusters forming the newel posts are miniature versions of those that might support the vaulting of a nave. Rare and valuable furniture in the same style includes a set of gothick chairs in dark oak in the long gallery that would be suitable props for a dramatisation of Mary Shelley's *Frankenstein* or Horace Walpole's *The Castle of Otranto*. T.F. Pritchard also had a hand in the similarly striking but quite different decoration of the Blue Room, where *trompe-l'oeil* gold rosettes stud blue Jacobean panelling. Family portraits hang in almost every room, including a beautiful study by Gainsborough of Elizabeth Cowper, wife of Sir Archer Croft, the colouring all brown and red, and works by Lawrence and Philip de Laszlo. Crofts also dominate the little church of rough local stone just east of the house. The most memorable of the many family memorials here is an early sixteenth-century altar tomb to Sir Richard and Dame Eleanor Croft, with realistic effigies showing the couple in extreme old age.

Thickly wooded parkland surrounds the castle, as it has done for centuries, the great avenues for which Croft is famous including a line of Spanish chestnuts, in which some of the trees may be 350 years old, stretching about half a mile (0.8 kilometre) to the west, and oaks and beeches flanking the long entrance drive. An ancient lime avenue that once shadowed the chestnuts has now been replanted. While most of the park escaped the attentions of an improver of the 'Capability' Brown school, the late eighteenth-century landscaping of Fish Pool Valley in the Picturesque mode was a direct reaction to his ideas. This little steep-sided glen planted with mixed deciduous and evergreen trees has a dramatic wilderness quality, which is in perfect accord with the castle's gothick interiors. Another notable feature of the estate is the Iron Age hill-fort of Croft Ambrey, set on a ridge a mile (1.6 kilometres) north of the house.

ABOVE Many members of the Croft family, who came to this beautiful place before the Conquest, are commemorated in the tiny medieval and Tudor church that lies close by the castle, its rough stone walls providing a pleasing contrast to the Georgian playfulness of the entrance front.
OPPOSITE Croome looks out over 'Capability' Brown's first naturalistic landscape park, with an artificial river winding by the house.

Croome

Worcestershire
9 miles (14 kilometres) south of
Worcester and east of the A38 and
M5, 6 miles (10 kilometres) west
of Pershore

Inheriting Croome Court and the surrounding estate in 1751, when he was only 29, the cultivated and wealthy George William, 6th Earl of Coventry set about transforming both the existing 1640s house, which he was determined to remodel as a fashionable Neo-classical mansion, and its surroundings. The two young men he engaged to realise his ambitions, Lancelot 'Capability' Brown, who came to Croome in 1751 at the age of 35, and Robert Adam, who was first commissioned by the earl in 1760, when he was 32, had yet to emerge as the leading designers of their day, but their work at Croome is totally characteristic. In his decorative schemes for the house, Adam designed everything, from the plasterwork, mirrors and marble chimneypieces to much of the furniture, while Brown's landscaping of the park, the first he was to create in a naturalistic style, employed all the devices for which he would become well known – from the artificial river which winds past the court to a pleasingly irregular lake and the artfully placed clumps of trees and shelter belts, to the classical eye-catchers in the pleasure grounds round the lake and the borrowing of the wider landscape, with which the park seems to merge. This is a design on an epic scale in which the house plays an integral part, both as a grandstand for admiring the landscape and as a focus for the views from a network of meandering paths and drives.

Brown, whose only previous experience had been as head gardener at Stowe, was first engaged to remodel the house, although it is likely that the gentleman-architect Sanderson Miller, who was a friend of the earl and had recommended Brown, also had a hand in the design. In the 1790s, after both Brown and Adam had died, the earl employed the renowned architect James Wyatt to remodel some of the existing garden buildings and add other decorative features, among them statues made out of Coade stone and eye-catchers beyond the park, one of which is like a fragment of a medieval castle.

The Coventrys owned Croome for another 250 years, but in 1948 the house and the land immediately around it were sold. In the years that followed the court became, successively, a Catholic school, a centre for the International Society of Krishna Consciousness and, briefly, a conference venue and a private house. The lake silted up, weeds and shrubs invaded the pleasure grounds, garden buildings fell into disrepair and much of Brown's park was ploughed up and his plantations ravaged by Dutch elm disease. In 1996, with the help of the Heritage Lottery Fund and Royal Sun Alliance, the National Trust acquired the pleasure grounds and park and has re-created Brown's grand design, incidentally providing visitors with a unique opportunity to see what his landscapes would have looked like while the planting was still immature. Since 2007, when the newly formed Croome Heritage Trust bought the court and leased it to the National Trust, house and park have been reunited.

The court, and a sizeable red-brick service wing also designed by Brown, is first seen from above, across the great sweep of grass which leads down from a ridge to the east. The central two-storey block with a balustraded roofline was built on the foundations of the existing house, but Brown added a

giant Ionic portico onto the south front, with a wide flight of steps guarded by sphinxes giving access to the park, and also extended the house at both ends, marking each corner with a large three-storey turret. All is in warm Bath stone, but the effect is heavy rather than elegant, particularly as the chimneys of the old house, which Brown retained, form a massive wall across the roof. The gothic church of St Mary Magdalene (not National Trust), which Brown designed up on the ridge in the late 1750s to replace a medieval building close by the house, is a more successful composition, its great west tower standing high above the valley. Adam was responsible for the delicate gothic plasterwork, intricately carved pulpit and other furnishings in the light and airy interior. This was his first commission for George William, and the earl was so pleased he engaged Adam to finish off and refurnish the interior of the house.

The 1640s building lives on in the basement, and here too there are intriguing traces – a window with leaded panes, cambered brickwork that may once have paved a courtyard – of what may have been a Tudor house on this site. A procession of grand, unfurnished reception rooms fills the principal floor above. From the stone-floored entrance hall, with its pre-Adam Palladian decoration, double doors give onto the saloon filling

BELOW These griffins are on one of the Coade stone plaques that decorate the little pavilion on the island in the lake.

the centre of the south front. Rising to a high coved ceiling and warmed by two marble fireplaces, this is the room where George III, Queen Charlotte and three of their daughters were given dinner in July 1768, their visit a reflection of how famous the Croome landscape, the first of its kind, had become. Hanging on the main staircase is a huge painting of a horse and groom, with a race in progress behind them, which has been loaned back to the house. Dating from 1680 to 1710, it is possibly the work of John Wootton.

Alas, the fittings of Adam's tapestry room off the saloon, including his delicate ceiling and carved chimneypiece, are now in the Metropolitan Museum, New York. The long gallery running down the west front, with a great bay window looking towards the pleasure grounds, has lost the statues of Greek goddesses by John Cheere which once filled the niches on the interior wall, but the plasterwork ceiling, designed by Adam and executed by Joseph Rose, is still here, as are two of the grisaille panels painted for the room and the marble chimneypiece decorated with life-size nymphs carved by Joseph Wilton.

Although the contents were disposed of in 1948, many of the most significant pieces, such as the window seats made for the gallery, were retained by the Croome Estate Trust so it may be possible in the future to return objects and paintings to the rooms from which they came. The lost fittings, some of which disappeared from the house in the years after 1948, are another matter. Some surprising colour schemes, such as the multi-coloured treatment of the dining-room decoration, were the work of the Hare Krishna movement.

The garden buildings, now largely restored, are essentially unchanged. Adam designed the pedimented, temple-like greenhouse of 1760, which was used to display tender exotics, and he may also be responsible for the classical pavilion built on an island in the lake in 1776–8. Brown's domed rotunda, built in 1754–7 on the ridge above the house, with stuccowork by Francesco Vassalli, is still shaded by some of the cedars that were planted to shelter it in the mid-eighteenth century, and his grotto, a curving wall of tumbled stone blocks, is still a feature of the path round the lake. And, for the energetic, there are longer walks beyond the park to visit the distant eye-catchers with which Wyatt enriched the landscape.

Dinefwr

Carmarthenshire
On the western edge of Llandeilo,
off the A483

At the western end of the Black Mountains, in the broad green valley of the River Tywi, an extensive and beautiful eighteenth-century landscape surrounds a tall, four-square house, with turrets at each corner. Newton House, former seat of the Rice family, Barons Dynevor, dates from the mid-seventeenth century but was remodelled in *c.* 1770 by George Rice and his wife Cecil Talbot, who added playful corner turrets and the crenellated parapet, and again in 1856–7, when the 4th Baron Dynevor enlarged the turrets, added other features and refaced the house in stone. The baron commissioned plans from the local architect Richard Kyrke Penson, but it seems these were not used and the designer of the alterations is not known. The main façade, with gothic arches over the windows, an Italianate *porte-cochère* and tall pyramidal roofs crowning the angle turrets, suggests a cross between a Venetian palazzo and a French château, while the garden side of the house is embellished with an arcade and a first-floor conservatory.

The original contents were dispersed in 1976, when the house was sold, but many period features remain and rooms have been re-created by the National Trust as they might have been in the Edwardian era. Ornamental plasterwork of 1660 adorns the sunny drawing room and the inner hall, hung with family portraits, still has what appears to be a seventeenth-century stair, with sturdy oak balusters. There is a show of Rice family portraits in the dining room, which is where the household gathered for prayers, and there are stunning views down the valley from the conservatory at the head of the stairs. Two intriguing arrow-loop windows in the ale cellar in the basement, where there is a full range of service rooms, may be survivals from a medieval building on this site. There are also some interesting paintings of the house as it was in the later seventeenth and early eighteenth centuries, showing the barns that are now incorporated in the service courtyard.

The ruins of a former castle (owned by the Wildlife Trust of South and West Wales) overlooking the valley reflect Dinefwr's and the Rice family's involvement in the early history of Wales. This stronghold, rebuilt in stone some time in the twelfth century, was the capital of Deheubarth, one of the three ancient kingdoms of Wales and seat of the great Rhys ap Gruffydd, ancestor of Henry Tudor and sponsor of the first recorded eisteddfod, held in 1176. Rhys was anglicised to Rice in 1547, following the return of family lands confiscated sixteen years earlier because of a trumped-up charge of conspiracy against Henry VII.

The naturalistic park, landscaped by George and Cecil Rice with some advice from 'Capability' Brown, who visited Dinefwr in 1775, stretches down to the banks of the Tywi. Mature oak woodland includes descendants of the ancient wildwood that was enclosed for a medieval deer-park. There are still fallow deer beneath the trees and the Trust has reintroduced Dinefwr's distinctive white cattle, a feature of the park for at least 700 years until the herd was dispersed in 1976, at the same time as financial difficulties forced the sale of the house and the home farm. With the help of local authorities and other organisations, the Trust acquired the park in the 1980s, Newton House in 1990 and, most recently, the former service courtyard.

ABOVE LEFT The Italianate arcade and conservatory on the garden side of the house.
BELOW At the heart of Dinefwr Park, an extensive eighteenth-century landscape in the Tywi valley, is Newton House, dating from the 1660s but much altered since.

Downhill Demesne and Hezlett House

Co. Londonderry
1 mile (1.6 kilometres) west of Castlerock and 5 miles (8 kilometres) west of Coleraine on the A2 Coleraine–Downhill coast road

The wild and beautiful Ulster coast, with broom, ling and blaeberry heath clothing cliffs of limestone and basalt that stand high above the Atlantic, was where the remarkable Frederick Augustus Hervey, Bishop of Derry and later 4th Earl of Bristol, chose to site his house. The construction of the mansion began in about 1775, and the bleak moorland round about was transformed into a landscape park, 'a green carpet sprinkled with white clover' as the bishop described it in an invitation to a friend. It is meadow grassland still. Thousands of deciduous and evergreen trees were planted to soften the wilderness.

The bishop's obsession with circular buildings, which reached its full flowering at Ickworth in Suffolk (see p.184), was heralded at Downhill. Perched right on the edge of the cliffs to the north of the house is Mussenden Temple, a small domed rotunda crowned with a huge urn and with sixteen Corinthian columns ringing the façade. The design, which was based on the Temple of Vesta at Tivoli, had been suggested to the earl-bishop by James Wyatt, although the long-suffering Irish architect Michael Shanahan, who had overseen the construction of the house, again executed the plans for his difficult client. The little building was named after the bishop's cousin, Mrs Frideswide Mussenden, who died shortly before it was completed in 1785, and it was fitted out as a library. Here Frederick could study undisturbed, the silence broken only by the screaming of the gulls, by the ceaseless roar of the waves breaking on the rocks below and by the Atlantic gales, which sometimes threaten to tear the building from its roots. In the late twentieth century, the temple was increasingly at risk from cliff erosion and in 1997 the National Trust carried out a major stabilisation programme to prevent the building being lost to the sea.

Downhill House is now only a shell, a bleak ruin in the middle of the demesne, but the eighteenth-century landscape park survives. From the grand triumphal arch forming the Bishop's Gate on the Coleraine road, a path leads north through an arboretum and along the steep wooded valley known as Black Glen, emerging on the edge of the cliffs. Mussenden Temple stands a little to the west and there

ABOVE Mussenden Temple, perched right on the edge of the cliffs, was built by the eccentric Bishop of Derry, who retreated here to read and study.

are glorious views beyond over Lough Foyle to the coast of Donegal. On the edge of the woods, framing the view south from the house, another triumphal arch on a pedestal is the remains of the mausoleum Frederick erected in memory of his brilliant eldest brother George, Ambassador to Madrid and Turin, Lord Lieutenant of Ireland and Lord Privy Seal.

About a mile (1.6 kilometres) south-east of Downhill, set back from the coast road, is a long, low, one-storey cottage with a thatched roof known as Hezlett House. Despite its Georgian sash windows, this cottage is one of the few dwellings of its kind in Ireland dating from before the eighteenth century. Probably built as a parsonage for the rector of Dunboe in 1691, it was acquired by Isaac Hezlett, a prosperous Presbyterian farmer, a century later and his descendants continued to live here for another 200 years.

Apart from its age, Hezlett House is also unusual for its cruck construction, involving a frame of curved lengths of wood stretching from the floor to the ridge of the roof. Relatively common in buildings of the same date in Cumbria, this technique is rare in Northern Ireland. The tiny cottage rooms are furnished with some eighteenth-century pieces, and one room has been left open to the roof to display the carpenters' work. There is also a period cottage garden.

Dudmaston

Shropshire
At Quatt, 4 miles (6.4 kilometres)
south-east of Bridgnorth on the
A442

Looking west over the River Severn to the Clee Hills, Dudmaston lies close to some of the most beautiful countryside in Britain. Built for Sir Thomas Wolryche in the late seventeenth century, it is an unpretentious four-square house attributed to Francis Smith of Warwick, with some later alterations. Sir Thomas's line died out in the eighteenth century, but descendants of his sister Anne, who took the name Wolryche-Whitmore, continued to live here. Today, the intimate family rooms are home to relatives of Rachel, Lady Labouchere, who inherited the property from her uncle, Geoffrey Wolryche-Whitmore, in 1952.

The entrance hall and a cosy sitting-room still have original eighteenth-century panelling, but elsewhere white walls, curtain fabrics and bed linen introduced by the interior designer Nina Campbell in the late 1960s reflect Lady Labouchere's taste and decorative schemes, while a scatter of family photographs, boots and shoes lined up by the front door, piles of books and magazines and a tea-maker in the visitors' bedroom are reminders that Dudmaston is still very much lived in, as Lady Labouchere wanted it to be.

The entrance hall, hung with portraits and with high-backed late seventeenth-century chairs and settees set against the walls, is where the family eat in the evenings, as the candles on the long eighteenth-century table suggest. And the beautiful library, with shelves of leather-bound books set into the walls and five long windows framed by replicas of Campbell's yellow curtains, has comfortable sofas either side of the fire and a discreet drinks' table. Another show of family portraits here includes a canvas by Tilly Kettle and there are glowing, closely observed flower paintings by the eighteenth-century Dutch masters Jan van Huysum, Jan van Os and Paul Theodorus van Brussel on the window wall.

Gallery-like rooms set up by Lady Labouchere and her husband, Sir George, beyond the more traditional part of the house are devoted to Sir George's unusual collection of twentieth-century painting and sculpture, described by Alan Bowness, Director of the Tate Gallery from 1980 to 1988, as 'one of the most important private modern collections in a country-house setting'. Small-scale sculptures include a seated figure by Henry Moore, two seed-like forms by Barbara Hepworth, boxing hares by Barry Flanagan and a show of maquettes, two of which are realised full-size in the gardens, by the local sculptor Anthony Twentyman. A head of a girl by Matisse, a colourful abstract by Alan Davie and a cubist

ABOVE There is a splendid view of Dudmaston from the walk around the lake known as the Big Pool.

piece like two playing cards by Ben Nicholson are among the eclectic collection of drawings and paintings on the walls. More sombre and more unusual are the works in the Spanish gallery, acquired by Sir George while he was British ambassador in Madrid in the 1960s. Colours here are muted, grey and black, green and brown, pieces by artists such as Antoni Tàpies, Manuel Rivera and Antonio Saura illustrating artistic responses to life under the Franco regime. Chinese porcelain and French furniture are also fruits of years in the diplomatic service, as is the splendid chandelier in the staircase hall.

Lady Labouchere was responsible for the collection of botanical art by such great exponents as Pierre-Joseph Redouté (1759–1840), P. Reinagle (1749–1833), G.D. Ehret (1708–70) and W.H. Fitch (1817–92). Formal studies by these masters contrast with the fresh, fluid approach adopted by Mary Grierson (1912–2012), who was the official botanical artist at Kew for twelve years, and some other twentieth-century approaches, among them delicate watercolours of a pink rhododendron and a white anemone by Lady Labouchere, who was a keen botanical artist herself, and a series of small-scale ink drawings by John Nash, whose courses at Flatford Mill in Suffolk she attended.

The old servants' rooms had been stripped of nearly all original features by the mid-twentieth century and are used for changing exhibitions. Objects from the collection, including a scrap of parchment that is the deed of *c.* 1127 granting the manor to one Harlewin de Butailles, from whom the estate passed, by inheritance and marriage, to the present day, illustrate a timeline of those who have lived here, linking ancient and modern.

West of the house, terraced lawns fall steeply to the lake known as the Big Pool, where a sandstone column by Anthony Twentyman stands beside the water. A short walk away is the deep cleft of the Dingle, a wooded valley laid out in Picturesque style in the eighteenth century. Around is the historic estate. Fragments of the ancient Forest of Morfe preserved in the Dudmaston woodland show the longevity of the place, which has never been sold since the time of de Butailles.

ABOVE A portrait of Lady Labouchere hangs on the elegant stone staircase that was created in the 1820s when the room was remodelled.

Dunham Massey

Cheshire
3 miles (4.8 kilometres) south-west of Altrincham, off the A56

This long, low red-brick mansion, set round two courtyards and embraced by a medieval moat, reflects long occupation by the Booth and Grey families and the gradual enlargement and remodelling of the Elizabethan and Jacobean house built by Sir George Booth, 1st Baronet. Apart from the entrance front, with its neo-Caroline stone centrepiece and Edwardian dormers, Dunham Massey's present appearance is largely due to the obscure John Norris, who refaced the house and carried out other extensive alterations for George Booth, 2nd Earl of Warrington in the first half of the eighteenth century.

The library which Norris designed for the 2nd Earl is little changed. The earl's cipher appears on many of the faded bindings in the oak bookcases and he acquired the finely crafted model of the solar system which is the centrepiece of the room and the arresting limewood carving of the Crucifixion that hangs over the fireplace. The clockwork model, made in *c*. 1730, shows how the six known planets (Uranus and Neptune were yet to be discovered) moved round the sun, while the dramatic carving, dating from 1671, is the earliest known work by Grinling Gibbons, who based his composition on a painting by Tintoretto and set his agonised figures in a tranquil floral border.

The low-ceilinged, oak-lined chapel, formed out of two rooms in 1655, reflects the Booth family's ardent Protestantism, as does the outstanding collection of Huguenot silver. Among the fine pieces now set out in the Rose Room are a water fountain of *c*. 1728 by Peter Archambo and a wine cistern made in 1701 by Philip Rollos, both of which have handles in the form of the wild boars of the Booth crest.

Sumptuous Edwardian interiors and colour schemes are the result of remodelling in the early twentieth century by William Grey, 9th Earl of Stamford, whose family acquired the estate through the marriage of George Booth's daughter, Mary, to the 4th Earl. With advice from the connoisseur and furniture historian Percy Macquoid, and the firm of Morant & Co., decorators to Edward VII, the 9th Earl and his wife created rooms that rival the appeal of those from 200 years earlier. In their long saloon with a bay window arching out into the garden, Grey family portraits hang against deep-green walls suggested by Macquoid, who also advised dyeing the

ABOVE Dunham Massey was refaced in brick in the early eighteenth century, when the original Elizabethan and Jacobean house was remodelled for the 2nd Earl of Warrington.

two mossy Donegal carpets and reupholstering the fine early eighteenth-century walnut chairs, from the same period as the walnut chests on show elsewhere in the house, to match the room. Yellow damask curtains hanging at the long sash windows give the final touch in a colour scheme that could well have been created for Bunthorne in Gilbert and Sullivan's *Patience*. The 9th Earl was also responsible for engaging J. Compton Hall to create the elaborate entrance front, which is loosely based on Sudbury (*see* p.326).

A remarkable series of early views of Dunham Massey, recording its gradual transformation from 1696 to *c*. 1750, hang in the great gallery, once the long gallery of the Tudor house, and here, too, is Guercino's early seventeenth-century *Mars, Venus and Cupid, with Saturn as Time*, which might have been purchased by the 2nd Earl of Warrington. Family portraits hang throughout the house, among them works by Cornelius

Johnson, Lely and Dahl, of the Booths, and by Reynolds, Hoppner and Cotes, of the Greys, and the young 5th Earl of Stamford, when on his Grand Tour, arranged for the two huge caricatures of his travels by Thomas Patch, who shows the earl and his friends in an irreverent light.

The main house is set round the larger of Dunham Massey's two courtyards. The secondary court, to the west, contains the kitchens and other domestic offices and there is a fine eighteenth-century stable block. A gabled building of warm red brick with mullioned windows beyond the stables is an Elizabethan water-mill. The only visible survival from the time of the 1st Baronet, the mill was originally used for grinding corn, but in c. 1860 it was refitted as a saw-mill and estate workshop. The overshot water-wheel is fed from a continuation of the lake in front of the house and the Victorian machinery,

including a big frame saw for cutting up trees known as the Dunham Ripper, is all in working order.

An ancient deer-park surrounding the house is enclosed by the 2nd Earl's high brick wall and still shaded by trees he established, some of which form a series of radiating avenues. Yews and oaks on the lawns to the east of the house were part of an informal Victorian and Edwardian layout. This has now been re-established and enhanced, with beds of rhododendrons and azaleas and a water garden along the stream feeding the moat. A curious mound just north-west of the house may be the remains of a Norman motte.

BELOW The great hall of the Tudor house was given a new guise in the eighteenth century and altered again in Edwardian times, when the walls were painted yellow.

Dunster Castle

Somerset
In Dunster, 3 miles (4.8 kilometres)
south-east of Minehead on the
A396, just off the A39

A few miles east of Minehead, a steep-sided tor stands high above the River Avill. Now a little way inland, in medieval times the tor was washed by the sea and it was this natural defensive site that the Norman William de Mohun chose for his castle. Besieged for 160 days by Cromwell's troops in the Civil War, Dunster was considered a major threat to the Commonwealth and the regime ordered its complete destruction, sparing only the Jacobean mansion, by the local stonemason William Arnold, which had been built within the walls. Although little trace of the medieval defences survives, Dunster still looks like a castle, with a tangle of towers and battlements rising romantically from the thickly wooded hill. But this is a house masquerading as a stronghold. Largely a nineteenth-century vision of what a castle should be, it was created by Anthony Salvin in 1868–72 for George Fownes Luttrell, whose ancestor Sir Hugh Luttrell came to live here in 1405. Salvin kept the Jacobean mansion, grafting on towers and battlements and remodelling much of the interior.

A steep approach from the village clustered below the tor leads to the fifteenth-century gatehouse. Beyond, a thirteenth-century gateway, the oldest surviving feature of the castle, gives access to what was once the lower ward. Across it, the north façade of the house is dominated by Salvin's great four-storey kitchen tower, with an octagonal staircase turret, complete with authentic medieval arrow loops, rising above it. The nineteenth-century work blends so well with the Jacobean walls to the right that only details in the sandstone masonry show where one ends and the other begins.

Two of the finest features of the interior were commissioned by Colonel Francis Luttrell in the late seventeenth century. He was responsible for the oak and elm staircase with naked cherubs and dogs racing through a thick acanthus undergrowth carved on the panels of the balustrade. The work is cunningly dated by the fact that one of the beasts leaps over a clutch of Charles II silver shillings from the 1683–4 issue.

The carving is of a very high standard, comparable with that on the staircase at Sudbury Hall (*see* p.326), and it may be that the distinguished Edward Pierce, who was engaged at Sudbury, also worked here. Craftsmanship of similar quality is displayed in the plasterwork ceiling in the dining room, thought to be by Edward Goudge and also dating from the 1680s, where a thick encrustation of flowers and foliage almost conceals the creatures hidden in the design. Here a cherub shoots a deer with a bow and arrow; there a winged horse bursts from a blossom. A spider's web of plaster in the hall, the only original Jacobean ceiling to escape remodelling, looks down on an allegorical portrait of Sir John Luttrell, dated 1550, in which he is shown emerging half naked from a stormy sea while sailors abandon a foundering ship behind him. Equally striking, and of international importance, is the rare set of seventeenth-

RIGHT One of the finest features of the castle is the carved oak and elm staircase commissioned by Colonel Francis Luttrell, who made many improvements to the house in the late seventeenth century.

century painted leather hangings illustrating the story of Antony and Cleopatra which fills Salvin's gallery, their brilliant, glittering colours produced by painting on embossed silver leaf. Made in the Netherlands, these hangings, which have been cut and altered to fit the space at Dunster, are believed to be the largest and most complete set of their kind in the United Kingdom. A complete contrast to these historic interiors is the 1950s kitchen with egg-shell blue Hygena units that was installed for Alys Luttrell.

A deliciously cool Victorian conservatory, a leafy extension of the airy, pale-green drawing room, leads out onto a sheltered south-facing terrace. Although the tor is exposed to westerly winds, the mild maritime climate allows tender plants and shrubs to grow along the steep paths curling round the hill below the castle. Huge conifers tower above willows, camellias, rhododendrons and moisture-loving species beside the River Avill in the depths of the valley. A path following the river round the base of the tor leads to Dunster water-mill and an eighteenth-century bridge over the water. There has been a mill on this site since medieval times, but the present building, which has been restored to working order and is used to produce flour, dates largely from 1779 to 1782.

From the grassy platform which was the site of the Norman keep, and subsequently a bowling green, and from many rooms in the castle, there are magnificent views over the surrounding countryside, where a patchwork of small hedged fields rolling away to the hills of Exmoor still looks very much as it is depicted in a set of early eighteenth-century landscapes hanging in the morning room. The eighteenth-century folly on Conygar Hill, now a prominent feature to the north of the village, was built after these were painted.

Dyffryn

Glamorgan
7 miles (11 kilometres) west of
Cardiff, via A4232 off the M4 and
A48, 1 mile (1.6 kilometres) south
of St Nicholas village

Dyffryn was one of the last great country houses built in Wales. Commissioned in 1891 by the *nouveau riche* magnate John Cory, whose fortune came from the family's involvement in local collieries and in shipping Welsh coal round the world, its design, by the Newport architect E.A. Lansdowne, draws on both English baroque and the great Renaissance châteaux of France, with a dash of Tudor magnificence thrown in. It is a statement building, intended to underpin the family's recently acquired status and social aspirations.

The long, south-facing garden front, where a magnificent *Magnolia grandiflora* flowers creamy white in early summer, has something of the grand hotel about it. Long sash windows light the two principal floors and a pedimented centrepiece rises the height of the house. Turret-like extensions at the ends of the façade, tall chimneys, urn-studded balustrades and prominent dormers contribute to an eventful roofline. By contrast, the entrance front is dominated by a huge traceried window, as if the end of a cathedral nave had been grafted on to the house.

Like the exterior, the interior was designed to impress and the principal rooms were fitted out with chimneypieces, and some panelling, salvaged from other great houses. The traceried window lights a Tudor-style Great Hall, which rises three storeys to a purely ornamental double-hammerbeam roof. Used by the family as a drawing room, this vast space was warmed by a baronial fireplace made up of pieces from elsewhere, the early seventeenth-century wooden figures on either side, for example, probably originating in Germany or Holland. Richly coloured stained glass in the window, by A.L. Moore, depicts Elizabeth I at Tilbury, where she made her Armada speech. The Tudor theme of the hall, designed to link the new house with the ancient manor that was once here, is continued in the billiard-room, where the Renaissance-style carved oak panelling was cut to fit, and in the Oak Room, where the carved six-winged cherubim either side of the fireplace may have come from a confessional.

The interconnecting drawing-rooms looking onto the Great Lawn on the south side of the house were fitted out with Victorian opulence. Chimneypieces of alabaster and marble dating from the late sixteenth or early seventeenth century may have come from the long gallery of the Elizabethan Loseley House, ceiling paintings include work by Thomas Wallace Hay and there are delicate gilt swags and some original silk hangings on the walls. A curved wall in the Blue Drawing Room, matched by one in the morning room, may be an echo of the house built by Thomas Pryce in 1749 which John Cory remodelled.

Upstairs, what was the master bedroom has a grandstand view over the Great Lawn, with its central canal leading the eye on into the tree-shaded depths of the garden. This setting, which is as important and contrived as the house, was realised from 1906 by Thomas Mawson, one of the most sought-after garden designers of his day, who created one of the grandest and most individual of Edwardian gardens at Dyffryn. His Great Lawn not only gives a sense of scale but also, by its sheer expanse, makes up for the lack of prospects to distant hills.

John Cory's third son Reginald, who was a passionate plant collector, was closely involved in the planning of the gardens and many specimens he brought back from travels to the Far East and elsewhere are now among the extensive collection of trees in the arboretum to the east of the house. West of the Great Lawn, and sloping gently downhill with the lie of the land, Mawson created an extraordinary sequence of outdoor rooms. Walled with clipped yew or stone, each is self-contained, with arched openings, narrow paths and flights of steps leading enticingly from one to another. Each has a distinct character, from the strongly architectural Pompeian garden, with colonnades and a loggia round a fountain pool, and the cool green space of the cloisters, to the lushly planted herbaceous borders at the top of the garden. With the help of delicate watercolours by Edith Adie, whom Reginald commissioned to paint the garden in the early 1920s, and Mawson's detailed master-plan, the gardens are being restored to their Edwardian grandeur.

The house, too, needed restoration after years of neglect. When the last of the Corys to live here, John's daughter Florence, died in 1936, the house was bought by Sir Cennydd Traherne, who leased it to Glamorgan County Council two years later. After years of institutional use, the house was acquired in 1996 by the Vale of Glamorgan Council, as the local authority was now called, who changed the name of the house from Duffryn, as it had been known, to the Welsh Dyffryn (meaning valley). But the future of this great mansion remained problematic and in 2013, after Dyffryn had been closed for some time, the National Trust acquired it on a 50-year lease.

The house came to the Trust without its original contents, which had been sold when Dyffryn was leased to Glamorgan County Council, and only a few rooms have been furnished. The restored principal rooms are being shown as informal and atmospheric spaces from which, on the south front, visitors can enjoy views over the Great Lawn. Grand pianos in the Blue Drawing Room and the Great Hall, which has a particularly sympathetic acoustic, are a tribute to the Cory family's love of music and visitors may well see the house to the accompaniment of a piano being played.

BELOW The south front of the house looks over the Great Lawn, where the central canal leads the eye into the tree-shaded depths of the garden.

Dyrham Park

South Gloucestershire
8 miles (12.8 kilometres) north of
Bath, 12 miles (19.3 kilometres)
east of Bristol

After recording the burial of John Wynter in 1688, the local rector drew a thick line across the page. He knew it was the end of an era. Two years previously John's only surviving child, his 36-year-old daughter Mary, had married William Blathwayt, a rising government official, and by the end of the century this energetic self-made man had totally transformed the Tudor manor his wife had inherited, creating this great mansion set beneath a spur of the Cotswolds. Despite his loyalty to James II in the Glorious Revolution, a rare fluency in Dutch coupled with an unusual gift for administration recommended Blathwayt to William III, for whom he acted as Secretary of State from 1692 to 1701.

Rebuilt in stages between 1692 and 1704, as and when money was available, Dyrham's contrasting façades reflect Blathwayt's rising fortunes, which were partly derived from involvement in administering the American colonies and from the slave trade. The earlier west front, with glorious views over the countryside towards Bristol, is an attractive building crowned with a balustrade. Low, one-storey wings, one of which forms a covered passage to the medieval village church, embrace a courtyard terrace. An Italianate double stairway descends from the terrace to a great sweep of grass, and the façade as a whole has continental overtones, as if its architect, the Frenchman S. Hauduroy, was planning a grand Parisian town house.

By the time Blathwayt constructed the east front with its state apartments, he was important enough to obtain the services of William Talman, Wren's deputy and rival, whose grand baroque façade is proudly surmounted by the Blathwayt eagle. The monumental greenhouse that extends the range to the south, successfully obscuring the service quarters in the view from the hill above the house, is also Talman's.

The elaborate formal Dutch water garden that once surrounded this palatial mansion has long disappeared. In its place is Charles Harcourt-Masters's beautiful late eighteenth-century park, with groves and clumps of beeches, chestnuts and cedars spilling down the hillsides. But the interior still reflects the taste for Dutch fashions inspired by the new king, which Blathwayt would have had ample opportunity to

ABOVE A late seventeenth-century tapestry showing Alexander the Great meeting the philosopher Diogenes, who lived in a barrel, sets off two exquisite Delftware pyramid vases.

see at first hand. In Talman's entrance hall, bird paintings by Melchior d'Hondecoeter hang against embossed leather made in Amsterdam. Door locks and hinges in the Balcony Room, where the carved panelling was originally painted to resemble marble, are engraved with tulips, daffodils, strawberries and other flowering plants, and characteristic blue-and-white Delftware, including two impressive pyramidal flower vases intended for the display of prize blooms, is seen throughout the house. Sumptuous crimson and yellow velvet hangings adorning the state bed in the Damask Bedchamber are typical of the rich fabrics and textiles with which Dyrham was once furnished. And then there are the paintings. Cool

ABOVE By the time William Blathwayt built Dyrham's east front, he was in a position to engage William Talman, the king's architect, who designed a grand baroque façade crowned by the Blathwayt eagle.

Dutch interiors, soft land- and seascapes and serene still-lifes, including works by Abraham Storck, Samuel van Hoogstraten and Cornelis de Heem, feature throughout the house. One of Hoogstraten's perspective paintings shows a view through an unmistakably Dutch interior, with tiled floors leading to a distant room, where a chair is set by a glowing fire. This painting, like others at Dyrham, came from the London home of Thomas Povey, Blathwayt's uncle, where Pepys, who was a frequent guest, much admired it, and the glazed bookcases in the hall, one of which also came from Povey's home (the other is a copy), are almost identical to those made for Pepys in 1666.

The Hoogstraten painting was bought back, together with the furniture and other pictures, by Colonel George William Blathwayt, who inherited Dyrham in 1844 after the contents had been dispersed. As part of his scheme to save the house, for which he took out a huge loan, he modernised the servants' quarters set round two courtyards behind the greenhouse, creating a suite of early Victorian rooms arranged around a long passage. Here are the bakehouse, kitchen, wet and dry larders and tenants' hall, where the most important estate tenants dined on rent days. A delicious dairy, with marble shelves and a stone fountain to keep it cool, is lined with blue and brown Delft tiles that were probably re-used from the 1698 domestic offices.

East Riddlesden Hall

West Yorkshire
1 mile (1.6 kilometres) north-east of Keighley on the south side of the B6265, on the north bank of the River Aire and close to the Leeds and Liverpool Canal

The modest seventeenth-century manor house set on a bluff above the River Aire on the outskirts of Keighley was once the centre of an extensive estate. Close to the house, on the other side of a sizeable duck pond, are the estate's two massive barns.

The smaller, 88 feet (27 metres) long, has been altered and is now used for events, but the Great Barn, said to be the finest in the north of England, has been little changed since it was built. Some 121 feet (37 metres) long, it still has its flagged threshing floor, some brick-floored cattle stalls and the original riven oak beams in the timber roof. These magnificent stone buildings, and the crenellated bothy by the manor, show East Riddlesden's former importance in the agricultural economy of this area of Yorkshire. There is still a lane running down to fields along the Aire where the manorial water mill once stood, but the estate, much reduced in size, is now a green oasis in urban surroundings.

The manor, built of soot-blackened local stone, was largely the creation of the rich clothier James Murgatroyd, who bought the estate in 1628 and set about transforming an existing medieval and Tudor building. He was responsible for the main block of the present house. The gables and mullioned windows are conventional enough, but more unusual are the striking castellated and pinnacled two-storey porches which dominate the front and back of the house. Classical columns frame the doorways and there are rose windows at the level of the first floor. A one-storey great hall, which was probably also built by Murgatroyd, forms a link to the one surviving façade of another substantial wing, now just a gabled wall ornamented with pedimented windows. James Murgatroyd never finished rebuilding East Riddlesden and this wing was the work of Edmund Starkie, James's great-grandson, who remodelled the original medieval hall in the 1690s.

Prosperity in the eighteenth century was followed by a period of decline in the nineteenth, when the hall's owners lived elsewhere, letting the estate to tenant farmers, and land was gradually sold off. At the same time, Keighley became industrialised and started spreading along the valleys towards

ABOVE The garden front of East Riddlesden Hall, showing one of the unusual castellated porches which James Murgatroyd added to the house when he remodelled it in the 1640s.

East Riddlesden. The manor survived unaltered, although most of the wing built by Edmund Starkie was demolished in 1905 and none of the original contents remain. Virtually empty when it was saved from dereliction by the Briggs brothers of Keighley in 1934 and given to the National Trust, East Riddlesden has been completely refurnished. The panelled intimate rooms are now filled with locally made oak pieces, among them a carved and canopied early seventeenth-century cupboard in the dining room, said to be the one described by Emily Brontë in the opening pages of *Wuthering Heights*, and a magnificent oak settle inlaid with ebony and boxwood

in the drawing room. A late sixteenth-century copper curfew for keeping in the embers of a fire overnight, a massive oak grain chest and a shepherd's chair designed with a hutch for a lamb or a dog under the seat are among a number of rare and intriguing objects in the house, and there are also displays of pewter, Dutch and oriental porcelain and some seventeenth-century stumpwork.

BELOW The impressive great hall at East Riddlesden Hall, with its carved stone fireplace and period oak furniture, would have been used for receiving visitors in the seventeenth century.

Erddig

Wrexham
2 miles (3.2 kilometres) south
of Wrexham

Visitors to Erddig are given a sense of the country house as a functioning community. Instead of being welcomed at the front door, they are taken through the extensive and atmospheric complex of eighteenth- and nineteenth-century brick outbuildings that formed the estate yards. Here, tools and equipment give a unique picture of how these households and their lands were nurtured day by day. Saws hang on the walls of the pit where timber was cut into manageable widths, the tools in the blacksmith's shop are the very ones that were used to repair the fine eighteenth-century ironwork screen in the formal garden, and the dry laundry sports a mangle in which sheets and tablecloths were pressed using the weight of a box of stones. Similarly, the tour of the house includes the spacious, airy rooms on the attic floor where the female servants slept.

Judging by the staff portraits in the servants' hall, which go back to the 1790s, life was agreeable here. One of the housemaids is depicted at the age of 87 and the 73-year-old estate carpenter looks spry enough to wield the axe he carries over his shoulder. The tradition of recording the servants seems to have been started by Philip Yorke I, who inherited the house in 1767. And it was Philip who added the poem supporting the abolition of slavery to a portrait of a black coachman. It is not known who this was, but it is possible the painting shows the 25-year-old John Hanby, who was coachman to John Meller, the successful London lawyer who acquired Erddig in 1716. Philip I was also responsible for re-facing the west front, which had been badly damaged by the westerly gales and driving rain that are a regular feature of the weather here. The rather severe Neo-classical composition of the 1770s on this side of the house contrasts with the warm brickwork of the garden front, where the original late seventeenth-century central block is

BELOW The warm red brick of Erddig's east front closes a view over the canal in the re-created early eighteenth-century garden.

ABOVE Erddig's west front was re-faced in stone in the eighteenth century to protect it from the westerly gales and driving rain which are a feature of life here. RIGHT The saloon in the centre of the east front, generously lit by sash windows looking onto the garden, is in the seventeenth-century part of the house and still has its original oak panelling.

flanked by wings added by Meller in 1721–4. The length of the façade and the uniform sash windows give this front the look of a row of town houses.

After the architecturally modest exterior, Meller's superb furniture and rich textiles are a surprise, his sets of silvered and walnut chairs and ornate looking-glasses all having been obtained from leading London cabinet-makers. Goblin-like masks smiling wickedly at each other across the head of the pier glass in the saloon are by the same hand as the carved and gilded birds on the tester of the sumptuous state bed, their exotic plumage echoed by a flock of diminutive painted companions, flashes of brilliant peacock-blue suggesting kingfishers on the wing. More birds perch in the borders of the summery Soho tapestries made for the principal bedroom.

Philip I created the library that now displays his passionate antiquarianism as well as his great-uncle's legal tomes, and he was also responsible for the delightful Chinese wallpaper in the room next to the chapel, with hand-painted cameos showing oriental labourers at work. Betty Ratcliffe, companion and maid to Philip I's mother, made the extraordinary Chinese pagoda decorated with mother-of-pearl and the other model buildings in the oak-panelled gallery.

Philip I's concern for the past also led him to preserve the then old-fashioned garden. Although William Emes was employed to landscape the park between 1766 and 1781, contributing the unusual circular waterfall known as the Cup and Saucer, the hanging beech woods and picturesque walks,

Philip deliberately retained the formal layout near the house, the essential features of which, such as the enclosing walls, date from 1718 to 1732. With the aid of an engraved bird's-eye view of 1740 based on a painting by Thomas Badeslade, the garden has been reconstructed as it was in the early eighteenth century and is a rare example of a design of the period.

A long gravel path stretching away from the east front, its lines emphasised by a double avenue of pleached limes, provides a strong central focus, which is continued by a canal. The decorative wrought-iron screen that was repaired by the estate blacksmith closes the vista at the far end and mature limes shade the water. To the north, apple trees planted in blocks mirror the orderly rows shown on the engraving. Plums, pears, peaches and apricots, most of them varieties listed as growing here in 1718, are trained on the walls, and there are old varieties of daffodils and narcissus in the borders below. A Victorian parterre immediately in front of the house is perfectly in tune with the formal eighteenth-century layout.

Farnborough Hall

Warwickshire
6 miles (9.6 kilometres) north of
Banbury, ½ mile (0.8 kilometre)
west of the A423

This honey-coloured stone house, home of the Holbech family for over 300 years, looks out over a well-wooded patchwork of fields and hedgerows to the scarp of Edgehill and the Malvern Hills beyond. It is still largely as created between 1745 and 1750 by William Holbech, who needed a setting for the sculpture and art he had collected on a protracted Grand Tour. Probably with help from his close friend, the gentleman-architect Sanderson Miller, who lived only a few miles away, Holbech remodelled the old manor house acquired by his grandfather, adding long façades with sash windows, pedimented doorways and a roofline balustrade to the earlier classical west front commissioned by his father. The result is harmonious, but there are some amateur touches too, such as floor-level bedroom windows.

The front door opens straight into the Italianate hall. Busts of Roman emperors and of goddesses from classical mythology look down on visitors from their niches high in the walls, there is magnificent rococo plasterwork on the ceiling by the Yorkshireman William Perritt and a copy of a view of Rome by Panini hangs over the fireplace. This fine interior is a prelude to the outstanding decoration in the sunny former saloon, now a comfortable sitting-room, which was designed specially to house four large canvases of Venice by Canaletto and two of Rome by Panini (now replaced by copies). Here, sinuous, three-dimensional rococo plasterwork, standing out white against the blue walls, clamours for attention. A cornucopia bursts with fruit and flowers over the wall mirror between the windows, a fully strung violin and guns, bows and arrows reflect William's musical and sporting interests, and little dogs with upturned noses are profiled on the plasterwork picture frames set into the walls. The ceiling decoration, white on white, is similarly arresting. Although this plasterwork is also by Perritt, whose bill for the room survives, some of the plaster detailing, such as the foliage curling over the mirror as if embracing it, suggests the work of Roberts of Oxford, or even the hand of the Italian Francesco Vassalli. The late seventeenth-century garland of fruit and flowers ringing the

ABOVE LEFT Antique Roman busts set on brackets adorn the walls of the staircase.
LEFT Farnborough Hall was remodelled in the 1740s by William Holbech, who was also responsible for the grassy terrace with panoramic views over the Warmington Valley which stretches away from the house.

ABOVE The former saloon, with its rococo plasterwork, was originally designed to take four large views of Venice by Canaletto and two of Rome by Panini, sadly now replaced by copies.

domed skylight above the stairs is also very fine, each plaster blossom, grape and pomegranate fashioned individually.

The south front surveys a stretch of grass and trees bordering a long ornamental lake, one of two in the eighteenth-century landscape park. To the south-west, William's striking grass terrace stretches three-quarters of a mile (1.2 kilometres) along a ridge high above the valley, its smooth sward, hedged with bushy laurel, wide enough for two carriages to pass with ease and adorned with what are probably Sanderson Miller's eye-catchers. A little pedimented temple, its Ionic columns pleasingly weathered, is almost hidden by trees. Further along the terrace, a curving stone staircase gives access to the upper room in a two-storey domed pavilion, where rococo plasterwork picked out in white against blue echoes the craftsmanship in the house. Perhaps the Italian prisoners treated at the military hospital set up here during the Second World War, who inscribed their names on the obelisk at the end of the terrace, appreciated the panoramic views, now alas spoiled by the routing of the M40 through the Warmington Valley below the house.

The terrace was a feature of the *ferme ornée* which William, probably with the help of Sanderson Miller, created round his house, combining a working farm with a designed landscape ornamented with garden buildings, cascades and obelisks. Views and vistas to these features from circular walks across the estate were enhanced by attractive farm buildings and by deep shrubberies and thick hedgerows emphasising the curve of a field. A rare surviving example of this approach to landscape, Farnborough's historic parkland is now being gradually restored by the Trust, with the help of Natural England, to its appearance on an estate map of 1772.

Felbrigg Hall, Gardens and Estate

Norfolk
Near Felbrigg village, 2 miles
(3.2 kilometres) south-west of
Cromer, off the A148 Holt Road

In 1738 William Windham II, accompanied by his multi-talented tutor Benjamin Stillingfleet, whose sartorial habits are the origin of the term 'bluestocking', set off on a protracted five-year Grand Tour. As soon as William succeeded to Felbrigg in 1749, he asked James Paine to remodel part of the interior to provide a suitable setting for the paintings he had acquired, some of the best of which now hang in the intimate Cabinet Room in the west wing. Here small Dutch and Italian canvases, including 26 delightful gouaches by Giovanni Battista Busiri, are set three deep on crimson damask, displayed in frames that William commissioned and in a carefully balanced arrangement which he worked out. By contrast, dominating the west wall, and showing William's taste for Dutch marine painting, is Simon de Vlieger's huge canvas depicting Dutch and Chinese ships engaging pirates in the dangerous waters of the South China Sea in 1630. The young William also acquired Samuel Scott's panoramic *Old London Bridge* and the companion piece of the Tower of London, both of which may have been painted for their present positions in the drawing room, and the two canvases by William van der Velde showing the Battle of Texel, the final sea battle in the Anglo-Dutch war of 1672–4, when the Dutch defeated the combined fleets of England and France.

Paine's sumptuous and beautiful eighteenth-century interiors, with some flowing rococo plasterwork by Joseph Rose the Elder, lie within a largely seventeenth-century building that was the work of William's great-grandfather, Thomas Windham, a descendant of the wealthy merchant who had purchased the estate in 1459, and his son William Windham I. Thomas

was responsible for Felbrigg's haunting Jacobean entrance front, the plaster-covered brick and flint with stone dressings of which it is built now attractively weathered and lichened. A projecting central porch, with classical columns framing the front door, rises the height of the house; a huge mullioned window incorporating fragments of English and continental stained glass lights the great hall to the left of the porch; and banks of octagonal brick chimneys rise from the roof. Huge stone letters carved into the parapet crowning the façade spell out GLORIA DEO IN EXCELSIS. This glorious composition is almost certainly the work of Robert Lyminge of Blickling (*see* p.57).

Paine's gothick library, with pinnacled cluster columns between the bookcases, was intended to complement this Jacobean work. The exceptional collection now housed here, which was started by William Windham II, owes much to his politician son, whose friendship with Dr Johnson is commemorated in books once owned by the learned lexicographer.

Although William Windham I was building only 50 years later than his father, a mid-century revolution in architectural styles resulted in an extraordinary contrast between the two

ABOVE A detail of the eighteenth-century Chinese wallpaper in one of the bedrooms (*see* p.142).

RIGHT The great hall was remodelled in a heavy Jacobethan style in *c.* 1840, when the plasterwork ceiling decorated with bulbous pendants was introduced.

phases of work. Walking round the house, there is an abrupt transition from the romantic Jacobean front to the ordered classicism of the late seventeenth-century west wing designed by William Samwell, with its sash windows and hipped roof. This austere exterior hides ornate plasterwork that is probably by the celebrated Edward Goudge, who is best known for his work at Belton (*see* p.49). Peaches, pears, grapes, apricots, lemons and other fruits moulded in sharp relief on the drawing-room ceiling are accompanied by lovingly detailed depictions of pheasants, partridges, woodcock and plover. More birds dart and perch amidst lotuses and peonies on the eighteenth-century Chinese wallpaper in one of the bedrooms, the relatively sombre plumage of a couple of ducks floating companionably on a pond contrasting with the brilliant-red tail feathers of a bird of paradise.

Birds also feature in the walled garden set on a gentle south-facing slope to the north of the drive, where a peacock weathervane crowns the octagonal brick dovecote at one end. Undulating parkland, studded with stands of mature woodland, comes right up to the front of the house. Thousands of trees – beeches, sycamores, oaks and maples – date from the time of William Windham I, who laid the foundations of the Great Wood which shelters the house from biting winds off the North Sea only 2 miles (3.2 kilometres) away. His work was continued by his son with advice from the improver Nathaniel Kent and possibly also from Humphry Repton, and was taken up again by the last squire of Felbrigg, who planted some 200,000 trees and formed the V-shaped rides commemorating VE day in Victory Wood. Memorials of a different kind, monuments to generations of Windhams, including some fine brasses, fill the little flint church in the park, all that remains of the village that once stood here.

ABOVE One of the bedrooms is hung with beautiful Chinese wallpaper, decorated with silver pheasants and birds of paradise.
RIGHT Weathering has enhanced the appeal of Felbrigg Hall's romantic Jacobean entrance front, with Doric columns framing the doorway and carved heraldic beasts along the parapet.

Fenton House and Garden

London
In Hampstead, on the west side
of Hampstead Grove

This charming William and Mary house with its secluded walled garden is hidden away in a leafy road just off busy Heath Street. A square two-storey building, with dormers in the steeply pitched roof and tall chimney-stacks, Fenton House is one of the earliest and architecturally most pleasing of the many mellow brick houses built in Hampstead in the late seventeenth century, when mineral springs on the hill attracted London merchants and lesser gentry to what was then a village in the country. A pediment crowning the south façade marks what was once the entrance front, from which a gravel path leads to an elaborate iron gate on Holly Hill. Records on the house are patchy, but it seems to have been built, in *c.* 1686, by William Eades, the son of a bricklayer, and is called after the Baltic merchant who owned the property by 1793.

Intimate rooms on two floors, most of them panelled and one still retaining its original closet, just a few feet across, for a close-stool, now display the outstanding assemblage of furniture, pictures, needlework and eighteenth-century porcelain bequeathed to the National Trust, together with the house, by Lady Binning, who lived here from 1944 until her death in 1952. Lady Binning inherited much of the collection from her uncle, the connoisseur and collector George Salting, who made important bequests to the Victoria and Albert Museum, National Gallery and British Museum, and from her mother Millicent Salting, who was George's sister-in-law, but Lady Binning also made acquisitions herself.

Mostly shown in glass-fronted cabinets, the porcelain includes an exquisite Meissen gold-ground tea and coffee service and ornamental pieces from a number of major German factories. There are two sets of Seasons from the short-lived Bristol and Plymouth works, Winter in one being represented by an old bearded man leaning on a stick, a bundle of faggots under his arm, while a wall of the sunny bedroom where Lady Binning slept, now furnished and decorated as it was in 1950, is filled with the blue-and-white Chinese porcelain that was to inspire the colouring of Delft pottery.

The pictures, including a delightful array of seventeenth-century embroidery pieces hanging in a little upstairs room,

animal paintings by Sartorius and works by William Nicholson on loan from the family of the late T.W. Bacon, are now augmented by a bequest from the actor Peter Barkworth, who left 55 works to Fenton House on his death in 2006. Featuring oil paintings by the Camden Town group and sea- and landscapes in pencil and watercolour, this collection now hangs throughout the house, with many works enhancing the dining room. On display are Charles Ginner's night-time view of nearby Flask Walk, where Peter Barkworth lived, works by Walter Sickert and Duncan Grant and a distant view of Rye, rising like an island from Romney Marsh, by James Bolivar Manson, who painted it while on holiday with Lucien Pissarro. Two pictures by Constable include one of his characteristic cloud studies.

The individuality of the house also comes from the early keyboard instruments that stand in nearly every room. Originally collected by the late Major Benton Fletcher, the instruments include harpsichords by the two most prominent makers in London in the later eighteenth century, Jacob Kirckman and Burkat Shudi, as well as earlier continental and English harpsichords and spinets. A virginal dated 1664 by Robert Hatley of London could have been the instrument Pepys saw being rescued by boat from the Great Fire on 2 September 1666. Most of the instruments are kept in working order and a visit to the house may be accompanied by the sound of distant music.

From a balcony reached through one of the attic rooms visitors can look down on the walled garden on the north side of the house, with its raised terrace walks, clipped holly and yew and little apple orchard, and out over the rooftops of Hampstead to the distant outlines of city skyscrapers.

The Firs – Birthplace of Edward Elgar

Worcestershire
Crown East Lane, Lower Broadheath, 3 miles (4.8 kilometres) west of Worcester, off the A44

Edward Elgar, one of England's greatest composers, was born in this little red-brick cottage looking out towards the Malvern Hills on a beautiful June day in 1857. Newbury Cottage, as it was then called, had been built in the early nineteenth century as a two-up, two-down to house farm labourers, with a ladder giving access to the upper floor. By the time the Elgars moved in, in the early 1850s, the cottage had been doubled in size and given a staircase. Gabled outbuildings alongside, said to have been built by Elgar's father and his Uncle Henry, housed the family's pony and trap.

Only two years after Elgar was born, the family moved into Worcester where Elgar's father ran a music shop with Henry, but the family continued to come back to Broadheath for their holidays and the glorious countryside of this part of the world, with its hills, deserted lanes and lovely villages, remained with Elgar for the rest of his life and fed into his music. When he was knighted in 1931, he asked to be known as Baron Elgar of Broadheath and he always lived within reach of the landscape he loved.

After his death, in 1934, his daughter Carice, who knew her father's last wish was to be remembered in his birthplace, persuaded the Corporation of Worcester to buy the cottage and preserve it. Here she displayed the memorabilia which formed the core of the present museum. Since then the collection has grown considerably. The cottage has been altered to accommodate it and, in 2020, three years after the birthplace was taken over by the Trust, a visitor centre with further exhibition space was added. Most of the original manuscripts and letters have been donated to the British Library, as Carice wanted, but the substantial collection of mementoes still here conjures up the man and his world. On display are Elgar's upright piano, made in Paris in 1874, which visitors can play;

the gramophone which HMV, his recording company, gave him in the mid-1920s; and the chair and desk which were in his study in Craeg Lea, his house in Malvern. Family treasures include scrapbooks, photographs and other memorabilia.

Carice also set out to return the garden to how it would have appeared in Elgar's childhood, as recorded in a painting of 1856 by John Chessell Buckler, a family friend. The standard roses, gravel paths, colourful borders and archway festooned with honeysuckle shown in the painting still feature in the garden today. The octagonal thatched summer-house came from Elgar's last home, Marl Bank in Worcester.

Overall, this evocative place is as much a tribute to Carice, who did so much to preserve and promote her father's legacy, as it is to Elgar, who lived with Broadheath in his heart.

OPPOSITE Serene Fenton House, with rows of elegant sash windows and a pediment marking the entrance front, is one of the most pleasing of Hampstead's many late seventeenth-century houses.
RIGHT The thatched summer-house which Edward Elgar had at his home in Worcester is now in the garden of the little brick cottage where he was born.

Florence Court

Co. Fermanagh
8 miles (12.8 kilometres)
south-west of Enniskillen, via the
A4 and the A32 Swanlinbar road

South of Lough Erne, the border between the Irish Republic and Northern Ireland runs across the wild and dramatic Cuilcagh mountains. These lonely hills were the backdrop for Sir John Cole's early eighteenth-century house, which he chose to build on a site 8 miles (12.8 kilometres) from Enniskillen, where the family had been established since 1607. His building, probably little more than a hunting lodge, has long been replaced, but the name he gave it, which was that of his wife, lives on. And it was Florence Cole's considerable fortune that enabled their son John, 1st Lord Mount Florence, to build much more grandly than his father.

The 1st Lord's dignified house, dating from the 1750s, now forms the heart of Florence Court. Seven bays wide and three storeys high, it is built of rendered brick with stone dressings and crowned by a parapet. Delightful baroque details enliven the entrance front, giving the house an archaic touch. On the garden façade, a projecting bay window lighting the staircase stretches the height of the building, with three massive scallop shells marking the top. Open colonnades with round-headed arches leading to one-storey pavilions on either side of the central block were added in 1771, probably to designs by Davis Ducart, the Sardinian-born architect, by William Willoughby Cole, later 1st Earl of Enniskillen.

The house was extensively restored by the National Trust after a fire in 1955, in which many family portraits were lost. The main feature of the interior is the riotous rococo plasterwork attributed to Robert West, the talented Dublin stuccadore. In the dining room, thick encrustations of acanthus foliage swirl round the central motif, where an eagle with outstretched wings is surrounded by puffing cherubs representing the four winds. Tendrils of foliage hang over the border of the design, as if new young fronds are outgrowing the frame. The acanthus theme is repeated on the staircase, where three panels filled with fluid foliage are set either side of the well. A donation of family portraits, a set of large landscapes of the area and other pieces belonging to the Enniskillen family, such as an eighteenth-century Italian specimen table, together with fine Irish furniture acquired by the Trust, including the marquetry desk prominently decorated with scallop shells in the study, have helped to re-create the atmosphere of a great Irish country house.

The extensive service rooms in the basement, including a stone-flagged kitchen with a fire-proof ceiling like a huge umbrella, look out onto cobbled courtyards on either side of the house, one a coach-yard, the other housing a dairy, laundry, drying rooms and other essential facilities. Beyond the house, a range of stone outbuildings once catered not just for the estate but also for the wider community. In the carpenter's workshop, dating from the mid-nineteenth century, wood from the estate was turned into wheels, ladders, gates and much else, including luggage barrows for the Great Northern Railway. There is a blacksmith's forge, remodelled in the 1840s, and down a lane to the south of the house, just above the river Larganess, is the eighteenth-century mill, where the giant Victorian wheel has been restored to working order. Converted into a saw-mill in the 1840s, as well as supplying the needs of the estate, the mill turned out railway sleepers and met a huge local demand for building timber.

A rose garden fills part of the walled garden beside the drive, and the old kitchen garden here is being returned to its 1930s layout. The pleasure grounds below the house, rich in azaleas, rhododendrons and exotic trees and shrubs, were created, probably to a design by James Frazer, in the 1840s. Beyond is the extensive tree-studded park first laid out in the eighteenth century.

LEFT A view to the Venetian window on the entrance front, showing some of Florence Court's exuberant rococo plasterwork.

F

Fountains Abbey and Studley Royal

North Yorkshire
2 miles (3.2 kilometres) west
of Ripon, off the B6265 to
Pateley Bridge

The ruins of Fountains Abbey lie hidden in the valley of the River Skell, framed by steep wooded slopes. The approach from the west follows a narrow lane past the mellow stonework of the late Elizabethan Fountains Hall, which was partly built with material from the abbey ruins. The hall's symmetrical, many-windowed façade, with a deeply recessed central bay and projecting towers at both ends, has echoes of Hardwick Hall (*see* p.169), and Robert Smythson, who designed Hardwick, may also have been involved here. Classical columns and delightful carved figures flank the porch and there is an impressive carved chimneypiece in the Great Chamber, with a panel depicting the Judgement of Solomon.

Beyond the hall, and the monastic water-mill, the lane suddenly opens out into a grassy court in front of the monastery. Ahead, the west end of the abbey church, with the outline of a huge window above the west door, is dwarfed by Abbot Marmaduke Huby's great tower projecting from the north side of the nave. Almost 172 feet (52 metres) high, the tower is so tall that it can be seen from far away, peering over the rim of the valley. To the right stretches the west range, as impressively long as Huby's tower is tall and extending over the Skell at one end. All is built of the greyish sandstone that outcrops just beside the abbey.

Fountains is the largest abbey in England and has survived remarkably complete, probably because it was too remote to be turned into a country house or extensively plundered for building stone after its dissolution in 1539. The impressive remains, centred on the cloister at the heart of the abbey, contain many telling reminders of the daily life and routines of the community that lived here for 400 years. Worn stone steps on the south side of the cloister once led up to the long dormitory where the monks slept and the room beside the stairs still has the two great fireplaces where a wood fire was kept burning from November to Easter, so the monks had

somewhere they could warm themselves. Stone benches by the refectory door once held the basins where the community could wash their hands before meals, drying them on towels from a cupboard built into the arched recess that can still be seen on the wall of the warming room. The stone supports for the tables in the refectory itself still protrude from the grassy floor, and a flight of steps built into the thickness of the wall leads up to the pulpit where devotional works were read to the brothers while they ate.

A group of idealistic monks who had rebelled against the relaxed atmosphere of their parent Benedictine house founded St Mary of Fountains in 1132 as a pioneering Cistercian community. The austere and simple lifestyle of the early days is reflected in the unadorned architecture of the oldest parts of the abbey, such as the huge tree-trunk pillars supporting the cathedral-like nave. But the very success of the community was to lead to the relaxation of the principles that had made it great. With the aid of lay brothers, who vastly outnumbered the monks themselves, the abbey eventually controlled huge estates, largely given over to sheep, stretching west into the Lake District and north to Teesside, the source of the wealth

ABOVE LEFT This little classical temple in the water garden was designed as a cool garden house on the shady side of the valley.
BELOW The rhythmic stone vaulting of the west range of the abbey.

that made it one of the richest religious houses in Britain by the mid-thirteenth century. Wool merchants who came to Yorkshire from Flanders and Italy were accommodated in self-contained suites in the guest houses that can still be seen on Abbey Green.

This prosperity financed later building, such as the early thirteenth-century Chapel of the Nine Altars at the east end of the church, with its soaring perpendicular window. But the greatest monument to earthly concerns, Marmaduke Huby's tower, was added in the community's final decades. A prodigy tower in the spirit of Sissinghurst or Tattershall (*see* pp.307 and 332), Huby's creation, erected to his personal glory, was in direct contravention of early Cistercian practice. A magnificent example of the strength of religious faith, Fountains is also a monument to lost ideals.

Downstream from the abbey is the eighteenth-century water garden of Studley Royal whose creator, John Aislabie, retired here in 1720 after involvement in the South Sea Bubble brought his political career to an abrupt end. Mirror-like ponds on the valley floor reflect classical statues and a Tuscan temple and walks threading the wooded slopes on either side give vistas to a gothic tower and other eye-catchers. Most memorably, from a high-level path through the trees there is a sudden view up a sweep of grass-framed water to the abbey ruins. The serenity of this part of the garden contrasts with a

ABOVE Marmaduke Huby's great tower, which dominates the ruins of the abbey, was added in the early sixteenth century, not long before the monastery was dissolved in 1539.

wilder landscape downstream, beyond a lake fed by the Skell. Here Aislabie's son William enhanced the natural drama of a gorge-like section of the river and planted beech woods to create an early example of a Picturesque landscape.

Running down to the valley of the Skell is an extensive deer-park where another spectacular building was an addition of the late nineteenth century. Silhouetted on the skyline at the end of a lime avenue which climbs slowly from gates on the eastern side of the park is the gothic church of St Mary the Virgin, with a spire soaring above the trees. Built for the 1st Marquess and Marchioness of Ripon from 1871 to 1878, this is a *tour de force* by William Burges. The exterior is relatively restrained but the interior is a riot of colour and rich carving in wood and stone. Angelic musicians set against a gilded background throng the sanctuary, the choir-stalls are carved with multi-coloured parrots, the organ case masquerades as a medieval house, complete with spiral staircase, and there is stained glass illustrating the Book of Revelation.

This sumptuous example of High Victorian taste adds to the richness and variety of what is overall an exceptional property, now designated a World Heritage Site.

Gawthorpe Hall

Lancashire
On the eastern outskirts of Padiham; ½ mile (0.8 kilometre) drive to the house north of the A671

Set on the edge of the Pennines, with peaceful views to distant hills, Gawthorpe seems magically detached from the urban sprawl along the Burnley road out of Padiham by which it is approached. It is a compact three-storey Elizabethan house, with three projecting bays on the entrance front, a glittering grid of mullioned windows and a staircase tower rising above the roof and giving wide views over the country around. The building of the house was supervised by the mason Anthony Whithead, but the design, which has strong similarities to that of Hardwick Hall (*see* p.169) and Wollaton in Nottinghamshire, has been attributed to the talented Robert Smythson.

Gawthorpe had been the home of the Shuttleworth family for some 200 years before the present house was started in 1600, financed by the fortune of the Elizabethan barrister Sir Richard Shuttleworth. Inside, original Jacobean ceilings and woodwork set off the nineteenth-century restoration by Sir Charles Barry, architect of the Houses of Parliament (*see also* pp.99 and 192), who also made some changes to the exterior, such as raising the height of the prospect tower. He and his collaborators, A.W.N. Pugin and J.G. Crace, were employed in 1850–2 by Sir James Kay-Shuttleworth, the great Victorian reformer, who had married the heiress to the property, Janet Shuttleworth, and took her name. Barry also laid out an Elizabethan-style formal garden, part of which still overlooks the River Calder on the north.

The interior has an atmosphere of crowded opulence. In the richly furnished drawing room, startling green curtains and settees upholstered in velvet are combined with a striking carpet strongly coloured in blue and red. Photographs in ornate silver frames clutter the rare octagonal table made by Pugin and Crace. Potted ferns on pedestals, fringed table covers and a florid pink and blue Italian glass chandelier complete the effect. With the addition of a few cobwebs, it would be a perfect setting for Miss Havisham. The Jacobean frieze, with ornate three-dimensional plasterwork in which mermaids and other half-human creatures are entwined amongst writhing foliage, adds to the overall restlessness.

The long gallery running the length of the south front on the second floor is equally evocative and still has the feel of a place where people came for exercise in inclement weather. Decorated with original plasterwork, it is hung with portraits of early seventeenth-century society figures. These pictures and many others in the house, including a rather unflattering depiction of Charles II's mistress, the Duchess of Cleveland, are on loan from the National Portrait Gallery.

Five rooms on the first floor display pieces from the Gawthorpe Textile Collection. Assembled by Miss Rachel Kay-Shuttleworth, the last of the family to live here, this unparalleled collection of needlework includes pieces from the seventeenth century to the present day, ranging from quilts and christening robes to waistcoats and samplers, and work in many styles, such as lace work, white work and embroidery. The displays are changed regularly to show something of the variety of the collection and the final room has work by contemporary textile artists.

BELOW The entrance front of Elizabethan Gawthorpe Hall is lit by a glittering array of mullioned windows.

George Inn

London
In Southwark, on the east side of
Borough High Street, near London
Bridge Station

A rather uninviting arch off Borough High Street leads into a courtyard flanked by the one surviving wing of a seventeenth-century inn. Looking down into the yard from the galleries fronting the first and second storeys, it is possible to imagine the noise and excitement when The George was a major terminus for stagecoaches to all parts of England in the eighteenth and nineteenth centuries. It is now the last galleried inn in London, but several similar staging-posts once stood nearby, among them The Tabard, where Chaucer set the beginning of his *Canterbury Tales*.

The George was built in 1677 on the site of a much older hostelry that had been destroyed by fire the year before.

Originally it enclosed three sides of the yard, but two wings were pulled down in 1889. A strong period atmosphere survives inside: the coffee room lined with private drinking compartments, the bar with an open fireplace and the panelled dining room all conjure up the kind of establishment described by Dickens, who certainly knew The George as he mentions it in *Little Dorrit*. Even today the open galleries are the only way to reach rooms on the first and second floors.

Although it is no longer possible to stay here, The George is still very much an inn. Occasional performances of Shakespeare's plays foster the legend that the bard himself once acted in the courtyard.

BELOW In the days when stagecoaches set out from London to all parts of England, the George was just one of several inns in Southwark that catered for this traffic.

Gibside

Tyne & Wear
6 miles (9.6 kilometres) south-west of Gateshead, 20 miles (32 kilometres) north of Durham between Rowlands Gill and Burnopfield

This atmospheric property in the leafy Derwent Valley is at its best at dusk, when the urns set along the roof of the chapel and the central dome are silhouetted against the setting sun. From the chapel, a wide avenue of ancient oaks runs just under half a mile (0.8 kilometre) towards a great Tuscan column that rises over 140 feet (40 metres) from the wooded hill at the far end. A statue of Liberty crowns the column. These features are part of an extensive eighteenth-century layout, now being revived, in which formal avenues and a series of garden buildings designed as focal points were set in a more natural wooded landscape.

The Gibside estate came into the Bowes family in the early eighteenth century and it was George Bowes, a coal baron who combined good living with more intellectual pursuits, who transformed his inheritance, as funds allowed, from 1729 to 1760. The chapel was the last building to be added to the landscape. Designed by James Paine, it was begun in 1759, the year before George Bowes died, and stands on a platform above his mausoleum. Built of creamy local sandstone, it is in the shape of a Greek cross, with a columned portico reached by a double staircase marking the entrance.

The interior has early nineteenth-century furnishings of the highest quality. A splendid three-tier mahogany pulpit stands

ABOVE The magnificent three-decker pulpit, made of cherrywood.
BELOW LEFT Gibside Chapel was begun in 1759 but was not finished until over 50 years later, when the elegant plasterwork was added.

behind the altar, its umbrella-like sounding board perched on an Ionic column ensuring that the preacher's message reached those seated below. On either side elliptical cherrywood pews for servants and visitors fill the semicircular apses in the arms of the cross and there are box pews for the owner, agent and chaplain.

The eighteenth-century stables and banqueting hall by Daniel Garrett also survive, the former with a grand Palladian façade, the latter, in gothick style, set high to enjoy prospects over the estate, but the monumental orangery added by Mary Eleanor Bowes, George's daughter, is now a ruin and the rambling Jacobean hall set on a shelf above the Derwent is just a shell.

As George's only child, Mary Eleanor had inherited a fortune and was married, for her money, by John Lyon, 9th Earl of Strathmore, who changed his name to Bowes-Lyon to secure his prize. The late Queen Mother, daughter of the 14th Earl, sometimes came to Gibside as a child from the Strathmores' house near Barnard Castle for a picnic in the park.

Goddards

York
27 Tadcaster Road, about
1½ miles (2.4 kilometres)
south of York city centre

Although not far from the centre of York, Goddards seems more like a place in the country. Beyond the brick gatehouse on the busy Tadcaster road, a drive framed by pollarded chestnuts leads down to the house, with birdsong replacing the noise of traffic. At the back, the garden borders the open green spaces of the racecourse, fostering the illusion that this is a rural retreat.

A long house of deep red brick with shallow wings on both fronts, banks of tall, Tudor-style chimneys, mullioned casement windows, a steep, red-tiled roof and diamond patterning in the brickwork, Goddards was built in the early 1920s for Noel Terry, joint managing director of the family confectionery business, Terry's of York, who wanted a new home for his wife Kathleen and their four children. More than that, he wanted a house close to the new works being built on the other side of the race course, close to the River Ouse along which barges brought the cocoa and sugar used in the making of Terry's chocolates. At Goddards, Noel could walk to the factory every day from the gate at the bottom of the garden. Although this was the 1920s, there was provision for servants too. To the north of the house, shielded from the rest of the building by a projecting verandah, is the former service wing, with dormers in the roof lighting what were servant bedrooms.

Goddards was designed by Walter Brierley, the leading Yorkshire architect of the day, in a loose Arts and Crafts idiom reminiscent of the Edwardian country houses designed by Edwin Lutyens. There is some fine craftsmanship, from the carved oak newel posts and balusters of the stairs and the intricate patterning of the leading in the staircase window to the ornamental brickwork of the chimneys and on the back of the house. Much of this detailing was by J. Hervey Rutherford, Brierley's partner, and Rutherford took over when Brierley, who was in his sixties when the house was begun, became ill. Brierley died in 1926, just as the roof was being put on.

Originally, except for the rooms used by the children, the family side of the house was filled with Noel Terry's outstanding collection of eighteenth-century furniture and clocks. Following Noel's death in 1980, the house was sold to the Trust, while the collection is now displayed in the eighteenth-century setting of Fairfax House in the centre of York. For many years, the Trust has used Goddards as a regional office and there are still Trust offices here; the principal rooms that are now on show, where much of the original decoration has survived, have been refurnished to evoke something of the atmosphere of Goddards in the 1930s.

A Tudor-style porch, with an oriel window above the doorway, leads into the wide oak-panelled hall linking the main rooms on the ground floor. At the far end, lit by windows on two sides looking onto the garden, is the beautiful drawing room, with subtle plasterwork by George Bankart covering a gently arched barrel ceiling and panelled walls painted a deep cream. In the study next door, a carved Georgian panel over the fireplace is all that remains of Noel Terry's collection of eighteenth-century pieces. Upstairs, displays in the former guest bedroom tell the story of the Terry family and their confectionery factory, which closed in 2005.

The compartmental garden, with hedges of clipped yew enclosing a series of outdoor rooms, slopes away from the broad terrace at the back of the house. Designed by the landscape architect George Dillistone, it becomes increasingly informal as it descends, with meandering paths through a rock and water garden at the lowest level. For the Terry family, the garden was an extension of the house. The shady verandah opening onto a garden room bounds one side of the terrace and there are areas for bowls and tennis. On warm nights the children were allowed to sleep in camp beds on the lawn, guarded by their terrier Timmy, and various unusual pets were encouraged to take up residence, among them midwife toads, which still inhabit the pools.

OPPOSITE The garden front of Goddards, showing the decorative brickwork which is a feature of the house. Visitors can take tea on the terrace, as the Terry family used to do.

Godolphin

Cornwall
Between Hayle and Helston, off a
zigzag road from Godolphin Cross
to Townshend

The Godolphin estate lies deep in Cornwall, in a well-wooded landscape of small fields, scattered settlements and twisting lanes, and with a sense of the sea near at hand. At its heart, beneath the cone of Godolphin Hill and shielded by woodland along the Hayle River, is this ancient house, one of the most atmospheric and haunting places in the West Country. Low, two-storey ranges, lit by stone-mullioned windows and built of local granite like the field walls and stiles on the estate, are set round three sides of a grassy courtyard. What was the great hall range on the south side, with an arched porch giving onto the court, is now a romantic ruin. A second courtyard that once lay beyond it was demolished, along with most of the hall, in the early nineteenth century.

The Godolphin family were living on this site from the twelfth century and a fortified manor with a large courtyard was built here in *c.* 1300. When Sir John Godolghan built a magnificent new house, set around two courtyards, a little to the north-west in 1475, the old house was ruinous and granite from it was used in the new building, one wing of which survived later alterations. By this time the family were people of substance, grown rich on the mining of rich seams of tin and copper on the estate and, through judicious marriages and loyal service to the Crown, gradually securing their position as one of the leading families of Cornwall. They continued to prosper under the Tudors, emerging as players on the national stage from the reign of Henry VIII. The old king, diseased and failing, knighted William Godolphin after the successful siege of Boulogne in 1544 and Sir Francis Godolphin I, who inherited in 1575, was the first of a line of Godolphins to be governor of the Scilly Isles, which were held for the king in the Civil War. As the family's status grew, so the house was enlarged, becoming the largest and grandest in Cornwall in the seventeenth century. This was the high point. By the time Sidney Godolphin, the 1st Earl, became Queen Anne's First Lord of the Treasury in the early eighteenth century, the family had a London house and their old Cornish seat was increasingly neglected. By the early nineteenth century, it had become nothing more than a slightly run-down farmhouse. Godolphin was lovingly restored by Sydney Schofield, son of the American landscape painter Elmer Schofield, and his wife Mary, who came here in 1937. The National Trust bought the estate from the Schofields in 2000, and in 2007 the house and garden were also acquired.

The north-facing entrance front, its stone now weathered and lichen-spotted, is approached across a forecourt paved with mossy cobbles. In the centre of this façade is a long Italianate colonnade, its weight carried on eight stocky Tuscan columns carved from the local granite. On the other side of what is only a screen wall, an identical colonnade looks onto the courtyard. This remarkable architectural flourish, an exceptionally sophisticated feature for its date in this part of the country, was added in the 1630s, together with the rooms above, by Sir Francis Godolphin III, whose plans for remodelling the whole house never got further than this range. A cultured and sophisticated man, whose brother was the poet Sidney Godolphin, Sir Francis would have moved in court circles and been aware of the new Italianate architecture in London, typified by Inigo Jones's Banqueting House. The lead drainwater heads on this front carry the double-headed eagle of the Godolphin arms and the leaping dolphin of the family crest, and a Tudor arch closed with original massive oak doors that was incorporated in the seventeenth-century work leads through into the courtyard.

The interior is a succession of light, airy rooms, the most glorious being the long chamber with windows on both sides

that runs above the colonnade. A room that was used by William Godolphin IV, friend of the diarists Pepys and Evelyn, still has its 1630s decorative frieze, original pine floorboards, and enchanting blue-and-white seventeenth-century Delft tiles featuring mythical beasts round the fireplace. The closet off, now a bathroom, was probably William's library and study. Seventeenth-century improvement also accounts for the lofty chamber in the west range with large mullioned windows looking onto the courtyard. Known as the King's Room, this is where Prince Charles, the future Charles II, is said to have rested when he was fleeing to the Scilly Isles and France in 1646 after his crushing defeat at the Battle of Naseby in 1645. The high coved ceiling has pendants of what may be Jacobean plasterwork and a richly carved oak overmantel on the south wall is thought to commemorate the wedding of William Godolphin III and Thomasine Sydney in 1604. Originally in the hall, it was moved to this room in the nineteenth century when the hall was demolished. On the other side of the courtyard is the medieval east wing, a remnant of Sir John Godolghan's house, where one of the intimate rooms has rich linenfold panelling and carved ceiling beams.

Godolphin came to the Trust with only a few furnishings and, although now a holiday let, has been sympathetically fitted out with pieces that, like the refectory table in the dining room, dating from 1750 to 1830, suit the spirit of the house. There are a couple of Godolphin family portraits as well as some striking paintings of Cornish fishermen by Walter Schofield, who used one of the rooms in the west range as his studio. A squint big enough to take a musket covering the entrance is a reminder of Cornwall's former lawlessness and of the Godolphins' support for Charles I in the Civil War, the expense of which probably prevented Sir Francis from completing the updating of his house.

A grand and beautifully proportioned stable block built in 1608 sits beside the house, its mullioned windows and rough cobbled floor, complete with drainage gullies, still unchanged. Behind the stables is the intimate, stone-walled King's Garden, while east of the house are the skeletal remains of a compartmental fourteenth-century garden, with raised walks and the depressions of former fish-ponds. This rare survival, the earliest garden in the care of the Trust, is thought to have once been part of a more extensive grid of garden enclosures surrounding the medieval manor. Nineteenth-century farm buildings, such as the cow barns south of the house, are gradually being restored, while in the woodland along the river and up on the hill are the pits, gullies, spoil heaps and other remains of former mining, now romantically deserted and overgrown.

Great Chalfield Manor

Wiltshire
3 miles (4.8 kilometres) south-west of Melksham, via Broughton Gifford Common

When Thomas Tropnell rebuilt his manor between 1467 and 1480, England was still being torn apart by the Wars of the Roses and no one could feel secure. His new courtyard house was approached through a defensible fourteenth-century gatehouse and encircled by a curtain wall and a moat. Visitors coming to the porch could be assessed through a squint from the parlour (now hidden behind panelling), and a little wicket in the ancient oak front door admits only one person at a time.

There is still a medieval gatehouse, a moat and the remains of the curtain wall, but seeing the house today, so peacefully set in the countryside only a few miles from Bath, it is difficult to connect it with the troubled times in which it was built. The honey-coloured stone, gabled façades and mullioned windows give it the look of a Cotswold manor and there are delightful stone carvings of griffins holding the Tropnell arms and soldiers in fifteenth-century armour crowning the gables on the entrance front. Across what was the outer courtyard, at right-angles to the house, is a little fourteenth-century church, which Tropnell enhanced with a bellcote and spire.

Inside, the great hall, lit by windows high in the walls, rises to what would have been a richly painted ceiling and arched openings lead to the fine first-floor rooms in the gabled wings on either side. Both these chambers are lit by beautiful oriel windows, but that lighting what was once Tropnell's solar is particularly striking, with delicate fan vaulting over the bay inside and a crest of decorative stonework on the exterior. This

room looks out on the little church and from here, too, the family could watch proceedings in the hall through two of the curious stone masks with cut-away eyes that hang in the room below – one a king with ass's ears, another a bishop in his mitre, the third a laughing face. Another curiosity is the mural painting in the dining room, showing a man with five fingers on each hand. This painting may depict Thomas Tropnell himself, a 'perilous, covetouse man'.

The house as it is seen today reflects Sir Harold Brakspear's restoration in 1905–12 for the Fuller family after about two centuries of neglect and disrepair, during which both the east and south wings that once closed the inner courtyard were demolished (although the foundations of the latter can still be seen in the garden). Sir Harold's sensitive and scholarly reconstruction used drawings made by Pugin's pupil Thomas Larkin Walker in 1836, when the manor was already dilapidated. The Fullers, whose descendants live here still, were also responsible for introducing the period furniture, Flemish tapestries and eastern carpets that now enhance the house. And, with advice from the watercolourist Alfred Parsons, they laid out the garden to south and east of the manor, with more formal areas near the house and a rough-grassed orchard, coloured with wild flowers in spring, running down to the moat on the south side.

Since its restoration, Great Chalfield has again been the hub of a rural estate that includes home farms, woodland, labourers' cottages and its own parish church. Little has changed on the land, where field names and boundaries are still as they are shown on a map of 1794.

LEFT At the back of the house, the garden slopes down to an arm of the moat that was dug to protect the manor in the Middle Ages.
ABOVE The hall is hung with seventeenth-century Flemish tapestries.

Greenway

Devon
Greenway Road, Galmpton,
on the east bank of the River Dart
off the A379

One of the most successful and prolific authors of all time, outsold only by Shakespeare, is Agatha Christie (1890–1976). As well as producing a library of ingenious detective stories and a number of other books, she also wrote several plays, one of which, *The Mousetrap*, has been running continuously on the London stage for almost 70 years. It seems appropriate that this exceptional woman, who knew how to conjure up suspense and mystery, should have fallen for this romantic and atmospheric place overlooking the magical Dart estuary. A luxuriant woodland garden, developed over the last 200 years and filled with many rare and tender plants and specimen trees, surrounds the house and plunges steeply to the water, adding greatly to Greenway's individual charm. On the other side of the river is the little village of Dittisham, from which ferries cross to the quay below the property, and there are spectacular views over the water and down the estuary to Dartmouth.

Although there was a late sixteenth-century Tudor mansion here, home to several generations of the adventuring Gilberts of Compton Castle (*see* p.106), the central block of the present white Georgian house was built, by an unknown architect, for the merchant adventurer Roope Harris Roope in 1771 on a site in front of the old Greenway Court. A tall stuccoed building, with an array of sash windows looking west over the river and a hipped roof, the house is tucked into the slope at the top of the garden. One-storey wings fronted by colonnaded porticoes on either side of the main block were added in 1815 by James Marwood Elton, whose father, another merchant adventurer, had bought the property in 1791.

Dame Agatha, whose childhood home in Torquay (now demolished) lay just a few miles away, bought Greenway with her second husband, the archaeologist Max Mallowan, as a holiday home in 1938, employing the young Guilford Bell

LEFT Agatha hung French ivory-framed mirrors above the bookcases in her bedroom.

to demolish a billiard-room wing that had been added in the later nineteenth century and make other alterations. Agatha's daughter Rosalind Hicks and her husband Anthony lived here from 1978 and in 2000 Rosalind and Anthony, together with Rosalind's son Matthew Prichard, gifted the property, with its shield of surrounding woodland and farmland, to the National Trust. The garden has been open since 2003 and the house, which came to the Trust with all its contents, opened in 2009.

Shown as it was in its heyday, as a holiday home in the 1950s, Greenway is a most attractive house, with light, well-proportioned rooms, their cream decoration being one of Guilford Bell's improvements, and a sense of comfort and serenity. Apart from some de-cluttering by the Trust, the furnishings are largely as recorded in the 1942 inventory and there are displays of family portraits and photographs and the kind of belongings that make a house feel lived in, from Anthony Hicks's hats to golf clubs, walking sticks and soft toys. All the family were great collectors and every table, chest and mantelpiece and every glass-fronted cabinet is used to display their rather individual treasures, among them ceramics, pocket watches, boxes made of scrolled paper and Tunbridgeware. Large built-in cupboards in the winter dining-room are stuffed full of further items, including modern studio glass and the Mallowans' collection of silver.

In the drawing room filling the west wing, a sofa and deep armchairs are set invitingly round the fire. This is where Agatha Christie used to read the manuscript of her latest thriller to family and friends, asking them to guess who the murderer in the story might be; she wrote letters at the mahogany bureau and played the Steinway grand that sits in a corner of the room. A portrait of Agatha aged four, painted by Douglas Connah in 1894, hangs in the room next door, and the doll she is shown clutching sits on the chair below. Upstairs, the writer's bedroom, with its large walk-in wardrobe and display of papier-mâché furniture, is largely unchanged, and a striking brightly coloured kimono here is the one being worn by her mother in a photograph downstairs. An adjoining room is now devoted to Max Mallowan's excavations in Mesopotamia, with a display of miniature pottery heads and other finds. A

ABOVE Greenway is an attractive Georgian house set high above the Dart estuary, with magical views over the river and downstream towards Dartmouth.

haughty ceramic camel dating from the Tang dynasty (AD618–906) in the dining-room was a present from Max to Agatha and other pieces in the house came from her childhood home.

Another aspect of Greenway's history comes through in the library, where an unusual frieze dates from the Second World War when the 10th Flotilla of the US Coastguard was based in the house and Greenway was caught up in the preparations for D-Day. Painted by Lt Marshall Lee in 1943 in what was then the officers' bar, the frieze depicts incidents in the flotilla's war, such as the hard-fought invasion of Sicily; a final tableau shows the house half-hidden in trees high above the Dart, with a naval vessel in the deep-water anchorage below.

A stable block tucked away to the north-west of the house, still with some original stalls and loose-boxes, also dates from the eighteenth century, but a bell tower and clock were additions of the 1850s. Down on the river, in leafy seclusion, is a substantial two-storey late Georgian boathouse. A plunge pool fed from the Dart fills with salt water at high tide, while above, with a balcony overlooking the river, is a roomy sitting-room, complete with fireplace. This is where Agatha Christie set the murder of Marlene Tucker in *Dead Man's Folly*, thus bringing the place she loved into her writing.

In keeping with Greenway's history as a much-loved retreat for Agatha and her family, the top of the house has been turned into a spacious holiday apartment.

Greys Court

Oxfordshire
3 miles (4.8 kilometres) west
of Henley-on-Thames, east of
the B481

This picturesque assemblage of old buildings set on a peaceful wooded hillside was caught up in one of the most notorious murders of the seventeenth century. When the poet Sir Thomas Overbury died in the Tower of London in 1613 in mysterious circumstances, James I's favourite, Robert Carr, Earl of Somerset, and his beautiful wife, Frances Howard, were found guilty of poisoning him. Reprieved by the king, the two were confined at Greys Court, the home of William Knollys, whose wife was Frances's sister.

There could be few more enchanting prisons. The modest Tudor house of the Knollyses, built of a pleasing mix of brick, flint and stone and with some unobtrusive eighteenth-century improvements, is set within the courtyard of the medieval manor of the de Greys, who gave the property its name. The gabled east front of the house, its mellow pink and grey walls half obscured by climbing plants, looks across a sweep of grass to two fourteenth-century towers, one now ruined, but the other, the Great Tower, still looking as it did when Edward III granted the 1st Lord de Grey a licence to crenellate in 1347. The foundations of two gatehouses and the walls of two courtyards appear as outlines in the grass in dry summers.

BELOW The modest late sixteenth-century house at Greys Court, built of a pleasing mix of brick, flint and stone, with the castellated bay window of the elegant drawing room added in *c.* 1750 protruding to the north.

Inside the house, intimate family rooms include an elegant classical drawing room, created in about 1750, where there is some exceptional plasterwork on the walls and ceiling that may be by Roberts of Oxford and where a fine marble chimneypiece replaced a sixteenth-century one in stone; the so-called school room, which also has elaborate plasterwork; and a kitchen with massive beams that appears to have survived from the medieval house.

There is late seventeenth-century and early eighteenth-century English furniture in mahogany, walnut and oak, and two large Swiss chests and sixteenth- and seventeenth-century Swiss stained glass in the window that lights the pine staircase reflect the fact that, in 1937, Greys Court was bought by Sir Felix and Lady Elizabeth Brunner and now contains pieces from the collection of Swiss artefacts acquired by Sir Felix's grandfather (the Brunners being an ancient Swiss family). Lady Brunner's theatrical background is reflected in portraits of her grandfather, the great Sir Henry Irving, and other Irving relatives and the view of the house from the north-west that hangs over the drawing-room fireplace was painted for her in 1993 by James Lynch. The Brunner family gave Greys Court to the National Trust in 1969.

A group of brick outbuildings to the south of the house includes an early Tudor wheelhouse with a massive donkey wheel. The largest still surviving in Britain, the donkey wheel raised water 200 feet (61 metres) from an ancient well and was used until 1914.

Across the grass from the house, the romantic ruins of the medieval fortifications form the skeleton of an enchanting garden. Ancient flint walls form the backdrop to a rose garden, planted with old-fashioned species, a White Garden against the Great Tower and a wisteria arbour, flowering profusely from craggy and monstrous stems that form a woody canopy above visitors' heads. An opening in the wall of an ornamental kitchen garden leads out to the maze centred on an armillary sphere that was added in 1981, its brick paths symbolising the journey through life. Where the garden is small-scale and inward looking, the grassy court in front of the house gives uninterrupted views south over the ha-ha and across a deep, tree-framed fold of the Chilterns.

Gunby Hall

Lincolnshire
2½ miles (4 kilometres) north-west of Burgh-le-Marsh, 7 miles (11.2 kilometres) west of Skegness on the south side of the A158

Set in the wide landscapes of rural Lincolnshire in one of the most remote corners of England, just a few miles from the North Sea, is this serene William and Mary house. The elegant main block, dating from 1700 and built of rose-red brick, rises three storeys above the basement to a roofline parapet. A broad flight of steps leads up to the front door and there are generous sash windows on every floor. Limestone dressings contrast with the mellow brickwork and there is a scrolled pediment over the front door and a Venetian window lighting the main staircase, but this is not a grand house, its modest rooms designed to be lived in rather than to impress. A two-storey wing to the north, the result of additions in 1873 and 1898, is in keeping with the character of the main house, its plate-glass windows disguised with false glazing bars. William Morris wallpapers, such as the 'daisy' pattern which decorates the back stairs, reflect the aesthetic taste of this period. Lawns dotted with ornamental trees lap three sides of the hall and on the fourth, just beyond the nineteenth-century wing, is a brick stable yard, with a cupola over the entrance arch.

Gunby was the home of the Massingberds, an ancient Lincolnshire family, from 1700 to 1967, with a descent that often passed through the female line. It was built by Sir William, 2nd Baronet, who decided to replace the family's medieval manor house which lay a short distance away across the fields, its site still marked by the moat that once surrounded it. Some of the bricks for the new hall may have been taken from the old manor, others made from clay dug from the estate, creating the pit that is now filled by the ice-house pond.

Gunby's warm, panelled rooms are filled with fine paintings, furniture, china and other precious things, most of which have been in the family for generations. The 2nd Baronet surveys visitors from a portrait in the hall, and also here are four lines of poetry by Tennyson, who was born at Somersby, only a few miles away, and knew Gunby well, its tranquillity perhaps inspiring his reference to 'a haunt of ancient peace'. There are two book-lined rooms. In the library off the hall, leather-bound volumes largely acquired by the Massingberds between 1690 and 1730 are one of the best surviving examples of a squire's

ABOVE Gunby's brick façades are echoed in the mellow brick walls of the garden.

library, while an important collection of military history housed in the study was assembled in the first half of the twentieth century by Field Marshal Sir Archibald Montgomery Massingberd, a brilliant strategist whose own writing on the First World War was highly regarded.

Diana, Sir Archibald's wife, following on from the tradition set by her brother and his wife, who had lived at Gunby before her, filled the house with music. In the elegant panelled music room that runs the length of the west front of the nineteenth-century wing, a Blüthner grand piano hints at the string groups she coached here and the local choirs who came to Gunby to rehearse. In 1943 Diana and Archie campaigned successfully to save Gunby when the air ministry wanted to demolish the house so as to give heavily laden bombers a clearer path from Spilsby airfield, which lay next to the estate. The music room has other associations too. Among the paintings here is Sir Joshua Reynold's fine portrait of his friend Bennet Langton, his long unpowdered hair falling in curls over his shoulders, whose son Peregrine married the heiress to the estate in 1784. Bennet Langton was also a friend of Dr Johnson and this connection accounts for the fact that Gunby has a very rare autographed copy of the first edition of Boswell's biography, one of only six known to have survived and the only one in England.

ABOVE Gunby's brick façades are echoed in the mellow brick walls of the garden.

A brick dovecot as old as the hall presides over the lavishly planted walled garden north-east of the house, filled with the blossom of roses and apples at the right time of year. More fruit trees – pears, plums, gages and figs – are espaliered on the walls of the adjoining kitchen garden, where traditional English vegetables are grown in a compartmental layout which has been unchanged for 200 years.

The estate, crossed by a network of paths and green lanes, incorporates three farms and a stretch of disused railway line. South-west of the hall, across the fields, is remote Monksthorpe Chapel, where local baptists came to worship at a time when non-conformists were persecuted and which is still used occasionally for services. Dating from 1701, but probably standing on the site of an earlier building, the chapel, roughly walled in brick, was intended to resemble a barn and was originally thatched. It was re-roofed with pantiles in the 1840s when the interior was refurbished. The baptismal pool, a brick-lined trough in which believers were fully immersed, lies outside the chapel beside the west end. It was last used in 1972.

Ham House

Surrey
On the south bank of the River
Thames, west of the A307,
at Petersham

Ruthless ambition created
this red-brick palace beside
the River Thames, with its
principal rooms still furnished
in the style of Charles II's court.
Elizabeth Murray, Countess of
Dysart, was not content with the Jacobean house she inherited
from her father, William Murray, 1st Earl of Dysart, despite the
improvements he made in 1637–9. A second marriage gave
her the opportunity to spend lavishly on remodelling. Even
before the death of her first husband, the countess's name was
being linked to the high-flying Earl of Lauderdale, a member of
Charles II's cabal ministry. When his wife conveniently died,
the two were married. In the same year, 1672, the earl received
a dukedom, and the couple set out to mark their position with
new building. He was at the height of his power, benefiting
from his appointment as Secretary of State for Scotland, which
effectively gave him license to run the country as he pleased,
and from an official position which connected him to the trade
in slaves, ivory and gold along the West African coast. The
countess, it was said, had complete ascendancy over him. The
haughty, rather unattractive couple confidently surveying the
world from Lely's portrait in the round gallery clearly deserved
each other and together they produced one of the most lavishly
appointed houses of their day.

Externally, Ham is sober enough. A long, three-storey block
of a house with tall chimneys, it is enlivened on the entrance
front with two projecting wings, each of which incorporates
a short colonnade, and with sixteen busts set in niches at the
level of the first floor. More busts are set round the brick wall
enclosing the forecourt. There were once wings on the south
front too, but these were engulfed when the Lauderdales
doubled the size of Ham by building new apartments along
this side of the house. The new rooms were given sash
windows, which had only recently been invented, but these
were designed to blend with the Jacobean casements.

Inside, there are few traces of the interiors created in 1610
for Sir Thomas Vavasour, Knight Marshal to James I, for whom

RIGHT The early seventeenth-century Green Closet is a rare survival of the
intimate rooms that were designed for the display of small paintings and
miniatures.
OPPOSITE Busts set in niches ornament the north front of Ham House.

Ham was built, but several rooms still display the taste of Elizabeth's father, which reflects the period love of rich effect. His great staircase, its details now bronzed but originally gilded, incorporates martial features – a drum, armour, a cannon with a pile of shot – on the carved and pierced panels and there are carved baskets of fruit crowning the newel posts. The stairs lead to the sequence of first-floor state rooms created by William Murray along the north front. His great dining room is now the gallery above the hall. Beyond lie his drawing room, hung with tapestry as he would have known it, and his refurbished long gallery, the first with original plasterwork, woodwork and marble chimneypiece, the second lined with gilded panelling divided by Ionic pilasters which the earl added to the Jacobean room.

Portraits in sumptuous gold frames line the gallery, among them several works by Lely and the portrait that Charles I gave to William Murray, who was one of his most loyal supporters. A rare survival is the intimate Green Closet off the gallery, where some 86 miniatures and small paintings framed in ebony and gilt are hung closely on brilliant green damask. Many of the pictures, which include miniatures by Nicholas Hilliard and Isaac Oliver, were hanging here in the seventeenth century. The ceiling paintings of cupids, nymphs and satyrs, in tempera, are by Franz Cleyn, who was principal designer for the Mortlake tapestry works.

Along the south front, arranged over two floors, are the apartments created by the Lauderdales. On the first floor, the long gallery leads into a suite of three rooms fitted out for Charles II's queen, Catherine of Braganza, in 1673. Although partly refurnished in the eighteenth century by the duchess's great-grandson, the 4th Earl of Dysart, many of the extravagant original fittings remain. There are hangings of silk damask and velvet, fire-irons ornamented with silver, intricate parquet floors and a carved wooden garland of subtle craftsmanship. Most of the seventeenth-century decor survives in the intimate closet at the end of the suite, which is still hung with winter hangings of 'crimson and gould stuff bordered with green and gould stuff' and has a baroque ceiling painting by Antonio Verrio, who had worked extensively for Charles II. More paintings by Verrio in the overblown style favoured at the time, such as a group of maidens representing the arts, also adorn the private closets in the two suites of rooms that the Lauderdales created for themselves on the ground floor of the south front. Here the flavour is more mixed. The Duchess's closet, where she would have retired for privacy, or to talk to her closest friends, is furnished with her tea-table and writing cabinet (the white crackled teapot in which she brewed her precious tea is also on show in the house), while survivals of the original decorative scheme include inset sea paintings by William van der Velde (in his rooms) and bird paintings by Francis Barlow (in hers). But her bedroom has had to be re-created as it might have appeared, and what was the duke's bedchamber has the 1740s furnishing scheme of the 4th Earl, who turned it into a drawing room. Tapestries here have an elegant French flavour, gilded chairs

ABOVE The Queen's antechamber still has its seventeenth-century damask wall-hangings, now a faded brown, lacquer chairs that were listed here in 1683, and inset pictures painted for the room in the 1670s.

and sofas upholstered in gold silk have X-frames in the style of William Kent, and a new carpet woven for the room, based on archive material, has been designed to pick up the strong blues and pinks in the tapestries.

The spirit of the house extends into the garden, where the formal seventeenth-century layout, in which the garden was devised as a series of contrasting compartments, has been re-created. The south front looks over a broad terrace to a lawn divided into eight uniform square plats and beyond to the wilderness. Looking from a distance like a well-ordered wood, this too has an architectural plan. Grassy walks lined by hornbeam hedges radiate from a central clearing, dividing the wilderness into a series of small enclosures, four of which contain little summer-houses. East of the house, a secluded

knot garden is flanked by the cool green tunnels of hornbeam alleys and a period kitchen garden has been restored in front of the wisteria-hung seventeenth-century orangery to the west. Outhouses include the eighteenth-century dairy, with marble shelves carried on cast-iron cow's legs, and the late seventeenth-century still house, where soaps, sweet-scented waters and ointments were prepared. Close by, beyond the trees screening the entrance front, is the Thames and the little ferry from Twickenham, which has for centuries brought visitors across the water.

Hanbury Hall

Worcestershire
4½ miles (7.2 kilometres) east of Droitwich, 1 mile (1.6 kilometres) north of the B4090; 6 miles (9.6 kilometres) south of Bromsgrove, east of the M5

James Thornhill was at the height of his career when Thomas Vernon, a successful Chancery lawyer, commissioned him to decorate the staircase of his new house in 1710. Although his work for St Paul's Cathedral was still in the future, Thornhill had completed the Sabine Room at Chatsworth in Derbyshire and was halfway through his magnificent Painted Hall at Greenwich. Like this masterpiece, the Hanbury staircase is exuberantly baroque, with mythological scenes illustrating the life of Achilles framed between classical columns on the walls and a host of deities set among clouds looking down from above. In the Great Hall below, where a bust of Vernon stands over the fireplace, the subtle monochrome ceiling, also by Thornhill, is painted with *trompe-l'oeil* domes and shells and, in each corner, with musical instruments and agricultural tools representing the seasons of the year.

Vernon's square red-brick house, begun in *c.* 1700 and probably designed by a local mason, is a typical example of Restoration domestic architecture, with dormers in the hipped roof and a central cupola. Pavilions in the French or Dutch style project from all four corners. The design of the striking pedimented entrance façade, with a central bay set between Corinthian columns and decorated with flowing carving, may have been influenced by the treatment of a grand house such as Thoresby Hall in Nottinghamshire, which had been remodelled in the 1680s for the Duke of Kingston. An unusual detached long gallery has two ornate Jacobean overmantels made up of carved woodwork brought from elsewhere. Domed gazebos at the corners of the entrance court are Victorian.

BELOW LEFT This marble bust of Thomas Vernon, in his wig and lawyer's bands, stands over the hall fireplace.
BELOW RIGHT Hanbury's staircase was painted by James Thornhill, one of the greatest decorative artists of his day.

Hanbury's original contents were mostly sold in 1790 after the dissipation of the family fortunes during the disastrous marriage between Emma Vernon and Henry Cecil, later Lord Exeter. Some family pieces, such as the two Dutch marquetry chests of drawers in the Blue Bedroom, have returned in recent years and all the portraits, including works by Kneller and John Vanderbank, are now back in the house, hanging in the Great Hall and Dining Room. Generally, most of the interiors have been re-created, but the essence of the early eighteenth century comes through in a panelled bedroom and dressing room known as the Hercules Suite, the latter still with its original corner chimneypiece. And in the smoking room at the back of the house, once Thomas Vernon's office, a painting of Hanbury, commissioned by Bowater Vernon, Thomas's heir, from John Wootton, shows the house in the setting of its early eighteenth-century landscape, with long avenues of trees stretching into the distance.

Nearby hangs a bird's-eye view of the estate in 1732 by Joseph Dougharty showing the avenues and Vernon's compartmental formal garden, both part of a grand design by George London. Later changes destroyed all but remnants of London's layout but, using this bird's-eye view and surviving plans, the avenues have now been replanted and the garden, with its sunken parterre, grove, wilderness, bowling green and fruit garden, re-created. The handsome orangery was commissioned by Bowater Vernon in 1733.

BELOW Serene Hanbury Hall, built of brick with stone dressings and finished off with a little cupola, is typical of the architecture of Restoration England.

The Hardmans' House (Mr Hardman's Photographic Studio)

Merseyside
59 Rodney Street, Liverpool

This substantial Georgian terrace house, with a long garden behind, was for years both home and workplace of Edward Chambré Hardman (1898–1988) and his wife Margaret (1909–70). Edward was Liverpool's leading portrait photographer from the 1920s to the 1960s, and Margaret ran much of the business, as well as being a gifted photographer in her own right. In the era before informal poses became fashionable and every family had the equipment to produce their own photographs, there was a demand for formal portraits that was met by commercial studios. Hardman catered for this market, photographing anyone who was anyone in Liverpool as well as a stream of distinguished visitors, among them Ivor Novello and Margot Fonteyn. He was also a skilled landscape photographer, capturing the Liverpool of his day and more distant places and countrysides. Working in the pictorial tradition, with much use of soft focus, retouching and other manipulative devices, Hardman created images that are moody and atmospheric. Many of them are now also of documentary interest. He never set out to make a record of the changes in the city around him, but his evocative images of the now-vanished Liverpool shipbuilding industry, such as photographs showing the use of wooden scaffolding in the yards, and of other aspects of the urban scene, are of great historical value. His achievements were fully recognised in his lifetime: he was one of only four photographers to receive a special medal to mark the London Salon's Golden Jubilee in 1959, and he was awarded an Honorary Fellowship of the Royal Photographic Society in 1980.

Hardman was born in southern Ireland and, following the example of his father, who was a keen amateur photographer, began taking photographs seriously as a child, winning his first competition at the age of 14. After serving in the army in India from 1917 to 1922, he decided to set up a photographic studio with a fellow officer, Kenneth Burrell, who seems to have been of value largely for his social connections and was not involved in the day-to-day running of the business (initially based in Bold Street). Soon, anyone of any pretensions or importance

ABOVE Hardman always kept the name of the original business, although his friend and partner Kenneth Burrell left Liverpool in 1929.

in the area was being photographed by Burrell & Hardman and Hardman began a series of portraits of actors appearing at the Liverpool Playhouse, among them, over the years, Richard Todd, Robert Donat, Patricia Routledge, Michael Redgrave and Beryl Bainbridge. Hardman married Margaret, who had joined the studio as an employee, in 1932, and the two of them would set off by train and bicycle into the countryside where they both photographed landscapes, many of which were commissioned as covers for *Cheshire Life* or the back page of the *Daily Post*.

The business prospered. Hardman opened a second studio in Chester and in 1948 moved to Rodney Street. But little more than a decade later the tide turned. With demand for formally posed portraits declining, he worked less and less, becoming virtually a recluse after Margaret died. On his death, the house and its contents passed to the E.C. Hardman Trust, which in turn gave everything to the National Trust in 2001.

ABOVE Hardman's dark room. He would often manipulate his images, removing blemishes and scraping in highlights, before carefully mounting them.

Still as it was when the Hardmans lived and worked here, 59 Rodney Street is a complete example of a period photographic studio and is full of furnishings and ephemera from the 1930s, '40s and '50s. At the front of the house are the clients' waiting room and changing room and Hardman's studio, the latter fully equipped with backdrops, cameras, lights, props and even drawers of toys to entertain younger sitters. Three darkrooms and areas for printing, cutting and mounting were where Hardman manipulated and finished his images, and the Hardmans themselves lived in the cramped and relatively frugal quarters at the back. Some of the furniture is in the style of Sir Gordon Russell, who was a pioneer of the Modern Movement in English furniture design, and there is a strong period feel, with many everyday items, such as tins of food and packets of soap and silk stockings, in the condition in which they were purchased over 50 years ago.

Hardwick

Derbyshire
6½ miles (10.4 kilometres)
west of Mansfield, 9½ miles
(15.2 kilometres) south-east of
Chesterfield

This cathedral of a house stands tall and proud on the top of a windswept hill, its distinctive, many-towered outline lifting the spirits of those hurtling past on the M1. As the huge stone initials set along the roofline proclaim, this is the house of Elizabeth Shrewsbury, better known as Bess of Hardwick, the resilient and resourceful squire's daughter who rose from relatively humble beginnings to become one of the richest and best-connected people in Elizabethan England.

Hardwick shows how far she had come. By the time the house was begun, Bess was already approaching 70 and had outlived four husbands. Her marriages had advanced her social position and increased her wealth, but it was Bess's shrewd business sense and wise investments that ensured she eventually became one of the richest women in England. Her last marriage was to George Talbot, 6th Earl of Shrewsbury, the head of the oldest, grandest and richest family in England. By 1583, when she bought the family estate from her brother James, the marriage had broken down, to her distress, and Bess initially embarked on remodelling the manor house where she had been born, the romantic ruins of which (in the guardianship of English Heritage) still crown the crest of the ridge just to the south-west of the New Hall. Although built piecemeal, on a cramped and awkward site, this first venture was in many ways a trial run for what was to come, incorporating features, such as the enormous windows lighting the Great Chambers on the top floor, which Bess would use again. This house was still unfinished when, in 1590, Bess's situation was transformed by the earl's death. It is possible the foundations for the New Hall had already been laid a few weeks before, but now Bess had the funds to fully finance

her new project. Whereas the Old Hall had been produced piecemeal, the New Hall rose on virgin land and was designed as one by Robert Smythson, the most original of Elizabethan architects. It is a prodigy house, in a class of its own, but it was never large enough for all Bess's household. Even after the new building was finished, in 1597, servants and guests were still accommodated in the Old Hall.

Both houses are built of limestone quarried from just down the hill, but whereas the gabled and irregular outlines of the Old Hall reflect the remodelling of an existing building, the profile of the New Hall is clean and symmetrical. Windows that become progressively larger up the house enhance the strong vertical thrust of the six towers, giving Hardwick the appearance of a glittering glass lantern. Inside, a broad, tapestry-hung stone staircase, to the same innovatory design as one in the Old Hall, weaves its way majestically to the state apartments lit by huge windows on the third floor. These rooms are still very much as Bess left them. Her High Great Chamber for the reception and entertainment of important guests was designed round the tapestries that still hang here, purchased new in 1587. The goddess Diana with her court on the three-dimensional plaster frieze above was intended as a tribute to Elizabeth I, whom Bess always hoped would visit Hardwick (she never did).

A tapestry-hung door leads into the atmospheric long gallery, where some of the 80 pictures covering the walls were here in Bess's time. Portraying royalty, family, friends and patrons – evidence of her good connections – they include three of Bess's husbands and a glittering representation of the queen herself, her famous red hair piled high and her dress decorated with sea creatures and birds and studded with pearls. Here, too, is a memorable painting of the philosopher Thomas Hobbes, tutor to Bess's grandson, the 2nd Earl of Devonshire. Hobbes is shown just a few years before he died at Hardwick in 1679, toothless in extreme old age.

Elizabethan tapestries and paintings are complemented by an important collection of embroideries dating from 1570 to 1640, many of which were worked on by Bess herself and which include pictorial wall-hangings made out of a patchwork of velvets and silks and exquisite cushion covers worked in cross-stitch. There is also some exceptional original furniture, such as the eglantine table in the High Great Chamber, inlaid

ABOVE These late seventeenth-century silk hangings are among Hardwick's outstanding collection of textiles.

with a mosaic of musical instruments, playing cards and board games, even the setting of a four-part motet, that was probably made to celebrate Bess's marriage to the Earl of Shrewsbury in 1568, and, in the adjoining room, an inlaid walnut table that is carried on carvings of sea dogs and tortoises.

Hardwick's unique character owes much to the 6th Duke of Devonshire, who inherited in 1811 and deliberately enhanced the antiquarian atmosphere of the house, promoting the legend that Mary, Queen of Scots stayed here and filling it with additional furniture, paintings and tapestries from his other properties, particularly from Chatsworth some 15 miles (24 kilometres) to the west.

Formal gardens to the south were laid out in the late nineteenth century. One section is a herb garden, another is a pear orchard and there are colourful herbaceous borders. A little Elizabethan banqueting house was used as a smoking room by the 6th Duke's private orchestra, who were forbidden to smoke in the hall itself. Buildings grouped round a stableyard beyond the garden include a smithy that existed in Bess's time, and a great barn (now the restaurant) and ox-house (now the shop) that date back to the early seventeenth century. Grain threshed in the barn would have been taken to be ground at the mill at Stainsby, in the northern part of the estate, where the present building, of 1849–50, has an iron water-wheel and other machinery that is still in working order.

The 1,990-acre (800-hectare) estate embraces two different landscapes. At the back of the hall, a formal stretch of grass focused on a central basin looks out across the flat, partly cultivated land on the limestone plateau east of the house.

To the west is the oak-wooded, hillier terrain of the former deer-park, with a series of fish-ponds and a partly restored duck decoy. Now a country park, it is grazed by rare breeds of cattle and sheep.

ABOVE With its six towers, advancing and receding bays and great array of glass, Hardwick is the most theatrical and dramatic of Elizabethan houses, standing tall on a windswept hill.

OPPOSITE The Blue Room on the top floor of the house is still hung with the Brussels tapestries listed in the inventory of 1601.

Hardy Country

Dorset
Hardy's Cottage is at
Higher Bockhampton, 3 miles
(4.8 kilometres) north-east of
Dorchester, ½ mile (0.8 kilometre)
south of the A35; Max Gate is
1 mile (1.6 kilometres) south-east
of Dorchester, off the A352

The Wessex of Thomas Hardy's imagination, which gives such a strong sense of place to all his novels, was rooted in the countryside of Dorset and the towns and villages set in a tapestry of lush valleys, untamed heath and open downland that he had known since childhood. The market town of Dorchester, which would be thinly disguised as Casterbridge, was the centre of both his real and fictional worlds. Just a couple of miles outside the town is the secluded and picturesque cottage where the poet and novelist was born, in the bedroom at the top of the stairs, in 1840, his hold on life so tenuous that he was at first thought to be dead. Here Hardy grew up, walking 6 miles (9.6 kilometres) to school in Dorchester and back every day. Although he set off for London in 1862 to work as an architect, he returned five years later to live with his parents while he practised locally, continuing to write in the little upstairs room with a window looking west to the monument on Black Down, 10 miles (16 kilometres) away.

OPPOSITE This delightful cottage, of cob and thatch, is where the poet and novelist Thomas Hardy grew up, drawing inspiration for his writing from the people and landscapes around him.
RIGHT The house Thomas Hardy designed for himself and built outside Dorchester, just a few miles from the cottage where he was born, is an unremarkable, red-brick suburban villa.

The cottage dates from 1800, when his family settled here. With its deep thatched roof, casement windows and cob walls covered in roses, honeysuckle and japonica, it is everyone's idea of what a cottage should look like. The sheltered old-fashioned garden, crowded with pansies, lupins, lavender, day lilies, pinks, marigolds and a host of other plants, is much as Hardy would have known it, although his father used to store materials for his building business on some of the space.

Many of the places and incidents Hardy describes so vividly are drawn from his life here. The cottage itself appears in *Under the Greenwood Tree*, in which the villagers' dance is set in the parlour to the left of the porch; the description of the musicians ousted by the new-fangled organ in Mellstock church echoes what happened in Stinsford church nearby, where Hardy's grandfather, father and uncle used to play the violin and cello for services; and Hardy used Egdon Heath behind the cottage, now largely tamed but once a wild and desolate expanse of bracken, heather and gorse stretching almost to the coast, as the setting for *The Return of the Native*.

In 1874, with the success of *Far From the Madding Crowd*, the fourth of his novels, Hardy took the decision to devote himself totally to writing. This was also the year in which he finally left the cottage to embark on his troubled marriage to Emma Gifford. For several years the couple moved restlessly from one place to another, a period during which Hardy produced only one major work, but in 1885 they returned to Dorchester to live in the angular red-brick villa on the south-eastern edge of town which Hardy had designed for himself and where he lived until his death, in 1928. In his study at Max Gate he wrote *Tess of the d'Urbervilles*, *Jude the Obscure* and *The Mayor of Casterbridge*, as well as the moving poetry rooted in the disintegration of his marriage and Emma's death, in 1912 (two years later, in 1914, he married Florence Dugdale). In his last years, a stream of literary visitors came to the house, among them T.E. Lawrence, whose Clouds Hill (*see* p.101) was nearby, W.B. Yeats, Robert Louis Stevenson and Virginia Woolf. There are several pieces of Hardy's furniture in the house although not, alas, his study, which was reconstructed in Dorchester County Museum, and there is a fine view. Some of the rooms are shadowed by the trees Hardy planted to protect his privacy; others, like the study, are filled with light. Hardy regularly walked back to Stinsford church from Max Gate and his heart is buried in the churchyard.

Hatchlands Park

Surrey
East of East Clandon, north of the
A246 Guildford–Leatherhead road

In the late 1750s Edward Boscawen, second son of the 1st Viscount Falmouth and Admiral of the Blue, used prize money from victories over the French in the Seven Years' War to finance a new house. The architect of his square red-brick Georgian mansion, probably Stiff Leadbetter, ingeniously designed it with seven different floor levels. Looking at the house from the south-west, three storeys on the west front change mysteriously into two on the south. Sadly, the admiral did not live to enjoy his new mansion, dying only a year or so after he and his wife, Frances, moved in.

Hatchlands contains the earliest recorded decoration in an English country house by Robert Adam, who was engaged in 1758, just after he had returned from his Grand Tour. Appropriately, his plaster ceilings in the saloon and library have nautical themes, the motifs featured ranging from mermaids, dolphins and seahorses to drums, cannon and anchors. At the end of the century Joseph Bonomi made alterations to the staircase and the garden entrance, and a hundred years later

ABOVE Hatchlands Park, with a little pediment marking the entrance front, was built in the 1750s for Admiral Boscawen.
BELOW LEFT The grandiose music room at Hatchlands, where recitals are given, was an addition of *c*. 1903 in the style of the late seventeenth century by the architect Reginald Blomfield.

Sir Reginald Blomfield added the music room in seventeenth-century style for Stuart Rendel, who was at one time a managing partner in London of Sir William Armstrong's engineering firm (*see* Cragside, p.117) and became Lord Rendel of Hatchlands.

Apart from a few pieces from the Rendel collection, such as the eighteenth-century gilt pier-tables in the saloon, Adam's interiors are now complemented by pictures, furniture and keyboard instruments lent by the collector and musician Alec Cobbe, who is the National Trust's tenant at Hatchlands. Red silk panels in the saloon set off works by Carlo Dolci, Rubens, Frederick de Moucheron and a rare sixteenth-century altarpiece by the Florentine Alessandro Allori, and a number of portraits in the house include canvases by Gainsborough, Angelica Kauffmann and Hoppner. Among the collection of keyboard instruments by European makers dating from *c*. 1750 to 1840 are an Erard pianoforte reputedly made for Marie Antoinette, one of the few French harpsichords to escape destruction in the years after the Revolution, and a very rare quadruple-strung piano by Conrad Graf. The collection is maintained for performance and visitors may be lucky enough to hear the distant sound of music by Mozart, Couperin or Schubert.

Hill Top

Cumbria
At Near Sawrey, behind the
Tower Bank Arms

As a child in London, where her domineering parents discouraged friendships with other children, Beatrix Potter led a very isolated existence, with only her brother Bertram for company of her own age. The brightest spot in a stifling regime was the annual family holiday, in her early years to Scotland, but from 1882, when she was 16, to the Lake District. These brief episodes, and the freedom they brought, fuelled a longing for the country which emerged in meticulously observed watercolours of wild creatures and plants and in the beginnings of the animal fantasies that have delighted children and adults for over a century.

Beatrix's purchase of this small, largely seventeenth-century farmhouse in 1905 was a momentous step. Presented to her parents as nothing more than a good investment (which it was), to their lonely 39-year-old daughter, the rough stone building with a view over Near Sawrey to the fells beyond represented the possibility of escape from an increasingly dreary and unchanging regime. Although she was only able to snatch weeks here in the eight years that followed, this period was to see her best work, with the production of thirteen of the stories in which rabbits, mice, squirrels, hedgehogs and other creatures become humans in miniature, all of them illustrated with Beatrix's charming and individual paintings.

Anyone who has read these nursery classics will recognise Hill Top and its well-furnished, homely rooms, filled with accumulated clutter. The long, sloping garden flanking the path to the house, with rows of vegetables on one side and a medley of traditional flowers on the other, is still as it appears in *The Tale of Tom Kitten* and *Pigling Bland*. The old-fashioned kitchen range with its crackling fire strikes a reassuring note in several animal holes and burrows, the nineteenth-century dresser is featured in *The Tale of Samuel Whiskers*, and the grandfather clock with a cheerful sun on its face was the model

LEFT Beatrix Potter illustrated the old-fashioned kitchen range in a number of her animal stories. Her hat lies on the chair beside the range, with her clogs underneath.

ABOVE Hill Top, the small farmhouse in the Lake District which Beatrix Potter bought in 1905 and which is featured in many of her stories, is approached through a long, richly planted cottage garden.

for the one in *The Tailor of Gloucester*. Peter Rabbit's red-spotted handkerchief and the doll's house food – dishes of oranges and pears and a large ham – stolen by Hunca Munca and Tom Thumb are in one of the upstairs rooms. Some grander pieces of furniture, striking an unexpected note, were acquired after Beatrix's mother died, and there is a room hung with her brother Bertram's landscape paintings.

For the last 30 years of her life, during which she was contentedly married to William Heelis, a local solicitor, Beatrix lived as a prosperous farmer in the nearby Castle Cottage (not open), reserving Hill Top, which was kept unchanged, for

ABOVE Hill Top, the small farmhouse in the Lake District which Beatrix Potter bought in 1905 and which is featured in many of her stories, is approached through a long, richly planted cottage garden.

those times when she wished to be alone with her memories. During this period, she became increasingly concerned about the conservation of the fells and began to buy land to save it from being broken up or developed. In 1895 her friend Canon Rawnsley founded the National Trust and her substantial landholdings, with their farmhouses and cottages, came to the Trust on the death of her husband in 1945.

Hinton Ampner

Hampshire
On the A272, 1 mile (1.6 kilometres) west of Bramdean village, 8 miles (12.8 kilometres) east of Winchester

Set on a low ridge looking south over terraced gardens and tree-studded parkland to the gently undulating fields and woods of the estate is what appears to be a red-brick Georgian manor, with sash windows lighting the two principal floors and a roofline parapet. But both the house and much of its setting date from the mid-twentieth century, when Ralph Dutton, the 8th and last Lord Sherborne, who looked back to the eighteenth century as a golden age, set out to create a suitable setting for his distinguished collection of furniture, *objets* and paintings. He had inherited Hinton Ampner, then a large and gloomy Victorian mansion, and the surrounding estate in 1935 and over the next few years, with the help of the architects Lord Gerald Wellesley and Trenwith Wells, he remodelled the house to create a pleasing neo-Georgian building. Then, on 3 April 1960, when he was walking in the park, he noticed smoke rising above the trees and returned to the house to find it in flames. The building, and most of the contents, were destroyed. Undaunted, Ralph Dutton immediately set about rebuilding and refurnishing as beautifully as before.

A true connoisseur, with a wide-ranging knowledge of architecture and interior decoration, Lord Sherborne chose everything for the house and composed the rooms to fulfil an overall vision. Running across the east end of the house, with long windows on two sides, is the elegant drawing room. A classical screen divides off one end, the walls are hung with opulent gold wallpaper and sea-green curtains frame the windows. The furnishings reflect Ralph Dutton's particular taste. An inlaid English cabinet of about 1800 and a giltwood side table with a top of white marble and bluejohn that was once part of Lord Curzon's collection in Carlton House Terrace reveal his love of hardstones; so, too, do the marble roundels and sleeping putto, and the porphyry chimneypiece and bust of Augustus Caesar, part of a collection of porphyry of which Ralph Dutton was particularly fond, in the hall. Similarly, a landscape by Locatelli hanging above the cabinet in the drawing room and canvases by Pellegrini in the hall show Lord Sherborne's appreciation of Italian seventeenth- and eighteenth-century painting and of Venetian art in particular. Two disturbing pictures by Fuseli hang in Ralph Dutton's intimate sitting room, where almost everything was saved from the fire. Some pieces were purchased on his travels abroad, others acquired at auction, from dealers, or from houses that

BELOW In remodelling the 'hideous' house he had inherited, Ralph Dutton set out to create a Georgian manor house, rebuilding again when fire destroyed his new home in 1960.

ABOVE The comfortable library at Hinton Ampner, lined with the fine collection of books which Ralph Dutton put together after the fire, is furnished with Regency pieces and a Savonnerie carpet of *c.* 1800.

had been or were being demolished. Two marble fireplaces and three doors came from Robert Adam's Adelphi Terrace, which was pulled down, and the dining room has a reproduction of a plaster ceiling, with original inset paintings, which Adam designed for a house in Berkeley Square.

The flavour of restrained opulence continues upstairs, where comfortable bedrooms, two with bow windows looking onto the garden, lie either side of a central corridor with a white marble urn in a niche at one end. Reflecting Ralph Dutton's desire to have a house with all mod cons, *en suite* bathrooms were provided for each bedroom, that for his own use fitted out with a shower and boldly decorated with black glass and strongly contrasting leaf pattern wallpaper, in red and white. There are pieces of rare green porphyry from Egypt; china by Sèvres, Meissen and Spode is displayed along the corridor; and a show of paintings includes Italianate landscapes by Poussin and work on copper by the seventeenth-century artist

Tobias van Nymegen. And always there are the views from the bedroom windows, over the garden and beyond.

Hinton Ampner's surroundings were all part of Ralph Dutton's vision. His formal garden, with long grassy walks, strategically placed eye-catchers, lichened steps leading from one level to another, topiary and clipped Irish yew, the lines softened by borders of roses and other flowering plants, descends into the landscape park. This too was carefully composed out of what had been a muddle of hedgerows and scattered trees to create an idyllic foreground to views over unspoilt chalk countryside.

An orchard marks the site of a Tudor manor that lay to the north of the present house and was demolished in the late eighteenth century.

The Homewood

Surrey
Portsmouth Road, Esher

Just outside Esher, set in a 7-acre (2.8-hectare) landscaped garden, is this striking and unusual country house. From the garden, it appears as a long white box on stilts, with an almost unbroken wall of glass lighting the first floor and open terraces either end. Inside, it is airy and spacious, with panoramic views of the garden and sliding glass doors leading onto a balcony. Completed in 1938, when the Modern Movement in Britain was still very much in its infancy, it is an early and important example of a house built under the influence of the continental avant-garde, in particular Le Corbusier and Mies van der Rohe. It was designed, for his parents, by the young Patrick Gwynne (1913–2003), who started working on the house when he was only 24. Gwynne had

begun his architectural training with John Coleridge, a former assistant of Sir Edwin Lutyens, but, inspired by what was happening on the Continent, he had joined the practice of the pioneering modernist Wells Coates, where he was introduced to new construction techniques, using reinforced concrete, and cutting-edge design. By the time he started on The Homewood he had also seen key modernist buildings abroad and had studied Le Corbusier's iconic Villa Savoie, outside Paris, which was a major influence on his thinking.

For his parents, who took the courageous decision to entrust the building of the new house to their son, Gwynne combined modernist architecture with a concern for living that was to

BELOW From the garden, the house looks like a white box on stilts, with a wall of glass lighting the main living area on the first floor.

ABOVE LEFT The Homewood was designed both for entertaining and for everyday living, with a cosy arrangement round the sitting-room fireplace for intimate evenings.

ABOVE RIGHT Gwynne's huge picture windows bring the garden into the house.

be a hallmark of all his residential work. Built of reinforced concrete and with a flat roof, the house consists of two unequal wings joined to a central block. One wing holds the bedrooms; the other, staff quarters and service areas. There is a dramatic spiral staircase, lit from below by a sunken spotlight. As at the Villa Savoie, the main living area is on the first floor and is carried by slender columns and lit by huge windows looking onto the garden. Although uncompromisingly modern, the house is based on a classical system of proportions and has a pleasing sense of order and harmony.

The sophisticated interior shows Gwynne's attention to detail and materials. The living room is a multi-purpose space for relaxation and entertaining. The maple floor is sprung for dancing and doors to the dining room and balcony beyond can be pushed back to create one huge room. Sliding doors in an interior wall hide a drinks cabinet and gramophone, a drop-leg table swivels out to serve as a bar, and food can be passed through a hatch from the kitchen. For more private living, there is a cosy arrangement round the fireplace and two loungers placed by the window give views over the garden. Stylish finishes include a wall of Levanto marble and tiny Murano glass wall-tiles lining the hall. Gwynne also designed much of the furniture, including a writing desk that doubles as a drawing board and the Chinese lacquered book table, and

there are many imaginative and witty touches, among them the round table in the dining room that has been provided with a central well for holding flowers or a low light.

The house owes much to its leafy setting, which was initially landscaped by Gwynne's father, and there is an oval pool designed by the young Denys Lasdun, with whom Gwynne worked at Wells Coates.

The Homewood was Gwynne's first independent commission. Returning to Esher after service with the RAF in the Second World War, Gwynne went on to design a series of private houses for distinguished clients, among them the hotelier Charles Forte and the actor Laurence Harvey, as well as a number of larger projects, such as the glass and concrete extension to the gothic Theatre Royal in York and the Serpentine Restaurant in London's Hyde Park, where he used glass lavishly to give the impression that diners were eating al fresco. He continued to live at The Homewood after his parents died and in 1999 gave the house with the majority of its contents and the garden to the National Trust.

Hughenden

Buckinghamshire
1½ miles (2.4 kilometres) north of
High Wycombe, on the west side
of the Great Missenden road

This substantial red-brick house set among beech woods on a spur of the Chilterns was the country home of Benjamin Disraeli, one of Queen Victoria's most able and visionary prime ministers, and his wife Mary Anne. Disraeli's greatest achievements came at the end of his long political career. Becoming Prime Minister in 1874, when he was 69, over the next six years he was responsible for progressive social reforms, while his diplomatic skills at the Congress of Berlin in 1878 did much to check Russian expansionism, one of the key issues of the day. More controversially, perhaps, from the perspective of the twenty-first century, it was his imperialist foreign policy that gained the queen the title of Empress of India. An established writer as well as a politician, he had dwelt on the condition of the poor some thirty years earlier in his novels *Coningsby* and *Sybil*.

Disraeli acquired Hughenden in 1848, the year after his election as MP for Buckingham and the year before he became leader of the Conservative Party. At a time when political power was largely in the hands of the landed aristocracy, he had increasingly felt the need for an estate to bolster his political ambitions, but he had only been able to make the purchase with the help of Lord Bentinck and his brothers, who loaned two-thirds of the sum involved. The grandson of an Italian Jew who had come to England looking for work, Disraeli had little in the way of financial resources himself. Marriage to Mary Anne, a wealthy widow twelve years his senior, had enabled him to pay off most of his debts, but her money did not stretch to the asking price for the estate.

Disraeli and Mary Anne, whose marriage of convenience became a love match, lived at Hughenden until their deaths, in 1881 and 1872 respectively. The plain, three-storey Georgian house they acquired was gothicised with the help of the individual architect Edward Buckton Lamb, a project

in which Mary Anne seems to have taken the lead. Stucco was removed to reveal the blue and red brickwork behind, stepped battlements and pinnacles were added, and the interior was enhanced with gothic fixtures and fittings and grained woodwork. In 1881 Hughenden passed to Disraeli's nephew Coningsby, who continued to make alterations to the house, adding a large wing in a similarly gothic style to the west. Richly coloured interiors reproduce some of the original decorative schemes that Mary Anne loved, such as the deep red walls of the hall and staircase, and portraits that were here in Disraeli's day, of friends and those Disraeli admired, as well as of close family, and original furnishings can be seen in almost every room.

A painting of Disraeli by Francis Grant, executed in 1852, presides over what is now the library, where floor-to-ceiling shelves hold works by Disraeli's father, the bibliophile and poet Isaac D'Israeli, as well as by Disraeli himself. A marble foot used as a paperweight on the desk is a copy of Mary Anne's left foot and two plaster statuettes on the mantelpiece, one depicting the faithful John Brown, were a gift from Queen Victoria, who became genuinely fond of Disraeli. The sombre, north-facing dining room is where Victoria was treated to

ABOVE LEFT This portrait of Disraeli by Sir Francis Grant, painted in 1852, hangs in the library.
BELOW When the Disraelis came to Hughenden in 1848, they set about giving the house a fashionable gothic flavour.

lunch in 1877, the legs of her chair cut down so her feet could reach the floor. Upstairs, the Disraelis' sunny, south-facing bedroom, all yellow and white, has been re-created with the help of the 1881 inventory, and the study where he conducted a lively correspondence and worked on his last three novels is largely as he left it. Watercolour portraits of his parents hang on the walls, the black-edged notepaper that he always used after his wife's death lies ready on his desk and his red dispatch box is to hand.

An obelisk on a near hillside, erected by Mary Anne in 1862 in memory of Disraeli's father, would have reminded him of the two people who influenced him most, and his writings show how he loved this place, valuing the solitude and escape it offered.

In recent years, Hughenden's vital secret role in the Second World War has come to light. Requisitioned by the Air Ministry in 1941 and codenamed Hillside, the house was used to produce maps for night-time bombing missions, among them the Dam Busters raid and the operation to sink the battleship *Tirpitz*. There were five drawing offices, where the maps were painstakingly compiled, one of which has been re-created in the west wing. Rows of drawing desks, each with its own Anglepoise lamp, are set side on to the large south-facing windows which, together with the white ceiling, gave maximum natural light. In producing the maps, all features helpful to pilots – woods, roads, rivers and lakes – were hand painted on foils and then combined to produce a map in shades of black and magenta which could be read at night at a height of 19,000 feet (5,791 metres) in a dimly-lit aircraft. The maps were photographed in what was Disraeli's ice house in the grounds, which has been fitted out to evoke its wartime role, and they were dispatched at night in trucks that were kept in the stable yard. Those stationed here, about 100 people, were required to work long hours, which could include evenings and weekends, and were billeted in local villages. Lunch was provided for one shilling and sixpence, but civilians had to find their own bicycles to get to and from their billets. A vast air-raid shelter carved out of the hill below the house for the use of those working here has been colonised by bats.

RIGHT Colourful island beds in the terraced garden below the south front of the house reflect the planting when the Disraelis lived here.

Ickworth

Suffolk
In Horringer, 3 miles
(4.8 kilometres) south-west of
Bury St Edmunds on the
west side of the A143

Frederick Augustus Hervey, 4th Earl of Bristol, must rank as one of the Church's more remarkable bishops. Appointed to the see of Derry, the richest in Ireland, in 1768 when only 38, his sympathy with both Roman Catholics and Presbyterians made him enormously popular, despite a sometimes light-hearted approach to his duties which once led him to organise a curates' race along the sands at Downhill (see p.124), rewarding the winners with vacant benefices.

A large income coupled with an inherited fortune allowed the Earl-Bishop to embark on extensive foreign tours, during which he amassed the works of art he intended to display in his new house on the family's Suffolk estate, to which he had succeeded in 1779. Ickworth is as grandiose and flamboyant as its creator. A larger version of the 4th Earl's earlier house at Ballyscullion, it was inspired, like the little Mussenden Temple at Downhill, by the circular Belle Isle on an island in Windermere. A huge domed rotunda decorated with classical columns and terracotta friezes is linked by curving corridors to rectangular wings, the whole building stretching some 600 feet (183 metres) from end to end. But Frederick was never to see his house completed. Work on Ickworth, based on designs by the Italian architect Mario Asprucci the Younger, which were adapted and simplified in England, began in 1795, but came to a halt on the 4th Earl's death from gout in an outhouse in Italy in 1803 (from where his body was shipped back to England, labelled as an antique statue). Tragically, the bishop had had his magnificent collection appropriated by Napoleonic troops in Rome in 1798.

The 4th Earl's ambitious plans were realised by his son, created 1st Marquess of Bristol in 1826. The superb paintings, porcelain and furniture now displayed in the house largely represent the slow accumulation of several generations of Herveys, who have owned the estate since the mid-fifteenth century. Many followed brilliant political careers, as did Frederick's gifted eldest brother George, the 2nd Earl, who acquired gilt furniture and paintings while he was on diplomatic postings to Turin and Madrid. It was the 1st Earl, Frederick's grandfather, another prominent politician, who bought the early eighteenth-century Huguenot pieces among the silver displayed in the Silver Room, the relatively restrained hand of Paul de Lamerie contrasting with more ornate rococo Italian work. One case here is devoted to a shoal of silver fish, some designed as ornamental pendants, others as scent containers, their realistic, scaly forms including a whale and a swordfish as well as more mundane species.

The 1st Marquess housed the bulk of the collection in the grand state rooms in the rotunda rather than in the wings, as his father had intended. The largest room in the house is the hemispherical library across the south front, notable for its rare late seventeenth- and early eighteenth-century political periodicals and ornamented with busts of four leading politicians: Pitt the Younger, Canning, Fox and Liverpool. Benjamin West's portrayal of the death of General Wolfe, which the artist painted specially for the Earl-Bishop, and Hogarth's *Holland House Group*, showing Frederick's father, Lord Hervey, in the centre of a group of friends that includes the 3rd Duke of Marlborough, are among a number of outstanding portraits in the house. A painting of a grave little boy with two greyhounds and a huge mastiff at his feet is Velázquez's study of the Infante Balthasar Carlos, son of Philip IV of Spain, and there is a full-length canvas by Gainsborough of the colourful Augustus John Hervey, Vice-Admiral of the Blue, who briefly succeeded as 3rd Earl between his two brothers. It seems this philanderer deserved his wife, Elizabeth Chudleigh, whose bigamous marriage with the Duke of Kingston in 1769 gave rise to one of the most famous scandals of the eighteenth century. Quite different in character is the charming self-portrait by Madame Vigée Le Brun, commissioned by the Earl-Bishop in Naples in 1791, the artist's severe black dress setting off a vivacious face crowned with a mop of curly hair that is loosely caught up in a white handkerchief. The most extraordinary exhibit is Flaxman's marble group, *The Fury of Athamas*, based on a scene from Ovid's *Metamorphoses*, which dominates the staircase hall. Commissioned by the 4th Earl, Athamas is here shown holding his young son over his shoulder by an ankle, about to dash him to death. A second child clings to their mother, terrified.

From the 1st Marquess's orangery in the west wing, floor-length windows lead out onto a terrace looking south over the heavily wooded garden, where tall cypresses, clipped yew

and evergreen oak create the illusion of an Italian landscape. Artfully contrived vistas give enticing glimpses of the rotunda. From the long raised terrace walk beyond the trees, created in *c.* 1870 to shield the garden, there is a sweeping panorama over clumps of mature beeches and oaks in the park. In the foreground, partly hidden in a dip, is St Mary's church, while

ABOVE The rotunda as seen from the garden. Asprucci's designs for Ickworth, sent from Italy, were executed by Francis Sandys, who simplified them.

an obelisk just visible above a wooded ridge on the far horizon was erected by the people of Derry in affectionate memory of their bishop.

Ightham Mote

Kent

6 miles (9.6 kilometres) east of
Sevenoaks, off the A25, and
2½ miles (4 kilometres) south
of Ightham, off the A227

A steep path from the car park leads down to this magical house set in a deep, wooded valley in the Kentish Weald, its walls rising sheer from the surrounding moat. Half-timbered upper storeys project from the façade here and there, a little hump-backed stone bridge crosses the water to an old wooden door, and the roofline is a medley of steeply pitched gables, massive brick chimneys and moss-stained tiles. Ducks paddle about beneath the walls.

Built round a courtyard and dating originally from the 1320s, Ightham Mote has retained its medieval appearance, despite many later alterations, because additions were piecemeal and made use of local oak and Kentish ragstone which were sympathetic to the ancient building. The great hall on the east side of the cobbled courtyard was the core of the early house and still has its early fourteenth-century timber roof. Tudor improvements, when the house was owned by the courtier Sir Richard Clement, account for the armorial glass in the great window of the hall which Clement inserted to advertise his loyalty to Henry VIII and impress the neighbours, on whom, in his position as Gentleman Usher, he kept an eye. The Tudor rose and the pomegranate of Catherine of Aragon, the king's first wife, which appear both here and on richly carved oak bargeboards facing onto the courtyard, must have been in place well before Henry cast Catherine aside and married Anne Boleyn in 1533, a ceremony at which Sir Richard Clement officiated.

Clement was also responsible for the decoration in honour of Henry and Catherine on the arched barrel ceiling of the long, half-timbered room on the first floor. The room is now a chapel, but it was probably originally designed as a grand guest chamber and the ceiling is exuberantly painted with vividly coloured badges and emblems in red, orange, green and white representing the royal houses of England, Spain and France. The colours have faded now, but it is easy to imagine how glowing they must once have been. The room appears to have become a chapel in the 1630s and seems to have been fitted out gradually, resulting in a beautiful array of fine woodwork – linenfold panelling, a richly carved pulpit, choir stalls and pews – of various dates. There is sixteenth-century stained glass in the windows and a remarkable late fifteenth-century oak door at the west end.

Across a landing from the chapel is the drawing room and an abrupt change in atmosphere and style. The room is dominated by a monumental Jacobean fireplace decorated with carved Saracen heads and painted in black and gold, and is lit by an eighteenth-century Venetian window. The walls are covered in hand-painted Chinese wallpaper of *c.* 1750 and the room as a whole has a distinctly exotic flavour, although, as in the rest of the house, the furniture, with the exception of a few pieces, has been added since 1951, when the original contents were sold.

The drawing room fills one end of the late fifteenth-century west range. On the other side of a central gatehouse tower are the simply furnished bedroom and dressing room that were used by Charles Henry Robinson, the American who bought Ightham Mote in 1953, having spotted a sale advertisement in a back number of *Country Life*, and gave it to the National Trust in 1985. The library, with its alcove bookshelves, is also as he had it. His desk sits in one of the alcoves and the pictures include drawings of his house in Maine.

Another American, Mary 'Queen' Palmer, whose husband rented Ightham in 1887, is depicted in a large-scale canvas by the Palmers' friend John Singer Sargent. Recently acquired for the house, Sargent's panoramic picture, painted in the garden in 1889, shows Queen, her daughter Elsie and friends playing bowls on the extensive lawn which stretches up the combe north of the house. A medieval stewpond here was fed by the stream that now crosses the grass to fill the moat. The stream also feeds a lake below the house and a raised walk fringing the lawn leads to another lake hidden in the trees beyond. Near the house a long border is crowded with traditional English flowers and there is a paved Fountain Garden. There are romantic views of the house from walks through the woodland and always there is the constant sound of running water, like soothing background music.

ABOVE The south front of the house dates from the late fifteenth or early sixteenth century, but the upper storey was given its attractive 'Tudor' studding only in *c.* 1904.
OPPOSITE A half-timbered range overlooking the cobbled courtyard at the heart of Ightham Mote has bargeboards carved with the emblems of Henry VIII and his first wife, Catherine of Aragon.

Kedleston Hall

Derbyshire
3 miles (4.8 kilometres) north
of Derby, easily reached and
signposted from the A38
Derby bypass

No one could describe this grand classical palace as homely. But then, it was always intended as a show place. On the impressive entrance front, looking north over a sweep of open parkland, a massive pedimented portico adorned with classical sculpture rises the full height of the three-storey central block. To either side are substantial rectangular pavilions, linked to the main building by curved corridors. A tower peeping above the west pavilion flags a medieval church, all that remains of the village that was swept away when the landscape park was created.

Sir Nathaniel Curzon, later 1st Lord Scarsdale, began the house in 1759, only a year after he had inherited the estate. A cultivated man who was interested in the arts, he saw it as a setting for his paintings and sculpture, a collection that was on view to visitors from the day the house was built. The formal reception rooms and guest suite filling the central block were never intended to be used except for the entertainment of important visitors. The family lived in one pavilion; the kitchen and domestic offices were in the other.

Although work began under the direction of Matthew Brettingham and James Paine, by 1760 these two architects had been superseded by the young Robert Adam, who had recently returned from Rome. Adam transformed his predecessors' rather conventional designs. His monumental Marble Hall, with ten alabaster columns like tree trunks framing the room on either side and classical statues in niches along the walls, is top-lit to suggest the open courtyard of a Roman villa. The adjoining rotunda known as the Saloon, its coffered dome rising to a height of 62 feet (19 metres), was based on the Pantheon in Rome, one of the most admired buildings of classical antiquity. To either side lie formal reception rooms, Adam's hand evident in virtually every detail of their decoration. Delicate plaster ceilings were executed by the Yorkshireman

Joseph Rose and paintings were grouped and hung according to Curzon's wishes; plaster frames built into the walls in some rooms ensure his arrangements have survived. The furniture, some of it designed by Adam, some designed and made by the London cabinetmaker John Linnell, some with inputs from both men, picks up on decorative themes. In the State Withdrawing Room, carved and gilded dolphins, merfolk and sea nymphs on the four great sofas echo nautical touches in the ceiling. Made by Linnell, they are based on an Adam design, but one that Linnell radically altered.

The paintings hanging double-banked in all the principal rooms, including a number of epic canvases such as Benedetto Luti's *Cain and Abel* and Salomon Koninck's

RIGHT Robert Adam enlivened Brettingham and Paine's north front with a more dramatic central portico. The windowless façade is ornamented with lead figures in niches and carved stone medallions as a backdrop to the columns.
OPPOSITE In the Music Room, Curzon took great care over the arrangement of his paintings, many of which hang in the fitted plaster frames designed for them by Adam.

Daniel before Nebuchadnezzar, illustrate Lord Scarsdale's taste for seventeenth-century Italian and Dutch Old Masters. Family portraits, some of which date back to the sixteenth century, adorn the guest apartments, among them a charming study by Nathaniel Hone showing the 1st Lord Scarsdale walking in the grounds with his wife Caroline. Thomas Barber's portrayal of the elderly Mrs Garnett, the housekeeper who took Boswell and Dr Johnson round Kedleston in 1777, is also memorable.

There is a collection of Blue John vases and ornaments in the house and Kedleston also has hundreds of objects – weapons, domestic religious artefacts and ceremonial gifts – that were acquired by Marquess Curzon of Kedleston in the early twentieth century during his travels in Asia and while he was Viceroy of India from 1899 to 1905. These are displayed in the Eastern Museum, in a presentation that was devised in the 1920s and is now a period piece, seen from the perspective of the coloniser and showing little concern for the cultural significance or meaning of objects. The displays are currently being reviewed and, drawing on the knowledge in local communities, will be re-presented and re-interpreted.

The long drive from the great arched gateway of Adam's North Lodge runs through the park devised by Nathaniel Curzon and the landscape designer William Emes, with input from the canal builder Hugh Henshaw, to set off the house. The park is planted with carefully placed clumps of trees and has a three-arched stone bridge, designed by Adam, to carry the drive across a chain of serpentine lakes. Adam also designed the Fishing Pavilion on the upper lake, a Venetian window facing north over the water reputedly enabling ladies to cast a line into the pool below while being shielded from the sun.

To the south of the house, a broad open lawn bounded by a ha-ha marks the eighteenth-century informal garden and there are uninterrupted views across the park beyond as it rises gently to a belt of trees. A hexagonal summer-house and orangery were both designed by George Richardson in the late eighteenth century and a pair of gates leads into a winding 3-mile (4.8-kilometre) circuit of the park.

Killerton

Devon
On the west side of the B3181,
formerly the A38, Exeter–
Cullompton road

This sprawling, two-storey house, home to several generations of the Acland family, sits below the steep wooded slopes of Killerton Clump, a volcanic outcrop rising high above the valley of the River Clyst and visible for miles around. Later additions mask the plain Georgian block that was built in 1778–9 for Sir Thomas Dyke Acland, 7th Baronet, to replace an Elizabethan house on more or less the same site. Sir Thomas had planned to build a grandiose Palladian seat by Robert Adam, but when this scheme came to nothing he turned to the equally fashionable James Wyatt to design his new mansion. Foundations were laid at a site higher up the hill, but family concerns and an increasing lack of confidence in Wyatt led Sir Thomas to call a halt to the project and work stopped in 1777. The foundations, hidden in woodland, have recently been discovered and partly excavated. The more modest building at the bottom of the hill ended up being the principal residence, and was considerably expanded in the early nineteenth century and again in Edwardian times. At the foot of the drive are William Spring of Exeter's magnificent stone stables, with an elegant cupola rising over the pedimented archway leading into the courtyard. A later Sir Thomas, the 10th Baronet, was responsible for the Victorian Norman Revival chapel by C.R. Cockerell to the north of the stables. This was built to supersede the tiny Elizabethan building on the other side of the hill that, along with a gatehouse, is almost all that remains of the original Acland seat at Columbjohn.

Killerton is not a show house. It has always been a family home, where generations of Aclands have been involved in the estate and in local and national politics and have paid little attention to acquiring fine furniture and paintings. The interiors, much altered over the years, are as unpretentious as the exterior and give a broad idea of domestic life between the First and Second World Wars. A music room in the centre of the house, lit by a window bay added in the 1820s, and dominated by the chamber organ that was given to Lydia Acland, wife of the 10th Baronet, by her father, was a focus of family life. Dinner in the dining room on the west front, looking onto the garden, was always eaten in evening dress,

with bare arms for the ladies however cold the weather and a place near the fire for the most privileged. The room is decorated with an eighteenth-century plaster frieze and is hung with generations of family portraits. Wooden columns frame a connecting door to the library, where two terracotta roundels by the Danish sculptor Bertel Thorvaldsen were acquired by the 10th baronet and his wife Lydia when they visited the sculptor in Rome in 1836. In a corner of the room is a set of false book-backs with fanciful titles. These interiors are adapted, to a greater or lesser extent, to fit in with Killerton's 'theme of the year', which may involve moving furniture and added interpretation.

A massive Edwardian staircase leads to the upper floor, where the rooms are used to display the Killerton collection of historic and contemporary fashion. This originated as the costume collection of Paulise de Bush, which was given to the Trust in 1978 and which included many eighteenth- and nineteenth-century pieces which she had rescued from a house in Berkshire during the Second World War. Exhibitions are

generally changed every year and the extensive collection is available for research and study.

Sir Thomas Dyke Acland, 7th Baronet, who built the Georgian house, also established the framework of Killerton's outstanding garden, with advice from Nathaniel Richmond and the help of the young John Veitch, who was not yet 21. Veitch, who went on to become one of the greatest nurserymen and landscape designers of his day, had a life-long association with Killerton, where the garden, and its exceptional collection of plants, continued to be developed by later members of the Acland family, for whom it was always of huge importance. Paths climb ever upwards through the trees in the arboretum on the slopes of Killerton Clump and a walk shaded by mature beeches follows the contours of the hill.

The 10th Baronet, who presided over Killerton from his coming of age in 1808 and who, with Veitch, did so much to nurture the garden, is remembered by the granite cross that stands high up on the western edge and which was erected by 40 of his friends in 1873.

ABOVE The modest Georgian house which forms the core of Killerton (right) was greatly extended in the 1820s by Sir Thomas Acland, 10th Baronet, who built new rooms for his children with direct access to the garden.
OPPOSITE The beautifully proportioned eighteenth-century corridor leading to Killerton's original front door, on the south side of the house, is little changed and still has its elegant Georgian fanlights.

Killerton sits at the centre of an extensive estate in the fertile valleys of the Clyst and Culm. A mix of farmland and sizeable areas of woodland, it also includes the villages of Broadclyst and Budlake. There are many traditional buildings, among them Marker's Cottage in Broadclyst, a small cob and thatch house dating back to the fifteenth century, which has a contemporary cob summer-house and some mid-sixteenth-century paintings on a wooden screen. A few minutes' walk away, on the River Clyst, is the working Clyston Mill, probably built in the early nineteenth century but occupying an ancient site, and half a mile (0.8 kilometres) north up the B3181 is Budlake village, where a small thatched cottage still has its 1950s Post Office Room.

Kingston Lacy

Dorset
On the B3082 Wimborne–
Blandford road, 1½ miles
(2.4 kilometres) west of
Wimborne

This great mansion in the heart of Dorset dates from 1663, when Sir Ralph Bankes built a house here to replace the earlier family seat at Corfe Castle (*see* p.107), 20 miles (32 kilometres) away, which had been destroyed in the Civil War. Sir Ralph's collection of pictures still hangs here, but Kingston Lacy as it is now was transformed between 1835 and 1841 by the handsome and original William John Bankes (1786–1855), friend of Byron, who engaged Sir Charles Barry, architect of the Houses of Parliament, to remodel the house and filled it with paintings and other works of art he had acquired during his extensive travels in the Mediterranean. Sadly, William had little

opportunity to enjoy what he had created. In 1841 he was accused of behaving indecently with a soldier in a London park and he fled to the Continent, where he spent the rest of his life. Nevertheless, although unlikely ever to see his house again, this extraordinary man continued to concern himself with its furnishing and decoration.

The exterior still retains the shape of the double-pile Restoration mansion built by Sir Roger Pratt for Ralph Bankes, but has been much altered. The hipped roof, pierced by prominent dormers, is crowned with a balustrade and cupola by Barry and his tall chimneys at each corner give the house the look of an upturned footstool. On the south front, Barry's broad Italianate terrace sweeps right across the façade, with central steps flanked by urns and guarded by lions descending to a lawn dotted with Venetian well-heads. His impressive marble staircase leading up to the principal rooms on the first floor is also of Italian inspiration. Bronze figures set in niches in the airy loggia on the half-landing include a depiction of brave Lady Mary Bankes, who twice defended Corfe Castle for Charles I in the Civil War. She is shown holding the key to the castle; what may be the actual keys are displayed over the fireplace in the library.

The principal floor still reflects the layout of Roger Pratt's house and some rooms are still as remodelled by R.F. Brettingham in the 1780s for Henry Bankes. The painted ceiling of 1790 by Cornelius Dixon in the saloon, with its delicate curves and spirals of foliage, arches over the room like elaborate wrapping paper. The paintings hanging two and three deep here include Rubens's portraits of Maria Pallavicino and Maria Grimaldi that were acquired by William: one encased in her gleaming wedding dress like an exotic beetle, both women wearing ruffs so big that their heads seem detached. The library, with a fine collection of leather-bound books dating from the mid-seventeenth century, is also largely as designed by Brettingham. A ceiling painting by Guido Reni that William Bankes acquired from a palazzo in Bologna in 1840 dominates the room. Executed in 1599, the painting illustrates the description of the first day in Genesis, when the darkness was separated from the light, and is a rare example of Reni's early work. Taken down from the ceiling when the National Trust took over Kingston Lacy in 1981, this fragile painting, one of the most significant in the house, was stripped of nineteenth-century retouching and painstakingly restored in 2007.

More recently, in 2010, a vast mythical painting by Tintoretto was restored and put on display for the first time in the dining room. Painted in 1570–9, it was probably acquired by Bankes from a Venetian palazzo and, like the Guido Reni, has been in store since 1981. Sebastiano del Piombo's unfinished *The Judgement of Solomon*, which hangs nearby, was painted about 50 years earlier and was probably also intended for a Venetian setting.

While the dining-room panelling dates from the late nineteenth century, the adjoining Spanish Room is as William created it, with works he procured during his travels in Spain at the time of the Peninsular War set against gilded leather hangings and seen beneath a sumptuous coffered ceiling, thought to be one of those Scamozzi added to the Palazzo Contarini on the Grand Canal in Venice. Papal power and splendour shine through Velázquez's portrait of Cardinal Massimi, clothed here in peacock blue.

A naturalistic late eighteenth-century landscape park, dotted with mature trees and grazed by Red Ruby cattle, surrounds the house. The Edwardian garden restored by the Trust includes a brightly coloured parterre to the west of the house and a Victorian fernery to the east. A cedar walk lined with trees planted by visiting notables, including Kaiser Wilhelm II, leads to the lime avenue and the newly restored Japanese garden, one of the largest in Britain. A pink granite obelisk, one of three in the garden, was brought here by William Bankes from a temple on the Nile.

Kingston Lacy is also the centre of an extensive agricultural estate in the valley of the River Stour. Including some twelve farms and parts of the villages of Shapwick and Pamphill, this is a historic rural landscape, dotted with earthworks, such as the Iron Age hillfort of Badbury Rings, and rich in vernacular buildings. White Mill, a substantial brick and tile corn-mill on the Stour, was largely rebuilt in 1776 but is probably on the site of one of the eight mills recorded on the river in Domesday Book. It still has its original and now very rare elm and applewood machinery.

RIGHT The upper flight of Barry's grand marble staircase linking the principal floors turns round a copy of a Roman marble candelabrum.
OPPOSITE The east front of Kingston Lacy looks out over a formal Dutch garden, with balls of golden yew, which was laid out in 1899.

Knightshayes

Devon
2 miles north of Tiverton
on the A396

The Luddite band who destroyed his Leicestershire factory on 28 June 1816 prompted the young John Heathcoat to move his revolutionary new lace-making machines to the safety of Devon, where he set up his works in one of the Tiverton mills left empty by the decline of the wool industry. The profits from what was to become the largest lace factory in the world enabled his grandson, John Heathcoat Amory, the 1st Baronet, to purchase the Knightshayes estate and to build the idiosyncratic gothic house that overlooks the little town in the valley below. Dating from 1869 to 1874, it is a singular place. Built of dark-red Hensley stone, the house rises forbiddingly from the terraces to the right of the drive in a frontage of pointed gables, large mullioned windows and prominent gargoyles.

A rare example of the domestic architecture of William Burges, the High Victorian medievalist who is much better known for his churches, such as the masterpiece at Studley Royal (*see* p.147), this rather dour exterior was planned to conceal interiors of exceptional richness. Although Burges's designs were mostly rejected by his client, who thought them too extreme, the schemes produced by his more conventional replacement, John Diblee Crace, were by no means subdued and, too bold and colourful for Sir John's taste, were largely covered up in later years. Where possible, the National Trust has sought to restore the nineteenth-century work. Maxims by Robert Burns and Chaucer in bold gold lettering run round the frieze in the dining room, where rich red and green wallpaper

LEFT The gothic south front of Knightshayes, with its gables and gargoyles and an oriel window tucked into an angle of the façade, looks over formal terraced gardens on this side of the house.
OPPOSITE ABOVE The boudoir ceiling, with its zodiac roundels, was repainted in 1981 by Ian Cairnie, who based his work closely on a scheme by Crace.
OPPOSITE BELOW A portrait of Alexandra Seymour, Lady Heathcoat Amory, whose son, Sir John, 3rd Baronet, gave Knightshayes to the Trust, hangs over the fireplace in the boudoir.

designed by Crace complements the dark half-panelling. Above is a beamed and painted ceiling supported on corbels carved with creatures from the Devon countryside: a badger, a fox and an otter with a fish. The medievalism of the hall, with its gothic arches, gallery, timber vault and whimsical carvings, is even more striking. This was the only room to be completed largely as Burges planned, but a bedroom has been decorated on the basis of his original drawings and shows clearly how rich the interiors would have been if his schemes had been followed. A wide painted frieze filled with birds perched on stylised branches echoes a motif used by Burges at his London house and a golden bed and painted cabinets, all on loan from the Victoria and Albert Museum, were also made to his designs.

The drawing room and morning room, both of which have boldly painted, compartmental ceilings, are hung with the nucleus of the art collection acquired in the years after the Second World War, when Knightshayes became a convalescent home for American airmen, by the 3rd Baronet (1894–1972) and his wife, the former golfing champion Joyce Wethered, whom Sir John had married in 1937. Vivid red poppies like a scarlet splash on the wall are one of two flower pictures once attributed to Constable, a misty river scene in Picardy by Richard Parkes Bonington is complemented by a copy of a Turner seascape, and a Madonna and Child by Matteo di Giovanni is one of a number of early religious works. The original fireplace having been lost, the restored nineteenth-century decoration in the drawing room is now set off by a massive carved marble chimneypiece which was designed by Burges for Worcester College, Oxford, where it remained until 1966, and which the college has given to the Trust.

Although based on a nineteenth-century design by Edward Kemp, the garden owes much to the 3rd Baronet and Joyce, who greatly enlarged it, creating the extensive woodland garden, and made it one of the finest in the county. A formal layout near the house includes a water-lily pool in a battlemented yew enclosure and a topiary hunt on the hedges framing the lawn to the south, one of the pursuing hounds shown gathering itself to leap a leafy obstacle. West of the house, a little valley has a show of daffodils in spring, and there is a large walled kitchen garden, with unique stepped walls, which was designed by Burges.

Knole

Kent
At the south end of Sevenoaks,
just east of the A225

A sudden opening between the buildings lining the main A225 through Sevenoaks signals the unpretentious gateway to Knole. The drive from this modest entrance emerges unexpectedly into the glorious park surrounding the house, scored with deep valleys, planted with ancient oaks, beeches and chestnuts, and grazed by herds of fallow and sika deer. As the road breasts a rise, there is a view of what looks like a compact hilltop town, with rabbit-cropped turf running almost up to the walls and a jumble of chimneys, gables, battlements and red-tiled roofs rising behind.

Sprawled round several courtyards like an Oxford college, Knole could house the retinue of a medieval prince. The main ranges are of rough Kentish ragstone, but hidden away in some of the minor courts are half-timbered façades, like those that can be seen in a hundred villages round about. Inside, in contrast to the rather plain and rugged exterior, are furnishings and decoration of great richness and rarity.

The core of Knole was built by Thomas Bourchier, Archbishop of Canterbury, between 1456 and his death in 1486, when he bequeathed it to the see of Canterbury. Three more archbishops enjoyed and improved the splendid residence Bourchier had created before Archbishop Cranmer was forced to give it to Henry VIII in 1538. By this time, Knole had been enlarged by the addition of an outer courtyard with a turreted gatehouse, but it seems the covetous king spent little or no time here. Knole was later held briefly by Elizabeth I's favourite, the Earl of Leicester, but by 1605 the freehold of the house and estate had been acquired by the late queen's cousin Thomas Sackville, 1st Earl of Dorset, who had also been Elizabeth I's Lord Treasurer (a post to which he was reappointed by James I). The earl's descendants, later Dukes of Dorset and then Lords Sackville, have lived here ever since. The 1st Earl transformed Knole, turning the medieval and Tudor palace into a Renaissance mansion. He employed James I's master plasterer, Richard Dungan, and, probably, the king's master carpenter, William Portington, to create the patterned ceiling and intricate carved screen in the great hall, and to decorate the ballroom. And he established a series of state apartments on the first floor, each with its own long gallery,

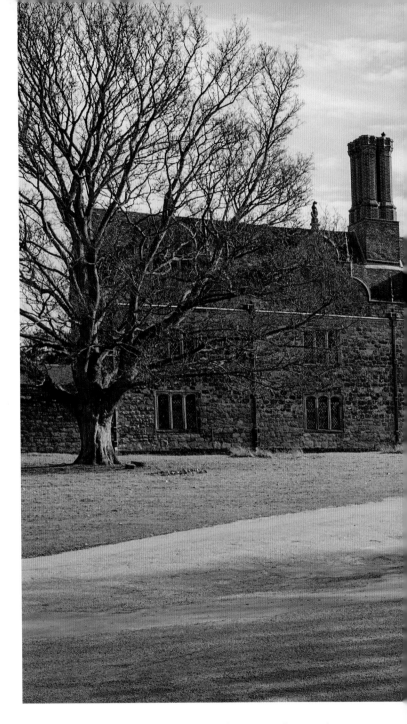

connecting them to the hall with a grand staircase decorated in grisaille. It was the 1st Earl, too, who added the Sackville leopards to gables all over the house, and his initials and the date, 1605, to lead downpipes in the courtyards.

All this remains and, in the late seventeenth century, after depredations during the Civil War, when Knole and its lands were seized and the contents largely sold, the house was

filled with an outstanding collection of seventeenth-century furniture and textiles by the 6th Earl. As Lord Chamberlain to William III, the earl was entitled to take away discarded furnishings from the royal palaces and he also enriched Knole with the furniture acquired by his grandfather, the Earl of Middlesex, who was Master of the Great Wardrobe to James I. As a result, Knole's galleries and bedchambers are filled

ABOVE Knole's long west front looking over the park, with its massive brick chimneystacks and turreted gatehouse, probably dates from the late 1400s, although the curved gables were later embellishments.

with state beds, tapestries, chairs and stools that would once have adorned the palaces of Whitehall, Hampton Court and Kensington. Blue damask chairs in the Brown Gallery are stamped WP for Whitehall Palace, brass locks in the Cartoon

Gallery carry William III's monogram, and a state bed hung with watery-green Genoa velvet that was made for James II may have been the one in which the king spent his last night in Whitehall Palace, on 17 December 1688, before fleeing to exile in France. Some of the rarest and finest pieces are displayed in the King's Room: a silver looking-glass, table and candlestands shine brilliantly in simulated candlelight, drawing the eye away from the magnificent great bed with its cloth of silver and gold and matching chairs and stools.

In the late eighteenth century, Knole was enriched again by the cultivated and handsome 3rd Duke, who added a notable picture collection of his own to the many paintings already in the house, among them portraits by Mytens, Dobson and Van Dyck from the early seventeenth century, and John Wootton's panoramic landscape in the ballroom, showing the 1st Duke

and his retinue arriving at Dover Castle in 1728, its period frame adorned with two prominent Sackville leopards. The 3rd Duke also acquired a number of Old Masters and patronised English painters of his day, in particular his close friend Joshua Reynolds, whose many canvases at Knole, most of them hung two deep in the Crimson Drawing Room, include a self-portrait which Reynolds gave to the duke, along with likenesses of Samuel Johnson and the playwright and poet Oliver Goldsmith, and of the Duke's Chinese page. In an age when great houses all over the country were being remodelled in the newly fashionable classical style, the 3rd Duke also stands out for his appreciation of the ancient mansion he had inherited, which he did not alter, and, less exceptionally, for his long relationship with the Italian dancer Giovanna Baccelli, who is immortalised in a plaster statue at the foot of the grand staircase, where her nude form, introduced at one time as that of 'a close friend of the family', reclines provocatively on a couple of tasselled plaster cushions.

Knole has recently undergone a £20 million programme of renovation and conservation which has greatly increased knowledge of the house, revitalised the historic show rooms and resulted in the opening of some additional areas. A small door by the entrance arch opens onto a steep and narrow spiral staircase in the gatehouse tower which leads up to the rooms lived in by Eddy Sackville-West, novelist, music critic and gifted pianist, from 1926 to 1940. A cousin of Vita Sackville-West, who thought he had 'a face like a Persian cat – all white and serious, with large violet eyes', Eddy moved in the same circles as Vita and Virginia Woolf, and was visited here by many notable literary and artistic figures, Cecil Beaton, Aldous Huxley and the composer Ethel Smyth among them. Stacked one above the other in the tower are Eddy's bedroom, with a bathroom ingeniously shoehorned into an adjoining turret, and music room, where he had his baby grand piano. Blue and pink colour schemes reproduce his original decoration. Never happy at Knole, Eddy eventually renounced his inheritance and went to live in Ireland, taking his piano with him. But he is still a strong presence here. His wind-up gramophone with a huge horn stands in a corner, a fire screen embellished with stylised flames is a copy of the one painted by his lover Duncan Grant, and another lover, the Surrealist artist John Banting, decorated a corner cupboard. A portrait of Eddy by Graham Sutherland hanging in the music room shows him as an anxious and apprehensive figure, hands tightly clasped.

Tours of the extensive attics above the Great Hall and Cartoon Gallery reveal a very different side of Knole. The high-ceilinged fifteenth-century kitchen can be glimpsed through an internal window and, running the width of the house from north to south on the top floor, is a stunning Jacobean long gallery, its ceiling covered with decorative plasterwork by Richard Dungan and a high-status painted staircase leading up to it from beside the ballroom. Long abandoned, its floor and walls have been pulled out of shape by the great clock that once stood on the roof above and is now on the inner gatehouse.

Also now on view is the airy, light-filled orangery created in 1823 that fills the south side of the outer court. Stone-floored, and with huge windows looking onto the Sackville-Wests' private garden, this is a restful, peaceful space.

OPPOSITE Knole's Spangle Bedroom takes its name from the silver and gold bed hangings. For long blackened, these have now been partly restored to their original appearance. The room is lined with fine Jacobean panelling and seventeenth-century Brussels tapestries.
RIGHT The 1st Earl's painted staircase formed an impressive link between the great hall and the state rooms on the first floor.

Lacock Abbey, Fox Talbot Museum and Village

Wiltshire
3 miles (4.8 kilometres) south of Chippenham, just east of the A350

This romantic house, with ranges of golden stone set round a grassy court, lies in a leafy pastoral setting beside the River Avon. Twisted Tudor chimneys break the roofline and a prominent octagonal tower juts out at one corner. This unusual and evocative place has a history going back almost 800 years, with many echoes of the nunnery for Augustinian canonesses founded in 1232 by the redoubtable Ela, Countess of Salisbury, in memory of her husband William Longespée. At its suppression by Henry VIII's commissioners in 1539, the nunnery was acquired by the duplicitous and self-seeking William Sharington, a rather unattractive man who seems to have behaved with more than the usual dishonesty in his public life, but who showed both sensitivity and imagination in converting his purchase into a house. Although he demolished the abbey church, the outlines of which are now marked by long grass in the south lawn, Sharington kept many of the nunnery's original rooms and also incorporated innovative Renaissance features that were rare in England at this date. Beautiful fifteenth-century cloisters, with carved bosses punctuating the stone vaulting, still frame the court at the heart of the house. The daughters of well-to-do families who formed the community sunned themselves on the stone seats set into the walls or stretched out their hands to the blaze in the great fireplace preserved in the warming room, one of a set of fine, mostly stone-vaulted thirteenth-century chambers, including the sacristy and chapter house, opening onto the east cloister walk. The ghost of the nunnery is also evident in the thirteenth-century vaulted undercroft in the west range, part of which became the servants' hall; in a huge blocked medieval fireplace in the kitchen; in wall-paintings of St Christopher and the crucifixion of St Andrew in the chaplains' room; and

in the Brown Gallery, which Sharington created out of part of the refectory and where original corbels still support the roof, although this is now hidden by the ceiling.

The wide Stone Gallery which Sharington fashioned from part of the nuns' dormitory to give views over his formal garden on the east side of the house is still much as he left it, lit by largely Tudor windows and with a delicately carved classical chimneypiece. Knowledge of the Renaissance also comes through in Sir William's three-storey octagonal tower, where a narrow angled passage leads to a high-ceilinged chamber on the first floor. A place where Sharington could keep important papers and display precious objects, this tiny cupboard of a room, possibly the only one of its kind surviving in England, was both a strong-room and an early equivalent of the *studiolo* of an Italian Renaissance prince, where books and treasured works of art would be kept. It is almost filled by an elaborate octagonal stone table supported on the shoulders of four satyrs and carved with the scorpions of the Sharington crest, their vicious tails and matchstick legs also recognisable in pendants studding the vaulted ceiling. This exceptional stone carving may be the work of John Chapman, who worked for Henry VIII, or by a foreign craftsman from the Tudor court. There is another stone table in the room above. Filling the top of the tower and only accessible from the roof, this was a banqueting house where Sharington would have entertained his guests, Sir John Thynne of Longleat among them. His scorpions appear again on the Tudor tiles which have been re-used in a Georgian stewing range in the kitchen.

The newest architectural fashions were again introduced to Lacock in the middle of the eighteenth century, when John Ivory Talbot, a descendant of Sharington's niece, made extensive changes to the house and grounds. Sanderson Miller's gothick hall, completed in 1755, is entered by a prominent double flight of steps on the west front. Below the painted heraldic ceiling, decorative niches with pinnacled canopies are filled with terracotta figures made in 1755–6 by the Austrian sculptor Victor Alexander Sederbach, whose strange company, two nuns, a bishop, a knight and a grisly skeleton among them, is dominated by Ela in heroic pose over the fireplace, a bird perching on her outstretched left arm. The adjoining dining room was also remodelled by John Ivory Talbot, in 1751–2, but here, in contrast to the drama next door, the decoration is coolly classical.

In the lovely South Gallery hung with family portraits, including a painting of Sir William dressed in black with a long, red beard, a brown, indistinct photograph placed by one of the oriel windows shows the bare outlines of the lattice panes. This blurred print was produced from a tiny negative, the world's first, made in 1835 by the pioneer photographer William Henry Fox Talbot, who inherited the estate as a baby in 1800. Although he did not come to live at Lacock until 1827, introducing the oriel windows in the South Gallery in *c*. 1830, he conducted many of his early experiments at the abbey. The earliest photograph was taken by Joseph Niépce in 1826, but Fox Talbot was responsible for inventing the negative–positive process, which paved the way for the development of modern photography.

The ground floor of the converted barn at the abbey gates is devoted to this exceptional man's life and work, displaying the skeletal forms of leaves and flowers captured in early experiments as well as portraits of his family and life at Lacock. Fox Talbot's achievements in other areas are also recorded, from his translation of the cuneiform inscriptions discovered in 1847 at the palaces of the Assyrian kings in what is now Iraq, to his work on microscopy, demonstrated by magnified insect wings and plant sections. Also a prominent mathematician and astronomer and a Fellow of the Royal Society, Fox Talbot's scientific interests were accompanied by an appreciation of the artistic possibilities of photography, as clearly illustrated by his plates in *The Pencil of Nature* (1844–6), the first book to include

photographs. The museum also exhibits examples of the work of other pioneers in this field, such as Louis Daguerre, Nicéphore Niépce and Thomas Wedgwood, and early photographic equipment.

Beyond the Fox Talbot Museum is the village of Lacock, now a picturesque assemblage of well-preserved buildings from the fourteenth to the late eighteenth centuries and primarily a tourist attraction, much used for filming period dramas, but for hundreds of years a busy and prosperous place. There has been a permanent settlement here since Saxon times and probably even earlier, but the present layout, with four main streets forming a square, dates from the thirteenth century, when a planned village was established for workers on the abbey estates. Its inhabitants grew rich on the medieval wool industry and the weekly market initiated by Ela. Lacock was ideally placed for both, being within a day's journey of prime grazing lands in the Cotswolds and on the Marlborough Downs and a staging-post on the road linking centres of the wool trade in the West Country. There was also access to the sea via the River Avon, which meanders past to the east. At its height in the late Middle Ages, Lacock's continued prosperity after the

OPPOSITE Shell-backed chairs dating from the 1630s in the Stone Gallery are painted with the lion of the Talbots, who lived at Lacock for centuries.
BELOW The three-storey octagonal tower which William Sharington added to Lacock Abbey contains a strong-room, with a massive iron door, where he kept his precious books and other valuables.

decline of the wool trade owed much to its position on a through route between Marlborough and Bristol, which brought wealth to the village and travellers to fill its many inns until the mid-eighteenth century. From then onwards Lacock stood still. Lack of development in the nineteenth century, when many nearby settlements expanded rapidly, was largely due to the Talbot family, who ensured no railway lines came too near the village. Lacock fossilised, resulting in one of the most pleasing and individual places in England.

Reflecting the village's origins, the irregular terraces that line the streets are all built on narrow medieval house plots running back from the frontages. There are timber-framed buildings with mullioned windows and jettied upper storeys, seventeenth-century stone cottages and elegant Georgian brick mansions, such as the two examples dated 1719 and 1779 in East Street, but many of the apparently later buildings are older than they look and were originally timber-framed. Lichen and moss encrust stone-slated roofs and gables, and dormers add to the pleasingly varied street façades.

Of the numerous inns, the timber-framed Angel in Church Street retains its medieval layout and the passage through which horses would be led to the yard behind, while the George in West Street has an original dog-powered spit.

A magnificent fourteenth-century tithe barn would once have stored rent paid to the abbey in the form of corn, hides and fleeces. Standing slightly apart is the battlemented and pinnacled church of St Cyriac. Largely rebuilt when the village was at its most prosperous in the fifteenth century, it contains the grandiose Renaissance tomb of Sir William Sharington. A narrow lane leads from the church to the eighteenth-century packhorse bridge over the Bide Brook and to the Avon beyond, where a medieval bridge crosses the river.

Fox Talbot's granddaughter Matilda gave the abbey and the village to the National Trust in 1944, and members of the Talbot family continued to live in the abbey until 2011.

Lamb House

East Sussex
In West Street, Rye, facing the
west end of the church

In 1726 a violent storm drove the ship carrying George I from Hanover to England onto the sands fringing the estuary of the River Rother, 2 miles (3.2 kilometres) from Rye. James Lamb, mayor of the prosperous little town, escorted the king to his house and offered him his bed, although his wife was heavily pregnant and in fact gave birth to a son that night. Heavy snow kept the king in Rye for three days and the Lambs, whose ignorance of German matched the king's lack of English, were rewarded with a silver bowl and 100 guineas as christening presents for their infant, who had the king as his godfather. The modest brick-fronted house that bears Lamb's name, one of many pleasing buildings lining Rye's cobbled streets, had been completed just two years earlier.

Some 200 years later the house was connected with another outstanding character, in this case the American novelist and critic Henry James, who bought it for £2,000 in 1900. Already in late middle age and well established in both Europe and America, James was to reach the height of his powers here. It was at Rye that he wrote his three greatest novels, *The Ambassadors, The Wings of the Dove* and *The Golden Bowl*, dictating them in a sonorous voice to his secretary, Theodora Bosanquet, in the garden pavilion in summer and in a small, sunny study in winter. Here, too, he entertained a stream of other established literary figures, including H.G. Wells, Ford Madox Ford, Rudyard Kipling, Max Beerbohm and Edith Wharton.

Remarkably, after James's death in 1916, Lamb House became the home of three other novelists, the brothers A.C. and E.F. Benson and, later, Rumer Godden. They, too, found the tranquil atmosphere conducive, with the neighbourhood and society of Rye forming the inspiration for E.F. Benson's *Mapp and Lucia* novels.

Since 1950, when Lamb House came to the National Trust without any contents, the Trust has been gradually retrieving items connected with Henry James and a collection of his books is now on show in the morning room.

The walled garden, much loved by those who have lived here, contains a rich variety of plants. Sadly, the eighteenth-century garden room, with a bay window looking down the street, was destroyed by a German bomb in 1940.

LEFT Lamb House, a modest Georgian building tucked away on the corner of a cobbled street in the delightful little town of Rye, has been lived in and visited by a stream of literary figures.

Lanhydrock

Cornwall
2½ miles (4 kilometres) south-east
of Bodmin, overlooking the valley
of the River Fowey

Lanhydrock is lost in a long Victorian afternoon. No one is at work in the cool, tiled dairy, or in the huge stone-flagged kitchen, and buckets and brushes are lined up in the housemaids' closet ready for the next day. No sound comes from the extensive servants' quarters, where a pair of black boots stands neatly by a bed and the footman's livery lies ready to wear, while in the nursery wing all is still. Pipes lie waiting in the masculine confines of the smoking room and the dining-room table is laid for ten, the menu already handwritten in French. The period feeling is so strong that it would be no surprise to meet a scurrying maid with a tray or to hear the Agar-Robartes family and their guests, or their nine children, coming in from the garden.

Lanhydrock's interiors vividly evoke gracious living in the 1890s. The house itself, with three battlemented ranges of silver-grey granite set round a courtyard and mullioned windows, is much older, but was largely rebuilt at the end of the nineteenth century after a disastrous fire in 1881. Although, to avoid the risk of another fire, no gas or electricity was installed. The designs by Richard Coad, a local architect who had trained in London, incorporated the latest comforts and conveniences, such as the massive radiators featured in almost every room. The hill behind the house was cut away to accommodate a full range of service rooms and a steam generator in the cellar powered the jets for scouring greasy pots in the scullery and a range of equipment in the airy, high-ceilinged kitchen, where butterscotch walls reflect the late nineteenth-century colour scheme. Ice was brought by train from Plymouth for the ice chests in the pantry and spring water from the hill above the house was channelled along runnels in the slate and marble slabs in the dairy where jellies and custards were put to stand.

At the same time, as he was instructed, Coad restored the Jacobean exterior of the rather old-fashioned house built here by John Robartes, later 1st Earl of Radnor, between 1634 and 1644, his new work merging beautifully with the one wing that was not extensively damaged in the flames. An enchanting detached gatehouse still stands at the head of a beech and sycamore avenue leading away across the park, as it has done since the seventeenth century, and obelisks crowning this little architectural conceit are echoed by more on the main building and on the low wall enclosing formal gardens around the house.

Only the north wing, which survived the fire intact, gives a flavour of the original interiors. A sunny 116-foot (35.5-metre) gallery running the length of the second floor and lit by windows on both sides suggests what might have been lost. The barrel ceiling arching overhead is covered with magical plasterwork dating from just before the outbreak of the Civil War. Although the 24 panels illustrating incidents from the Old Testament take centre stage, the delightful creatures surrounding them are far more memorable: furry porcupines, bears, armadillos and peacocks rubbing shoulders with mythical beasts, such as dragons and centaurs. The gallery is hung with portraits, including works by Thomas Hudson, who was a West Country painter, and George Romney, and cases

house an exceptional collection of sixteenth- and seventeenth-century books, among them a four-volume atlas of 1694 with delicate watercolour maps showing the Cornish landholdings of the 2nd Earl of Radnor, and also 28 works printed before 1500.

Like Coad's interiors, Lanhydrock's garden reflects Victorian taste. In front of the house, clipped yew marks the corners of six geometric shapes planted with roses in George Truefitt's formal layout of 1854 and more yew studs his intricate parterre beside the north wing, bedded out twice a year. Beyond the obelisks and castellations of the surrounding parapet, a large informal garden dating from the 1860s covers the steep slopes rising above the house. Winding paths through shrubs and trees, including exceptional displays of large Himalayan magnolias, rhododendrons and camellias, lead ever upwards,

ABOVE A disastrous fire in 1881 destroyed most of the main house at Lanhydrock, but the delicious gatehouse, built in 1651 as a hunting lodge from which to watch the pursuit of deer, was untouched.
OPPOSITE In the dairy, spring water from the hill above the house was channelled along runnels in the marble and slate slabs to keep butter, cheeses and puddings cool.

past the well used by the monks of St Petroc's Priory at Bodmin, who held Lanhydrock before the Dissolution, and the spring feeding the stream that runs down the slope. Vistas over the house and the wooded valley of the Fowey culminate in magnificent views from the broad terrace walk at the top of the garden and there is a network of paths across the wood- and parkland of the estate.

Lavenham Guildhall

Suffolk
Market Place, Lavenham

The medieval town of Lavenham, with streets of crooked half-timbered houses and a glorious late fifteenth-century church, is a monument to the prosperity brought by the Suffolk cloth industry, at its height in the fifteenth and early sixteenth centuries. Apart from the church, one of the finest buildings is the guildhall, which is prominently sited in the market square. Traditional timber-framing, its exuberant carving now heavily weathered, is limewashed to a pleasing silvery-grey, the upper floor is jettied out over the lower and both are lit with oriel windows. An ornate two-storey porch projects into the square and the building as a whole rests on a brick plinth, which deepens as the ground slopes away behind.

The hall was built in 1529 by the Guild of Corpus Christi, one of four religious and social guilds in the town. Less than 20 years later, when Henry VIII turned against the Roman Catholic Church, the guild was dissolved, and the guildhall was subsequently used as a town hall, prison and workhouse before being restored in 1887. The former meeting rooms of the guild, with moulded ceiling timbers and a floor of ancient oak, are at street level. The rooms above (probably let as storage to cloth merchants) now house a local history museum. Drawing on first-hand accounts, displays here tell the story of Lavenham from the boom years of the medieval cloth trade to the nineteenth century, when many buildings in the town were neglected and in a parlous state. The most unusual exhibit is a mummified cat that had been placed in a nearby roof to ward off evil spirits.

Dye plants in the walled garden were used in the production of medieval cloth. There is also a restored nineteenth-century lock-up and mortuary and a Newsham fire engine, thought to be the oldest in East Anglia.

ABOVE The wealth created by the Suffolk cloth industry in the fifteenth and early sixteenth centuries financed many buildings in Lavenham, among them the fine half-timbered guildhall in the market square.

Leith Hill Place

Surrey
On slopes of Leith Hill, south
of the A25 via Hollow Lane, ½ mile
(0.8 kilometre) north of the B2126

This tall, many-windowed house, with three-storey pedimented wings either side of a lower central block, lies high in the Surrey hills, with panoramic views over rolling wooded countryside to the far distant hump of the South Downs. This was a site chosen for its dramatic potential. The house is boldly set on a grassy platform below which, beyond another terrace and a ha-ha, the park falls sharply away. Behind the house, slopes rise steeply to Leith Hill, the highest point in south-east England. The most imposing façade, faced in stone, looks south towards the view. Here, a pedimented porch leads on to the terrace and pediments ornament the first-floor windows in the wings, but a tall, off-centre brick chimney disturbs the symmetry and there are homely dormer windows with horizontal sashes in the roof.

Originally a many-gabled Elizabethan mansion of local sandstone, some walling from which is exposed on the west side of the house, Leith Hill Place was remodelled in the early eighteenth century by Lieutenant-General John Folliot, who, although still often away on military campaigns, bought the estate in 1725, probably to establish himself as a country gentleman. As well as giving the exterior a fashionable Palladian coat, he also improved the interior, adding corridors on both the ground and first floors, so rooms could be accessed independently, and introducing some of the classical chimneypieces. A later owner, Richard Hull, built the tower which now crowns Leith Hill (see p.412) in 1765.

Apart from its glorious position, much of the interest of the house lies in its connection with the Wedgwood and Darwin families, and with the composer Ralph Vaughan Williams, whose mother was a Wedgwood. The association began in 1847, when Josiah Wedgwood III, known as Joe, grandson of the founder of the celebrated pottery firm, bought the house and moved there with his wife Caroline, née Darwin, and their three young daughters. The naturalist Charles Darwin was Caroline's brother and often came to the house. Charles fired his nieces with his intellectual curiosity, recruiting them to help with his observations of earthworms on Leith Hill. Caroline herself was a keen plantswoman and botanist, and it was she who established the Rhododendron Wood on the slopes of the

hill, either side of what was then the main carriageway to the house. She transformed two fields, planting them with the rhododendrons and azaleas that now, together with bluebells, form such a vivid springtime display, and she was probably also responsible for the giant redwoods towering above.

Ralph Vaughan Williams was Caroline's grandson. When his mother, Caroline's daughter, was left a widow in 1875, only seven years after she had married the Reverend Arthur Vaughan Williams, she decided to take her three young children, one of them the two-year-old Ralph, back to Leith Hill Place to live with her parents. Here Ralph spent his childhood. His aunt Sophy taught him to sing and to play the piano, and the Surrey countryside, with its lanes and woods, and the folk songs he heard on his wanderings, were to have a deep influence on his music.

It was Ralph who gave the house to the Trust when he inherited it on the death of his elder brother in 1944. Since then, until the Trust took it over again in 2008, the house has been tenanted, first by Wedgwood cousins, who were here until the 1960s, and most recently by Hurtwood House School, who boarded pupils in the house.

Today, the airy, well-proportioned main rooms, lit by long sash windows and furnished with comfortable sofas and two

BELOW Originally a many-gabled Elizabethan mansion, Leith Hill Place was given a fashionable Palladian exterior in the early eighteenth century.

grand pianos introduced by the Trust, are places to relax, to drink in the view, and to savour the unusually informal atmosphere. Ralph Vaughan Williams's music plays in the background. No original contents remain, but Ralph's 1903 Broadwood upright, its case the colour of rich honey, on which he composed most of his important works, among them *The Lark Ascending* and *Fantasia on a Theme by Thomas Tallis*, has been given to the house. And in the entrance hall, where Ralph once practised on a small organ while a servant pumped the bellows for him, is a bust of the composer by Maurice Juggins and an endearing sculpture of Ralph's cat, Foxy, who is shown purring beneath his master's hand.

Today, Leith Hill Place is a place in transition, as yet still showing the scuffed floors, tired paintwork and cracked plaster of years of neglect. All is being gradually renovated and school partitions have been removed from the drawing room on the first floor, where three long windows look out over what must be one of the best views in England. And visitors can treat themselves to scones baked in the kitchen at the east end of the house, where the original Aga is still in use.

BELOW From the terrace on the back of the house, there are panoramic views south over rolling wooded countryside to the distant hump of the South Downs.

Lindisfarne Castle

Northumberland
On Holy Island, 6 miles
(9.6 kilometres) east of the A1,
across the causeway

Accessible only by a causeway that is submerged for several hours at high tide, Holy Island feels like a place apart, a visit here like an adventure into the unknown. The castle is set on a dolerite crag at the far end of the island, its stone walls continuing the lines of the rock as if rising naturally from it. A cobbled approach curves steeply up the face of the crag to the entrance high above, a precipitous drop on one side, a cliff-like wall on the other. With views south to Bamburgh Castle and east over the water to the Farne Islands, this is an entrancingly romantic place, even when lashed by winter gales sweeping in from the North Sea.

Created in 1903 by the young Edwin Lutyens out of the shell of an originally Tudor fort, Lindisfarne's small rooms look backwards rather than forwards. There are Norman-style pillars, huge fireplaces, deeply recessed mullioned windows and rounded stone arches, and the castle's very individual charm is enhanced by the varied materials and floor levels that are characteristic of Lutyens. Herringbone brick floors are juxtaposed with stone, timber and slate. Some rooms are austerely whitewashed; in others, such as the dark Ship Room in the bowels of the building, where massively thick vaults arching overhead once protected the castle's magazine, the stone is left bare. With the exception of the kitchen, where a high-backed settle and armchairs are grouped round the leaded range, none of the rooms could be described as cosy, although carved English and Flemish oak furniture, blue-and-white Delftware and richly coloured carpets give a feel of seventeenth-century Dutch interiors.

The old fort would probably have been left to gradually decay if Edward Hudson, the founder of *Country Life*, had not happened upon it on a visit to the island and employed Lutyens to turn it into a summer retreat. Hudson was a hospitable man who loved to entertain, often holding house parties at the castle at which the celebrated cellist Madame Suggia used to play for her fellow guests.

A little walled garden lies on a sheltered south-facing slope to the north of the crag. The original planting scheme designed by Gertrude Jekyll, flowering in a mass of purple, grey, pink and burnt-orange in high summer, has been re-created.

Following major work to restore the fabric of the building, the contents of the castle are not all on show. Key pieces are celebrated in a rolling programme of exhibitions.

ABOVE Although Lindisfarne Castle's rooms are small and intimate, the use of much bare stone and slate and of Norman-style pillars gives the interior of the house an austere atmosphere.
RIGHT The castle is romantically set on Holy Island off the Northumbrian coast.

Little Moreton Hall

Cheshire
4 miles (6.4 kilometres) south-west
of Congleton, on the east side of
the A34 Newcastle road

The prosperous Moretons of Little Moreton Hall were powerful local landowners who profited, like many others, from the opportunities to acquire land after the Black Death of 1348, which almost halved the population, and after the dissolution of religious houses in the 1530s, when former monastic property was sold off. Between *c.* 1504, when the house was begun, and the mid-sixteenth century, the family doubled the size of their estates. As the Moretons grew richer, they enlarged their timber-framed, moated manor house, building additions that gradually embraced a central courtyard. The last major extension, adding a bakehouse and brewhouse, was in *c.* 1610. Most striking is the south range, erected in the 1560s. Whereas most of the hall is of two storeys, this range rises to a third floor, which is filled with a magnificent long gallery. Probably added as an afterthought while building was in progress, the gallery perches top-heavily on the house like a stranded Noah's Ark and has pulled the supporting timbers out of shape, so that the hall looks as if it might topple over. A projecting gatehouse links this range to the bridge over the moat.

Apart from three pieces, all the original furniture has disappeared and the rooms are mostly unfurnished. Nothing distracts from the quality of the building itself. Constructed in an age when wood was plentiful, the hall seems to have been devised to display the full range of the joiner's and carpenter's art, with timbers arranged in a huge variety of patterns to glorious effect. The confidence and pride of the carpenter who carried out work in 1559 is proclaimed in the inscription he left on one of the prominent bay windows built for William Moreton II: 'Rycharde Dale Carpeder made thies windovs by the grac of god.' The leaded panes are similarly unusual, with glazing patterns varying from room to room and even window to window. This craftsmanship in wood and glass, a testament to the ingenuity and skill of Tudor workmen, gives Little Moreton Hall its unique character.

The interior is a corridor-less warren, with one room leading into another and four staircases linking different levels. Some rooms are little more than cupboards and plainly decorated; others are much grander, with fine chimneypieces and panelling. There is a simple chapel, to which worshippers are still summoned on Sundays by a bell in the courtyard. Texts from the Bible painted on the chancel walls were probably added in *c.* 1580 at the same time as the decoration of the parlour, where a frieze crowning the elaborate painted panelling, the whole composition a rare example of sixteenth-century painted decoration, illustrates the story of Susannah and the Elders, a favourite Protestant theme. Characters are shown in contemporary Elizabethan dress, the blues and reds of their costumes still fresh and bright. In the long gallery, where the massive weight of the roof is taken by huge curved beams morticed and tenoned into the rafters, plasterwork picked out in orange and green at either end of the room depicts the virtues of hard work and the power of knowledge over superstition.

A hedge of hornbeam, holly, thorn and honeysuckle edges the moat, enclosing a lawn planted with fruit trees and a reconstruction of an Elizabethan knot garden, with box-edged compartments filled with gravel. Two prominent mounds were probably vantage points for surveying the surrounding countryside.

LEFT The south range is covered with decorative timber framing and pulled out of shape by the long gallery, with its immensely heavy roof of stone slates, that runs the length of the top floor.

Llanerchaeron

Ceredigion
Off the A482, 2½ miles
(4 kilometres) south-east
of Aberaeron

Just inland from Cardigan Bay and the sea, in the pastoral wooded valley of the Afon Aeron, is a rare survival of the small gentry estates that were such a mainstay of the economy of rural Wales in the eighteenth and nineteenth centuries. In the same family for ten generations, Llanerchaeron reflects a self-sufficient, country-oriented way of life that has largely vanished. By 1700, the estate had passed to the Lewis family and it was Colonel William Lewis, soon after he inherited in 1789, who commissioned the young John Nash to replace a mid-seventeenth-century house. Nash, who had retreated to Wales to recover from bankruptcy and was turning out a number of villas for the Welsh gentry at this time, incorporated the existing building in his plans and set the new house to take full advantage of views across the park. It is a charming mix of the conservative and the unexpected. The plain, well-proportioned late Georgian exterior, with stuccoed walls and a slate roof, is unexceptional, but Nash included decorative oval rooms on the first floor and a dramatic top-lit staircase, and there is subtle detailing, such as in the design of the plaster friezes, each of which is different.

The interior still has a sense of the family. Stuffed fish and woodcock, and an array of fox and otter heads, reflect their passion for hunting. The drawing room, with its ebonised cabinets and chairs by a late nineteenth-century Manchester cabinetmaker, is hung with family photographs and portraits, one a pastel by Lawrence of Colonel William, and the books in the library, assembled since 1918 when many of the contents of the house were sold, reflect their interest in the outdoors. Upstairs, one of the oval rooms is a boudoir with deliciously feminine plasterwork, the other a dressing room. Both have curved doors and a niche in each corner and the dressing room still has the mahogany cupboard and chest of drawers that were made for it in the eighteenth century.

A bell corridor flanked by the butler's pantry and the original light and airy kitchen leads to Nash's elegant service courtyard, ringed by a slate-slabbed walkway that is sheltered by deeply overhanging eaves. Eighteenth-century fittings still survive, among them solid slate cream pans in the dairy and original cheese presses. Beyond the courtyard is the detached, stone-walled billiard-room that was built in 1843 and which was designed with a prominent lantern in the centre of the roof to give an even light on the billiard-table beneath.

The surrounding park was landscaped in the spirit of the Picturesque, and ornamented with gothicised cottages. A church beside the drive was used as an eye-catcher in the views from the house and the now-abandoned track of the railway to Aberaeron, which the family encouraged, runs through the park. The family's sporting lifestyle comes through again in the home farm, where the buildings round the yard, mostly contemporary with the house, include kennels for otter hounds and elegant stables. Their importance in the local economy is seen in the little church, where estate employees once filled 40 of the 60 seats.

House, gardens and grounds have been restored by the National Trust. Vegetables, fruit and herbs are grown in the two walled gardens and the estate is run as a working farm. There are extensive walks across the park and estate.

RIGHT Deeply overhanging eaves shelter the slate walkways round Nash's elegant service courtyard.

Lodge Park

Gloucestershire
3 miles (4.8 kilometres) south-east
of Northleach, across the A40
from Sherborne village

On the open Cotswold plateau east of Cheltenham, with sweeping views towards the Thames Valley, is a unique survival of an early seventeenth-century grandstand set in a sporting landscape. The building is exquisite, its main façade positively crammed with architectural detail. Pedimented windows set shoulder to shoulder across the first floor carry bearded and moustachioed heads, there are exaggerated quoins, shell-headed niches and a columned portico supporting a wide balcony, and a massive classical chimneystack breaks the balustraded roofline.

This compact architectural caprice, more box than house, was built to overlook a broad, grassy track edged with dry-stone walls that still runs over a mile (1.6 kilometres) south from the A40. From the roof and balcony of the lodge, the well-to-do would watch and bet on dogs chasing fallow deer along the course, which finished at a shallow ditch in front of the grandstand. The lodge was built in the 1630s for the colourful John 'Crump' Dutton, a habitual gambler who was

effectively providing himself with his own race course. The interior had just two large rooms, one on each floor, above a basement kitchen, with a grand staircase to take the company up to the Great Room opening onto the balcony. Here they ate and watched the deer coursing, or went on up to the viewing platform on the roof. The designer of the lodge is believed to be Balthazar Gerbier, but the local mason-architect Valentine Strong may well have directed the work, drawing some of the detail from pattern books that illustrated the kind of Italianate features favoured by Inigo Jones. Crump had created a deer park too, but in the early eighteenth century the lodge was made the focus of a landscape by Charles Bridgeman, who planted wooded enclosures for the deer, artful clumps of trees and a double lime avenue leading away behind the building. This landscape is being restored.

At about the same time as Bridgeman's landscaping, the lodge was refurbished, probably to a scheme devised by William Kent. In later years, it was converted into estate cottages and, in the nineteenth century, when the gate lodges were added, turned into a house. The National Trust has returned it, as far as possible, to its original configuration, with a reconstructed Jacobean-style oak staircase leading to the Great Room and a lively modern re-creation, carved by masons of the Hereford Cathedral workshop, of the great hooded fireplace that was once here and which was moved to Sherborne House in the nineteenth century. There is a show of Dutton portraits on the walls. In the hall downstairs there are two of the side tables that were made for the lodge in *c.* 1730 and an atmospheric landscape by George Lambert depicts the open, well-wooded countryside of the 1740s, without the regular stone-walled fields that now dominate the view from the roof.

Lodge Park is part of the 4,106-acre (1,662-hectare) Sherborne estate. Straddling the A40 and the serene Windrush Valley, this largely agricultural holding includes much former parkland and most of Sherborne village. Strung out along

LEFT The Great Room at Lodge Park, designed for entertaining visitors, opens onto a wide balcony where guests enjoyed a grandstand view of deer coursing on a track in front of the house.
OPPOSITE Although isolated on the windswept Cotswold plateau, Lodge Park, built in the 1630s, has a main façade that is crammed with innovative Italianate detail in the latest fashion of the day.

the valley, this is a charming collection of mainly nineteenth-century, estate-built cottages in a Cotswold vernacular style, with gabled stone-tiled roofs and stone-mullioned windows. Most are south-facing, with gardens separating them from the road. The big house, seat of the family since the sixteenth century, was sold away in 1970, and the 7th Lord and Lady Sherborne lived at the lodge, where the fortune Lady Joan had inherited from her father, the Canadian multi-millionaire Sir James Hamet Dunn, financed a colourful lifestyle. On the 7th Lord's death, in 1982, the Sherborne estate came to the Trust; the peerage, which dates from 1784, died with the 7th Lord's cousin, Ralph Dutton of Hinton Ampner (*see* p.177).

Lyme

Cheshire
On the south side of the A6;
6½ miles (10.4 kilometres)
south-east of Stockport, entrance
on the western outskirts of Disley

Used to the blinding sun and hard shadows of his homeland, the Venetian architect Giacomo Leoni must have found it hard to contend with the grey skies and misty distances of the bleak Peak moors at Lyme when Peter Legh XII engaged him to remodel his largely Elizabethan mansion in 1725. Leoni responded by bringing a touch of Italy to the English countryside.

The courtyard of the Tudor house was ringed by shady arcades and given a double flight of steps rising to the pedimented entrance, as if it were the *cortile* of a grand *palazzo*. The Mediterranean effect was later enhanced by the addition of a marble pavement and an Italian Renaissance wellhead. The long south front is entirely Leoni. Built of rose-tinted local gritstone, it is dominated by a classical portico extending the full height of the house. Giant lead figures of Venus, Neptune and Pan set along the pediment stare at their reflection in the lake below and six bays separated by pilasters stretch away on either side. Something of the grand Elizabethan house survives on the north, where a towering Tudor gateway leads into Leoni's courtyard.

Despite much later remodelling, two Elizabethan interiors survive: a light and airy panelled long gallery hung with seventeenth- and early eighteenth-century portraits and the richly panelled former great chamber, now a drawing room. In the eighteenth century, although he was primarily involved with the exterior of the house, Leoni also created some internal spaces, of which his oak-panelled saloon, lit by windows looking over the park through the columns of his portico and adorned with a gilded rococo ceiling, has all the elegance of the period. Pale three-dimensional limewood carvings decorating the panelling were introduced from elsewhere in the house by Lewis Wyatt, whose alterations in the early nineteenth century were done with great sensitivity. One of these realistic compositions, which are traditionally attributed to Grinling Gibbons, cunningly intertwines an artist's palette and brushes,

a partly folded chart and navigation instruments. In another, an embroidered lace handkerchief falls in naturalistic folds.

A full-length portrait of the Black Prince in Leoni's grand classical entrance hall is a vivid reminder that the land of Lyme was won for the Legh family in 1346 on the battlefields of France. Lyme was to remain the home of the Leghs for nearly 600 years and many other aspects of the family history are

RIGHT The Venetian architect Giacomo Leoni, who was commissioned to remodel Lyme Park in the 1720s, was responsible for the Italianate south front, with its massive Ionic portico overlooking the lake.

reflected in the contents. A copy of Velázquez's *Las Meninas* portrays the celebrated mastiffs that were bred here until the twentieth century and were traditionally presented as royal gifts to the courts of Europe. The ancient Greek sculptures in the library, one of the interiors fashioned by Wyatt, were excavated in the early nineteenth century by the intrepid Thomas Legh, whose portrait in Turkish or Greek dress enlivens the staircase.

His grandest find, a stele of Melisto and Epigenes of *c.* 350BC, has pride of place over the fireplace, but the little tombstone of the same date in the window bay, commemorating a mother and her newborn babe, is more memorable. A tragedy of a different kind is recalled in the Stag Parlour, where faded red covers on the Chippendale chairs were reputedly made from the cloak Charles I wore on the scaffold. In the late twentieth

century the house was enriched by the magnificent collection of seventeenth- and eighteenth-century bracket and longcase clocks acquired by Sir Francis Legh, who was born at Lyme in 1919, the earliest of them an instrument by Ahasuerus Fromanteel of 1658, which was one of the first pendulum mechanisms ever produced. Five clocks by the outstanding London maker Thomas Tompion from the collection of Mr M.H. Vivian are now also on display. Most recently, the rare illuminated Missal that was printed for William Caxton in 1487, and probably acquired by Sir Piers Legh V on publication or soon afterwards, has returned home to Lyme.

There has been a garden on this unpromising site, carved out of moorland, since the seventeenth century. But the present layout and planting are essentially Victorian and owe much to William John Legh, 1st Lord Newton, who inherited in 1857 and took advice from the garden writer and theorist Edward Kemp. A sweep of grass running down to a naturalistic lake below the terrace on the south front, and the informal semi-wild area along the deep ravine carved by the stream feeding the lake, contrast with a series of formal gardens with massed bedding, one of which is overlooked by an orangery designed by Lewis Wyatt.

From the south and west terraces there are views across the lake to Lyme's medieval deer-park, 9 miles (14.4 kilometres) in circumference and already walled in Elizabethan times. Set dramatically on a windswept ridge high above the grazing herds broods the Cage, its stark outlines relieved by little domed turrets at each corner. Probably built to designs by Leoni as a hunting tower and banqueting house, it was modified in the early nineteenth century by Lewis Wyatt. This arresting eye-catcher is the building that approaching visitors see first.

Lytes Cary Manor

Somerset
1 mile (1.6 kilometres) north of
the Ilchester bypass on the A303

This enchanting manor house built of warm local limestone and set round a courtyard in the depths of rural Somerset bears the name of the family who lived here for 400 years, from the fourteenth to the eighteenth century. Rounded topiary yews line the flagged path leading to the entrance, where the swan of the Lyte family, wings half raised, crowns the gable of the porch. To the left is the oldest feature of Lytes Cary, the simple chapel built by Peter Lyte in *c.* 1343, attached to the house but only accessible from the outside. Family coats of arms in red, white and yellow stand out prominently on the painted frieze added in 1631 that enlivens the whitewashed interior and there is some medieval stained glass in the windows.

Although the appearance of the house today owes much to Sir Walter and Flora Jenner, who acquired it in a dilapidated state in 1907 and lovingly restored it, rebuilding the north and west ranges in an unobtrusive late seventeenth-century style and filling the rooms with appropriate furniture and china, Lytes Cary has a feeling of great age, of a place that has grown out of its surroundings. The Tudor great hall between the porch and the chapel, with a little oriel off it where the family would eat in privacy, away from their servants and retainers, rises the full height of the house to an open timber roof with carved angels on the ends of the rafters. On show in the hall is a copy of Henry Lyte's *Niewe Herball*, first published in 1578, which was translated from the work of the renowned Flemish herbalist Dodoens and dedicated to Queen Elizabeth I. Subsequently known as the *Lytes Herbal*, it was still being reprinted in 1678. Henry would have enjoyed the splendid plaster ceiling in the great chamber on the floor above, added by his father in the 1530s, the interlaced hexagons and diamonds studded with armorial bosses heralding Elizabethan plasterwork of a generation later. This room also has a fine interior porch covered in linenfold panelling and crested with trefoils.

Neglected after the departure of the Lytes in 1755, the house was being used to store cider and farm equipment when the Jenners bought it. The medieval and Tudor core is shown as Walter and Flora had it, furnished with high-quality

ABOVE With the exception of the eighteenth-century farmhouse wing to the right, the east front of Lytes Cary, with the traceried window of the little chapel on the far left, is medieval and Tudor.

seventeenth- and early eighteenth-century oak pieces and with fabrics in authentically medieval browns, olives and muted reds. Seat covers and panels decorated with vaguely Elizabethan embroidery are the work of Walter's sister-in-law, Nora Jenner, who, with her husband Leopold, Walter's brother, had bought the similarly neglected Avebury Manor (*see* p.33) in 1902.

Sir Walter and Flora also laid out the beautiful compartmental garden, with clipped yew hedges enclosing a series of outdoor rooms. A vivid mixed border punctuated with urns set between buttresses of yew leads to a long raised walk overlooking an orchard planted with the crab apples, medlars and quinces that the Elizabethans loved. Other yew compartments frame smoothly mown lawns and a fountain pool.

Lyveden

Northamptonshire
4 miles (6.4 kilometres)
south-west of Oundle via the
A427, 3 miles (4.8 kilometres)
east of Brigstock

Stretching up the side of a valley in an empty, rolling countryside of woods and meadows is one of the most important Elizabethan gardens in England, re-created by the Trust from what had been bumps and watery hollows in the grass. Laid out by Sir Thomas Tresham between 1595 and his death in 1605, the garden was designed to link his manor house deep in the valley with his new garden lodge, perched high on the ridge half a mile (0.8 kilometres) above. Sir Thomas was an ardent Catholic and both garden and lodge were devised to be symbolic as well as ornamental. From the manor, an orchard walk leads to a water garden with canals, a broad, raised terrace giving views over the valley and prospect mounds. A labyrinth path symbolising the pilgrimage through life is cut in the long grass of the central plot, echoing what is thought to have been Tresham's layout, and originally there would have been raspberries and roses too, recalling the blood and thorns of Christ's Passion.

Beyond is the lodge, an arresting roofless shell finely built of local limestone. The large mullioned and transomed windows are glassless, but would have given panoramic views over the countryside. Designed to be habitable, with a well-equipped basement kitchen and room for a small library, the lodge is also an expression in stone of Tresham's deeply held faith and the Elizabethan love of riddles and devices. It is built in the shape of an equal-armed cross and almost every feature alludes to numbers of religious significance. Five-sided bay windows refer to Christ's five wounds on the Cross, the seven instruments of the Passion are carved on the frieze between the ground and first floors, and the fragmentary remains of an 81-letter inscription running round the top of the building are a play on the number three, which refers both to the Trinity and the three-leaved clover of the Tresham emblem.

The lodge was intended to be a place of retreat and secret worship, but work on the building proceeded slowly, partly because Tresham's reckless elder son was a financial burden, and partly because of penalties for recusancy. Although loyal to Queen Elizabeth, after 1581, when the Catholic threat to England was at its greatest, Tresham was fined heavily and frequently arrested. He continued to direct operations from prison, but the lodge was never finished.

The gabled manor where visitors enter the garden was rebuilt by Tresham's son Lewis and has been much altered since. Its recent acquisition by the Trust means that manor, garden and lodge have been reunited for the first time since the seventeenth century and visitors can once again experience Lyveden as an upward journey, as Tresham intended.

LEFT The haunting roofless shell of the garden lodge, where the huge windows would have given panoramic views over the countryside around.

Melford Hall

Suffolk
In Long Melford on the west
side of the A134, 14 miles
(22.5 kilometres) south of
Bury St Edmunds, 3 miles
(4.8 kilometres) north of Sudbury

Set into the high brick wall bordering Long Melford's village green is a delicious octagonal banqueting house, with finials rising like brick fingers at every angle and from all eight gables. This giant doll's house, probably a survival from an early seventeenth-century formal garden, faces along a grassy terrace – the former bowling-green – to one of the most satisfying Tudor houses in East Anglia.

Looking east over the park, its back towards the village, is a U-shaped mansion of mellow pink brick, with two long gabled wings flanking the courtyard on the entrance front. A dramatic array of soaring chimneystacks and fanciful turrets crowned with onion domes breaks the roofline and there is also a two-storey Renaissance-style porch decorated with fluted pilasters. Although neither the builder nor the date of building is certain, the hall probably dates largely from the early sixteenth century, when the abbot of the great Benedictine house of St Edmundsbury (now known as Bury St Edmunds) enjoyed the estate as his private domain. By the Dissolution it had passed to Sir William Cordell, a shrewd and upwardly mobile lawyer, who at first leased the hall but was granted the property outright by Queen Mary in 1554. Despite subsequent alterations, such as the removal of the gatehouse range that once closed the courtyard, the disappearance of part of the moat, and the insertion of some early eighteenth-century sash windows, the exterior is still very much as Queen Elizabeth I must have seen it when she was entertained lavishly here in 1578. The interior was substantially altered twice, first in the 1730s, when the principal rooms were given fashionable rococo decoration, and again in the nineteenth century, when Thomas Hopper injected Regency touches in a Greek Revival style.

The house was ransacked during the Civil War, when looters left the cellars knee-deep in beer, and suffered a devastating fire in 1942, which destroyed most of the rococo decoration, but

ABOVE When the north wing of the Hall was rebuilt after being gutted by fire in 1942, it was redecorated in Scandinavian style, with white walls and uncarpeted floors, reflecting the taste of Lady Ulla.
LEFT The staircase in the north wing of Melford Hall has three balusters to a tread, each carved to a different pattern, and other fine decorative detail.

recovery from both disasters was swift and there are still echoes of the Cordells, who were here for 250 years, and a strong sense of the seafaring Parker family, notable for producing no fewer than three admirals, who bought the hall, with most of its furnishings, in 1786. Although transformed by Hopper, who introduced the grand processional staircase, the panelled great hall still has its Tudor shape and is hung with a collection of seventeenth-century portraits. The old oak furniture, which also seems so fitting, was introduced by the antiquarian Sir William Parker, 9th Baronet, in the late nineteenth century. Also here is the survey of the estate that Sir William Cordell commissioned in 1580; every field is named and the long strip of the village green with the church at one end is clearly shown.

Hopper was also responsible for the splendid Regency Library with its curved oak bookshelves, florid Greek couches and armchairs appropriately decorated with owls. Paintings by Dominic Serres of historic naval engagements fought by

the 5th Baronet, Vice Admiral Sir Hyde Parker, and his second son, also an admiral, line the library walls, one of the most memorable showing fireships drifting on the tide towards a British fleet on the Hudson River on 16 August 1776, during the American War of Independence. The 5th Baronet, who ran away from school to join the merchant navy and worked his way up through the ranks to become the most technically skilled admiral of his day, appears as a larger-than-life figure in a portrait by Romney in the little octagon off the main library. This exceptional man was also responsible for much of the Chinese porcelain displayed in the house, which he took as prize booty from a Spanish galleon laden with gold and precious things that he captured in 1762. Twenty-one years later, aged 70, the 5th Baronet set sail from England to take up the East Indies command, but, after calling in at Rio de Janeiro, his ship was never seen again; with him on board was his grandson Harry, who was only 14 years old.

A dining room in the part of the house that was damaged by the fire was decorated in Scandinavian style, with cool white

ABOVE Melford Hall's west front, with later corner blocks framing the octagonal turrets and soaring chimneystacks of the Tudor building, provides a dramatic backdrop to the garden.

walls and a polished stone floor, by Ulla, the Danish wife of the 11th Baronet, and the house also has connections with Beatrix Potter, whose cousin married the 10th Baronet. Some of the illustrations for *Jeremy Fisher* were sketched at the hall's old fish ponds and on show is the room where Beatrix slept, her menagerie of animals being accommodated in an adjoining turret, and the model of Jemima Puddleduck, neatly dressed in a blue poke bonnet, which she gave to the Hyde Parker children.

Lawns studded with domes of box and planted with specimen trees set off the mellow brickwork of the west front and are framed by an undulating crinkle-crankle wall on one side and by the bowling-green terrace on the other. The north arm of the moat is now a sunken garden by the terrace but the west arm still runs along the village green, past some intriguing topiary figures outside the garden wall.

Mompesson House

Wiltshire
In Salisbury, on the north side of Choristers' Green in the Cathedral Close, near High Street Gate

Salisbury's leafy cathedral close, bordered by an array of dignified old houses, seems the perfect setting for Anthony Trollope's Barsetshire novels. Mrs Proudie, the bishop's domineering wife in *Barchester Towers*, would certainly have been at home in Mompesson House, with its beautiful sash-windowed Queen Anne façade rising to a hipped roof. In early summer, two white magnolias soften the grey Chilmark limestone that faces the house. Inside, elegant airy rooms with eighteenth-century plasterwork and marble chimneypieces look over the close towards the cathedral spire soaring above the rooftops.

The house was built in 1701 by Charles Mompesson, whose initials adorn the hopper heads, but the sumptuous stucco decoration by an unknown hand was commissioned by his brother-in-law and heir Charles Longueville. The most spectacular plasterwork is in the staircase hall, where the bold and florid design includes flowers, fruit, satyrs' masks and the head of King Midas with ass's ears. In the Green Room,

an eagle with outspread wings crouches in the middle of the ceiling, ready to pounce.

Later residents have also left their mark. Cool seascapes and a scene of peaceful domesticity are among several watercolours by Barbara Townsend, one of the three daughters of George Barnard Townsend, a local solicitor who came to Mompesson in the mid-nineteenth century. Living on here until her death at the age of 96 in 1939, Barbara became a legend in the close, continuing to sketch and paint right up to the end of her life, a tiny figure wrapped in layers of shawls, scarves and veils. In 1952 Mompesson was purchased by the architect and connoisseur Denis Martineau, who restored the house and left it to the National Trust in 1975. Coming to the Trust without any contents, Mompesson has been refurnished with pieces appropriate to its Georgian heyday and now displays the Turnbull collection of over 370 English eighteenth-century glasses and eighteenth-century English porcelain figures from the William Bessemer Wright collection.

The high wall of the close bounds the secluded garden at the back of the house, where a wisteria- and rose-covered pergola provides welcome shade on hot summer afternoons. The old privy is hidden behind a tree in one corner.

LEFT The beautiful Queen Anne façade of Mompesson House, looking onto the cathedral close at Salisbury, is built of grey Chilmark limestone and is half-smothered by two venerable magnolias.

Monk's House

East Sussex
4 miles (6.4 kilometres)
south-east of Lewes, off the former
A275 (now the C7) in Rodmell
village, near the church

This modest weather-boarded house at the far end of Rodmell village was the home of one of the most innovative novelists of the twentieth century. By 1919, when Virginia Woolf and her husband Leonard bought the property as a retreat from London life, Virginia's first two novels had been completed, but the experimental work that was to establish her reputation, in particular *To the Lighthouse, The Waves* and *Mrs Dalloway*, was still in the future. Two years earlier, at their house in Richmond, she and Leonard had founded the Hogarth Press, whose outstanding list, which included works by T.S. Eliot, Katherine Mansfield, E.M. Forster and Sigmund Freud, was to make a major contribution to literary life. Retreating to Monk's House enabled the Woolfs to indulge their passions for gardening and walking. Surrounded on all sides by the chalk hills of the South Downs, for Virginia this was somewhere she could 'spread out her mind', as she wrote in her diary on 11 June 1922.

The house looks as if the Woolfs were still living here and is full of reminders of the talented circle in which Virginia

and Leonard moved. Painted furniture in a post-Impressionist style by Virginia's sister Vanessa Bell and the artist Duncan Grant, who lived with Vanessa at Charleston across the Downs, includes a table and chairs in the sitting room: muted abstract designs picked out in blue and olive-green by Vanessa set off a panel of suns painted on the front of each chair back. Books are piled on one of Duncan's tile-topped tables and a formidable portrait of Einstein in old age, his face only half-lit, is one of a number of telling photographs. Ceramics on the mantelpiece were decorated by Duncan Grant, Vanessa Bell and her son Quentin, and their work also fills the top half of the dresser in the tiny kitchen.

Every room is hung with paintings by the family circle, including Italian and Sussex landscapes and tranquil still-lifes, apples or a jug of flowers, by Vanessa, as well as some of her distinctive portraits, one of them a haunting likeness of her sister. Flowering potted plants come from the greenhouse where Leonard nurtured the begonias, lilies and gloxinias with which he filled the house. A fish tank behind the sitting-room door recalls his habit of looking after ailing fish from the garden ponds, and the dogs' blue pottery water bowl is still in its place.

In these modest rooms the Woolfs entertained some of the best-known literary and artistic figures of the day, among them Vita Sackville-West, John Maynard Keynes, Lytton Strachey, E.M. Forster, David Garnett and Roger Fry. A black Chinese silk shawl embroidered in pink and green that is casually thrown over a chair in Virginia's sunny bedroom at the east end of the house was a present from Lady Ottoline Morrell. Many visitors were members of the Bloomsbury Group, which Virginia and Vanessa had founded with their brother Thoby Stephen and which was to give the sisters an influence far beyond their own work.

Near the house, Leonard turned the remains of outbuildings into a series of garden rooms. Informal cottagey plantings spill over brick paths and busts of Virginia and Leonard sit on the flint wall of the former piggery. The garden continues into grass and trees; there is a dewpond, an orchard and the lawn where the Woolfs played bowls. Here the view opens out, and from the weather-boarded shed where Virginia wrote there is a wide panorama east towards the River Ouse and a spur of the South Downs beyond. Her battered desk still fills the room.

ABOVE Virginia Woolf loved her sunny bedroom at the east end of Monk's House, from which she could look out on the garden, and which has tiles decorated by her sister Vanessa round the fireplace.

OPPOSITE Virginia wrote in a weather-boarded shed at the end of the garden, looking out towards the Ouse and the South Downs beyond.

Montacute House

Somerset
In Montacute village, 4 miles (6.4 kilometres) west of Yeovil, on the south side of the A3088, 3 miles (4.8 kilometres) east of the A303

This prodigy house is one of the most magical of Elizabethan buildings. Constructed of local honey-brown Ham stone to an H-shaped plan, and with a huge display of glittering glass, it was built for Sir Edward Phelips, an upwardly mobile lawyer who would become Master of the Rolls and Chancellor to the Household of Prince Henry, Charles I's ill-fated elder brother. Almost certainly designed by a local stonemason, the gifted William Arnold (*see also* Dunster Castle, p.129), it was probably started in *c.* 1595 and finished by 1601.

Long façades facing east and west rise three storeys to a roofline fretted with delicate chimneys, parapets and pinnacles and adorned with curved Flemish gables. Classical details on the entrance front, such as the nine curiously lumpy statues in Roman dress, betray the influence of the Renaissance, slowly filtering north from its beginnings in Italy. The other side of the house is even more engaging. In 1786 a new two-storey west front was slotted in between the existing wings to provide linking corridors on both floors. Internally, this meant the bedrooms on the first floor, which had previously led one into another, now had privacy, while externally the new wall surfaces were animated with ornamental stonework salvaged from Clifton Maybank, a splendid sixteenth-century mansion nearby that was being partly demolished. Heraldic beasts on pedestals crowd the parapet of the 1780s addition, enhancing the sculptural quality of the whole façade. Montacute's fantasy outline is continued in the spiky balustrade and the two delightful Elizabethan pavilions topped with obelisks that border the entrance court.

The decline in the Phelipses' fortunes led to Montacute being put up for sale in 1929. It was rescued by Ernest Cook, who was able to draw on the fortune made from the sale of his grandfather's travel company, and presented to the Trust. But, apart from some family portraits, the contents had been sold. Following an appeal in *The Times*, the house was refurnished with loans and gifts, among them fine period furniture, tapestries and pictures bequeathed by the industrialist Sir Malcolm Stewart.

These donated clothes contribute to Montacute's individual character. In the great hall, the early morning sun casts richly

ABOVE The local honey-coloured limestone of which Montacute is built is now attractively weathered and lichened.

RIGHT Montacute's east front, with ornate Flemish gables on the projecting wings and great windows lighting every floor, reflects a new vogue for symmetry, but the interior plan, with a great hall at the centre of the house, is conservative.

OPPOSITE Early seventeenth-century plasterwork in the great hall shows a village drama, in which a man is being punished after his wife caught him drinking when he should have been minding the baby.

coloured pools through the heraldic glass in the east-facing windows. Phelips family portraits hang above the original panelling and an elaborate stone screen with columns framing rusticated arches runs across one end. Rams' heads with extravagant curling horns are carved on the capitals of the columns. A rare early seventeenth-century plaster panel on the north wall gives a tableau of rural life: a hen-pecked husband caught by his wife drawing beer from a barrel rather than attending to the baby is punished by being paraded round the village astride a pole.

The room where Lord Curzon slept when he leased Montacute in the early twentieth century has an ingenious bath concealed in a Jacobean-style cupboard and the former great chamber, with its majestic carved stone chimneypiece, the finest in the house, has the only original furniture, a set of six early eighteenth-century walnut cane-back armchairs. A rich collection of hangings includes a fine fifteenth-century French

millefleurs tapestry showing a knight on horseback against a beautifully detailed carpet of flowers, and the importance of domestic needlework in past centuries is illustrated in a changing display of samplers from the collection formed by Dr Douglas Goodhart, which ranges in date from 1609 to the twentieth century.

A magnificent long gallery, the largest surviving Elizabethan example in Britain, runs the length of the third floor. This cool and airy room, over 170 feet (50 metres) long, is lit by an array of windows looking east towards the park and by oriels at both ends. It is shown sparsely furnished, as it would have been, as a space for walking and for enjoying the views from the windows. At night, with candles lit, the top of the house would have looked like a glittering lantern. Former bedchambers to either side, and the spacious corridor linking rooms on the floor below, are hung with Tudor and Jacobean portraits, most of which are on loan from the National Portrait

ABOVE In the 1780s, the Elizabethan west front of Montacute was embellished with ornamental stonework from another Tudor house, which gives this façade a dramatic and theatrical quality.

Gallery, in a display that echoes the family's connections and significance.

Among key figures of the age portrayed here are Bess of Hardwick, builder of another great Elizabethan house (*see* p.169), the poet Thomas Wyatt, who briefly held the lease of monastic lands at Montacute, and the diplomat and scholar Sir Edward Hoby, seen in a portrait by George Gower. Particularly memorable is the likeness of the seven-year-old Henry, Prince of Wales, the child's creamy pallor emphasised by his rich crimson dress. Rush matting running the length of the long gallery mirrors that on which the prince is standing. Of particular significance is the portrait of James I that was probably presented to Sir Edward Phelips by the king. Sold by the Phelips family in the 1980s, it was recently bought at auction thanks to the generosity of Moira Carmichael. Fine paintings elsewhere in the house, including portraits by Gainsborough, Reynolds and Lawrence, were part of the Stewart bequest.

Although now incorporating both nineteenth- and twentieth-century features and planting schemes, the extensive garden still follows the outlines of the original layout. The oriel window at the north end of the long gallery looks down on a formal rectangle of trees and grass which lies on the site of the Elizabethan garden. Raised walks framing the sunken lawn with its nineteenth-century balustraded pond probably date from when the house was built and a border of shrub roses under the retaining wall includes species in cultivation in the sixteenth century. The cedar lawn, with an arcaded garden house to which Lord Curzon may have added the Elizabethan façade, lies on the site of an old orchard.

An avenue of mature cedars, beeches and limes, fronted by clipped Irish yew, frames the west drive created in 1851–2, its lines continued in the wide grassy ride edged with limes which stretches away across the park to the east.

Moseley Old Hall

West Midlands
4 miles (6.4 kilometres) north of
Wolverhampton; south of the M54
between the A449 and the A460

In the early hours of 8 September 1651, five days after his defeat at the Battle of Worcester, Charles II in the guise of a woodcutter came through a gate at the end of the garden and moved silently up the flagged path leading to the house. Waiting in the dark outside were Thomas Whitgreave, the owner of Moseley, and his priest, Father John Huddlestone. The king was escorted through the heavily studded back door and, by the light of a candle, directed up the narrow stairs to the priest's room, now known as the King's Room.

Here he sat sipping a glass of wine while his sore feet were soothed, watching the firelight playing over the hangings of the four-poster bed where he was to spend his first night in comfort since the battle. Here, too, he was shown the hiding place, too small for a man to stand, which was concealed under a trapdoor in the cupboard to the right of the fireplace. Here Charles crouched when the Parliamentarians came to the house two days later. The night after this traumatic experience, the king mounted a horse brought to the orchard stile and rode away, disguised as a serving man, on the first leg of his long and hazardous journey to safety on the Continent.

Visitors retrace Charles's route on that fateful night 370 years ago when the Stuart cause was nearly lost. Although the half-timbered Elizabethan house that the king would have seen was encased in brick in 1870 and the mullioned windows have been replaced by casements, Moseley still has its tall Elizabethan chimneys, much of the original panelling and timber framing survives inside, and seventeenth-century oak furniture, including the bed on which Charles slept, and contemporary portraits of the king and those who helped him, all contribute to an evocative atmosphere, miraculously not yet destroyed by noise from the nearby M54 and creeping urbanisation. If you could stand at the window of Whitgreave's study over the front porch, as he and the king did, it would be possible to imagine that the remnants of the defeated Stuart army would shortly appear, straggling up the lane on their long walk back to Scotland. Mementoes of those perilous days include a proclamation of 10 September 1651, offering a £1,000 reward for the capture of the king, and Charles II's letter of thanks to Jane Lane, who accompanied him when he rode away from Moseley.

The house is now surrounded by a reconstructed seventeenth-century garden. In the knot garden, based on a design of 1640, delicate box hedges trace out a geometric pattern like a wrought-iron screen. Each compartment is filled with coloured gravels and stones and some are studded with box spheres. The orchard has been planted with old varieties of fruit trees; quinces, mulberries and medlars frame the path from the Nut Alley to the house, and more box hedges embrace a little herb garden. Perhaps the king saw a similar garden from the chapel windows when John Huddlestone took him to visit the oratory in the attic, now adorned with an eighteenth-century painted barrel ceiling. Charles was certainly to remember Moseley, giving Thomas Whitgreave a pension of £200 a year on his restoration in 1660 and summoning Huddlestone to administer the last rites of the Catholic Church when he lay dying in 1685.

BELOW Moseley Old Hall is where the young Charles II, on the run from the Parliamentarians, was sheltered for two days after the devastating defeat of his army at Worcester in 1651.

Mottisfont

Hampshire
4½ miles (7.2 kilometres)
north-west of Romsey, ¾ mile
(1.2 kilometres) west of the A3057

Those lucky enough to acquire monastic houses when they were dissolved in the 1530s were then faced with the problem of transforming the buildings into a domestic residence. Most chose to adapt the monks' living quarters, but a few ambitious men sought to incorporate the monastery church into their conversions. One such was William Lord Sandys, Lord Chamberlain to Henry VIII, who was granted the priory of Mottisfont in exchange for the villages of Chelsea and Paddington and whose descendants were to move here from The Vyne (*see* p.357) after the Civil War. The north front of his Tudor house, built of silvery stone, runs the full length of what was the nave of the church, ending in the truncated crossing tower. The outline of the arch leading to the north transept shows clearly on the wall of the tower. Original mullions survive on the ground floor, but sash windows were inserted above as part of extensive Georgian alterations. These also account for the eighteenth-century stone balls crowning the medieval buttresses, transforming them into ornamental pilasters.

The cultured world of the 1740s is far more pronounced on the south side, where an elegant red-brick Georgian façade with a central pediment is framed by two shallow bayed wings stepped out from the main body of the house. Three storeys here, in contrast to two on the north, reflect the sloping site.

Few traces of the Tudor interior escaped the Georgian remodelling, but the ghost of the priory emerges in the atmospheric early thirteenth-century cellarium, where columns of Caen stone, now partly buried, support a vaulted roof. The most individual feature of the house, the Whistler Room over the cellarium, is a much later addition. This enchanting drawing room takes its name from Rex Whistler's elaborate *trompe-l'oeil* murals, imitating gothick plasterwork, which he painted in 1938–9, after the completion of his mammoth work at Plas Newydd (*see* p.272). More theatrical backdrop than room decoration, Whistler's work includes the illusion of a smoking urn and of a paint pot abandoned high on a cornice. He was also asked to design the furniture for this room, but he never returned from the Second World War to complete his assignment.

Whistler had been commissioned by Mottisfont's last owner, Maud Russell, who bought the estate, with her husband Gilbert, in 1934, restored and modernised the house, creating comfortable interiors, and invited artists, writers and politicians for legendary weekend parties. Whistler's sketches for the drawing-room murals, and some idyllic landscapes that were offered as an alternative decorative scheme, are now part of a wider assemblage of late nineteenth- and twentieth-century art shown in the house. Apart from the Whistler drawings, these are all from the collection of the artist Derek Hill (1916–2000), who was a friend of Maud Russell. Consisting largely of intimate pieces, many of them drawings, pastels or gouaches, the collection includes works by Bonnard, Vuillard, Seurat, Corot and Degas, but the main focus is on British artists, among them L.S. Lowry, Barbara Hepworth, Graham Sutherland and Augustus John, who is represented by a gentle portrait of his sister Gwen, and paintings by Hill's former students at the British School in Rome, where he was art director in the 1950s. There are also landscapes by Hill himself. The collection is shown in a rotating display hung in the library, morning room, entrance hall and west corridor and further twentieth-century works and contemporary art can be seen in changing exhibitions in the light and airy gallery on the top floor of the house.

Lying low on sweeping lawns by the River Test, the abbey is the centrepiece of beautiful wooded gardens. Many of the mature walnuts, sycamores, Spanish chestnuts, beeches and cedars for which the property is now famous were part of the eighteenth-century grounds, but some are even older. A little gothick summer-house also dates from the eighteenth century and incorporates medieval floor tiles and a corbel from the priory.

Mr and Mrs Gilbert Russell, who came to Mottisfont in 1934, introduced features designed by Geoffrey Jellicoe

OPPOSITE The medieval
priory that was established at
Mottisfont in 1201 emerges
most clearly in the cellarium,
where columns of Caen stone,
now partly below floor level,
support a fine vaulted roof.
RIGHT A former entrance
hall at Mottisfont Abbey was
decorated in 1938–9 by Rex
Whistler, whose *trompe l'oeil*
fantasy, set off by the rich green
velvet curtains, includes trophy
panels painted in grisaille.

and, later, Norah Lindsay, among them the paved octagon surrounded by clipped yew and the box- and lavender-edged parterre. There is also a magnolia garden and a beech circle, and two walled gardens contain Mottisfont's renowned collection of roses. On the far side of the grounds, crystal-clear water still gushes from the spring that attracted the Austin canons to this sheltered spot nearly 800 years ago.

BELOW Although the south front of Mottisfont Abbey largely dates from the 1740s, the house incorporates the remains of a medieval priory, the cloister of which was on the site of the box parterre.

Mount Grace Priory

North Yorkshire
6 miles (9.6 kilometres) north-east of Northallerton, ½ mile (0.8 kilometre) east of the A19 and ½ mile (0.8 kilometre) south of its junction with the A172

The simplicity and austerity of this little Carthusian priory on the edge of the wooded Cleveland Hills is far removed from the splendour of Fountains, which is only some 20 miles (32 kilometres) to the south (see p.147). Whereas the remains of the Cistercian house speak of an increasing relaxation of the principles on which it was founded, Mount Grace reflects the pursuit of asceticism, untouched by worldly concerns. The Carthusians were more hermits than monks, living apart from each other as well as in isolation from what went on outside the priory walls. Whereas other orders ate, prayed and slept together, each Carthusian was mostly alone in his cell, to which meals were brought.

The main feature of Mount Grace is an extensive grass cloister, measuring some 270 feet (82 metres) on its longest side. Ranged around it, and along one side of an outer court, are the remains of the stone-built, four-roomed cells where the little community – there is provision for only 21 monks – spent long hours in prayer and contemplation and in copying out devotional works. Most of the cells still show the hatch through which food was served from the cloister, the right-angled bend ensuring that monk and server did not see one another. And each monk had his own walled garden, some 20 feet (6 metres) square, with his own garderobe at the far end. Perhaps some of the community allowed themselves to sit here and doze in the sun on warm summer afternoons.

On the north side of the cloister is the diminutive church, a plain, simple building that was rarely used except on Sundays and feast days, its little battlemented and pinnacled tower a telling contrast to Marmaduke Huby's soaring monument at Fountains Abbey.

But although Mount Grace turned its back on the world, the community was not averse to modern conveniences. Arched recesses still visible in the cloister walls of some cells once held taps fed from springs on the hillside above the priory. Spring water was also channelled to flush the drain serving the garderobes, some of which still project from the garden walls on the north side of the precinct.

Mount Grace was founded in 1398 by Thomas de Holland, Duke of Surrey and Earl of Kent, and is one of only nine Charterhouses established in England, most of them part of the great Carthusian expansion between 1343 and 1414. It was surrendered quietly to Henry VIII's commissioners in December 1539. Lord Darcy Conyers, who acquired Mount Grace by marriage in 1616, was probably responsible for converting the range housing the priory's guest accommodation and kitchens into the long gabled manor house flanking the outer court. The projecting two-storey porch was added in 1654 and in 1900–1 the architect Ambrose Poynter remodelled the manor in Arts and Crafts style for Sir Lowthian Bell. Restored interiors on show include the drawing room, which boasts an original William Morris

carpet, and visitors can also see the attics which were used as a nursery in the 1920s and '30s. Sir Lowthian Bell also built the reconstructed cell, like a tiny, two-storeyed cottage, on the north side of the cloister, the fireplace in its living room suggesting a degree of comfort in winter. It has since been rebuilt by English Heritage, who manage the property. For those who lived like hermits here, physical privation was probably not the greatest challenge. The cells would have been a spiritual sanctuary for the strong and resolute, but a prison for those who found they could not live with themselves or began to doubt their faith.

Mount Stewart

Co. Down
15 miles (24 kilometres) east
of Belfast on the A20
Newtownards–Portaferry road,
5 miles (8 kilometres) south-east
of Newtownards

Set on the Ards peninsula overlooking Strangford Lough, and surrounded by the most magical of gardens, Mount Stewart has one of the most beautiful positions of any house in Ireland. Home of the Vane-Tempest-Stewarts, Marquesses of Londonderry, it is alive with the spirit of Edith, Marchioness of Londonderry, the vivacious and brilliant wife of Charles, the 7th Marquess, who redecorated and furnished most of the house between the First and Second World Wars and, together with her head gardener, Thomas Bolas, created the exceptional gardens. A bust in the Black and White Hall portrays the linen merchant Alexander Stewart who acquired the estate in 1744, and whose descendants live here now. However, the 7th Marquess's immediate predecessors, although they still visited Ireland, generally lived elsewhere, and it was only when Edith and Charley decided to make Mount Stewart a more permanent home in the 1920s that it became a family house once again. As a result of a recent £8 million restoration, Mount Stewart has been returned to how it was in its heyday, from the 1920s to the 1950s, when Edith held convivial house parties here. Following the death of the 9th Marquess in 2012, this memorable place has also been enriched by a loan of over 700 items from the estate of the Marquess of Londonderry. This outstanding collection includes 11 portraits of the family by Sir Thomas Lawrence, furniture, sculpture, ceramics and other pieces, such as the silver now displayed in the former gun room.

The long, two-storey main block, built of dark grey local stone and with a huge classical portico looking onto the balustraded entrance court, was created in the 1840s, when Charles, 3rd Marquess, and his wife, Frances Anne Vane-Tempest, daughter of a coal-mining magnate, decided to remodel and enlarge the original eighteenth-century building. It is possible that the renowned Irish architect William Vitruvius Morrison was involved in the design, but the local architect-builder Charles Campbell, who was in charge of

RIGHT The early nineteenth-century west front, by John Ferguson, a local builder-architect, overlooks the sunken garden.

the work, undoubtedly had a hand in the plans. Filling the centre of the house is a dramatic octagonal hall, lit from above by a huge dome and ringed by double pairs of wooden Ionic columns, painted to imitate marble. Classical statues are set off by stone-coloured decoration replicating the scheme that was here in the 1840s and the original stone floor, which had been hidden under black-and-white linoleum, has been uncovered. The vast drawing room divided by screens of green Ionic columns is similarly imposing and gave Edith just the setting she needed for her lavish entertaining.

The west wing, built for Robert, the 1st Marquess in the early nineteenth century, and constructed of the same grey stone as the later work, has a lighter and more intimate touch. Robert approached the Neo-classical architect George Dance the Younger to design the new wing, but although Dance advised on the plans, the detail was worked out and executed by another local man, the builder-architect and joiner John Ferguson. Edith and Charley created private suites in this wing, installing a new spiral staircase to link their sitting rooms on the ground floor with bedrooms and bathrooms above. The least changed of the interiors in this part of the house is the Breakfast Room, where a beautiful parquetry floor by Ferguson is a composition in oak, holly and mellow bog fir. Delicate plasterwork on the ceiling reflects the design. Double doors lead into the elegant staircase hall where George Stubbs's intriguing painting of a racehorse, *Hambletonian, Rubbing Down*, hangs half way up the stairs. Commissioned by Frances Anne's father, Sir Henry Vane-Tempest, who owned the horse, it commemorates Hambletonian's win at Newmarket in 1799. The 75-year-old Stubbs, whose masterpiece this was, thought the animal had been driven too hard and shows him after the race in a state of exhaustion. Hambletonian dominates the painting, towering over the stable boy who is rubbing him down in an image that suggests the power and strength of the horse as well as his fatigue.

The principal bedrooms called after European cities (Rome, Geneva, Paris) and 22 giltwood Empire-style chairs used during the Congress of Vienna in 1814–15 recall Viscount

RIGHT George Stubbs's painting of the racehorse Hambletonian, shown in a state of exhaustion after winning a race at Newmarket in 1799, hangs half way up the main staircase.

Castlereagh, son of the 1st Marquess and British Foreign Secretary for ten years. The main architect of the Act of Union of 1801 that united Great Britain and Ireland until the creation of Eire in 1921, Castlereagh went on to play a major role in the war against Napoleon and in the Congress of Vienna that concluded it, regarded as the world's first summit. The European boundaries established at this time lasted until the start of the First World War. The kneehole Austrian Empire desk at which the Treaty of Vienna was signed now stands in the Drawing Room, with Lawrence's full-length portrait of Castlereagh, by now 2nd Marquess of Londonderry, in his garter robes above it, his confident bearing showing nothing of the strains that would lead him to take his own life in 1822.

The 6th and 7th Marquesses also followed prominent political careers, and both Edward VII and the future George VI were entertained at Mount Stewart. As Secretary of State for Air from 1931 to 1935, the 7th Marquess promoted the development of the Hurricane and Spitfire fighter planes which were to prove so crucial in the Battle of Britain in 1940, and introduced legislation to establish air corridors. And in the late 1930s he made several private visits to Germany to meet Hitler and other Nazi leaders in an effort to promote Anglo-German understanding.

Leading politicians, among them Sir Arthur Balfour, Harold Macmillan and Ramsay MacDonald, featured at the celebrated house parties that Edith gave in the interwar years. Her original 1920s decor, with most rooms decorated in cream and off-white, was replaced in the last decade of her life by rich and flamboyant colour schemes and these now give Mount Stewart much of its special character. Salmon-pink walls in the Drawing Room set off a green grand piano and comfortable chairs and sofas are spread invitingly on the pink Aubusson carpets. Subdued low-level lighting comes from lamps of every description, some made out of classical urns, others once altar candlesticks. Chinese tea caddies converted into lamp stands, chinoiserie screens and other oriental pieces were brought back from a trip to China in 1912.

A great beauty, Edith's charm is if anything enhanced by the drab khaki she is wearing in the portrait by de Laszlo in the Black and White Stone Hall showing her in the uniform of the Women's Legion, which Edith founded. One of three likenesses of Lady Londonderry by de Laszlo, this painting is part of an exceptional collection of family portraits now in the house. Apart from the works by Lawrence, there are portraits by Sir John Lavery, who was a frequent visitor, and also by the less well known Edmond Brock, who used one of the bedrooms as a studio and, among other things, produced four enchanting studies of Edith's youngest daughter Mairi, then a little girl, who was later to inherit Mount Stewart and gave it to the Trust, together with much of the contents, in 1976.

Mount Stewart's enchanting 97-acre (39-hectare) garden flourishes with subtropical luxuriance in the mild microclimate of the Ards peninsula. Edith sponsored every plant hunter of her day and acquired exotic plants and seeds from everyone she could, filling the garden with rare and tender species. Many of the trees and shrubs cultivated here are rarely seen elsewhere in the British Isles and an abundance of rhododendrons and lilies reflects Edith's particular fondness for these plants. Around the house a formal garden is laid out as a series of varied outdoor rooms. An Italian garden, with steps descending to fountain pools, was designed by Edith, her delight in the whimsical showing in the row of pillars carved with the faces of orang-utans. Equally singular are the friendly stone animals sitting on a terrace on the south front, where four plump dodos, a grinning dinosaur, a hedgehog, a frog and other creatures recall some of the friends, a mix of politicians, military men, writers and artists, who came to Lady Edith's weekly dinners at the family's London house during the First World War. These deliberately light-hearted occasions, designed as a respite from the cares of war, became known as meetings of the Ark. Each guest was given a frivolous name, usually with an animal connection. So, Winston Churchill was Winnie the Warlock, Lord Hailsham was Hailsham the Hog and the beautiful Lady Diana Cooper was Diana the Huntress. Appropriately, Lady Londonderry was Circe the Sorceress. An ark made of cast concrete sits on the balustrade of the terrace. The more intimate sunken garden to the west of the house has rose-hung pergolas and scalloped beds, and the secluded, shady Mairi Garden, named after Edith and Charley's youngest daughter, has a summer-house with a dovecote set on its roof.

Away from the house the planting is informal, with magnificent trees, shrubs and herbaceous plants lining the walks round the lake created by the 3rd Marquess, part of a nineteenth-century layout which Edith enriched. Conical roofs glimpsed above the trees on the summit of the wooded hill beyond the lake mark the Londonderrys' private burial ground, named Tir n'an Og, Land of the Ever Young, where Edith and Charley and other members of the family are buried.

The octagonal Temple of the Winds, on a prominent knoll in the woods to the east of the house, is the only building in Ireland by the pioneering Neo-classical architect James 'Athenian' Stuart and survives unaltered. Like its counterpart at Shugborough (*see* p.303), it was inspired by the Tower of the Winds dating from the second century BC in Athens. Erected for the 1st Marquess and completed in 1796, it was designed as an eye-catcher and banqueting house. The sumptuously

decorated upper room has another parquetry floor by John Ferguson, the star-like design again echoed in plaster on the ceiling, and a dew-drop chandelier hangs from the central medallion. On the floor below, long sash windows can be lowered into the basement to give an uninterrupted view over the island-studded waters of Strangford Lough to the prominent silhouette of Scrabo Tower on the north shore, built in memory of the 3rd Marquess.

BELOW The theatrical octagonal hall filling the centre of the house is lit from above and ringed by wooden columns painted to look like marble.

Mr Straw's House

Nottinghamshire
5–7 Blyth Grove, Worksop

To look at, this bay-fronted, three-storey Edwardian villa is like a thousand other red-brick suburban semis built for well-to-do tradesmen and professionals in the early years of the twentieth century. But the Straw brothers – William and Walter – who lived here for over 50 years were anything but ordinary. Perhaps never quite recovering from the deaths of their parents, William and Florence, in the 1930s, and maybe naturally private and conservative, they preserved the house as it was when their father and mother were alive, ignoring many modern conveniences, such as central heating and the telephone, and the advent of radio and television.

Today, 5–7 Blyth Grove is partly a shrine to William senior and Florence, partly a uniquely well-preserved example of interwar middle-class living. Completely refurbished before the family moved in, in 1923, the house boasts 1920s Sanderson wallpapers with decorative borders, doors and other woodwork painted to simulate oak, and period carpets and lino, including a fashionable Egyptian-style carpet. Furnishings are heavy, the rooms cluttered, with the parents' belongings still in their customary places. William senior's coats and hats still hang in the hall, and in William and Florence's bedroom, where the brass bedstead remains, covered with newspaper, the dressing-table still has the box for William's detachable collars and drawers of personal belongings, such as the blue sunglasses Florence wore on her annual holiday in Scarborough. The period detail includes trade calendars advertising the grocery business that William built up, and an unheated, starkly functional 1920s bathroom. The kitchen, where bread was baked every Saturday night, is similarly uninviting, although, as a small nod to modernisation, the brothers did put in a 1950s gas stove.

The boys seem to have fitted in round their parents' space, living largely in the south-facing dining room, one of only two rooms where a fire was regularly lit in cold weather, and, in William junior's case, sleeping in a small atticky bedroom at the top of the house. An ordered routine, unchanged for 40 years, included the Sunday outing to church, where the brothers always sat in the same pew, and the Sunday afternoon walk into town to inspect their grocery store and other property, while every weekday, after the shop closed, Walter would call in at his cousin's house over the road from the shop to listen to the 6 o'clock news on the radio. Both brothers liked to work in the little garden, which still has its outside privy. It seems William, who read English at university and taught for some years in London, was the dominant personality, resisting innovation and refusing to let Walter bring the car he bought in the 1960s to the house. It was William, too, who became the custodian of Blyth Grove, leaving notes around the place to record details about the family and its possessions. But he was by no means unworldly. Savings from his teacher's salary were invested in Marks & Spencer shares, worth over £150,000 at his death in 1990.

RIGHT The Edwardian villa where William and Walter Straw lived for over 50 years, preserving the house as it was when their parents were alive, still has William senior's coats and hats hanging in the hall.

Needles Old and New Batteries

Isle of Wight
West of Freshwater Bay
and Alum Bay

The threat of a French invasion in 1858, fuelled by Lord Palmerston's aggressively nationalistic foreign policy, threw Britain into a panic, not least because the coastal defences, little changed since the time of the Battle of Trafalgar in 1805, were clearly inadequate. This magnificently sited little fort, set 250 feet (76 metres) above the sea on the far western point of the Isle of Wight, was one of the new artillery works built to guard the approaches to the Solent and the major naval base at Portsmouth.

A walk of about a mile (1.6 kilometres) across the downs leads to the dagger-shaped headland, with precipitous chalk cliffs falling to the jagged outlines of the Needles, where the fort was built. On the other side of a ditch cut to protect the landward approaches is the only entrance, a massive archway dated 1862. A tunnel-like passage emerges in the parade ground, where five semicircular gun emplacements, two of them now mounted with guns rescued from the sea by the National Trust in 1983, face west and north. Built into the rock are underground chambers for storing gunpowder, shells and cartridges: the ingenious arrangements that allowed candles or oil-burning lanterns to be used without danger of igniting the powder and the system of ventilation ducts that kept the ammunition dry can still be seen. From the parade ground, a steep spiral stair descends to a long, brick-lined tunnel leading to the look-out positioned on the very tip of the headland, where a searchlight was set up in 1899. The views are breathtaking: down onto the points of the Needles, with their wheeling colonies of cormorants and seagulls, and across the bay to the mainland, where the outline of Hurst Castle marks the western arm of the Solent. Just up the hill, on the site of the original Needles lighthouse, are the remains of the Needles New Battery, built in 1893–5 and finally closed in 1954 when the guns were scrapped.

Although the Needles batteries saw little active service, they have played an important role in military history. A massive iron ring in the parade ground of the Old Battery marks the site of the world's first anti-aircraft gun, set up here in 1913. And some concrete terraces set vertiginously above the sea near the New Battery are where the engines of the Black Knight rocket were tested in 1956, before the rocket was launched at Woomera in Australia.

BELOW From the look-out on the very tip of the headland, there are spectacular views of the Needles and of the mainland over the water.

Newark Park

Gloucestershire
1½ miles (2.4 kilometres)
north-east of Wotton-under-Edge,
1½ miles (2.4 kilometres) south
of the junction of the A4135 and
the B4058

This unusual and atmospheric house stands high on a spur of the Cotswolds, with panoramic views to the south and west over steep wooded slopes plunging to the valley of the River Severn. Buttresses, battlements and Georgian sash windows attributed to James Wyatt, who remodelled Newark in the 1790s, only partly disguise the modest four-storey Tudor hunting lodge built by Sir Nicholas Poyntz in c. 1550.

A romantic dragon weathervane dating from Tudor times, its long coiled tail silhouetted against the sky, still surmounts the building. Like his father and grandfather before him, Sir Nicholas was prominent at court, becoming Groom of the Bedchamber to Henry VIII after 1539. His hunting lodge was built on land which had formerly belonged to the Abbey of Kingswood in the vale below and which was granted to him by the king after the monastery was dissolved.

ABOVE Apart from the battlements, which were added in the 1790s, the east front of the house, with its classical doorway, has changed little since it was built in c. 1550.

Some materials from the former abbey were incorporated in Newark.

The Tudor building emerges most strongly on the east, where Wyatt's sympathetic hand did not destroy original features. Although Sir Nicholas's architect is unknown, this tall, symmetrical façade, with huge mullioned and transomed windows lighting the upper floors, reflects the sophisticated world of the court rather than local building styles, and suggests something of the Elizabethan prodigy houses that were to follow at the end of the century. A prominent three-light oriel projects from the centre of the building and a pedimented doorway flanked by Doric columns is a remarkably pure Renaissance feature for its date. The first floor of the lodge was originally a banqueting room, with wide

views over the deer-park around the house and the wooded countryside beyond, and from the roof, which was designed as a viewing platform, Sir Nicholas and his guests could watch deer being hunted in the valley below.

Internally, Wyatt left the lodge more or less as it was and Tudor fireplaces still warm some of the rooms in this part of the house, but he remodelled a second block added in the late seventeenth century, introducing Neo-classical interiors. More Doric columns divide the unusual hall he inserted between the two parts of the building, with ox skulls prominent on the frieze decorating the screen.

Formal axial gardens to the north and east were laid out by Mr Robert Parsons, the Texan architect who rented the house from 1970 to 1994 and began to restore it, but there are still remnants of the wild bulb garden and rock gardens created in the late nineteenth century on the wooded slopes below the lodge. Here paths descend steeply to a secluded lake with a late eighteenth-century brick summer-house looking over the water.

BELOW Winding paths lead down to the lake at the bottom of the garden, where this eighteenth-century summer-house looks over the water.
BELOW RIGHT The bay window that originally lit the banqueting room on the first floor is filled with late eighteenth-century painted glass.

Nostell

West Yorkshire
On the A638 out of Wakefield
towards Doncaster

There are two eighteenth-century mansions at Nostell, one of which is only a few feet high. Commissioned in *c.* 1735, at much the same time as work began on a new house for Sir Rowland Winn, 4th Baronet, this precious object, like the similarly fine example at Uppark (*see* p.352), is one of very few dolls' houses to survive from the eighteenth century and is exquisitely made. Nine rooms on three floors are fully fitted out in period style. Marble chimneypieces are thought to have been copied from plates in James Gibbs's *Book of Architecture* of 1728, carved mouldings and cornices are picked out in gilt, silk curtains hang at the windows of the grandest rooms and a mahogany drop-leaf dining table is surrounded by beautifully made walnut chairs. There are even working brass locks in the doors, bureau drawers that can be opened, tiny silver plates and glasses, and ornamental Chinese porcelain. Grandly dressed figures are looked after by servants in the Winn livery of grey and yellow, and there is a glass mouse under the kitchen table. This house in miniature, although it enchants children, was not a plaything. It was probably ordered, as a shell, by Sir Rowland for his young wife Susanna, who, together with her sister Katherine, decorated and fitted out the rooms, buying finely crafted toy furniture in London and using dress fabrics for upholstery and costumes. This not only gave the women an occupation but also enabled them to try out room decoration and other skills before doing them for real. Nearly three centuries later, the dolls' house is a unique and unaltered example of the fashionable decor of the day. Although it is not known who made the dolls' house, it may have been designed by James Paine, the young architect who was commissioned by Sir Rowland.

The Winns, who made a fortune as textile merchants in London, acquired the estate in 1654, six years before a baronetcy was granted by Charles II, and lived here for the next 350 years. The present house was built to replace an earlier building that had been formed out of the Augustinian priory that was once here. Paine's severe classical main block, based on plans by the local architect Colonel James Moyser which Paine modified and adapted, is relieved only by the Ionic portico attached to the entrance front, with a pediment breaking the roofline. Two service pavilions – one since demolished – were joined to the south end of the house by curved corridors and Paine had intended to add pavilions to the north end as well, but the 4th Baronet died before these could be executed and most of the state rooms too were left unfinished. The family wing, like a Palladian villa attached to one end of the entrance façade, was designed by Robert Adam, who was hired by Sir Rowland's son, the 5th Baronet, in 1765 to complete the house. Adam was also responsible for the substantial terrace reached by two flights of gracefully curving steps which lifts the entrance façade.

The interior, with superb ornamental plasterwork and one of the largest collections of Chippendale furniture in the world, is a many-layered composition of great richness, reflecting the changes caused by interruptions to work on the house and the employment of outstanding craftsmen of the day. Stylistically, there is a strong contrast between Paine's fluid rococo decoration for Sir Rowland and Robert Adam's Neo-classical designs for Sir Rowland's son, who wanted his house finished in the latest fashion. Like Paine's schemes, though, Adam's designs were never fully carried out, the untimely death of the 5th Baronet in a carriage accident bringing work to a halt, leaving Adam and his craftsmen unpaid. A generation later another layer was added by the collector Charles Winn, 1st Baron St Oswald, who acquired paintings, antique furniture and books for the house, and his son, Rowland, the 2nd Baron, who, during a nineteenth-century heyday, used wealth from mining on the estate to refurbish Nostell and complete Adam's wing.

Adam's beautiful Top Hall lacks the statues and grisaille paintings with which he had hoped to embellish it, but it is a serenely graceful room, with delicate plasterwork by Joseph Rose the Younger picked out against a subtly darker background. His library, decorated with nine stylised classical

ABOVE LEFT This gilded ho-ho bird perches on the corner of a chinoiserie mirror, part of a suite that Chippendale supplied for the state apartment in 1771.

paintings by Antonio Zucchi and with the Winn family's important collection of books housed in the pedimented bookcases, still has all the furniture designed for it by Chippendale, including the massive desk which dominates the room.

Adam's restrained treatments only serve to heighten the opulence of Paine's earlier decorative schemes, of which that in the dining room, with plasterwork by Joseph Rose the Elder, is the most impressive. Zucchi's playful cherubs in the elaborate panels over the doors and the plaster frieze of vines and satyrs' masks suggest an appreciation of the good things in life. Paine was also responsible for the splendid ceiling, with its trio of music-making cherubs, in what was originally a private music room for guests. Redecoration for the 5th Baronet accounts for the exquisite Chinese wallpaper, with brightly coloured birds of all sizes and varieties perching on branches laden with flowers and foliage, that Chippendale chose to complement his rich green and gold lacquer furniture when the room was turned into a dressing room. The Tapestry Room, originally intended by Adam and Chippendale to be a drawing room, which had been left unfinished, was transformed by Charles Winn, who installed the Brussels tapestries.

Fine paintings hang throughout the house. Among them are a large-scale copy of Holbein's group portrait of Thomas More and his family, a characteristic landscape by Pieter Breughel the Younger, with a procession of diminutive figures accompanying Christ on his way to Calvary (saved in 2011 by public appeal and support from the Art Fund and National Heritage Memorial Fund), and a self-portrait of 1791 by Angelica Kauffmann, in which she portrays, in classical symbolism, her decision to abandon a promising operatic career in favour of painting.

The 1st Baron was responsible for buying a clock made in 1717 by the young John Harrison, who was the son of the estate carpenter at Nostell and went on to make his name by inventing the first timepiece that was accurate enough to enable seamen to determine their longitude. Harrison made the mechanism of the clock almost entirely out of wood, the movement, frame and wheels of oak, the pendulum of mahogany and the spindles and pinions of boxwood.

RIGHT Adam's scheme for Nostell was never fully realised. His plan had been to balance the family wing to the right of the main block with one on the other side.

Nostell's interiors are a celebration of the craftsmen who worked here as much as of the key men involved. Surviving accounts reveal that the plasterer Joseph Rose the Younger employed a skilled workforce of up to seven men at the house, their various job titles, 'plaisterer', 'ornament plaisterer', 'labourer' etc., indicating specific roles in the casting, fitting or free modelling of the ornamental plasterwork. Moulds could be used to produce symmetrical, low relief designs, but anything complex, such as the semi-circle of oak leaves on the ceiling of the Top Hall, was created by hand. Similarly, the huge range of pieces, from servants' chairs and a chopping block to the green and gold chinoiserie suite, which Chippendale supplied from his premises in London, relied on skilled labour conversant with gilding, veneers, marquetry and imitating lacquer with paint as well as working wood. The fashion-conscious and socially aspiring Winns, keen both to reflect their increasing wealth and to improve their position in society, drove the building and fitting out of Nostell, but they relied on the skills and dedication of others to realise their dreams. As things turned out, only the dolls' house was completed all of a piece. By contrast, the building, decorating and furnishing of the main house never went according to plan and took over a century to complete. New displays on the upper floor have been devised to help visitors unpick the styles and changes in taste which can be seen in the house today.

Nostell's setting was as carefully planned as the interior and, like the mansion, required generations of estate workers to create and maintain it. The house is set off by a pastoral landscape that still has traces of Stephen Switzer's formal design of 1730 for the 4th Baronet, but which was developed in a more naturalistic style over the next hundred years. The main view from the house looks across a great tree-framed sweep of grass and a chain of lakes is crossed by the many-arched bridge that was built in 1759–61 to carry the main Wakefield to Doncaster road. A gothick menagerie that was probably designed by Paine but has additions by Adam stands in the pleasure grounds to the west of the lake. Adam also designed three lodges for the 5th Baronet, one of which is in the form of a pyramid.

LEFT Ancient coins and seals collected by the 5th Baronet and his grandson Charles Winn were kept in the medal cabinet which Chippendale designed for the library.

Nuffield Place

Oxfordshire
On the A4130 between Wallingford
and Henley-on-Thames

The little village of Nuffield sits at the western edge of the Chilterns, where the hills fall away towards the Thames. Surrounded by trees on the edge of the village is the unpretentious and comfortable house where the industrialist and philanthropist William Morris, 1st Lord Nuffield, lived for 30 years. A self-made man who left school at 15, Morris, who started in business by repairing and building bicycles, made his fortune by producing one of the first affordable family cars. His prototype model was designed in 1912, when Morris was in his mid-30s, but it was only after the First World War, when he applied the kind of streamlined manufacturing techniques developed in America to the mass production of cars at his Cowley works in Oxford, that output took off and vehicles could be sold at prices that a wide sector of the population could afford. By 1925 the factory was producing 56,000 cars a year, owning one was no longer the preserve of the very rich and Morris was well on the way to becoming one of the wealthiest men in the world.

William and his wife Elizabeth bought Nuffield Place in 1932, the year before Morris became Lord Nuffield. Designed by Oswald Milne, a pupil of Lutyens, as an L-shaped building of red and grey brick, the house was built in 1914 as a country retreat for the shipping magnate Sir John Bowring Wimble.

BELOW The attractive west front of Nuffield Place, with green shutters framing the windows, deep eaves and a sundial set into the brickwork.

Alterations by Lord Nuffield, in particular the addition of a capacious billiard-room, have blurred the original lines, but the many-windowed façades looking onto the garden, with their deep eaves, tall chimneys breaking the sweep of the tiled roof and green shutters, show the character of Milne's work.

The interior is essentially as it was when Lord Nuffield died in 1963, with furnishings that reflect a certain kind of 1930s taste, and a strong sense of William Morris the man and of the couple's lifestyle. Apart, perhaps, from the billiard-room, with its Art Deco burr walnut cocktail cabinet, there is nothing showy here, although the reproduction furniture that was made for the Nuffields in the 1920s and '30s, much of it by the local firm Cecil A. Halliday of Oxford, and the richly coloured oriental rugs, are all of the highest quality. A love of the historic and traditional comes through in the limed oak panelling lining the hall and first-floor landing and in the copies of antique pieces, among them a 'Tudor' oak food cupboard made of genuinely old timber in the dining room and a high-backed carved settle in the hall. The table in the dining room, also made by Hallidays, is laid for dinner with the Nuffields' striking blue bohemian glassware, but, except when entertaining, William and Elizabeth preferred to sit in the much more modest room next door, Scottie dogs at their feet. A television cabinet tucked away in one corner, with a period wireless perched on top, was bought in 1955.

Lord Nuffield's love of things mechanical comes through in the four longcase clocks in the hall, which he kept in perfect working order, in the automatic match dispensers in the drawing room and, above all, in the capacious built-in tool cupboard, crammed with screwdrivers, spanners, saws and an array of other useful things, from materials for repairing shoes to coils of wire, in his bedroom. The carpet here is patched together and there is a tangle of flex round the reading light rigged up over the bed. In summer, Lord Nuffield often slept in the little room next door, created out of a balcony on the corner of the house, where a long window gives a panoramic view north-west over the Thames valley to Wittenham Clumps on the other side of the river.

Rooms are hung with flower paintings, prints, or watercolours of Oxford, and there are three portraits of the great man, the most memorable painted by Henry Gates in 1931, but there are no fine works of art here. Lord Nuffield

ABOVE Lady Nuffield's car, a 1946 Wolseley four-door saloon, is garaged close to the kitchen garden.
OPPOSITE Lord Nuffield rigged up the reading light over the bed in his bedroom and kept the many clocks in working order.

was the ultimate philanthropist, preferring to use his fortune to benefit others rather than to spend lavishly on himself. An ultra-violet sun lamp like those he provided for night workers in his factories in the Second World War and a huge iron lung like the hundreds he provided for hospitals throughout the Commonwealth reflect his particular interest in health and medicine. In 1937 he founded Nuffield College in Oxford, but by far the most important of his many benefactions was the gift of £10 million for the setting up of the Nuffield Foundation for medical, scientific and educational research in 1943. At his death, the house and estate passed to Nuffield College and in 2011 the college gave the house and some of the land to the National Trust.

Nunnington Hall

North Yorkshire
In Ryedale, 6 miles
(9.6 kilometres) south-east
of Helmsley; 1½ miles
(2.4 kilometres) north of the
B1257 Malton–Helmsley road

For much of its history, this tranquil house on the banks of the River Rye was a secondary residence, lived in by stewards or tenants of influential men rather than being in the mainstream itself. One grandee was William Parr, brother of Catherine, Henry VIII's sixth queen, who forfeited Nunnington to the Crown in 1553 when he unwisely supported the plan to put Lady Jane Grey on the throne. Another was Robert Huicke, physician to Henry VIII, Edward VI and Elizabeth I, who told the queen she would never have children. The earliest parts of the present building, visible on the west front, are Elizabethan, dating from Parr's time. The house was much improved and extended by the Norcliffe family, who lived at Nunnington in the early seventeenth century, but when Parliamentary troops billeted here during the Civil War badly damaged the hall, Thomas Norcliffe, after first removing various desirable fittings, gave up the lease.

Richard, 1st Viscount Preston, who inherited Nunnington from his great-uncle in 1685, restored and remodelled the hall, largely creating the house as it is today. A convert to Rome, Lord Preston was Master of the Wardrobe to James II and one of five peers entrusted with the government of the country when James fled in 1688. Apprehended on the fishing boat he had hoped would bear James triumphantly back to England, Preston was taken to the Tower of London and saved from execution only by the pleadings of his youngest daughter Susannah. Stripped of his offices and disgraced, he returned to Yorkshire, where he died a few years later.

Preston is traditionally attributed with Nunnington's finest architectural feature: the long, two-storeyed south front with projecting gables at either end. Unusually, two central doors stand one above the other, with a charming wrought-iron balcony round the upper one, and the whole composition appears both welcoming and refined.

Inside, the house is cosily elegant, its panelled rooms filled with period furniture, tapestries and porcelain collected by the last owner, Mrs Fife, and her husband Colonel Fife, who came to live here after she inherited the hall in 1920. The grandest room is Preston's oak hall, with its elaborate chimneypiece

supporting his coat of arms joined with those of his wife and a three-arched classical screen leading to the great oak and pine staircase climbing round three sides of a well. Preston emerges again in the two large ceiling canvases, curiously depicting various family coats of arms against a cloudy sky, that he commissioned for a small upstairs room, and in the little oratory adjoining a bedroom in the west wing, a reminder of his adopted Roman Catholicism and of the family's continued recusancy in the eighteenth century. Part of the attic above now

ABOVE The first-floor balcony on Nunnington's late seventeenth-century south front is an unusual feature to find in a country house of this period.

houses the collection of miniature rooms, fully furnished in different period styles, formed by Mrs T.M. Carlisle between 1933 and 1970.

The walled garden to the south of the house is a rare survival from the seventeenth century, which still bears traces of the original formal layout. A rusticated stone gateway inserted in the south wall in the 1920s marks the site of the *clairvoyée*, a railing on a low wall extending the view beyond the garden which is shown on a rough sketch by Samuel Buck of *c*. 1720.

A lawn is flanked by rectangles of spring-flowering meadows and an orchard is planted with old varieties of fruit trees. Eccentrically individual arches and gates through which the garden is approached have bold rustication in a French style that Lord Preston may have seen when he was Ambassador to France for Charles II.

Nymans

West Sussex
On the B2114 at Handcross,
4½ miles (7.2 kilometres) south
of Crawley, just off the M23/A23
London–Brighton road

The enchanting garden that was devised and nurtured by three generations of the Messel family is set high, looking out over the Weald towards the South Downs. It is laid out round an apparently ancient house. Now largely a picturesque ruin, with climbers smothering the buttressed walls, mullioned windows that are now glassless and empty and roofless gable ends, this romantic backdrop is all that remains of the southern side of a pastiche Tudor manor that was built here in 1928 by Leonard and Maud Messel. Leonard's father, Ludwig, had created the original garden and he and his wife Annie, who had come to Nymans in 1890, had enlarged an existing early nineteenth-century villa, which was given an Italianate tower, a huge conservatory and other improvements, such as a billiard room. The architect Sir Ernest George was involved in some of the alterations, but most of the work was based on plans by Ludwig's brother

Alfred. Leonard and Maud, on the other hand, who inherited Nymans in 1916, longed to live in a West Country manor and they engaged Norman Evill and subsequently Sir Walter Tapper to transform the existing building into a convincing reproduction of a medieval and Tudor house. Tragically, in February 1947, in the middle of an exceptionally hard winter, the house caught fire and, the standpipes being frozen, the flames could not be brought under control until water was pumped up from a pond at the bottom of the park. The whole southern side of the building, with the Great Hall and other principal rooms, was gutted and almost all the contents, including a valuable collection of botanical books, were lost. Although damaged, the north and west parts of the house survived and the family rooms were re-created in a more intimate setting with furniture salvaged from the fire and with other pieces that were brought down to Sussex after the Messels' London house was sold. Miraculously, much of the planting on the south front also withstood the flames, including the great *Magnolia grandiflora* that now smothers the end of the ruined Great Hall.

After Leonard's death in 1953 and that of his wife in 1960, their daughter Anne and her second husband, the 6th Earl of Rosse, came to live at Nymans and did much to nurture and enrich the garden. The house is shown as the countess had it. There are many echoes of her brother, the theatre designer Oliver Messel, and of her son by her first marriage, the photographer Lord Snowdon, who advised on the arrangement of the rooms. A door in the ruined wing opens into a long, wide, low-ceilinged corridor, more hall than passage, which leads to the main rooms in the range beyond. Arched openings reveal a comfortable sitting room, known as the Garden Hall, with a Broadwood grand piano, custom-made for Ludwig, covered in family photographs at one end, and the little Book Room, where the television that belonged to Maud Messel has been given curtains and a proscenium arch by her son Oliver, as if it were a theatre. There are irregular stone flags in the hall, heavy arched wooden doors, great fireplaces and other period touches, such

LEFT An ornamental urn in the garden with the glassless windows of the Great Hall behind.
OPPOSITE An octagonal dovecot sets off the west wing of the house. This became the Messels' family home after the southern side of the building was destroyed by fire.

as a timber partition in the Gun Room, which were brought here from ruined medieval buildings to add character.

The atmosphere of antiquity is enhanced by the Messels' collection of tapestries and seventeenth-century furniture, and by a Flemish panel painting of Christ blessing the children, with figures in robes of luminous scarlet. These pieces are mixed with many twentieth-century touches, among them Norman Evill's drawing of the house, a sketch of the actress Merle Oberon by Oliver Messel and a dramatic self-portrait by Lord Snowdon. This last is among another show of family

photographs in the comfortable library, complete with drinks trolley, at the end of the passage. The countess, who died in 1992, used to write here at the desk under the window that looks out onto the little stone-walled court on the west side of the house, graced with an octagonal dovecote in one corner.

Exhibitions relating to Nymans and the Messels are shown in a gallery on the first floor. Further rooms, including the countess's bedroom, will gradually be opened over the next few years, and visitors can now go inside the walls of the Great Hall, where a new garden is being created.

Ormesby Hall

Middlesbrough
3 miles (4.8 kilometres)
south-east of Middlesbrough,
west of the A171

Sir James Pennyman, 6th Baronet, and his aunt Dorothy were clearly people of taste. Although 'Wicked Sir James', a spendthrift in the best eighteenth-century manner, ran through the fortune he inherited in 1770 in eight years, he spent his wealth on enlarging the Ormesby estate and enriching the house his aunt had built some 30 years earlier. Unfortunately, he was then obliged to surrender the property to the bailiffs.

Probably completed by 1743, Ormesby was designed by an unknown architect in a characteristically plain Palladian style then popular in North Yorkshire. The rather severe outlines of the tall, three-storey main block rising to a hipped roof are relieved only by a heavy cornice and pediments on the two main façades. Projecting porches were Victorian additions.

The interior of the main block is a complete contrast. Ormesby is not at all grand, but the most talented of local craftsmen were employed to create the rich plaster decoration and woodwork that are such a feature of the house. Ionic columns screening both ends of the hall and Palladian motifs here and in the library are of Dorothy's time, but Sir James introduced the delicate Adamesque ceilings attributed to Carr of York in the drawing room and dining room. Plain family rooms on the first floor contrast with some decorated guest rooms on the north side, one adorned with carved festoons of fruit and foliage. These rooms are served by a notably ornate gallery, essentially a glorified landing, which runs across the house. Some of the finest eighteenth-century carving at Ormesby is on the sumptuous pedimented doorcases here, with subtle variations in the design indicating the status of the chamber beyond.

The house is now filled with Regency and Victorian furniture, and a number of family portraits reflect the generations of Pennymans who continued to live at Ormesby despite the 6th Baronet's extravagance.

A two-storey service wing on the east was formed out of the earlier Jacobean house, thought to have been built in about 1600, its low façades an interesting contrast to the later building. Although most of the original features of the service wing have been lost, one fine ornamented Jacobean doorway has survived, with the crest granted to James Pennyman in 1599 proudly displayed on the coat of arms above. Model railway displays now housed here are a unique addition to the Trust's collections.

Sir James's dignified stables, crowned with a cupola and probably also designed by Carr of York, stand close by and a small rose garden and mixed beds and borders, some planted in cottage-garden style, set off the house. A holly walk shows off fancy-leaved varieties, and naturalised spring bulbs carpet the woodland towards the church, where William Lawson, author of several gardening books, was vicar in the early seventeenth century.

ABOVE Ormesby Hall was designed in a severe Palladian style that was popular in North Yorkshire in the mid-eighteenth century.
LEFT Talented local craftsmen were employed to create the rich plaster decoration which is such a feature of Ormesby.

Osterley Park

Middlesex
Just north of Osterley station,
on the western outskirts of
London (Piccadilly tube line)

This grand Neo-classical villa was created in the mid-eighteenth century out of a mansion built for Sir Thomas Gresham, Chancellor of the Exchequer to Elizabeth I. The ghost of the sixteenth-century courtyard house still lingers on in Osterley's square plan, with three ranges of warm red brick looking onto a central courtyard. But the delightful corner turrets crowned with cupolas, somewhat reminiscent of those at Blickling (*see* p.57), are later additions. There is nothing Elizabethan about the sash windows and balustraded roofline, and on the fourth side of the courtyard, where once there would have been another range, a wide flight of steps leads up to a magnificent double portico stretching between the wings. The courtyard itself is raised, to give direct access to the principal rooms on the first floor.

Although there were alterations to Gresham's mansion in the late seventeenth and early eighteenth centuries, the house was transformed from 1761 by Robert Adam, who spent 20 years working on Osterley for the Child family. Statues of Greek deities standing in niches and 'antique' vases on pedestals in Adam's cool grey and white entrance hall introduce the classical theme of the house. In the airy library, paintings depicting the world of ancient Greece and Rome by Antonio Zucchi are set into plaster frames built into the walls above the pilastered and pedimented bookcases. Marquetry furniture attributed to John Linnell includes a pedestal desk inlaid with trophies representing the arts, and there is a delicate Adam ceiling. Close by is an eating room arranged in the eighteenth-century way, with the chairs against the walls

BELOW Elegant curved stairs descend from the gallery on the west side of the house, which forms a pleasing contrast to the theatrical entrance front.

ABOVE The decoration in Adam's Etruscan dressing room at Osterley was created by Pietro Maria Borgnis, who painted the motifs on paper and then pasted them on canvas for fixing to the walls and ceiling.

and no large central table. The kitchen in the basement below, where five servants were employed in the mid-eighteenth century, was set in the opposite corner of the house, so diners were not disturbed by noise and cooking smells.

Adam also designed the three rooms that form the state apartment on the south front. One of his most ambitious pieces of furniture, a domed eight-poster bed, dominates the state bedroom, but the most original decorative scheme is in the Etruscan dressing room, where ochre-coloured dancing figures and urns set beneath arches look as if a series of Greek vases has been flattened on the walls. In contrast, and despite its Adam ceiling, the first room in the sequence has a French flavour. All claret and gold, it is hung with Gobelins tapestries designed by Boucher, their installation, almost certainly at Adam's suggestion, prompted by the tapestry room created at Croome (see p.121) in 1771. A badger, a porcupine and other creatures depicted in the borders are representatives of the menagerie that Mrs Robert Child kept in the grounds and her wide-brimmed garden hat has also been included in the design.

Unlike most of the interiors on the principal floor, the gallery that stretches the length of the garden front has decorative features which pre-date Adam, such as the marble fireplaces carved by Joseph Wilton from a design by William Chambers. Adam, though, was responsible for the pea-green wallpaper, the Ionic doorcases and the four large pier-glasses, which were almost certainly made by John Linnell.

Red-brick Tudor stables just north of the house, with original staircase turrets in the angles of the building, survive largely intact, apart from some alterations to doors and windows and the addition of a clock tower in the eighteenth century. Behind are the eighteenth-century pleasure grounds, where a Doric temple and Adam's semicircular garden house are set off by lawns, serpentine gravel paths and a re-creation of a Regency flower garden. The park stretches away, with majestic cedars planted in the eighteenth century shading a lake and cattle grazing beneath the trees in the Great Meadow to the west, where the pasture has never been ploughed. Despite the proximity of Heathrow and the M4, Osterley still feels like a country estate.

Adam was employed by Francis Child, whose grandfather had purchased the estate in 1711 after rising from obscurity to found one of the first banks in England (now subsumed in the Royal Bank of Scotland). After Francis's early death at the age of 28, his brother Robert completed Osterley, but he also died prematurely, perhaps partly as a result of anxiety about his only child Sarah Anne, who eloped with the 10th Earl of Westmorland at the age of 18. When mildly rebuked by her mother, another Sarah, who pointed out she had better matches in mind, the high-spirited girl replied, 'A bird in the hand is worth two in the bush.' The father forgave his only child, but altered his will to leave Osterley and most of his fortune to Sarah Anne's second son, or eldest daughter, thus cutting out the Westmorland heir.

In the event, Osterley passed, through Sarah Anne's daughter, to the Earls of Jersey, and it was the 9th Earl who gave the house to the National Trust in 1949. Sadly, a collection of exceptional paintings, including works by Rubens, Van Dyck and Claude, which had been displayed in the gallery were almost all destroyed in a fire while *en route* to the earl's new home in Jersey. The present hang in the gallery, based on loans and gifts, has been devised to conjure up the eighteenth-century arrangement and is strong on later seventeenth- and eighteenth-century Venetian painting. Some enormous eighteenth-century Chinese jars and vases spaced down the room, fruits of the family's involvement in the East India Company in the first half of the eighteenth century, are part of an important collection of ceramics in the house.

Since 2015, the house has been enriched by the return, on a ten-year loan from the trustee of the Earldom of Jersey, with the backing of the 10th Earl, of significant family paintings and rare pieces of furniture. Portraits of the two men who employed Adam, Francis and Robert Child, the first by Ramsey, the second by Romney, now hang in the house and a flamboyant self-portrait by William Dobson, who succeeded Van Dyck as court painter to Charles I, has also returned to Osterley. A companion portrait, in a matching oval frame, by Van Dyck, now in the National Portrait Gallery, used to be here too, both pictures having been purchased by a 'Mr Child' in 1712 for a grand total of 80 guineas. Further family portraits hang upstairs, among them a pastel of Sarah Anne with her parents, the girl holding her father's hand affectionately. Recently, Carlo Dolci's painting of St Agatha, which was sold in the 1930s, was bought back for the house.

Overbeck's

Devon
1½ miles (2.4 kilometres) south-west of Salcombe, signposted from Malborough and Salcombe

A narrow, winding lane leads steeply up from the Kingsbridge estuary and the resort of Salcombe to this elegant Edwardian house set on a slope above the sea. Like the small Victorian villa it replaced, it was for long known as Sharpitor after the craggy line of rocks just offshore, but it now bears the name of Otto Overbeck, the eccentric scientist, artist and inventor who lived here from 1928 to 1937 and left the house to the Trust. His most important invention was his popular electrical rejuvenator, a device which he claimed enabled people to defy the ageing process, and it was this that gave him the money to acquire the house.

Overbeck's was built, just before the First World War, by Adam Hannaford Shepherd, a local man, for Captain George Medlicott Vereker and his wife Frances. When their son Robert was killed just 22 days into the war, aged 21, the Verekers offered it to the Red Cross in his memory and, from August 1915 to January 1919, Overbecks was a convalescent hospital for British

ABOVE From the garden of Overbeck's, set high on the cliffs above Salcombe on the coast of south Devon, there are panoramic views up the wooded Kingsbridge estuary, where the water is speckled with sailing boats in summer.

and Allied troops. It was run entirely by volunteers, including the Verekers. The drawing-room fitted out in Edwardian style, with comfortable chairs in the bay window looking onto the garden, is shown as it might have been at that time and autograph books, photographs and pictures, most of them lent by the son of Annie Yeoman, who was a volunteer nurse at the hospital, conjure up those years. The present tea-room, with a painting of Otto over the fireplace and original panelling, is where the convalescing soldiers played billiards.

Beyond the upper lawn around the house, the 6-acre (2.5 hectare) garden slopes steeply towards the sea in a series of sunny, sheltered terraces. Many rare and tender species thrive in a microclimate that is almost Mediterranean. Far below there is the constant backdrop of the sea. Cliffs across the bay run south to the dramatic headland of Prawle Point, while inland there are views to Salcombe and up the wooded reaches of the estuary.

Owletts

Kent
1 mile (1.6 kilometres) south of the A2, at the west end of Cobham village, at the junction of roads from Dartford and Sole Street

This red-brick, two-storey Charles II house, with dormer windows peering over the parapet and massive chimneys rising high above a steeply pitched, hipped roof, was built for a prosperous Kentish farmer, Bonham Hayes, in 1683. His initials and those of his wife Elizabeth are cut into the brickwork of the chimneys and also figure prominently in the bold plasterwork over the staircase. The finest original feature of the interior and very unusual in such a modest house, this decorative stucco, probably created by Italian craftsmen, features realistic three-dimensional flowers and fruit and carries the date of the work, 1684.

A bird-bath in the garden formed of Corinthian capitals from the old Bank of England recalls the architect Sir Herbert Baker, who was born at Owletts in 1862. He and his wife Florence gave the house, with much of its contents, to the National Trust in 1938. Known today for his imperial London buildings – India House, South Africa House and the Bank of England – and for his collaboration with Sir Edwin Lutyens in the design of New Delhi, Sir Herbert made his name in South Africa, where he built Groote Schuur for Cecil Rhodes in 1896 and the Union Buildings in Pretoria, where Nelson Mandela

was installed as president, in 1912. He was largely responsible for creating Owlett's present historic atmosphere. Among other improvements, he extended the library, opened up the hall and ornamented it with symbolic plasterwork, stripped the paint from the original pine doors and introduced the cedar panelling in the dining room.

The contents reflect the architect's travels and talents. Sir Herbert's carved dining room chairs are decorated with creatures symbolising the family, a Dutch grandfather clock and chest were brought back from Cape Town, and there is a memorable strip cartoon of his journey from Delhi to Owletts, with one frame showing Sir Herbert and Lutyens together on an elephant. The living room is hung with watercolours by Sir Herbert, but the most remarkable feature here is the blue and gold wall-clock which was made by his son Henry and which shows the time in the countries that once composed the British Empire.

This airy, sunny room looks onto the garden, where broad lawns and a tennis court emphasise that this is a family place. Figs and peaches ripening above rows of vegetables in the walled garden to the east of the house recall the dangling grapes in the plasterwork over the stairs.

BELOW This attractive, red-brick Carolean house was the home of the architect Sir Herbert Baker, who was born here in 1862.

Oxburgh Hall

Norfolk
At Oxburgh, 7 miles
(11.2 kilometres) south-west of
Swaffham, on the south side
of the Stoke Ferry road

This romantic moated house is set on what was once an island in the East Anglian fen. The land around is now criss-crossed with drainage dykes and cultivated, but when Edward IV gave Sir Edmund Bedingfeld licence to build his fortified manor house at Oxburgh in 1482, the site was on a promontory in the marsh. Apart from a period in 1951–2, when Oxburgh was briefly in the hands of a property developer before the family managed to buy it back and give it to the Trust, Bedingfelds have lived here ever since. The gradual impoverishment of the estate that resulted from their adherence to the Catholic faith ensured that the house survived unaltered through the sixteenth and seventeenth centuries.

Even in this remote corner of England, Sir Edmund was more concerned with display and comfort than defence. The best-preserved part of his fifteenth-century courtyard house is a piece of early Tudor showmanship: a flamboyant towering gatehouse with battlemented turrets and stone-mullioned windows rising sheer from the moat. Flemish-style stepped gables and twisted terracotta chimneys on the brick ranges to either side, which contribute so much to the romantic character of the place, seem to be all of a piece; in fact they were added by J.C. Buckler as part of extensive restoration in the mid-nineteenth century for Sir Henry Paston-Bedingfeld, the 6th Baronet. Buckler was also responsible for the beautiful oriel window that fills two storeys of his convincingly medieval battlemented tower at the end of the east range.

The interior of the house includes both Tudor survivals and atmospheric Victorian rooms. Henry VII came to Oxburgh in August 1498. The room in which he slept no longer exists, but a brick-walled room warmed by a great fireplace in the Tudor gatehouse tower is now known as the King's Room to commemorate the royal visit. A priest's hole in the floor of a former garderobe off this room is an evocative reminder of the family's religious sympathies, and these come through again in Oxburgh's most prized possession, needlework by the Catholic Mary, Queen of Scots. Rich embroidery set onto green velvet was wrought by the queen and Bess of Hardwick while Mary was in the custody of the Earl of Shrewsbury after her flight to England. Mostly devoted to delightful depictions of a wide assortment of beasts, birds and fishes ranging from the unicorn to the garden snail, these enchanting pieces are very rare illustrations of the skill of both women.

The nineteenth-century interiors, with designs by J.C. Buckler and J.D. Crace, are rare survivals of romantic High Victorian taste. Crace's heraldic ceiling in the drawing room incorporates delicately painted foliage and flowers in blue, pink and green. More heraldic devices – crimson fleurs-de-lis – are woven into the carpet of the low-ceilinged library, picking up the red in the flock wallpaper. A neo-Tudor fireplace dominating this room has a carved overmantel made up of medieval fragments from continental churches, including

LEFT Brightly coloured embossed leather on the walls sets off the portrait of Sir Henry Bedingfeld, 2nd baronet, at the head of the north staircase.
OPPOSITE Dating from 1482 when the Wars of the Roses were at their height, Oxburgh is one of the most romantic of houses.

some delicate fan vaulting. The small dining room is another rich Victorian interior. The dark lustre of the panelling and of the elaborate sideboard with its crest of writhing birds is relieved by vivid blue, orange and red tiles round the fireplace.

In the chapel, which was built in 1836 for the 6th Baronet, Victorian and medieval craftsmanship are again combined. The heraldic glass in the south window, dominated by a great red Bedingfeld eagle, was commissioned from Thomas Willement, but the splendid altarpiece is crowned by a sixteenth-century painted and carved triptych, purchased by the Bedingfelds in Bruges in about 1860.

Apart from the nineteenth-century Wilderness Walk to the

west of the chapel and mown grass around the moat, most of the garden lies to the east of the house, where Buckler's tower looks out over a florid French-style parterre flowering in swirls of blue and yellow. A yew hedge beyond the parterre fronts a colourful herbaceous border. Behind is the fanciful, turreted wall of the Victorian kitchen garden, now planted as a formal orchard with climbers on the walls.

In 2016 a dormer window collapsed and crashed into the courtyard below. Investigation uncovered structural weaknesses in the roofline and in 2019 an ambitious project to repair the roof, windows, chimneys and medieval gatehouse, and thus to secure Oxburgh's future, was begun.

Packwood House

Warwickshire
2 miles (3.2 kilometres) east
of Hockley Heath on the A3400,
11 miles (17.6 kilometres)
south-east of central Birmingham

This tall, many-gabled house looking over a grassy forecourt was built in the late sixteenth century for John Fetherston, a prosperous yeoman farmer. The original timber-framing has now largely been rebuilt in brick and rendered over, but the house still has its massive Elizabethan chimneystacks and there is an array of mullioned casement windows and a delightful red-brick stable block at right-angles to the house that was added by another John Fetherston in *c.* 1670. Never a prominent or county family, the Fetherstons, it seems, lived quietly here, although they were caught up in the Civil War, apparently offering shelter and succour as seemed expedient. Cromwell's general, Henry Ireton, slept here the night before the Battle of Edgehill in 1642 and there is a family tradition that Charles II was given food and drink at Packwood after his defeat at Worcester in 1651.

When it was sold by the last of the Fetherstons in the later nineteenth century, the house had been greatly altered, with sash windows replacing the original casements and other 'improvements'. In 1905, when it was sold again, it was also much in need of repair. The buyer was the wealthy industrialist Alfred Ash, a genial man who owned a string of racehorses and is said to have viewed life 'from the sunny side – and from the interior of a gorgeous Rolls-Royce'. His son, Graham Baron Ash, a connoisseur and collector, used his father's fortune to restore the house in the 1920s and 1930s, sweeping away Georgian and Victorian alterations and painstakingly acquiring features that would give Packwood a period feel, rescuing leaded casements, floors, beams and chimneypieces from other old buildings. To complete his romantic vision of how a Tudor house should be, he also added the splendid long gallery and fashioned the great hall, complete with oriel window, out of an existing barn, leaving the room open to the original rustic timber roof. He filled Packwood with period furnishings, including fine Jacobean panelling and an exceptional collection of tapestries, such as the seventeenth-century Brussels hanging depicting a cool terraced garden with splashing fountains and urns filled with orange trees. A long oak refectory table in the great hall and a Charles II oak cupboard inlaid with mother of pearl in the dining room are two of the many pieces that Baron Ash bought from the Ferrers family, whose moated manor house, Baddesley Clinton, is just 2 miles (3.2 kilometres) away (*see* p.36) and who, in the 1930s, were much in need of funds.

The house Graham Baron Ash created is as contrived and self-conscious as a work of art. The garden, too, is a showpiece. On the south side of the house, across a large sunken lawn, brick steps lead up to a terrace walk. Beyond, through a

LEFT At Packwood, Graham Baron Ash created a great hall out of a former barn, using the hayrack to make a balustrade for the gallery at one end and hanging fine tapestries on the walls.
OPPOSITE Although originally Elizabethan, and still boasting massive period chimneystacks, Packwood House is largely a creation of the 1920s and '30s and represents an idealised vision of a Tudor manor house.

decorative eighteenth-century gateway, is the exceptional topiary garden where a throng of mature clipped yews, most rising well above the heads of visitors, is said to represent the Sermon on the Mount. At the far end of the garden, a mound is crowned by a single yew tree; twelve more, similarly massive, are crowded below. These, representing the Master and his disciples, were part of the seventeenth-century garden, but many of the multitude dotting the smoothly mown grass below, each tree characterised by its own lumps and slants, were planted in the mid-nineteenth century.

A sunken garden in front of the house, also dating from the seventeenth century, has brick gazebos at each corner, one ingeniously designed so that its fireplace can be used to warm fruit trees growing on an adjacent wall. There are yew-hedged enclosures, walls and steps of mellow brick, wrought-iron gates, some with glimpses into the park, and a vivid herbaceous border.

Paycocke's

Essex
On the south side of the A120
West Street, the road to Braintree,
not far from the centre of
Coggeshall, next to the Fleece Inn,
5½ miles (8.8 kilometres) east
of Braintree

The wealth generated by the East Anglian cloth trade in the fifteenth and sixteenth centuries financed some of the most beautiful churches in the British Isles. It was also used to enrich the homes of the merchants themselves, many of whom invested their fortunes in fine half-timbered buildings advertising their enhanced status. Paycocke's, dating from around 1500, is one of these, its long brick and timber street façade, the upper floor jettied over the lower, incorporating carpentry and carved woodwork of the highest quality.

Vertical timbers limewashed a silvery-grey are set expensively close along the front of the house, with brick filling the spaces that would once have been packed with wattle and daub, the two together forming distinctive pink and white stripes. There are five oriel windows on the first floor and beneath them an intricately decorated wooden beam running the length of the façade carries a series of delightful cameos, such as a dragon depicted upside down and a small person apparently diving into a lily. Larger, naturalistic figures frame the fine oak gates through which a carriageway leads to the back of the house. As indicated by the four family tombs in the parish church, the Paycockes were people of substance, the house John Paycocke built on the occasion of his son Thomas's marriage to Margaret Harrold (commemorated by the initials TP and MP carved on both interior and exterior woodwork) standing out from its more modest neighbours along West Street.

Inside, it is clear that Paycocke's was a place of work and business. Peg holes in the studs of the walls were once used to hold the warp thread of the looms, wool was stored in the roof space and the lengths of cloth were probably stretched out to dry in the garden. A display of Coggeshall lace includes a device that used water-filled flasks to intensify candlelight, thus allowing four lace-makers to work by the light of one candle.

LEFT Massive doors carved with linenfold decoration and flanked by wooden figures fashioned in the frame of the gateway give access to the carriageway leading to the back of Paycocke's.
OPPOSITE Wealth from the East Anglian cloth trade financed the richly decorative street façade of this medieval merchant's house, which was built by John Paycocke for his son in the early sixteenth century.

Peckover House

Cambridgeshire
On the north bank of the River
Nene, in Wisbech

Changes in the coastline of the Wash have taken Wisbech further and further from the sea. It is now some 12 miles (19.2 kilometres) away, but only 250 years ago the River Nene was navigable into the heart of the town and there was a substantial port here, involved in a prosperous trade with the Netherlands. Although the sea traffic has long since died, imposing red-brick merchants' houses still line the river, giving this sleepy little town an elegance and importance out of all proportion to its present status. Dutch gables and hipped roofs reflect influences from across the North Sea and, as in Holland, there was a spirit of religious toleration here that fostered a substantial Quaker community in the town, many of whom, as elsewhere in East Anglia, were prominent in local affairs.

One such was Jonathan Peckover, a tradesman and campaigner for the abolition of slavery, who has given his name to the elegant, three-storey Georgian town house on the North Brink of the Nene which he bought in 1777. Five years later, in association with the Gurneys, another leading Quaker family, he established the local bank of Gurney, Birkbeck and Peckover in a wing adjoining the house, from where the business was run for almost a century until the bank merged with Barclays in 1896. Peckovers continued to live here until the mid-twentieth century, when Alexandrina Peckover was persuaded by her nephew Alec Penrose, one of whose brothers was the artist Roland Penrose, to gift Peckover to the National Trust in 1943. Alexandrina stayed on until her death in 1948.

In contrast to the rather plain exterior, the panelled rooms have fine Georgian fireplaces and a wealth of wood- and plasterwork by local craftsmen. The decoration includes both Neo-classical motifs and more exuberant rococo features, among them the magnificently fluid carving surrounding the mirror above the drawing-room fireplace, where festoons of drapery are suspended from an eagle with outstretched wings. In recent years, the vast library that was added onto the east

ABOVE LEFT The drawing room, where the eye-catching rococo decoration framing the mirror over the fireplace was probably carved for the room.
LEFT The stone-flagged kitchen, part of the servants' quarters in the basement, has a 1930s range.
OPPOSITE Peckover House is one of a number of fine eighteenth-century buildings on the banks of the Nene that reflect Wisbech's former prosperity.

end of the house in 1878, and that had been denuded of its contents, has been refitted with reproductions of the original bookshelves, wallpaper and other features and filled with books. The banking wing has now also been opened and there is a rolling programme of exhibitions.

After the built-up river frontage, the spacious walled garden, which extends behind several buildings along the Nene to the west, comes as something of a surprise. It is a surviving example of the Victorian 'gardenesque' style, in which the display of individual plants is as important as the overall effect. A spacious lawn is shaded by fine specimen trees and flanked by a bosky wilderness walk. Colourful flower-beds mark a more formal area and there are spectacular climbing roses, an orangery and a cool green fern house.

Penrhyn Castle

Gwynedd
1 mile (1.6 kilometres) east of
Bangor, at Llandegai off the A5

From the long upward climb off the Bangor road there is a sudden view of Penrhyn's great four-storey keep rising above the trees, with battlemented turrets at each corner. The rest of the creeper-clad building stretches away across a bluff in an impressive array of towers, battlements and crenellations. Round-headed windows ornamented with a carved zig-zag motif seem to have been lifted from a Norman church. The interior, where a grand hall with soaring Romanesque arches suggests the transept of a cathedral, is even more dramatic. There are long, stone-flagged corridors, high ceilings and heavy doors and panelling. Carved stone is everywhere: surrounding arches and doors and forming bosses, corbels, friezes and capitals.

Seen against the backdrop of Snowdonia, and set prominently above the River Ogwen with views over the Menai Strait to Anglesey, this romantic neo-Norman fantasy was built to impress, but is a castle in appearance only. Built from 1820 to 1832 by Thomas Hopper, a fashionable architect who had been employed by the Prince Regent to add a conservatory to one of his London residences, Carlton House, it was commissioned by George Hay Dawkins-Pennant to replace the gothic house, by Samuel Wyatt, he had inherited

from his uncle Richard Pennant. Both men had the advantage of huge wealth, initially generated by the family's sugar plantations in Jamaica, which were first established in the seventeenth century and which, by 1805, were worked by some one thousand enslaved Africans. In addition to the money coming from Jamaica, G.H. Dawkins-Pennant also enjoyed a sizeable income from the family's slate quarry in Snowdonia, where it forms a great bite out of the hills. Richard, whose entrepreneurial activities included devising ways to diversify the triangular slave trade on which the Jamaican estates depended, had turned the quarry into a major concern and by 1792 it was exporting over 12,000 tons of slate a year.

Like the workers in the slate quarry, the stonemasons, carpenters and other craftsmen who built and decorated the castle were local men, and this unique building is as much a monument to their skills as to Hopper's designs. Using Welsh oak, limestone from Anglesey and slate from the family quarry, these men interpreted the architect's vision and translated his decorative motifs, some of which were taken from marginal illustrations in manuscripts, others from a book on England's medieval architecture, into stone and wood, sometimes, it seems, contributing ideas of their own. The great staircase, where almost every surface is covered with patterning, is a *tour de force* of carved stone. A strange population looks down from the slender pillars of a blind arcade: here a bearded wild man,

OPPOSITE Penrhyn Castle, with an impressive array of towers and battlements set against the backdrop of the Welsh mountains, is an early nineteenth-century vision of a Norman stronghold.
RIGHT The riot of carved decoration on the grand staircase is typical of the quality of stonework seen throughout Penrhyn, all of which, like the similarly impressive woodwork, was executed by local craftsmen.

there an elf with pointed ears, somewhere else a gargoyle with interlocking teeth. Looking closely, writhing foliage becomes a contorted face. At the foot of the staircase, the curve of the door into the drawing room is echoed by a semicircle of carved hands round the arch.

Hopper also designed Norman-style furniture for the house, much of which was put together by the estate carpenters. Slate was used lavishly, as in the slate billiard table with cluster-column legs in the library and the extraordinary slate bed weighting over a ton in one of the bedrooms, a piece that was probably carved by someone more used to producing headstones for the churchyards round about. Hopper even designed carpets to match. Exceptional stained glass, such as that filling the windows of the grand hall, was supplied by Thomas Willement, the leading designer of the day, and there are some notable textiles too, such as the rich green and crimson velvet used for the curtains and upholstery in the Ebony Room, named after its oppressive ebony furnishings. Morris wallpapers in the family rooms were introduced in the late nineteenth century, but essentially the castle has survived unchanged.

In the mid-nineteenth century, the house was greatly enriched by the Spanish, Italian and Dutch paintings collected by Edward Douglas-Pennant, 1st Baron Penrhyn of Llandegai, among them a Canaletto of the Thames at Westminster, Aert van der Neer's moody riverscape, lit by a full moon veiled by clouds, Palma Vecchio's *Holy Family*, and a delightful painting of St Luke sketching the Virgin and Child from the studio of Dieric Bouts, the arches behind the apostle framing a sylvan landscape with a distant walled town.

The servants' quarters are shown as they were after rebuilding in 1868. A warren of rooms giving onto an inner courtyard is centred on the kitchen, where gastronomic dinners of eight or nine courses were prepared when the future Edward VII was entertained here in 1894. Penrhyn slate forms cool work surfaces in the pastry room and dry larder and tops the butter table in the dairy larder, where milk, cream, butter and eggs were delivered from the home farm every morning. In the outer court, close to the back gate, is the Ice Tower, where a deep pit was packed with ice in the winter, some of it cut from a lake high in Snowdonia, for use in the warmer months.

In the sizeable stable block, designed to hold 36 horses, slate again features prominently, forming the mangers and stall divisions. A museum of industrial locomotives associated with the slate industry accommodated here includes *Charles*, a saddle tank engine that once worked the railway serving the family's quarries. This railway was one of the improvements introduced by Edward Douglas-Pennant, who also added greatly to the estate, providing new farmhouses and other buildings for his tenants, and introduced agricultural reforms. The emancipation of the Pennants' African slaves in Jamaica in 1833, for whom the family had received compensation, meant that the quarry, where 3,000 men were employed in the 1890s, was now the main source of income. Bethesda, where most of the quarrymen lived, had grown into a substantial settlement. But the Douglas-Pennants' paternalistic regime was increasingly under strain. Years of dissatisfaction with pay and working conditions and George, the 2nd Lord's opposition to a union boiled over in 1900 and the ensuing strike lasted until 1903. When it ended, because of a slump in the industry, not all the workers could be re-engaged and this whole episode has left a residue of bitterness and resentment.

The estate, some 72,000 acres (29,000 hectares) at its height, is now 40,000 acres (16,200 hectares) of mountain and upland pasture. In the pleasure grounds surrounding the house, fine specimen trees are mixed with mature beeches and oaks, and there is a ruined gothic chapel placed as an eye-catcher on a prominent knoll. A terraced walled garden sloping steeply into a valley below the castle shelters many tender shrubs and plants, and includes a water garden at the lowest level.

Petworth House

West Sussex
In the centre of Petworth

A luminous landscape by Turner at Petworth shows the park at sunset. Dark clumps of trees throw long shadows over the lake and in the foreground a buck stoops to drink, its antlers silhouetted against the sun-tinged water. Turner was inspired by 'Capability' Brown's masterpiece, one of the greatest man-made landscapes created in eighteenth-century Europe. Brown's sublime wooded park, with its serpentine lake, enfolds a late seventeenth-century palace filled with an exceptional collection of works of art, including fine furniture, *objets* and sculpture as well as paintings. This great house, in a French baroque style, was the creation of the unlikeable Charles Seymour, 6th Duke of Somerset (the Proud Duke), who set about remodelling the manor house of the earls of Northumberland, probably to designs by Daniel Marot, on his marriage to Elizabeth Percy, the daughter of the 11th and last earl. Petworth's impressive west front, with projecting bays at each end, stretches over 300 feet (90 metres) and is decorated with the phoenix wings of Somerset's ducal crest. Although, apart from the Grand Staircase, only two seventeenth-century interiors survive intact, these fully reflect Charles Seymour's self-importance. The major feature of the florid baroque chapel is the theatrical family pew filling the west end. Supported by classical columns, it is surmounted by carved and painted drapery on which Somerset's arms and coronet are prominently displayed, as if this were a royal box. His coldly formal marble hall with its black-and-white chequered floor on the other side of the house must have quelled the spirits of the few thought worthy to set foot in the Proud Duke's house.

As well as remodelling the house, Charles Seymour also added to the art collection established by the earls of Northumberland, which included a series of portraits by Van Dyck and works by Titian and Elsheimer. And he commissioned Grinling Gibbons to produce the limewood carvings of flowers, foliage, birds and classical vases which now cascade down the walls of the Carved Room, and Louis Laguerre to paint the Grand Staircase.

On the death of the 7th Duke in 1750, the estate passed to his nephew Charles Wyndham, 2nd Earl of Egremont, and it was he who employed Brown to landscape the park. A cultivated man who had profited from the Grand Tour and time in the diplomatic service, he was largely responsible for Petworth's collection of Italian, French and Dutch Old Masters. He also acquired the impressive array of ancient sculpture from Greece and Rome. Now of particular importance because it is one of only three such collections of the period to have survived intact, it includes the sensitively sculpted head

BELOW Carved limewood of exceptional quality, by Grinling Gibbons and John Selden, frames portraits and forms festoons and swags in the Carved Room.

fashioned in the fourth century BC known as the Leconfield Aphrodite, and some good Roman portrait busts and copies of Greek originals. The 2nd Earl's son, the philanthropic and benevolent 3rd Earl, who presided over Petworth for 74 years, from 1763 to 1837, left his stamp on almost every room, enriching them with his purchases of contemporary art and sculpture, and altering and rearranging furnishings and picture hangs in pursuit of the perfect scheme. Best known as the patron of Turner, for whom he arranged a studio at Petworth, the 3rd Earl also acquired works by Thomas Gainsborough, Joshua Reynolds, Henry Fuseli and Johann Zoffany. And he augmented his father's sculpture collection, for which he twice extended the existing gallery, with works by English contemporaries, such as Sir Richard Westmacott and John Rossi, and by the Irish sculptor J.E. Carew. One of the most striking pieces is the vividly fluid representation of St Michael and Satan by John Flaxman that was finished in 1826, the year in which the sculptor died. Except for the spear that St Michael is about to plunge into his grovelling adversary, this powerful work, which cost the 3rd Earl £3,500, was all carved from one piece of marble.

In spite of a family tradition that paintings should be left as the 3rd Earl had them, many changes were made to the way they were arranged by Sir Anthony Blunt, then the Trust's Honorary Adviser on paintings, after Petworth came to the National Trust in 1947. In recent years, helped by generous loans of pictures from the present Lord and Lady Egremont, the Trust has re-created the spirit of the 3rd Earl's crowded and eclectic displays. In some cases it has been possible to reconstruct the hangs as recorded in watercolour and gouache sketches painted by Turner when he was staying here. Thus, on the south wall of the square dining room, a large canvas by Reynolds is now framed on three sides by columns of small paintings and crowned by a Reynolds self-portrait, just as it was some 200 years ago. Similarly, four landscapes by Turner have been returned to the Carved Room for which they were commissioned. At the same time, again with loans from Lord and Lady Egremont, additional contents have been brought in, such as the copper *batterie de cuisine* in the impressive servants' quarters.

Although the great storms of 1987 and 1989 brought down hundreds of trees, the park is still much as Turner painted it, with deer grazing beneath clumps of beeches, chestnuts and oaks. Trees still frame Brown's serpentine lake below the west front and crown the ridges shading imperceptibly into Sussex downland. Far in the distance on the horizon is the outline of a turreted gothick folly, possibly designed by Sir John Soane. Brown's pleasure grounds to the north of the house, with serpentine paths winding through rare trees and shrubs, echo the boundaries of a vanished Elizabethan layout. A little Doric temple was probably moved here when the pleasure grounds were created, but the Ionic rotunda, perhaps designed by Matthew Brettingham, was introduced by Brown. Here, too, are some of the carved seventeenth-century urns on pedestals which the 3rd Earl placed strategically in the gardens and park.

LEFT This grand marble-floored hall, with carved woodwork by John Selden, formed the entrance to the Proud Duke's house.
OPPOSITE Petworth's palatial west front, built for the 6th Duke of Somerset, looks out across the landscape park created by 'Capability' Brown.

Plas Newydd

Anglesey
1 mile (1.6 kilometres) south-west
of Llanfairpwll and the A5 on the
A4080, 2½ miles (4 kilometres)
from the Menai Bridge, 5 miles
(8 kilometres) from Bangor

'I tried repeatedly in vain ... to get some use made of my drawing.' So Rex Whistler explained his decision to join the Welsh Guards in 1940. Four years later he was dead, killed by a mortar bomb in Normandy at the age of 39. Plas Newydd, which has a substantial collection of Whistler's work, is where this talented artist spent some of his happiest and most creative hours. His *tour de force*, a panoramic seascape, 58 feet (18 metres) wide, fills an entire wall of the dining room. Painted on a single piece of canvas that Whistler had had specially made, it looks across the choppy waters of a harbour to an Italianate town 'bristling with spires, domes and columns' set at the foot of wild and craggy mountains, a vision that echoes Plas Newydd's own setting on the shores of the Menai Strait, with the mountains of Snowdonia rising steeply from the water on the other side.

Reproductions of this painting never capture the sweep and scale of the composition or the wealth of detail it includes, with plentiful allusions to buildings the artist had seen on his continental travels and to the family of his patron, the 6th Marquess of Anglesey, of whom he was very fond. Every corner contains some delightful cameo. At the far end of the *trompe-l'oeil* colonnade on the left-hand side people are going about their business in a steep street running up from the water. Two women gossip; an old lady climbs slowly upwards with the help of a stick; a boy steals an apple from a tub of fruit outside a shop. A girl leaning out of an upstairs window to talk to a young man below, as if she were Juliet and he Romeo, alludes to Whistler's unrequited love for the beautiful Lady Caroline, the marquess's eldest daughter, and the artist has portrayed himself as the gardener sweeping up leaves in the colonnade.

Whistler's mural was part of Lord Anglesey's extensive changes to Plas Newydd in the 1930s. He and his wife converted the house into one of the most comfortable of their day, following the 6th Marquess's maxim that 'every bathroom should have a bedroom', and employed Sybil Colefax to create Lady Anglesey's feminine pink and white bedroom, furnished with pink muslin curtains and white bed-hangings and with a pink ribbon setting off the white bedspread. The long saloon with a view over the Menai Strait to Snowdon is also much as the 6th Marquess and his wife arranged it, with two large and comfortable settees either side of the fire and four pastoral landscapes by Ommeganck dominating the pictures.

Architecturally, Plas Newydd is intriguing. The original sixteenth-century manor built by the powerful Griffith family was substantially remodelled in the eighteenth century, most importantly in the 1790s for the 1st Earl of Uxbridge by James Wyatt and Joseph Potter of Lichfield, who produced the uncompromising mixture of classical and gothick. There is a classical staircase leading to a screen of Doric columns on the first floor and a classical frieze by Wyatt appears boldly white against blue in the ante-room and against red in the octagon, but in the hall there is fan vaulting, with elaborate bosses at the intersection of the ribs. This stately room rising through two storeys with a gallery at one end opens into the even more splendid gothick music room, the largest room in the house and probably on the site of the great hall of the manor.

An early artificial limb and mud-spattered Hussar trousers recall the 1st Earl's son, who was created 1st Marquess of Anglesey for his heroism at the Battle of Waterloo in 1815, where he lost a leg. He is also remarkable for the fact that he had 18 children and 73 grandchildren. Other members of the family gaze down from a fine array of portraits, including works by John Hoppner, George Romney and Thomas Lawrence and a Grand Tour painting of the 1st Earl, a rather plump young man in a salmon coat. Many of these pictures came from Beaudesert, the family's Staffordshire house that was dismantled in 1935 and which was also the source of some of the fine furniture.

Plas Newydd is first seen from above, when the path leading down from the car park suddenly reveals the gothick west front covered in red creeper and magnolia. Sweeping lawns and mature woodland set off the building, the mix of native

ABOVE In this detail of the magnificent mural he painted for the house, Rex Whistler shows Neptune's trident, complete with a frond of seaweed, leaning against the central urn and his golden crown abandoned on the plinth, as if the sea-god had just come out of the water.

OPPOSITE This spiral staircase at Plas Newydd leads from the gothick hall to the comfortable bedroom fitted out in pink and white in the 1930s for Lady Anglesey, wife of the 6th Marquess.

trees and exotics here include many fine sycamores, beeches and oaks that pre-date the planting undertaken with Humphry Repton's advice. A Venetian well-head and Italianate urns in the formal terraced gardens evoke a warmer sun than that which reddens the peaks on the far side of the water in the evening.

ABOVE Plas Newydd is gloriously set above the Menai Strait, with views over the water to the mountains of Snowdonia, and has its own private harbour, built in the 1790s.

OPPOSITE Plas yn Rhiw's homely interiors are full of the belongings of the three Keating sisters, who bought this little house on the Llŷn peninsula in 1938 and lovingly restored it.

Plas yn Rhiw

Gwynedd
12 miles (19.2 kilometres) from
Pwllheli, on the south coast road
to Aberdaron

The long Llŷn peninsula, which shields Cardigan Bay from the full force of the Atlantic, is a windswept claw of craggy moorland and tiny fields. Only in the far south-east, which is protected by the tor of Mynydd-y-Graig, is there shelter enough for woodland to thrive. Plas yn Rhiw sits in this wind-shielded pocket below the hill, with views over the bay to Cadair Idris and south along the coast to Fishguard. On clear nights the lights of Aberystwyth beckon across the water. A Georgian frontage hides a much older building behind. Thick granite walls in the tiny parlour and the remains of a stone spiral staircase are survivals of a Tudor dwelling on this site. As the date stone on the front of the house proclaims, it was first extended in 1634; two wings built into the hillside, Georgian sash windows and the slate-floored Victorian verandah were additions of the early and mid-nineteenth century, turning the farmhouse into a gentleman's residence.

Plas yn Rhiw's homely interiors reflect the three forceful and indomitable Keating sisters, Eileen, Lorna and Honora, daughters of a successful Nottinghamshire architect, who bought the property in 1938 and lovingly restored it after almost 20 years of neglect. A white hat and gloves lie neatly on the patchwork quilt covering one of the simple wooden beds. A shoe rack is filled with Honora's fashionable footwear from her days in London and a successful career in the social services. Elegant Georgian chairs, fur coats and family portraits speak of comfortable gentility, and an extensive collection of popular classics suggests many evenings spent listening to the old gramophone in the parlour. Gentle watercolours hanging three and four deep on the stairs, their muted colours recording local views and landmarks, recall Honora's days at the Slade and her youthful ambition to be an artist.

The little terraced garden sloping down towards the sea, with thickly planted beds framed by box hedges, dates from the 1820s. Organically managed, it is a mix of tender and exotic species and indigenous wild flora and there are bulbs in the rough meadow grass and woodland behind the house.

The sisters, who are still a legend in the neighbourhood, worked tirelessly to protect the natural beauty of the peninsula. They were often seen, wrapped up warmly, tramping the lanes to check on rubbish tips and illegal caravan sites. Fiercely outspoken in defence of their beliefs, the Keatings were personally self-effacing, little realising that the words with which they chose to honour their parents – 'there is no death while memory lives' – would serve as their own memorial.

Polesden Lacey

Surrey
5 miles (8 kilometres) north-west of Dorking, 1½ miles
(2.4 kilometres) south of
Great Bookham, off the A246
Leatherhead–Guildford road

Polesden Lacey is alive with the spirit of Margaret Greville, whose vivacious portrait greets visitors to the house. Those she invited to the legendary weekend parties held here from 1906 until the outbreak of the Second World War included Indian maharajahs, literary figures, such as Beverley Nichols, Osbert Sitwell and Harold Nicolson, and prominent politicians. Edward VII was a close friend of the elegant society hostess, as was Queen Mary, the latter often telephoning in the morning to invite herself to tea that afternoon. In 1923, the year after Margaret Greville was made a dame, the future George VI and Queen Elizabeth spent part of their honeymoon at Polesden Lacey. After 1908, when her husband died, Mrs Greville presided over the house alone.

Set above a deep valley on the edge of the North Downs, with views across the combe to sheep-grazed fields and hilltop woods, the house is a comfortable, two-storey building sprawling round a courtyard. The white frames of generous sash windows on both floors stand out attractively against honey-coloured stucco. The flavour of the Regency villa built in the 1820s by Joseph Bonsor to the designs of Thomas Cubitt still lingers on the south front with its classical colonnade, but the house was much enlarged and the interior transformed after 1906 by Mewès and Davis, the architects of the Ritz Hotel, as an essential step in the realisation of Margaret Greville's social ambitions. Here she displayed her outstanding collection of paintings, furniture and other works of art, the nucleus of which she had inherited from her wealthy father, William McEwan, founder of the Scottish brewery that still bears his name.

The range and richness of the collection, which includes Flemish tapestries, French and English furniture, English, continental and oriental pottery and porcelain, and European paintings from the fourteenth to the eighteenth centuries, gives Polesden Lacey its extraordinarily opulent atmosphere, vividly evoking the charmed life of the Edwardian upper classes. Some of the finest pieces were intended for very different settings. In the sumptuously decorated drawing room, glittering mirrors reflect carved and gilt panelling that once adorned an Italian palace. A richly carved oak reredos in the hall, a masterpiece by Edward Pierce, was originally intended for Sir Christopher Wren's St Matthew's church, just off Cheapside in London, which was demolished in 1881. From her father, Margaret Greville inherited some Dutch seventeenth-century paintings, but she acquired most of the British portraits in the dining room, among them Raeburn's charming study of George and Maria Stewart as children, the little girl shown holding a rabbit in the folds of her dress, and was also largely responsible for the best of the collection shown in the corridor round the central courtyard. The pictures hanging here include several early Italian works, such as an exquisite early fourteenth-century triptych of the Madonna and Child, sixteenth-century portraits in the style of Corneille de Lyon and a number of atmospheric Dutch interiors and landscapes, among them Jacob van Ruisdael's skyscape of the Zuider Zee in which diminutive figures on the shore are dwarfed by wintry grey clouds piled overhead.

Invitation cards, scrap albums and other mementoes collected by Margaret Greville conjure up the world in which she lived. The menu book records the *salade niçoise* and orange mousse on which Ramsay MacDonald dined on 17 October 1936 and the *aubergines provençales* given to the Queen of Spain the following day. The same names appear again and again in the visitors' book and the same faces recur in the photographs, statesmen and royalty, such as Grand Duke Michael of Russia and Kaiser Wilhelm II, rubbing shoulders with figures from the worlds of entertainment and literature, a memorable shot showing Mrs Greville in Hollywood with Wendy Barrie and Spencer Tracy. Upstairs, her bedroom apartment runs along the south front. The view over the valley from here is even more spectacular and there is a marble bath in the bathroom.

The atmosphere of the house extends into the garden, where spacious lawns are shaded by mature beeches, cedars

and limes. Although much of the layout is a twentieth-century creation, the long terraced walk is a legacy from the years when Polesden Lacey was the home of the playwright Richard Brinsley Sheridan. A series of more intimate walled and hedged enclosures to the west of the house include an iris garden and a rose garden centred on an Italianate marble well-head. Margaret Greville's garden ornaments are everywhere, from the griffins on the terrace in front of the house to vases, urns and sundials and the statue of Diana on the croquet lawn. She is buried in a yew-hedged enclosure beside the rose garden.

ABOVE Polesden Lacey, set high above a deep valley on the edge of the North Downs, is where the society hostess Mrs Margaret Greville entertained lavishly in the early twentieth century.
OPPOSITE Carolus-Duran's vivacious portrait of Margaret Greville greets visitors from the half-landing above the hall.

Powis Castle

Powys
1 mile (1.6 kilometres) south
of Welshpool, signposted from
the A483

Some time around 1200 the Welsh lord of Powys began building a new stronghold on this splendid defensive site, a great outcrop of limestone plunging steeply to the south with panoramic views over the River Severn to the hills of Shropshire. Although long since converted into a country house, Powis still has the trappings of a castle. Seen from across the valley, a massive Norman-style keep with three projecting towers rises to a battlemented skyline. To the left, a long range flanking the entrance court was created out of the substantial curtain wall that defended the inner bailey. In front of the castle, grand baroque terraces blasted out of the rock fall to a vast expanse of lawn.

A wide flight of steps closely guarded by twin drum towers leads up from the entrance court to a gothic archway. Here the house takes over. The front door opens into seventeenth-century grandeur and opulence and the magnificent interiors

fitted out for William Herbert, 3rd Lord Powis, 1st Earl, Marquess and titular Duke from the 1660s onwards. A staunch supporter of the Stuart cause, Lord Powis spent his last years in exile with James II. The most remarkable of his formal apartments, possibly designed by the gentleman-architect William Winde, is the richly gilded state bedroom. A deep alcove is almost filled with the canopied state bed, hung with crimson velvet and separated from the rest of the room by a finely carved balustrade. The only one of its kind in Britain, this barrier is a direct link with the formal etiquette of Louis XIV's Versailles that was closely imitated by the British aristocracy. Velvet-covered and marquetry furniture, a painted ceiling and rich tapestries contribute to the opulent effect,

OPPOSITE The library was formed in the early nineteenth century, probably to house books that had belonged to the Empress Josephine, consort of Napoleon, many of which were subsequently sold.
BELOW Although long since converted into a country house, Powis Castle, standing high above a series of magnificent Italianate terraces, still looks like the medieval stronghold it once was.

ABOVE The Clive collection of Indian treasures displayed at Powis includes a tent of painted chintz which belonged to Tipu Sahib, Sultan of Mysore.
OPPOSITE Opulent interiors at Powis, such as this grand painted staircase hall, were created in the late seventeenth century for William Herbert, 3rd Lord Powis, who died in exile in France with James II.

although not everything in the room is contemporary. A huge and much more accomplished ceiling by Antonio Verrio, based on Veronese's *Apotheosis of Venice*, with an assembly of deities seated on clouds, dominates the 1st Marquess's grand staircase.

There is no hint of this pomposity in the only surviving Elizabethan interior, a beautiful T-shaped long gallery dating from Sir Edward Herbert's acquisition of the castle in 1587. Young trees and tendrils of foliage branch across the plasterwork ceiling above the rather indifferent family portraits set against early seventeenth-century *trompe-l'oeil* panelling and the polished silver sconces forming pools of light down the room. A table carries a more than life-size marble cat, crouched aggressively over the body of a snake, ears pricked as it looks back over its shoulder, teeth bared and muscles rippling beneath its fur. This remarkable ancient Roman sculpture, perhaps modelled on a wild animal, came to Powis through the marriage of Lady Henrietta Herbert to Edward, the eldest son of Robert Clive of India, in 1784.

The house contains an important collection of Indian artefacts acquired by Robert, who amassed a fortune in the employ of the East India Company at a time when it was taking control of much of the Indian subcontinent. These objects are supplemented by those collected by Henrietta and Edward, who was Governor of Madras (now Chennai). Some of the most spectacular artefacts were taken as spoils of war in 1799 after the defeat and death of Tipu Sultan, ruler of Mysore, who had been involved in a series of hostilities with the East India Company. There are jewelled slippers that once adorned the Sultan's feet, a gold tiger's head from his throne, a jewelled hookah encrusted with rubies, diamonds and emeralds, and sumptuously decorated padded armour. There are plans to re-present the collection so that its links to British involvement in India are clearer.

A curiously elongated ballroom, originally almost twice as long, in the range flanking the courtyard, was commissioned from T.F. Pritchard in 1775. The final alterations to the castle were made for the 4th Earl of Powis in 1902–4 by G.F. Bodley, who was responsible for the Jacobethan-style panelling, plaster ceilings and other features in the dining room and oak drawing room, and for inserting mullioned windows to replace some existing sashes.

Powis's four great Italianate terraces ornamented with lead statues and urns hang over the valley below, forming a giant staircase descending the rock. Who designed them and when is unclear, but it is likely they date from the 1680s and were the inspiration of William Winde, who created the grand arcaded terrace at Cliveden (*see* p.99), with some of the work being carried out by the French gardener Adrian Duval in the early years of the eighteenth century. Clipped yews cluster closely below the castle, some lapping the terrace wall as if about to flow downhill. Rare and tender lime-tolerant plants flourishing here contrast with those planted in the wilderness laid out in the eighteenth century on the ridge across the valley, where the soil is acidic and where there are panoramic views of the castle from winding wooded walks.

A wooded medieval deer-park surrounds Powis, its naturalistic contours and planting partly reflecting alterations by 'Capability' Brown's disciple William Emes, who was engaged to landscape it in 1771 and diverted a public road away from the castle. Although most of the great beeches, sycamores and limes were planted between 1800 and 1850, some of the massive oaks may be as much as 800 years old.

Quarry Bank

Cheshire
1½ miles (2.4 kilometres) north of Wilmslow off the B5166, 2 miles (3.2 kilometres) from the M56, exit 5, 10 miles (16 kilometres) south of Manchester

In 1769 Richard Arkwright started a revolution in the textile industry when he invented a water-powered machine that could spin cotton. In the 1780s there was another watershed when the patents protecting his invention were challenged and overthrown, opening the way for a huge expansion in factory-produced yarn. One of the first to take advantage of the new opportunities was the young Samuel Greg, who in 1780 had inherited one of the largest textile businesses in Manchester. He found a suitable site for a water-powered mill in the isolated Bollin Valley some 10 miles (16 kilometres) south of the city and had built his first mill here by 1784. As the mill prospered, it was enlarged, weaving looms were introduced and water power was augmented with steam. Rows of red brick cottages to house the growing labour force were added to the little village of Styal nearby, and a shop, two chapels and a school were built for the community. Everything survives and, following a four-year restoration project, visitors can experience every aspect of life in this early industrial settlement.

This unique complex lies at the centre of over 300 acres (120 hectares) of well-wooded park following the River Bollin.

The surroundings are delightfully rural, with grass and trees setting off the red-brick mill, its soaring chimney and the bell tower that was used to ensure strict timekeeping. Impressive rows of multi-paned windows lighting every floor contribute to what is one of the finest brick-built Georgian façades in the country. Taken on by the Trust in a derelict state, the mill is now a working museum of the cotton industry, with four floors for visitors to explore. At its heart is a giant iron waterwheel, the most powerful in Britain. Spinning machines and weaving looms restored by the Trust rest on wooden floors, their weight supported by giant beams and iron columns. The clatter and vibration when the machinery is being demonstrated, and the lack of space, give some idea of what it must have been like to have been employed here during the mill's heyday. Conditions were tough. Quite apart from the danger of injury, workers had to endure working in the hot, humid environment that cotton needed, with little ventilation in the early years. Many suffered lung disease from inhaling cotton dust or cancer of the mouth from sucking cotton thread through the shuttle.

A short walk from the mill is the Apprentice House, a double-gabled, three-storey building constructed in 1790 to accommodate the children who, being much cheaper than adults, initially made up more than half the mill's workforce. Up to a hundred pauper apprentices were housed here. Brought in from workhouses, most of them were on contracts to work twelve hours a day, six days a week. The dormitories where they slept, girls on one side of the house, boys on the other, have been recreated as they might have been in the late eighteenth century, with straw-filled mattresses on the beds, chamber pots underneath and cloaks and hats hanging on wooden pegs. Neat rows of vegetables in the garden, including the red-veined leaves of cottagers' kale, illustrate the traditional produce which the children were required to tend after their shift in the mill, and which supplemented their staple diet of bread, milk, porridge, potatoes and bacon. On Sundays, they went to church, walking across the fields to Wilmslow.

LEFT Quarry Bank, one of the earliest water-powered factories in England, was built in the isolated Bollin valley and still lies in an unspoilt sylvan landscape.
OPPOSITE The entrepreneurial Samuel Greg lived with his family in this elegant white Georgian house beside his cotton mill; later generations of the family, though, moved further away from the works.

From the early nineteenth century, the apprentice system declined and there were increasing numbers of adult workers, many of whom lived in the rows of terraced red-brick cottages which Samuel Greg built specially for them between 1806 and 1822. Tiny two-up-two-downs, with steps up to the front door and down to a separate basement, these picturesque buildings were home to at least two families, one housed in two rooms in the basement, the other in the main cottage above, where the second bedroom was often rented out to lodgers. The long gardens attached to each cottage, now bright with flowers, were once allotments where the cottagers grew vegetables. Most of the cottages have been updated and modernised, but No.13 Oak Cottages, which was probably built in *c.* 1820, has been left as it was in the 1970s when it was last occupied. Visitors can now take guided tours through its unfurnished, atmospheric rooms with their plank doors, descend to the stone-floored basement, and step out into the back yard where each cottage had a privy and water butt. Down the street is the former village bakery, which now houses a permanent exhibition on life in Styal and the workers who lived here. Some thatched, half-timbered buildings, including the impressive Oak Farm which once provided the village with fresh dairy produce, are remnants of a medieval settlement.

Samuel Greg, his wife Hannah and their family lived in the elegant white Georgian house next to the mill, in the heart of the factory community. On the other side of the works is a smaller but no less comfortable residence that was inhabited by the mill manager, who controlled the flow of water powering the factory. The Gregs had been living in Manchester, and at first just spent their summers at Styal, but Hannah longed to make the beautiful and peaceful Bollin valley their permanent home. Quarry Bank House was begun in the 1790s. Initially a modest villa, it was extended in 1803 and again in 1814, but was always a home rather than a show place. Here Hannah created a tranquil and cultivated haven for herself and her thirteen children. None of Samuel and Hannah's possessions are still here, but using drawings, inventories and descriptions of Quarry Bank and similar houses, the Trust has decorated and furnished the rooms on show, including a light and airy drawing room looking onto ornamental gardens running down to the Bollin, as they might have been in the early nineteenth century. Hannah's writings and other exhibits introduce the family's social circle and her interest in self-improvement and debate. The upper, kitchen garden, dramatically set above a sandstone cliff with spectacular views over the valley, has some of the earliest surviving cast-iron glasshouses, probably dating from the early 1820s, which were used for growing vines and peaches. Later generations of Gregs moved to a grandiose Victorian house high up on the side of the valley.

Quebec House

Kent
At the east end of the village of
Westerham, on the north side of
the A25, facing the junction with
the B2026 Edenbridge road

A high brick wall on the road from Westerham to Sevenoaks conceals the unpretentious gabled façades of Quebec House, where James Wolfe spent the first eleven years of his life. His parents rented the house, then known as Spiers, in 1726, and James was born a year later. The house, which is sixteenth century in origin, was subsequently extensively altered but has now been returned to its seventeenth-century appearance. Basically square, it is built of a pleasing mixture of brick and Kentish ragstone and has three distinctive gables on each façade. It is a modest place, homely and welcoming, with low-ceilinged, panelled rooms.

Mementoes of General Wolfe and his victory at Quebec in 1759 during the Seven Years' War with France, when he defeated the French by scaling the Heights of Abraham above the town but was mortally wounded in the attack, are on display. A pencil sketch of Wolfe in the Bicentenary Room was drawn by his aide-de-camp on a page torn from a pocket book while they were in the field. The curiously pointed profile, a caricaturist's dream, is easily recognisable in a number of other paintings in the house.

Wolfe's travelling canteen in a corner of the same room gives a glimpse of the comforts enjoyed by an officer on campaign in the mid-eighteenth century. Clearly the finer things in life were not entirely discarded, as the canteen contained glass decanters as well as more mundane objects, such as a griddle and a frying-pan. Also here is the finely quilted banyan, a loose-fitting garment like a dressing-gown, in which Wolfe's body is said to have been brought back to England from Quebec.

A seventeenth-century staircase leads up to a tranquil panelled drawing room on the first floor, furnished with period pieces and a Broadwood square piano of 1788, and warmed by an open fire on cold afternoons. A striking portrait of James Wolfe's mother, Henrietta, hangs on the walls and her recipe book is also on display.

An exhibition in the old coach-house across the walled garden describes the Quebec campaign, which was key to establishing British colonial supremacy in North America, and its background and gives details of Wolfe's life. Three niches in the south wall of this building are thought to be bee-boles where bees were kept in straw skeps, or hives, possibly to aid the pollination of fruit trees on the wall.

ABOVE James Wolfe, who defeated the French at Quebec in 1759, spent the early years of his life in this modest building of brick and Kentish ragstone.

Rainham Hall

London

The Broadway, Rainham, just
south of the church, 5 miles
(8 kilometres) east of Barking

This early Georgian house
adjoining the graveyard of the
Norman parish church survives
from a time when Rainham
was a small village close to the
Thames, set amongst fields and
marshes and with a tidal creek
running down to the river. Built

in the Queen Anne style and completed in 1729, as the date on
a rainwater hopper proclaims, the Hall's red-brick façades rise
three storeys above a basement to a roofline parapet. Beyond
the fine wrought-iron railings shielding the house from the
street, steps lead up to a carved wooden porch carried on fluted

BELOW When Rainham Hall was built, London had not spread so far east and the
house was part of a small village set amongst fields and marshes beside the Thames.

Corinthian columns and there are round-headed sash windows, some of which are blind, on every floor. An attic storey, lit by oversized dormers protruding above the roofline parapet, was added in the 1920s by the solicitor William Murray Sturges.

Rainham is not grand. Apart from the spacious entrance hall, with its chequered marble floor, carved doorcase and marble fireplace, and the elegant staircase beyond, this is an intimate place of small panelled rooms and inviting window seats, with views onto the walled garden behind, over the lime trees at the front of the house, or down onto the churchyard.

Its builder, John Harle, was a merchant and shipowner from South Shields, at the mouth of the Tyne, where his father was a part-owner of ships carrying coal to London. John and his brothers had gradually extended the family business, and by the 1720s John was settled in London and overseeing trade between the Baltic and Mediterranean. He bought land at Rainham in 1728 and also acquired the wharf on the creek, from where he shipped agricultural produce to London and landed building materials and coal for the area around. This, too, is where he is likely to have unloaded the Caribbean mahogany used for the handrail and twisted balusters of his grand staircase. Not yet a fashionable wood in the early eighteenth century, the mahogany is likely to have come to England as ballast in a ship returning from the Caribbean. After John's death in 1742, and that of his second wife in 1749, the Hall was rented out and its contents auctioned. The *trompe l'oeil* panelling on the stairs, ornamented with hanging garlands and fluted columns, is thought to date from the 1780s, when his daughter-in-law owned the hall.

Some of the decoration and other details were introduced in more recent years. The plaque with the Harle coat of arms over the fireplace in the hall was installed by the restorer and antique collector Colonel Herbert Hall Mulliner, who bought the Hall in 1917 and copied the coat of arms from John's monument in the church. Mulliner may also have been responsible for some of the charming blue-and-white Delft tiles that line many of the fireplaces and he had much of the softwood panelling painted to resemble oak. And in the 1960s the eccentric society photographer Anthony Denney gave the house an individual gloss. Panelling and skirting in the hall, including the plug sockets, was painted to look like marble and gilding was added to the carved decoration, while he had the softwood panelling in his bedroom painted a delicate pale blue, since deepened to a darker hue.

Beside the former stables, now the café, stands a large Victorian dog kennel, with finials ornamenting its gabled roof.

The Hall reopened in 2015 following a major project of conservation and interpretation and former residents are being brought to life in a programme of changing exhibitions.

LEFT The elegant staircase of Caribbean mahogany was put in by John Harle, who built the house, but the *trompe l'oeil* panelling above was a later addition.

Red House

Kent
Red House Lane, Bexleyheath

In the midst of the sprawl of south London, behind an undulating brick wall, a tranquil, leafy garden sets off the small house in the country that the young Philip Webb designed for his friends William Morris and his wife Jane, who were just starting out on married life. It was Webb's first commission and was finished in 1860, in what was then a gentle Kentish countryside of orchards, fields and meadows. An unpretentious L-shaped building of deep-red brick with a steep tiled roof, also startlingly red, it is part Kentish farmhouse, part sleepy French manoir, part medieval monastery. Gothic porches shelter heavy wooden doors, sash windows are topped off with brickwork arches, a buttress is corbelled out to carry an oriel window, and the roofline is broken by two massive brick chimneystacks, by the steep pyramidal roof with a finialled cap which marks the staircase tower, and by gables and dormers. Everything is at different levels, and the sashes are mixed with casements and round bull's-eye windows. This individual place, so different from the stuccoed villas favoured by his contemporaries, embodied Morris's yearning for a pre-industrial world and his romantic ideas about the good life and the value of hand-craftsmanship. Morris stayed here only five years, but the house and the way it was fitted out were to have an enduring influence on later approaches to domestic architecture and ideas of good taste. This was the birthplace of the Arts and Crafts movement, of which both Morris and Webb were leading figures.

When Red House was built, Morris was only in his twenties. He had met Webb during a short stint in the offices of the gothic revival architect G.E. Street and he had also become friendly with two of the leading figures of the Pre-Raphaelite movement, Edward Burne-Jones, whom he had met while a student at Oxford, and Dante Gabriel Rossetti. It was Rossetti who, on the look-out for models with the kind of unconventional beauty valued by the Pre-Raphaelites, had spotted Jane Burden, whom Morris married in 1859. Both Burne-Jones and Webb were closely involved in the fitting out of Red House, which was decorated with rich embroidered hangings, medieval-style stained glass and tiles and specially made furniture, designed by Webb to be both practical and in tune with Morris's vision. Weekend visitors, collected from the nearest station by horse-drawn wagon, were put to work painting ceilings and furniture and the textiles, too, were all produced in the house, to Morris's designs. In 1861, some half-dozen of these friends became the core of the firm of decorators and designers which Morris founded, and which took his romantic ideals and artist-craftsman principles to a much wider audience. Jane, who was an accomplished embroiderer, became closely involved in the company, eventually, as it expanded, managing the embroidery department.

The interior, which is centred on the sturdy oak staircase set in the angle of the L, has long since lost most of the furniture made for it, but some important pieces remain, or have returned, and sympathetic later owners, in particular Ted and Doris Hollamby, who lived here for half a century, have preserved other original features and introduced Morris & Co. wallpapers and innovations in keeping with the house. Although now largely unfurnished, it is welcoming and well lit. There are abstract painted ceilings; richly coloured Persian carpets on the floors; exposed brick fireplaces in every

BELOW A detail from the painted decoration in the drawing room of Red House, one of the three scenes based on a medieval romance by Froissart that Burne-Jones completed in 1860.

room; painted panelling and a selection of Morris papers in cool greens and blues, their designs shaped by the flowers growing outside in the garden. The hall, where the family and their many visitors occasionally ate, and where Morris would appear from the door to the cellar clutching several bottles of wine, still has the tall settle designed by Webb, with painted panels thought to be by Morris. The dining room to one side is furnished with Webb's massive red dresser, topped off with a gothic canopy, and his large oak refectory table, and is hung with an unfinished embroidery of Aphrodite designed by Morris. One of twelve originally planned for the room, of which only seven were begun, it is thought to have been worked by Bessie Burden, Morris's sister-in-law.

Two of the main rooms are upstairs. The beautiful drawing room, with a high barrel ceiling going up into the roof, has another settle, designed by Morris, and an oriel window looking onto the garden, with a window-seat where the ladies of the house sat to work on their embroidery. The adjoining wall has three murals on a medieval theme by Burne-Jones, all that he completed of the proposed cycle of seven. At the end of one wing is Morris's airy L-shaped studio, lit by windows on three sides. Ted Hollamby, who worked as an architect,

designed the desk that fills the bay window and there are examples of the blocks used for printing Morris wallpapers.

Webb designed the compartmental garden as a natural extension of the house, although little remains. Apples and pears trained on the house and an evocative gnarled orchard evoke the Kentish countryside that was once all around and one of the garden rooms designed by Morris has been recreated. Sadly, Morris did not enjoy his dream for very long. The demands of his work took him back to London in 1865 and he is thought never to have visited Red House again. Many of the furnishings ended up at Kelmscott Manor, the Oxfordshire farmhouse he rented with Rossetti as a country retreat, and his idealism contributed to the founding of the Society for the Protection of Ancient Buildings, which directly inspired the formation of the National Trust.

Rufford Old Hall

Lancashire
7 miles (11.2 kilometres) north of Ormskirk, in the village of Rufford on the east side of the A59

Set in the low-lying, watery landscape of south-west Lancashire, close by the Rufford branch of the Leeds and Liverpool canal, is a peaceful L-shaped building dating back to the sixteenth century. The oldest part, all that remains of the H-shaped, timber-framed manor built here by Sir Robert Hesketh in c. 1530, is the magnificent Great Hall filling one arm of the house, on which no expense was spared. Some 46 feet (14 metres) long and 22 feet (6.5 metres) wide and built to impress, it rises to a richly carved hammerbeam roof. Angels, all but one now wingless, look down from the ends of the supporting beams and there are carved roof bosses, some of them displaying the arms of the great Lancashire families with which the Heskeths were allied.

Instead of a partition separating the hall from the screens passage, as was usual in houses of this date, there is a massive, intricately carved wooden screen. Three soaring finials look as if they might have come from a pagoda, but are in fact integral to the screen. This deliberately theatrical set-piece, backed by blind quatrefoils lining the upper wall of the passage and placed within a wooden arch supported by ornate octagonal pillars, is the only one of its kind known to have survived intact. The lord and his guests would have sat at high table under the canopy that curves over the far end of the room, their special status further emphasised by the great bay window, where fragments of heraldic stained glass still survive. A long refectory table, richly carved oak chests, and pieces from the Hesketh collection of arms and armour add to the hall's atmosphere. The exterior is similarly fine, an impressive display of studding, quatrefoils and wood-mullioned windows greeting visitors as they come up the drive.

A Carolean wing juts out at right-angles to the medieval Great Hall, its symmetrical gabled façade built of warm red brick contrasting strongly with the black-and-white half-timbering. A castellated tower peering over the angle between the two ranges is a later addition, a feature of the nineteenth-century building in Tudor gothic style that joins the Great Hall to the Charles II wing. This part of the house was partly formed out of a 1720s rebuilding, using sixteenth-century timbers, of

the east range, and includes a spacious Drawing Room rising to an open timber roof that stretches the full length of the first floor; a spy-hole looks down into the Great Hall below. As elsewhere in the house, richly carved press cupboards, oak settles and other period furnishings add to the antiquarian atmosphere, although not all are genuinely old. The tripod table on display in the Drawing Room, for example, is a nineteenth-century piece in seventeenth-century style.

Although they did not always live here, the Heskeths continued to own the Old Hall until it was given to the Trust in 1936. A show of family portraits includes Sir Godfrey Kneller's imposing likeness of the Thomas Hesketh, who rebuilt the east wing, and a number of landscapes are dominated by a huge canvas by the Flemish artist

OPPOSITE In 1662, a gabled three-storey wing with a datestone set into the brickwork was built at right-angles to the Tudor Great Hall range.
BELOW The hammerbeam roof in Rufford's Great Hall is decorated with carved angels.

Gommaert van der Gracht, whose still-life is set against a distant formal garden and walled town beyond.

Eighteenth- and nineteenth-century buildings around the estate yard, including a former cattle shed and a piggery, show the Old Hall's close connection to the land. Its links to the local community are reflected in the objects from the unique Philip Ashcroft collection that illustrate a rural way of life in this part of the world that has now disappeared. Household utensils, ceramics and other smaller items are distributed round the house, while agricultural equipment is on show in the stables.

St Michael's Mount

Cornwall
½ mile (0.8 kilometre) south of the A394 at Marazion

East of Land's End, round the southern headlands of the Penwith peninsula, the coast of Cornwall turns sharply northwards to embrace Mount's Bay. Prominent in every view across the bay is the island of St Michael's Mount, rising dramatically from the sea. Formed by an outcrop of granite, its steep-sided profile is crowned by the battlements and towers of one of the most unusual of country houses. At low tide, a causeway links the island to the shore, but at high water the only way to reach the Mount is by boat.

This atmospheric place is part religious retreat, part fortress, part elegant country house. The Mount has been associated with Christianity since the fifth century, when St Michael is said to have appeared to some local fishermen, and in 1135 a Benedictine priory was established here as a daughter house of the much grander Mont St Michel, set on another rocky outcrop some 150 miles (240 kilometres) across the Channel. The Mount became an important place of pilgrimage in the Middle Ages, when the attraction of the saint's shrine was enhanced by one of the priory's relics, the jawbone of St Appolonia of Alexander, which was said to cure toothache. A fourteenth-century granite church built on the highest point of the island is the most important survival from the priory. Lighting the west end of the building is a beautiful fifteenth-century rose window in which the flowing robes of a company of angels form swirls of olive-green, blue, red and orange.

The Chevy Chase Room in the earliest part of the castle was originally the monks' refectory and is now called after the hunting scenes on the unusual plaster frieze that runs round the walls. A piece of early seventeenth-century craftsmanship, the frieze shows men with spears and guns pursuing rabbits, boars, stags, a bear and a fox. Some of the dogs are perched mischievously on top of the frieze. The room is furnished with an oak refectory table of c. 1620 and a royal coat of arms displayed prominently over the fireplace was set up here to celebrate the restoration of Charles II. The massive granite walls are probably those built in the twelfth century, but the arching timber roof dates from 400 years later. The windows on the east side of the room, sheltered from the westerly gales, are filled with Flemish and other continental stained glass.

The guardroom in the entry range, the garrison room embedded in the rock, an old sentry box overlooking the steep cobbled path up to the castle and gun batteries pointing out to sea are legacies of the time the Mount was a fortress and played an important role in protecting the Cornish coast. In 1588, when it was the first link in England's defences against the Spanish Armada, a beacon was lit on the church tower to give warning of the approaching fleet. Some 60 years later it was one of the last royalist strongholds in the Civil War, finally surrendering to parliamentary forces in 1646. The Parliamentarian Colonel John St Aubyn, who was appointed governor the following year, bought the island in 1659 and began converting the fortress into a private house. His descendants live here still. Sir John St Aubyn, 4th Baronet, transformed the ruined lady chapel into the elegant Blue Drawing Room, where early rococo gothic plasterwork picked out in white against the blue walls, niches filled with monumental pink vases in jasper and alabaster and fine Chippendale furniture upholstered in blue conjure up the cultivated world of Georgian England.

Far below, on the steep and exposed lower slopes of the island, is the St Aubyn family's terraced rock garden and eighteenth-century walled garden. Despite the sea gales, rare tropical and subtropical plants flourish here.

From the castle terraces there are magnificent views along the Cornish coast and inland to rolling granite moors, while far below a thread of ant-sized people crossing the causeway leading back over the sands to Marazion at low tide could be a procession of medieval pilgrims. A row of whitewashed and stone cottages stands above the claw-shaped harbour on the sheltered north side of the island, where sailing ships once loaded Cornish tin and copper for the Continent.

OPPOSITE St Michael's Mount, set on a rocky outcrop just off the Cornish coast that is islanded by the sea at high tide, is one of the most picturesque of the Trust's properties.

Saltram

Devon

2 miles (3.2 kilometres) west of Plympton, 3 miles (4.8 kilometres) east of Plymouth city centre, between the A38 Plymouth–Exeter road and the A379 Plymouth–Kingsbridge road

Anyone who has travelled by train from Plymouth to London will know the pleasure of seeing the Saltram estate shortly after leaving the city, when the line suddenly emerges on the banks of the Plym estuary and the wooded slopes of the park rise on the other side of the water. With a view over Plymouth Sound to the trees of Mount Edgcumbe, this is a perfect position for a house and the building created here lives up to its setting. Although dating back to late Tudor times, Saltram is essentially a product of the eighteenth century, the rooms and their original contents summing up all that was best about that elegant age.

The remodelling of the house was the work of John and Lady Catherine Parker, who wrapped three classical façades round the mostly Jacobean core, fragments of which are still visible in an interior courtyard, and the three-storey seventeenth-century block which John's father had purchased in 1712. Their son, John Parker, 1st Lord Boringdon, who inherited in 1768, was responsible for amassing the outstanding collection of pictures and for inviting Robert Adam to redesign some of the principal rooms. Already at work on Kedleston Hall (*see* p.188) and Osterley (*see* p.253), Adam was at the height of his career and his interiors at Saltram, in which he was responsible for almost everything, including the door handles, are exceptional examples of his style. In the great Neo-classical saloon, delicate plasterwork attributed to Joseph Rose stands out white against the eggshell blue and burnt yellow of the coved ceiling. Blue damask lines the walls, setting off the four great looking-glasses and a show of portraits, Old Masters and Old Master

copies, hung as Adam intended. A magnificent Axminster carpet echoes the design of the ceiling and gilded chairs and sofas attributed to Chippendale line the walls. Double doors at the north end of the room give a vista into the equally elegant dining room, originally designed as the library, where romanticised depictions of ruins and rocky landscapes set into the walls and lunette paintings in Adam's delicate plasterwork ceiling are the work of Antonio Zucchi.

Another aspect of the eighteenth century is reflected in the more intimate and relaxed Red Room, where a quartet of cloud-based cherubs makes music in the rococo plaster ceiling. Paintings hang triple-banked in the fashion of the day, their gilded frames glowing against red velvet.

Although many of the 1st Lord's pictures are no longer in the house, the fine collection that remains includes several portraits by Sir Joshua Reynolds, who came from the nearby village of Plympton. The artist was a friend of the Parkers. He visited Saltram and painted many portraits of the family, his likeness of Lord Boringdon's second wife, Theresa, being particularly admired when it was exhibited at the Royal Academy. The majority of the purchases from Reynolds were in the six years of John and Theresa's marriage, from 1769, when members of the family are frequently recorded in the painter's pocket books.

The 1st Lord's other acquisitions include several works by Angelica Kauffmann, for whom he had sat in Naples in 1764 when on his Grand Tour, and a number of Italian, Dutch and Flemish paintings. Characteristic history paintings and scenes from classical mythology by Kauffmann hang on the main staircase, and here too is her portrait of Reynolds; it shows the artist in seventeenth-century dress with a bust of Michelangelo, whom Reynolds particularly revered, seen dimly behind him. On the landing above, a painting of a goggle-eyed youth in shining armour is Rubens's likeness of Vincenzo II Gonzaga, Duke of Mantua. A comfortable Regency library created by John Foulston for John and Theresa's son, the 1st Earl of Morley, on the south-west corner of the house has another show of portraits hanging above the bookcases, which are filled with leather-bound volumes largely dating from the time of the 1st Earl.

Other delights at Saltram are the eighteenth-century Chinese wallpaper, some of it depicting those curiously elongated figures so familiar from Japanese prints, which

ABOVE A detail from the ornate boulle writing desk in the library, decorated with an inlay of brass and shell.

OPPOSITE Robert Adam was responsible for almost everything in the saloon at Saltram, from the carpet echoing the design of the ceiling to the hang of the paintings.

ABOVE Saltram's Palladian west front dates from the remodelling of the rambling Tudor and Jacobean house in the mid-eighteenth century.

decorates some of the first-floor rooms, and a show of topographical watercolours by Frances Talbot, who married the 1st Earl in 1809. A light and airy late eighteenth-century kitchen looking onto a rough-walled internal courtyard has a 1,000-piece array of gleaming copper pans and moulds.

A sweeping lawn to the west of the house links the eighteenth-century façade to a series of colour-themed borders. Beyond are wooded glades and walks and an early Georgian terrace cut into the hillside. An octagonal mid-eighteenth-century gothic belvedere at the end of a long lime avenue was probably built by Harry Stockman, the estate's talented carpenter, as was the elegant pedimented orangery of 1775 by the house. Stockman also created the chapel nearby, adding battlements, buttresses and pointed windows to what was

originally a barn. The extensive deer-park formed in the mid-eighteenth century was landscaped in the style of 'Capability' Brown, but most of the magnificent views depicted in William Tomkins's delightful landscapes in the garden room have now been affected by Plymouth's urban sprawl. Shelter belts planted by the National Trust help to hide this intrusive reminder of the twenty-first century, but passengers on the main Plymouth to London line can still enjoy a glimpse of the amphitheatre, a mid-eighteenth-century folly nestling in the woods above the Plym estuary.

Sandham Memorial Chapel

Hampshire
4 miles (6.4 kilometres) south of Newbury, ½ mile (0.8 kilometre) east of the A34

Service in Macedonia and in a military hospital during the First World War inspired the visionary and touching paintings by Stanley Spencer that fill this chapel. These are not scenes of combat but cameos of everyday activities, conveying a sense of human companionship and providing a kind of modern equivalent to the 'labours of the months' seen in medieval art. Soldiers in Macedonia are shown filling their water bottles, dressing under mosquito nets, cooking breakfast in the open and picking bilberries. In the hospital they sort laundry, polish taps and make beds. Spencer's greatest work, *The Resurrection of the Soldiers*, entirely fills the altar wall. A stream of white crosses leads towards Christ seated in the middle distance, gathering crosses from the fallen in his arms. Soldiers emerge from their graves, shake hands with their comrades, clean buttons and wind puttees. Here, as throughout this powerful cycle, everyday life is touched by the immortal.

The 1920s red-brick chapel was built to Spencer's instructions by John Louis and Mary Behrend specially to house the paintings, which were created, on large seamless canvases, between 1927 and 1932. It is dedicated to Mary's brother Lieutenant H.W. Sandham, who served in Macedonia during the First World War and died of an illness contracted there.

Scotney Castle

Kent
1½ miles (2.4 kilometres) south of Lamberhurst on the A21

The magical garden created by Edward Hussey III from 1837 in a deep valley of the Kentish Weald owes much of its charm to the romantic buildings incorporated in the design. At the top of a steep bluff overlooking the valley is a nineteenth-century vision of an Elizabethan house, all gables, tall chimneys and mullioned windows, while far below, encircled by a lake-like moat beside the River Bewl, are the ruins of a genuinely ancient castle. Flowering trees and shrubs on the slopes frame carefully contrived views over the valley and from one building to another.

In a move against the fashion of the time, which was swinging away from the naturalistic layouts that had been in vogue since the eighteenth century, Edward Hussey, who had inherited the estate from his father while still a child, created an outstandingly successful example of the Picturesque style, whose exponents promoted artfully created landscapes, ideally including a romantic building or two, which gave the illusion of the beauty of nature untamed. At Scotney, the castle was the perfect eye-catcher. In fact the remnants of a fortified house that Roger Ashburnham constructed here in *c.* 1378–80 during the troubled decades of the Hundred Years' War, when men of substance in this part of England lived in fear of French raids, the castle consists of a massive round tower rising from the lake-like moat, with a projecting parapet at roof level, and a ruined gatehouse. A brick Elizabethan range adjoining the tower is all that survives of sixteenth-century additions, and jagged walls with gaping windows mark the remains of a substantial seventeenth-century wing.

Instead of living in the castle, where his father had contracted the typhoid that killed him from the drains, the

LEFT Looking towards the altar wall in Sandham Memorial Chapel, where a stream of white crosses leads towards the seated Christ.
ABOVE The wallpaper designed by Thomas Willement in the library at Scotney was originally brightly coloured, but has faded over the years.

young Edward, still in his 20s, built a new house in 1837–43, engaging the architect Anthony Salvin, who was known for his work in an Elizabethan Revival style, to design it in a neo-Tudor idiom. But the shaping of the surroundings and the actual site of the house were determined with the advice of the artist and landscape gardener William Sawrey Gilpin, who was a disciple of Richard Payne Knight and Sir Uvedale Price, the leading exponents of the Picturesque style. The natural drama of the valley was enhanced by the creation of a deep quarry, from which the streaky golden sandstone for the house was obtained, and the seventeenth-century wing of the castle was partly demolished, to focus the eye on the older remains and make them seem more romantic.

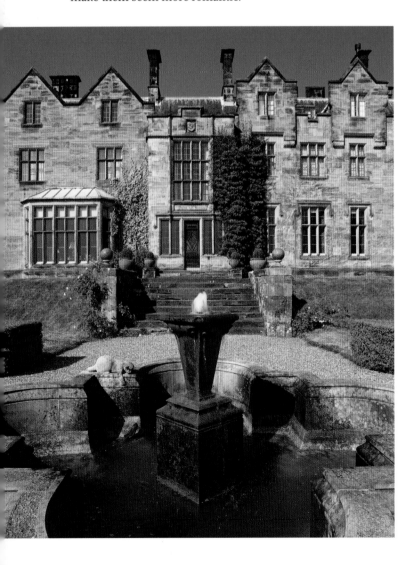

The new building, the design of which took 33 meetings between architect and client before Edward was satisfied, was devised to be both picturesque and practical. The tall, many-gabled façades are enhanced by a battlemented tower like a Northumbrian pele that dominates the entrance front and by the chimneys rising above the roofline, and there are great mullioned and transomed windows lighting the stairs and filling the bays looking over the garden. There are arresting details, too, such as the lead rainwater hoppers designed by the heraldic artist Thomas Willement, who is better known for his stained glass.

The interior, with stunning views from most of the main rooms, has been little altered since it was built and still has many of Salvin's decorative schemes and several pieces of furniture that he designed for Scotney. Most recently, the new house has been the home of the architectural historian and writer Christopher Hussey, Edward Hussey III's grandson, who inherited the estate in 1952 and gave it to the National Trust. The garden has been open since his death in 1970, and the house passed to the Trust, with all its contents, on his wife Betty's death in 2006. It is being presented as a welcoming and lived-in home, as Christopher and Betty had it, and with nineteenth-century furnishings blended with twentieth-century additions. There are inviting sofas and a drinks trolley in the spacious library, where the faded Willement wallpaper and the Jacobean-style plasterwork ceiling are both original, as are the bookcases designed by Salvin. In the book-lined study next door, where Christopher Hussey wrote his many articles for *Country Life* and other works, the ornamental ceiling features local Kentish hops, and there is more plasterwork by Salvin in the more formal dining room, where the huge buffet sideboard Salvin made for Edward Hussey III matches the richly carved panelling.

A few rooms were substantially altered by Christopher and Betty. Their sunny bedroom, with a bay window looking over the garden, was fitted with a walk-in wardrobe and en-suite bathroom in the 1950s and a restful blue and green bedroom,

OPPOSITE Scotney is an outstanding example of a Picturesque landscape, with carefully contrived vistas between the old castle on the valley floor and the new house, built in neo-Tudor style in 1837–43, far above.
LEFT The new house at Scotney, built in Elizabethan style, has a huge stone-mullioned window lighting the stairs on the garden front.

redecorated by Betty, is furnished with bamboo pieces purchased in 1951. Betty's sense of colour comes through again in the remodelled kitchen, where shelves are filled with her vibrant red and white china. The many paintings include likenesses of Christopher and Betty by their friend John Ward and views of both the new house and the old castle by John Piper, whom they also knew well, as well as family portraits, a market scene by the sixteenth-century Flemish artist Joachim Beuckelaer and a fantasy by the Italian baroque painter Faustino Bocchi, which Christopher Hussey bought while he was a student at Oxford. Most enchanting is the little room giving access to the garden, where blue-and-white Delftware vases are set against old Flemish panelling in the style of the seventeenth century.

One of the best views of the garden is from a semicircular bastion below the new house, which gives a vista down over the quarry and the slope of the valley, thickly planted with trees and shrubs, to the moated remains of the old castle.

Seaton Delaval Hall

Northumberland
2 miles (3.2 kilometres) north of
Whitley Bay, off the A190 between
Seaton Delaval and Seaton Sluice

This arresting baroque house, set less than a mile (1.6 kilometres) from the sea on a bleak and windswept coast, was designed by Sir John Vanbrugh, that most theatrical of architects, for Admiral George Delaval, who commissioned Vanbrugh in c. 1718. Arcaded wings framing a deep and gently sloping forecourt set off the tall central block. Placed by Vanbrugh on a raised platform, it is four-and-a-half storeys high, symmetrical, and designed for dramatic effect. Huge Doric columns, supporting nothing, frame the entrance, there are massive chimneys and heavy keystones over the windows, and the pedimented top storey resembles a classical temple. Playful details, such as the harpoons, sea creatures and other devices carved into the stonework, and the oculus windows

BELOW Vanbrugh's monumental entrance hall is decorated with blind arcading and statues representing the arts, including geography and astronomy.
OPPOSITE Seaton Delaval was designed for theatrical effect, with huge Doric columns framing the entrance, windows weighed down with heavy keystones and a penthouse like a classical temple.

resembling portholes, are allusions to the admiral's career. Vanbrugh, an architect of genius and the greatest exponent of the English Baroque, was both looking back to prodigy houses such as Hardwick Hall (see p.169) and setting out to create 'something of the castle in the air', a playhouse that could also be lived in. Gutted by fire in 1822, this central block is now an architectural shell, with a dramatic Piranesian interior of huge spaces, vistas to upper levels and shafts of light. Beyond the lofty entrance hall, with statues of the muses set into blind arcading at the level of the first floor and an original marble pavement, is the monumental saloon, 75 feet (23 metres) long and 29 feet (9 metres) wide. Running the length of the south front, this great room looks out through a grand Ionic portico to a great obelisk half a mile (0.8 kilometres) away across the former park. Slender cast-iron shafts dividing the saloon, replacements for eight stone columns destroyed in the fire, were inserted by the Newcastle architect John Dobson, who roofed the ruined building in 1860 and carried out essential restoration. Two oval stone staircases wind up through the house to either side of the hall and descend to the Stygian, stone-vaulted basement, sections of twisted iron handrail at the top of both stairs showing how fierce the fire must have been.

Sadly, neither the admiral, who died after a fall from his horse in 1723, nor Vanbrugh, who died in 1726, lived to see the house finished, and the completion of the work was overseen by George's nephew, Captain Francis Blake Delaval. The wings flanking the forecourt were built at the same time as the central block, but not entirely to Vanbrugh's published design. There was once an imposing wing south-east of the central block too, but this was gutted by the fire and demolished.

In the later eighteenth century, the flamboyant and profligate Sir Francis Delaval, eldest son of Captain Francis, turned the hall into a party house, pursuing a life of unrestrained pleasure while his younger brother John managed the estate and the coalmines, glass works and other enterprises which had made the family rich. Sir Francis and his seven brothers and four sisters became known as 'the Gay Delavals'. Indulging his love of the theatre, he put on lavish productions in London, and his wild parties at the house became notorious, not only for their extravagance but also for the tricks played on unsuspecting guests. Some of the parties were held in the monumental stables created by Sir Francis in

the east wing, where vast arches of stone span a great vaulted hall. The names over the stalls – Hercules, Julius, Zephyrus, etc. – refer to beasts housed here in *c.* 1800.

When Edward Delaval, the last of his line, died in 1814, the house passed to a nephew, Sir Jacob Henry Astley, whose main seat was at Melton Constable in Norfolk. After the fire, it was Sir Jacob's son, created 16th Lord Hastings in 1841, who employed John Dobson, although plans for fully restoring the house were never realised, leaving the shell that is seen today. The hall grounds were used for garden parties and church fetes, and prisoners of war were housed here in the Second World War, but the family rarely came to Seaton Delaval until, in the 1950s, the 22nd Lord Hastings and his wife Catherine decided to restore the hall and make the west wing, originally designed as the kitchen and servants' quarters, their home. The west wing had various uses before Lord and Lady Hastings finally settled here in 1990.

Seaton Delaval came to the Trust in 2009, two years after the deaths of Lord and Lady Hastings. Following a huge programme of restoration and conservation, the house and grounds are being presented in a way that conjures up the hall's eighteenth-century heyday and the spirit of the Gay Delavals. To the sound of laughter, music and footsteps, visitors will experience illusionistic effects and surprises, among them hidden peepholes, an upside-down room, and mirrors that distort and deceive. A few pieces that survived the fire will be on show, among them two marble-topped pier tables in the manner of William Kent, portraits of Sir John Hussey Delaval and his family by the local artist William Bell, paintings by Rhoda, the eldest of the Gay Delaval siblings, and, in the grounds, sculptures of David and Goliath and Samson slaying a Philistine from the workshop of John Cheere. Also on display, either in the rooms or in a specially created 'open' store in the west wing which visitors can wander through, will be fine furniture, paintings and ceramics brought here from Melton Constable by the 22nd Lord Hastings, a collection that includes family portraits by John Vanderbank and Francis Cotes, a likeness, after Reynolds, of Sir Francis Delaval, and a portrait of Admiral George Delaval by Kneller. Other treasures include pieces from a lovely Meissen tea and coffee service of *c.* 1750, a set of George I walnut chairs, and an ebony and ivory cabinet dating from *c.* 1650. Paintings of the north and south fronts of the hall are by Arthur Pond, who taught Rhoda Delaval.

The grounds, too, are being reimagined. Apart from the existing rose garden, and the topiary parterre north-west of the hall that was designed by James Russell for the 22nd Lord and his wife, work that was masterminded by Lady Hastings, the surrounding landscape, with the guidance of the estate map of 1781, is being reimagined and original sight lines restored. A stone shepherdess has been reunited with the stone flock that were found scattered around and positioned to make visitors smile.

Shaw's Corner

Hertfordshire
At the south-west end of the village of Ayot St Lawrence, 2 miles (3.2 kilometres) north-east of Wheathampstead

Narrow, winding lanes lead to the leafy village of Ayot St Lawrence and this red-brick Edwardian villa in an Arts and Crafts idiom that was bought as a country retreat by George Bernard Shaw and his wife Charlotte in 1906. A celebrated playwright, critic and political activist, Shaw was 50 and at the height of his fame when he and Charlotte came to Ayot St Lawrence and many of his views, such as those on social injustice, still have resonance today. Shaw lived in the house until his death in 1950 and some of his best-known works were written here, including *Major Barbara*, *Saint Joan* and *Pygmalion*.

Shaw wanted the house to be a 'living shrine' and it remains much as he and his wife had it, full of their possessions, some of which were specially brought from their London flat, and of echoes of his individuality and genius. His many hats, including the miner's hat he wore when chopping logs, hang in the hall. He wrote at the desk in the study, reference books to one side, littering the floor with scraps of paper as he worked; a smaller desk in the corner of the room was for his secretary, Blanche Patch. Among many pieces of sculpture is a bronze bust of Shaw by Rodin in the drawing room, the craggy head with its prominent nose caught to perfection, and an equally memorable portrait by Augustus John hangs in the dining

ABOVE The red-brick Edwardian house that Shaw and his wife Charlotte bought as a country retreat is set off by a sizeable garden where they loved to walk together, deep in conversation.
OPPOSITE Treasure from a Spanish galleon captured in the 1740s helped to finance the transformation of the Anson family's old seat into a substantial country house.

room. In later years, after eating his vegetarian dinner, Shaw would often sit by the fire and listen to broadcasts on the radio; photographs of Gandhi, Lenin and Stalin above the dining-room fireplace reflect his socialist sympathies.

Doors lead out to the extensive garden, where the Shaws would walk together deep in conversation, following the same route every time, and where Shaw would bury himself in the little rotating shed where he did much of his writing, safe from interruptions. When they had visitors, the Shaws would invite their guests to sit with them on the south-facing terrace on sunny days, the wide circle of friends who came here including the socialists Beatrice and Sidney Webb, William Morris, who gave Shaw one of the walking sticks in the hall, Apsley Cherry-Garrard, who had been on Scott's last Antarctic expedition, the alluring actress Mrs Patrick Campbell, and T.E. Lawrence, who became close to Charlotte. Only the museum room, in what was originally Charlotte's bedroom, has been created since Shaw's time, the collection of memorabilia on show here including the Oscar that he was awarded in 1938 for the screenplay of the film version of *Pygmalion* and the Nobel Prize for literature he received in 1926.

Shugborough Estate

Staffordshire
6 miles (9.6 kilometres) east of
Stafford on the A513 at Milford

The two Anson brothers born in the 1690s took very different paths in life. George, who went to sea at the age of 12, rose to be 1st Lord of the Admiralty and gained both fame and fortune on an epic four-year circumnavigation of the globe in the 1740s, during which he captured a Spanish galleon laden with £400,000 worth of silver, nearly a third of which George purloined. Much of the admiral's wealth went to help his cultivated elder brother Thomas improve the three-storey, late seventeenth-century house on the banks of the River Sow which he had inherited in 1720. Among other changes and enlargements made in the late 1740s and '60s, Thomas added charming domed pavilions with semicircular bay windows by Thomas Wright of Durham to frame the central block. The massive two-storey portico dominating the entrance front was a later addition, part of Samuel Wyatt's alterations for the

1st Viscount Anson at the end of the century that obliterated much of the earlier work. Similarly, Wyatt was responsible for the central bow on the garden façade, and for the verandahs on either side fronting the links to the pavilions, which he extended.

Thomas Anson was a leading spirit of the Society of Dilettanti, which promoted the art of classical antiquity. This interest in the ancient world comes through in features that survive from his time, such as the medallion heads representing Greek and Egyptian deities in the plasterwork by Vassalli in the dining room, and the huge, Piranesi-like paintings of classical ruins by Nicholas Thomas Dall seen in various parts of the house. In Thomas Wright's low-ceilinged library, with a shallow arch set on Ionic columns dividing the room, marble busts set along the bookcases include a number of antique sculptures, among them likenesses of Plato and Hercules, as well as delightful nineteenth-century portraits of various members of the family, one of whom is depicted holding a rabbit.

Neo-classical motifs also mark Wyatt's interiors. Giant yellow scagliola columns punctuate the walls of his curiously elongated saloon, their reflections in the pier-glasses on the end wall making the room seem even larger than it is. Joseph Rose the Younger's coved ceiling in Wyatt's impressive Red Drawing Room is decorated with delicate compositions reminiscent of a Wedgwood vase. This room also displays the few paintings that remain from Thomas Anson's once renowned picture collection, most of which was dispersed, with the rest of the contents, in the 1842 sale precipitated by the extravagance of the 2nd Viscount, created 1st Earl of Lichfield. Among them is a Murillo-inspired *Immaculate Conception*, a late work by Meléndez, painter to Philip V of Spain, and two paintings that were thought to be by Guido Reni (sadly, they are not) and which were bought back at the sale. A number of pictures connected with the estate have also survived, including two portraits of Corsican goats. Noble-looking beasts with corkscrew horns, these were part of a herd of this rare breed that was established by Thomas Anson. Some fine eighteenth-century French furniture in the principal rooms was acquired by the 2nd Earl when he set about rescuing the house in the 1850s.

A gold repeater, a snuffbox made of wood from one of his ships, Spanish coins and his commission from George III are among several mementoes of the gallant admiral. One of his officers designed the little Chinese house by the Sow, set off by a pagoda tree and other oriental shrubs, but the rococo plaster ceiling and Chinese painted mirrors that once adorned it are now in the house, complementing the oriental porcelain and other chinoiserie acquired by the brothers.

Shugborough came to the Trust in 1960 but until 2016 it was administered by Staffordshire County Council. In November of that year the estate was handed back to the National Trust, who have embarked on a major programme of change and restoration which is likely to continue for many years to come. Inside the house, the interior decoration will remain the same, but furniture and paintings will be moved around so they can be displayed more prominently. In the longer term, the plan is to move away from the traditional portrayal of a Georgian country house and to introduce a more creative presentation of its history and associated stories.

The rooms lived in by the Lichfield family, situated mostly on the upper floors, will remain largely as they are. Open to visitors

LEFT A number of classical features in the grounds of Shugborough include this Doric temple, attributed to James Stuart, that was probably designed as the entrance to the kitchen garden.
OPPOSITE The Red Drawing Room at Shugborough, the most impressive room in the house, was created in 1794 and is hung with the remains of a once renowned picture collection, most of which was sold in 1842.

since the death in 2005 of the 5th Earl, the society photographer Patrick Lichfield, these are more intimate and lived-in spaces which contrast with the grandeur elsewhere and show Shugborough in a different light. They are full of mementoes of the 5th Earl and his glittering 40-year career, during which he immortalised iconic figures of the 1960s such as Mick Jagger and Joanna Lumley, caused a stir by photographing the singer Marsha Hunt in the nude, and also took memorable images of his royal relatives (he was the Queen's cousin), among them shots of the exiled Duke and Duchess of Windsor and the official photographs of the wedding of the Prince of Wales and Lady Diana Spencer in 1981.

In the kitchen, which was fitted out in the late 1970s, a cupboard door is covered with business cards, and jams made from fruit grown on the estate, which Lichfield particularly enjoyed, are lined up on the window-sill of the light and airy circular breakfast room. Some of his most personal belongings, such as his spectacles and the boots and helmet he wore to ride his motorbike, are in the green sitting room, and here too is the collar of his dog Drum, beside the chair in which the 5th Earl used to sit. The bathrooms still have early twentieth-century plumbing and the elegant boudoir has the only hand-painted ceiling in the house and wallpaper inlaid with silver leaf. Treasures on display, some brought out of storage and being shown for the first time, others on loan, include a collection of enamelled and gilded jardinières and urns that are said to have come from the Summer Palace in Peking.

And then there are the photographs. Some of them, as in the green sitting room, are of close family, others are of celebrities, among them some images taken on the Shugborough estate which have not been seen before. Also on show is Lichfield's studio from Oxford Gardens in west London, which has been faithfully reconstructed with his cameras and other equipment.

Formal terraced gardens lead down to the Sow, where the family's arboretum on an island in the river, formerly private, is now accessible. The picturesque ruin on the banks of the Sow, a crumbling array of columns and walls topped by the statue of a druid, is outclassed by the classical monuments based on buildings in ancient Athens in the park that Thomas Anson commissioned from James 'Athenian' Stuart. A triumphal arch set on the highest point of the park acts both as an eyecatcher and as a memorial to the admiral, who died in 1762,

and his naval achievements. A gentle roar from the ground here signals the Stafford to Stoke railway that is buried in a tunnel beneath the arch. Two pedimented porches with fluted columns project from the octagonal Tower of the Winds in the valley below and a shady knoll is crowned with the circular columned structure of the Lantern of Demosthenes. As part of their planned changes, the Trust will be giving greater access to the park, with improvements to footpaths so visitors can explore the estate more widely.

Shute Barton

Devon
3 miles (4.8 kilometres) south-west of Axminster, 2 miles (3.2 kilometres) north of Colyton on the Honiton–Colyton road

Set on a wooded hill above the Axe valley a few miles from the Devon coast, Shute Barton is a rare survival of an unfortified medieval manor. As the arresting castellated gatehouse on the road suggests, the L-shaped building here now is a remnant of a once much larger house, most of which was pulled down in the late eighteenth century to provide stone for the grand Palladian mansion on the hill. What was left, originally the service quarters, became a farmhouse.

The two surviving ranges, battlemented and gargoyled and built of stone rubble and flint with ashlar dressings, frame the north and east sides of a tiny cobbled courtyard,

with a stair turret in the angle between the wings. An array of mullioned and transomed windows includes two pairs of original trefoil-headed lights, but there are also some sashes and other indications of a complex history of alteration and improvement, such as blocked openings and windows inserted in earlier apertures. On the south side of the court is the original gatehouse, now just giving access to the farmyard but once leading through to an extensive outer court with stabling, barns and staff accommodation.

The earliest parts of the building are in the east range. A sixteenth-century doorway from the inner court leads into the original stone-flagged kitchen, one end of which is filled with an enormous fireplace, over 22 feet (6.5 metres) wide. On a floor inserted over the kitchen, which was once much loftier, is an elegant, panelled seventeenth-century room and at the top of the house, reached by the newel stair in the angle turret, are the original servants' quarters, now a spacious chamber extending over most of the third floor and open to a medieval timber roof. There is a garderobe closet to one side of the fireplace.

Despite many vicissitudes, including the confiscation of the Shute estates during the Wars of the Roses, and involvement in the mid-sixteenth-century plot to put Lady Jane Grey on the throne, which led to the loss of the lands for a second time, descendants of Lord William Bonville, who built the fifteenth-century manor, have continued to be associated with the house. A few years after it was confiscated from the Greys, to whom Shute had passed by marriage, the estate was sold back to another descendant of the Bonvilles, Sir William Pole, in 1560 and it was he who built the gatehouse. The Poles were loyal to the king in the Civil War and suffered as a result, but their fortunes revived in the eighteenth century when Sir John William de la Pole, a close friend of the Prince Regent, succeeded in vastly increasing the size of the estate and built the new house on the hill; the future George IV was entertained there in 1789. Another branch of the family inherited the serenely beautiful Antony (*see* p.18), in Cornwall, which had been the home of the Carews for centuries, prompting a change of name to Pole Carew, and it was Sir John Carew Pole (he altered his name again on succeeding to the Shute baronetcy) who gave Shute to the National Trust in 1959 and Antony in 1961. Shute is now a holiday let but has some open days.

Sissinghurst

Kent
2 miles (3.2 kilometres)
north-east of Cranbrook,
1 mile (1.6 kilometres) east of
Sissinghurst village on the A262

The lovely garden set high on a Wealden ridge owes much of its charm to the Tudor buildings of mellow pink brick around which it was created and which form a romantic backdrop to the planting. These evocative remains are all that survive of the great Tudor and Elizabethan courtyard house of the Baker family, who came to Sissinghurst in *c.* 1490. There is also the ghost of an older manor here, its site marked by an orchard framed by three arms of a medieval moat.

Visitors approach Sissinghurst through a gabled archway crowned by three slender chimneys that was built in *c.* 1535 by the high-flying Sir John Baker, who rose to be Chancellor of the Exchequer and made the family rich. The long ranges to either side, originally used for stabling and servants' lodgings, may be Sir John's too. Beyond, across a grassy court, rises the brick prospect tower that forms the focal point of the garden. Four storeys tall, with slender octagonal turrets, this glorified gatehouse was built by Sir Richard Baker in 1560–70 as part of a wholesale reconstruction of his father's house and once led into a courtyard lined by tall, gabled ranges. Elizabeth I, who stayed here for three days in 1573, would have ridden through Sir John's archway to be greeted by Sir Richard under the tower. A fragment of the Elizabethan mansion is now a cottage in the garden and there is a little sixteenth-century building where the family's private chaplain may have lived. From the mid-seventeenth century, when the Baker family lost much of their wealth in the Civil War, Sissinghurst went into a long decline. Let to the government in 1756 as a camp for prisoners taken during the Seven Years' War, it was made even more ruinous by the 3,000 or so French naval officers imprisoned here, who responded to brutal treatment by destroying panelling and fireplaces and devastating the garden. They are also responsible for Sissinghurst being referred to as a 'castle', which is a corruption of the French *château*. After the war, the

old house was so damaged that in 1764 it was largely pulled down. Despite the 200 years of neglect and decay that followed, the evocative remains inspired the novelist and biographer Vita Sackville-West to purchase the property in 1930 and, with the help of her husband, Sir Harold Nicolson, the diplomat and literary critic, to create one of the most individual and influential gardens of the twentieth century. The old walls and hedges were used to create a series of intimate open-air rooms, each one planted differently, and long linking walks provide a unifying framework.

OPPOSITE The east front of Shute Barton, which is a very rare survival of an unfortified medieval manor.
ABOVE RIGHT This room in the tower, where Vita retreated to read and write, accompanied only by one of her Alsatians, is still filled with her books, furniture and ornaments.

The buildings were transformed into a singular and eccentric house for the Nicolsons and their two sons, its various parts scattered round the garden. The stables in the long north wing of the entrance range were formed into an atmospheric library, lined with thousands of books, many of which were Harold Nicolson's review copies. The fireplace, which now has a de Laszlo portrait of the young Vita (disliked by her) hanging above it, was made out of Elizabethan fragments found in the garden and the furniture includes copies of pieces from Knole (*see* p.196), Vita's childhood home. The family had their dining room and kitchen in the priest's house and Harold Nicolson worked in South Cottage, but the tower was Vita's retreat. Reached by a spiral staircase, and now viewed through a grille, is the cluttered room where she wrote, its walls still lined with the books on gardening, history

and travel that reflect her special interests. When he came to live at Sissinghurst, her son Nigel, a prolific author like his mother, would retreat to the octagonal gazebo in a corner of the orchard to write when the weather was warm enough. Vita saved summer days for gardening, and then wrote into the night. From the roof of the tower there is a bird's-eye view of the garden and wider prospects over woods, fields and oast houses to a distant ridge of the North Downs, with the spire of Frittenden church in the middle distance.

ABOVE A brick arch frames a view of the White Garden, where the central rose flowers profusely in July.
OPPOSITE The romantic Elizabethan tower that stands at the heart of Sissinghurst garden is a remnant of the great courtyard house that once stood on this site.

Sizergh

Cumbria
3½ miles (5.6 kilometres) south
of Kendal, north-west of the
A590/A591 interchange

Sizergh is dominated by the fourteenth-century tower at its heart. The Stricklands, who have been here for 750 years, were one of the great military families of the north, and the house they constructed in about 1340 reflected their wealth and also the vulnerability of their estate. Sizergh is only about 50 miles (80 kilometres) from the Scottish border as the crow flies and lies in the lowland corridor that leads south between the Lakeland hills and the inhospitable North Yorkshire moors, an area which, for centuries, suffered raids from north of the border. The massive tower that forms the core of the house, designed to be both lived in and defensible, rises almost 60 feet (18 metres) to the battlements. Its limestone rubble walls are still formidable despite the later mullioned windows and other alterations which have softened its appearance.

Elizabethan additions, partly hidden by a Georgian veneer, adjoin the tower and long, low Elizabethan service wings with soaring chimneys flank the entrance courtyard. Large medieval-style double doors open onto a Victorian carriageway running through the castle on the site of the great hall, with a grand stone and oak staircase rising from one side.

Early Elizabethan woodwork in several of the rooms gives Sizergh its special flavour. Superb panelling of *c.* 1575 inlaid with Renaissance motifs in poplar and bog-oak was sold to the Victoria and Albert Museum in 1891 but was returned in 1999 and can once again be seen in its former glory in the Inlaid Chamber. Craftsmanship of similar quality is displayed in the five intricately carved armorial chimneypieces, four of which date from 1563 to 1575. The rest of the panelling is also very fine, the oldest in the house being the oak linenfold work dating from the reign of Henry VIII in a passage room. Intriguingly, a lozenge design on the woodwork in the old dining room and a bedroom reappears on the backs of three Elizabethan oak chairs in the tower. Here, too, there are carved oak benches with unusually rich mid-sixteenth-century decoration.

A number of Stuart portraits and personal royal relics advertise the Stricklands' adherence to the Catholic faith and their loyal devotion to the Stuart cause. Refusing to desert the royal family after 1688, Sir Thomas Strickland and his wife Winifred accompanied James II into exile in France, where Lady Strickland was governess to the king's young son.

Terraced lawns, their retaining walls softened with shrubs and climbers, lead down from the south front to an ornamental lake that mirrors the castle in its glassy waters. Orchids and wild daffodils flowering in the grass of the meadow above the lake are part of a native limestone flora which reflects the rock outcropping all over the estate in screes, cliffs and pavements. An extensive rock garden was constructed of Westmorland stone in 1926 by Hayes of Ambleside, who arranged the little stream tumbling across it into the lake in a series of pools and falls.

ABOVE LEFT This bedchamber is lined with exquisite Elizabethan oak panelling inlaid with bog oak and poplar. Sold to the Victoria and Albert Museum in 1891, it was returned in 1999.
LEFT The massive tower that forms the core of the house is mirrored in the lake below the south front.

Smallhythe Place

Kent
At Smallhythe, 2 miles
(3.2 kilometres) south of
Tenterden, on the east side
of the Rye road

ABOVE This timber-framed sixteenth-century farmhouse at one end of Smallhythe village was bought by the spirited actress Ellen Terry in 1899 and is full of her theatrical mementoes and treasures.

This modest half-timbered sixteenth-century farmhouse belonged to the legendary actress Dame Ellen Terry for nearly 30 years, from 1899 until her death here on 21 July 1928. Appropriately, she first saw Smallhythe in the company of Henry Irving, the manager of the Lyceum Theatre in London's Covent Garden, with whom she had a theatrical partnership that lasted for 24 years.

Her attractive house stands at one end of Smallhythe, its steep, red-tiled roof and sturdy brick chimneys outlined against the Kentish marshes on all sides. With the sea 10 miles (16 kilometres) away as the crow flies, it is difficult to believe that the stream bordering the garden was once the route of the River Rother and that a thriving shipyard existed here where ships were built and broken and which catered for a procession of boats unloading at the wharves along the creek. At one time, Smallhythe was a royal dockyard and both Henry V and Henry VIII had ships built on this site.

Now preserved as a theatrical museum, the house is full of mementoes of Ellen Terry's life and of the world in which she moved. In the large beamed kitchen which she used as a dining room, with traditional wheelback chairs ranged round the walls, a refectory table in the middle of the warm red-brick floor and a high-backed settle by the fire, two walls are devoted to mementoes of David Garrick and Sarah Siddons. Other exhibits connected with famous names from the past include an affectionate message from Sarah Bernhardt – 'Merci, my dearling' – written with a flourish on the cover of a dressing-table; Sir Arthur Sullivan's monocle, with his autograph on the glass; a chain worn by Fanny Kemble and a visiting card from Alexandre Dumas, whose *La dame aux camélias* inspired Verdi's *La Traviata*. A letter in Oscar Wilde's languorous scrawl in an adjoining room begs Ellen Terry to accept 'the first copy of my first play', adding 'perhaps some day I shall be fortunate to write something worthy of your playing'. Here, too, is her make-up box; a sponge, a mirror and a large swatch of grey hair are prominent among the notably sparse contents, which seem barely adequate for someone of Terry's stature.

Upstairs there are displays of the lavish silk and velvet costumes, much criticised for their extravagance, that Irving created for Terry. The more private face of the great actress is revealed in her simple, low-ceilinged bedroom, with a view out over the marshes from the casement windows. Brightly patterned rugs cover the bare boards of the floor and there are rotund pottery pigs on the mantelpiece. Kate Hastings's pastel portraits of Terry's mother and of her two children, Edith and Edward Gordon Craig, offspring of her relationship with the architect and theatrical designer Edward Godwin, hang above the bed with its theatrical curved Empire ends. Godwin himself designed the modest dressing table and the wooden crucifix that Edward Gordon Craig made for his mother stands on the bedside table, next to a worn copy of the Globe Shakespeare annotated in her distinctively generous hand. Something of the great actress's integrity and resolution also emerges in a much-read edition of Robert Louis Stevenson's 'Christmas Sermon', one of the many underlined passages exhorting 'If your morals make you dreary, depend upon it they are wrong.'

Snowshill Manor

Gloucestershire
3 miles (4.8 kilometres)
south-west of Broadway, 4 miles
(6.4 kilometres) west of the
junction of the A44 and the A424

The Victorian grandmother who showed her young grandson the family treasures hidden away in her Cantonese cabinet on Sunday afternoons could not have known that those cherished things would inspire one of the most extraordinary collections ever assembled by one person. Charles Paget Wade, born in 1883, grew up to be an exceptional man. A talented artist and craftsman as well as a professional architect, once he had inherited the family sugar plantations in the West Indies he devoted his life to restoring the Cotswold manor house he bought in 1919 and to amassing the wide-ranging exhibits now displayed here.

Snowshill is an L-shaped building of warm Cotswold stone, with a warren of rooms on different levels leading one into another. The Tudor hall house of *c.* 1500 at its heart, still evident in the huge fireplace on the ground floor and in two ceilings upstairs, was substantially rebuilt in about 1600 and altered again in the early eighteenth century, when the

RIGHT When Snowshill's south front was extended in 1720, the left-hand side of the façade was given Georgian sash windows, but the old stone-mullioned and transomed casements were kept on the right.
OPPOSITE This eccentric display in Seraphim sets an array of Balinese and Javanese dancing masks against a collection of fine cabinets.

oddly attractive south front was created. Here, Georgian sash windows on the left side of the pedimented main entrance contrast with mullioned and transomed casements to the right, giving the house a rakish air.

Every corner from ground floor to attics is devoted to Charles Wade's acquisitions, which are packed into rooms with intriguing names such as Dragon, Meridian, Top Gallant and Seraphim. Wade did not set out to accumulate things because they were rare or valuable, but saw his pieces primarily as records of vanished handicrafts. As a result, the Snowshill collection is unique, displaying an unclassifiable range of everyday objects, from tools used in spinning, weaving and lacemaking to baby minders (one for use on board ship), prams, early bicycles, exquisite bone carvings made by French prisoners of war, eighteenth-century medicine chests cunningly contrived to carry a mass of little bottles and gaily painted model farm wagons. One room is devoted to pieces connected with the sea, such as compasses, telescopes and

ship models, another to musical instruments, arranged as a playerless orchestra, and yet another (his Seventh Heaven) to many of the toys Charles had as a child. Perhaps the most remarkable spectacle is in the Green Room, where suits of Japanese Samurai armour topped with ferocious masks greet visitors in a theatrically staged display. A sense of order everywhere shows that this is no random, magpie collection but a reflection of a serious purpose.

The steeply sloping terraced garden was largely designed by Wade's friend M.H. Baillie Scott, a fellow architect with whom he had worked when employed by Raymond Unwin in London before the First World War, but Wade altered and adapted the original structure. It is laid out as a series of interconnecting but separate garden rooms, with arches and steps leading from one to another. There are flagged paths, carefully contrived vistas down and across the slope, and many features and centres of interest, among them a medieval dovecote with birds roosting on the steeply pitched roof and a replica of Wolf's Cove, Wade's

ABOVE The Turquoise Room, in the part of the manor that was remodelled in 1720, is lined with ornate cabinets like the one that fascinated the young Charles Wade.

model of a Cornish fishing village, with cottages and a pub set round a rough-walled harbour, that has been recently laid out in the spot where Wade had it. His original buildings, and some of the delightful figures with which he peopled his creation, are on display inside the manor. Old-fashioned planting schemes reflect the influence of the Arts and Crafts movement, with its preference for cottage-garden styles. And always there is the backdrop of a far wooded hillside across the valley.

At the top of the garden, just below the manor house, is the little cottage where Charles Wade and his wife, Mary, lived. They had no electricity, a fireplace with two bread ovens being the only means of heating and cooking, and the walls and even the ceiling of the kitchen/living room are covered with a multitude of useful objects, from bowls and tankards to farm tools. Seeing these spartan conditions and the workshop where Wade spent so many happy hours, it is easy to believe, as Queen Mary said after visiting Snowshill in 1937, that the most notable part of the collection was Mr Wade himself.

Speke Hall

Merseyside
On the north bank of the Mersey, 8 miles (12.8 kilometres) south-east of the centre of Liverpool, 1 mile (1.6 kilometres) south of the A561, on the west side of the airport

A carved overmantel in the great parlour depicts the three generations of the wealthy gentry family who were largely responsible for this magical half-timbered moated manor house. Henry Norris to the left, accompanied by his wife and five children, carried on the building started by his father on inheriting the estate in about 1490. In the centre sits Sir William, whose considerable additions in the mid-sixteenth century may be explained by the nineteen children grouped at his feet (the son killed in battle is accompanied by a skull and bones). To the right is Edward, who recorded his completion of the house with an inscription dated 1598 over the entrance, and is shown with his wife and two of their children.

These men built conservatively, each addition merging perfectly with what had gone before and with no hint of the Renaissance influences that were becoming evident further south. Four long, low, half-timbered ranges enclose a cobbled courtyard. Gables jettied out over the floors below and topped with finials project unevenly and apparently haphazardly from the façades, rough sandstone slabs cover the roof and leaded panes show up as dark patches in a riot of black-and-white timberwork that is amongst the finest in England. An Elizabethan stone bridge crosses the now grassy moat to the studded wooden doors leading into the courtyard. Walking through is a surprise: two huge yews known as Adam and Eve shadow the cobbles, their branches rising above the house.

Surviving Tudor interiors live up to the promise of the exterior. In the light and airy T-shaped great hall rising to the roof, a number of plaster heads look down from the crude

BELOW A bridge over the moat leads to this romantic house dating from the fifteenth century, where each façade is decorated with a riot of timberwork.

gothic chimneypiece stretching to the ceiling. The naïve decoration here contrasts with the sophisticated carving on the panelling at the other end of the room, where busts of Roman emperors represented in high relief are set between elegant fluted columns. In the great parlour next door, panels in the fine early Jacobean plaster ceiling are alive with pomegranates, roses, lilies, vines and hazelnuts; bunches of ripe grapes and other fruits dangle enticingly and rosebuds are about to burst into flower. A spy-hole in one of the bedrooms and hiding places throughout the house reflect the Catholicism and royalist sympathies that almost ruined the Norrises in the seventeenth century, when parts of the estate were sold.

After years of neglect following the death of the last of the family in 1766, the house was rescued in the late eighteenth century by Richard Watt, who had made his fortune in the transatlantic slave trade. His descendants introduced the heavy oak furniture in period style which contributes to Speke's unique atmosphere. The more intimate panelled Victorian rooms in the north and west wings were created by the shipping magnate F.R. Leyland, who leased the house and

carried on restoring it during the minority of Watt's daughter Adelaide, who was a child when her father died. A noted patron of the arts, Leyland was responsible for hanging the early William Morris wallpapers that are now a feature of Speke, and he also entertained the painter James McNeill Whistler here.

The house lies buried in bracken woodland beside Liverpool airport, forming a green oasis in the heart of industrial Merseyside. A wide ride leads to the great embankment that shelters the property to the south. Those who struggle up the steep grassy slope are rewarded by a panoramic view of the River Mersey stretching away in a shining sheet of water to the smoking stacks of Ellesmere Port on the other side of the estuary.

ABOVE When the shipping magnate Frederick Leyland lived at Speke in the 1860s, he invited some 80 children from the estate to a Christmas meal in the great hall, built in the 1530s.
OPPOSITE ABOVE Stylistically, Springhill is a mixture, with a rear façade that does not repeat the symmetry of the entrance front.
OPPOSITE BELOW Past hostilities, among them the 105-day siege of Londonderry in 1689 which probably interrupted the building of the house, are conjured up by this show of weapons in the Gun Room.

Springhill

Co. Londonderry
1 mile (1.6 kilometres) from
Moneymore on the Moneymore–
Coagh road (B18)

A long-gun used in the defence of Derry in 1689, when James II's army besieged the town, is among many mementoes on show in this modest manor house which recall the staunchly Protestant family who built it and lived here for 300 years. The name of Conyngham has been associated with the area since 1609, and the land was granted to the family in 1658. The core of the present house dates to some thirty years later, when 'Good' Will Conyngham's marriage articles of 1680, a copy of which hangs in the hall, bound him to build 'a convenient dwelling house of lime and stone' for his 16-year-old bride, Ann Upton. The house was completed in the 1690s.

Springhill's peaceful whitewashed frontage, with long sash windows and a steeply pitched slate roof, is attractively set at the end of a long, straight avenue. Hexagonal one-storey bays added in the eighteenth century extend the house on either side, and detached pavilions of the same date as the house with charming Dutch gables flank the entrance courtyard. These were once used as service buildings.

Springhill's eighteenth- and nineteenth-century interiors have many echoes of the Conyngham family and their connections. 'Good' Will's kinsman Sir Albert Conyngham, who raised the Inniskilling Dragoons to fight for King William, was presented by the king with Kneller's portraits

of William and Mary, which hang in the entrance hall, for his services to the Protestant cause. And the medicine chest full of bottles and drawers in the library was used by the 3rd Viscount Molesworth, who was connected to the Conynghams by marriage, during the War of Spanish Succession (1701–14), when he was the Duke of Marlborough's aide-de-camp. The nationally significant collection of books, mostly acquired in the eighteenth century, includes a very early edition of Gerard's *Herbal* (first published in 1597) and first editions of Hobbes's *Leviathan* (1651) and Raleigh's *History of the World* (1614). Walnut William and Mary splat-back chairs surround an Irish table in the dining room, where a painting attributed to John Brown depicts the antiquary and art dealer James Byres guiding a group of young men on the Grand Tour in the early 1770s.

A gateway from the entrance court leads into the laundry yard, which still has its turf shed and what is believed to have been a slaughterhouse. The old laundry is used to show a changing exhibition of historic dress from the important collection of colourful and unusual pieces from the eighteenth to the early twentieth century. The little walled garden beyond the outbuildings, where herbs surround a tiny camomile lawn, is overlooked by a seventeenth-century barn, its interior spanned by roughly hewn oak beams.

Standen

West Sussex
2 miles (3.2 miles) south of
East Grinstead

Standen is a most unusual house, built in 1892–4 and yet not at all Victorian, built all of a piece and yet seeming to have grown out of the group of old farm buildings to which it is attached. This peaceful place on the edge of the Weald was designed by Philip Webb for the successful London solicitor James Beale, who wanted a roomy house for his large family for weekends and holidays. Standen was one of Webb's last commissions and, like Red House (see p.287), which was his first, is among the few unaltered examples of his work. A lifelong friend and associate of William Morris, for whom Red House was built, Webb shared Morris's views on the value of high-quality materials and craftsmanship. His aim was to design good, plain buildings, with comfortable interiors that could be lived in, an ambition that Standen fulfils in every respect.

As shown in Arthur Melville's delightful watercolour, painted when he visited the Beales for a weekend in 1896, Standen sits on a terrace, with views south to the wooded hills of Ashdown Forest. The attractive five-gabled garden front is partly built of creamy sandstone from the hill behind, but the upper storeys are weather-boarded and tile-hung in the Wealden fashion, producing a red and white effect. An arcaded conservatory is joined onto this front and there are tall brick chimneys rising almost to the height of the tower holding the water tanks.

The light, airy rooms are furnished with Morris's wallpapers and textiles, with richly coloured William de Morgan pottery, such as the red lustreware in a cabinet in the drawing room, and with a pleasing mixture of antiques and beautifully made pieces from Morris's company. The house was lit by electricity from the beginning, and most of the original fittings still exist. Webb's delicate wall lights in the drawing room hang like overblown snowdrops, casting soft pools of light on the blue and red hand-knotted carpet and on the comfortable chairs that were supplied from Morris's workshops, the pink velvet in which they were covered now a faded green. A sunflower motif on the wallpaper is echoed in the embossed decoration on the plates supporting the light brackets and in the swirls of foliage and sunflowers on the fender and on the copper cheeks of the fireplace. A view through to the conservatory from this room shows cane furniture set enticingly amidst a profusion of plants. All the rooms reflect Webb's meticulous concern for detail. The dining room at the end of the south front has an east-facing breakfast alcove, designed to catch the sunshine in the early morning, where oak dressers lined with china were just the right height for Mr Beale to carve the joint. Curiously, the first floor reveals that the Beales were expected still to rely heavily on washstands and hip baths: only two bathrooms were provided for the entire house, which had twelve family bedrooms.

The steep, south-facing garden reflects changes over several decades by a number of different hands. A fussy, gardenesque layout by the London landscape gardener G.B. Simpson, who

LEFT Standen has always been lit by electricity and many of the original fittings are still in the house, among them the delicate lights in the hall by W.A.S. Benson, William Morris's protégé.
BELOW Furnishings from Morris & Co. in the drawing room include a six-legged pie-crust table and most of the easy chairs.

ABOVE Standen's garden front, with its attractive gables and tile-hung upper storey, looks south to the wooded hills of Ashdown Forest.

was employed before Webb and planned his design to focus on a differently sited house, was then modified by his successor, who favoured a simpler approach concentrating on grass and trees and was responsible for the terraces that descend the hill in giant leaps, their outlines followed by hedges of clipped yew. The planting, on the other hand, was undertaken by James Beale's wife Margaret. The end result, although based on no coherent overall plan, is both individual and charming, with many changes of level linked by flights of steps. The little quarry from which the stone for the house was taken is now an attractively leafy corner of the grounds.

Staunton Harold Church

Leicestershire
5 miles (8 kilometres) north-east of Ashby-de-la-Zouch, west of the B587

This splendid church set in parkland on the edge of a lake is one of the very few that were built in the 20 years between the outbreak of the Civil War and the restoration of Charles II. Constructed in 1653, it was an act of defiance by the young Sir Robert Shirley, 4th Baronet, who was strongly opposed to Cromwell's Puritan regime and fully identified with the High Church Anglicanism of the martyred Charles I. Unfortunately for him, the church advertised both his audacity and his wealth. The incensed Cromwell retaliated by demanding money for a regiment of soldiers, throwing Sir Robert into the Tower of London when he refused to comply. There he died, aged only 27.

Staunton Harold is Sir Robert's memorial. Built in the revived gothic style that symbolised continuity with the old Church, its prominent pinnacles, embattled parapets and imposing tower are consciously medieval in spirit, but there is also a classical west doorway, with an outspoken inscription by the young baronet above it.

Fine carved woodwork by a joiner named William Smith survives unaltered inside. Oak box pews fitted with original brass candlesticks fill the nave. Oak panelling lines the walls and faces the columns of the nave and a magnificent Jacobean screen supports the organ loft at the west end. The organ itself, which pre-dates the church, is one of the oldest English-built instruments still in its original condition. Swirls of blue, black and white representing the elements in chaos draw the eye high overhead to a wonderfully abstract version of the Creation, dated 1655. The Puritans would have regarded both this display and the fixed altar in the chancel as idolatrous. The only two later features in the church are Robert Bakewell of Derby's ornate wrought-iron screen in the chancel arch that was an addition of the early eighteenth century and the marble tomb to Robert Shirley's great-grandson, who died of smallpox in 1714. The young man lies propped on his right elbow, as if eagerly surveying the world he has left.

ABOVE A splendid pinnacled and buttressed tower stands over the west door of Staunton Harold Church, where an inscription records that this singular building was the work of Sir Robert Shirley in 1653.

Stoneacre

Kent

At the north end of Otham village, 3 miles (4.8 kilometres) south-east of Maidstone, 1 mile (1.6 kilometres) south of the A20

Prosperous squires, farmers and other people of moderate means in the late Middle Ages built their houses to a standard pattern, with a central hall open to the rafters and an adjoining block, or blocks, with smaller chambers on two floors. An upper room, known as the solar, is where the family would retreat from the rest of the household. This layout, which endured for generations, reconciled increasing pressures for privacy with the traditional communal life.

This attractive half-timbered Wealden house, dating from about 1480, was typical of its time. But Stoneacre's individual character, created by Aymer Vallance, biographer of William Morris, in the early twentieth century, sets it apart. Impressive timberwork spans the great hall, with a rare and beautiful king-post, devised as a cluster of columns, supporting the ridge of the roof from the gigantic tie beam which stretches the length of the room. A massive brick chimney built in the 1920s rises the height of the hall from the fifteenth-century fireplace introduced by Mr Vallance on the south side, a collection of warm-toned Hispanic plates along the chimney breast enhancing the soft pinks of the brickwork. Twelve-light windows with leaded panes, some with stained glass designed by Vallance, face east and west, bringing both morning and evening sun into the hall.

In the adjoining parlour, where the Tudor fireplace was rescued from a house that was being demolished, the Arts and Crafts fabric making up the curtains, with a repeated motif of an angel blowing a trumpet, was designed by the artist and writer Herbert Horne in *c.* 1884 for the newly formed Century Guild, devoted to the promotion of traditional crafts.

This fifteenth-century core with its solar block to the south is now the centrepiece of a much larger place. Using timber, windows and furnishings from dilapidated Tudor houses, some of which were acquired as complete buildings, Mr Vallance created half-timbered wings in complete harmony with the genuinely medieval work. Badly neglected before he began his restoration, Stoneacre is a fascinating example of creative scholarship.

ABOVE Stoneacre's gabled, half-timbered façades seem all of a piece, but much of the house was created in the 1920s by Aymer Vallance, who re-used material from other Tudor buildings.

Stoneywell

Leicestershire
10 miles (16 kilometres)
north-west of Leicester, 5 miles
(8 kilometres) south of
Loughborough, east of the M1,
junction 22

Set amongst the crags, woods and bracken of ancient Charnwood Forest, but only a mile from the M1, is this most romantic of cottages. Constructed of rough local stone and slate and built into steeply rising ground, Stoneywell looks rooted in the landscape, at one with the granite outcropping nearby. There is a massive chimneystack at one end, casement windows are set at different levels, and an intriguing bulge in the back wall accommodates a spiral staircase.

Despite its appearance, Stoneywell is little more than a hundred years old. It was built in 1898 by the Arts and Crafts architect and designer Ernest Gimson for his brother Sydney, who was a director of the family engineering company in Leicester. Sydney used to come out to Charnwood Forest for camping weekends when he was in his teens and in 1897 he bought a 3.5-acre (1.4-hectare) plot in a spot where he and his friends used to picnic and asked Ernest to design a summer-house for him. Ernest created a place of great character and charm, in which the vernacular style, use of natural materials, deceptively simple design and attention to craftsmanship reflect the ideals of William Morris and his friends a generation earlier (see Red House, p.287, and Standen, p.318). Ernest's friend and fellow architect Detmar Blow directed the work and gathered the stone for the house from what is now the garden and fields round about, sometimes liberating an attractive piece from a dry-stone wall. Massive slate lintels over the fireplaces and front door came from the abandoned Swithland quarry nearby. There are chunky Swithland slates on the roof too, but these only date from restoration work in 1939, after a fire destroyed the original thatch.

Inside, the cottage is a place of irregularly shaped whitewashed rooms with low, beamed ceilings, inviting window-seats and deep window-sills of polished stone or wood. There is a small landing on the first floor, but mostly the rooms lead one into another, with steps connecting the many different levels. Everything is all of a piece, from the steep staircases with slate treads and rope handrails to the plank doors with their heavy wooden catches and the wooden pegs for coats. Everywhere there are quirky details, from a protruding slate

which Sydney used as a shelf for his tobacco jar to an alcove fashioned in the thickness of a wall and the seat tucked away to one side of the inglenook fireplace in the sitting room, with a tiny window to give views over the garden.

As well as Stoneywell, Ernest also built Lea Cottage on an adjoining plot for his brother Mentor and, ten years later, Rockyfield Cottage for his sister Margaret, but only Stoneywell still has its original character. Unlike the other two cottages, Stoneywell remained in the family, passing first to Sydney's son Basil, who lived here from 1947, and then to his grandson Donald, who came to live here with his wife Anne in 1953 and brought up his family in the cottage. In keeping with Ernest's design, Sydney and his wife Jeannie furnished Stoneywell with Arts and Crafts pieces, many of them made by Ernest or his friends and collaborators Ernest and Sidney Barnsley at the workshop they all shared at Sapperton in the Cotswolds. Despite alterations after the fire and the installation of a bathroom and other conveniences, such as a modern kitchen and central heating, the interior is little changed, with much of the original Arts and Crafts furniture still in place and other pieces on loan from the family and from Leicester Museum and Art Gallery. The overall effect is spare, but there are homely touches too.

Sidney Barnsley's solid oak table in the dining room and Ernest Gimson's ladder-back rush-seated chairs set around it all came from the Cotswold workshop, their attractive simplicity reminiscent of Shaker designs. A battered gardening hat sits on a chair and the slate stairs leading up to the sitting room carry a collection of stone hot water bottles, much in use before the central heating was installed, and a pair of Wellington boots which were used for visiting the pantry dug into the rock when the floor flooded, as it often did. Pottery on the dresser with a pattern picked out in rust and deep blue was designed by Sidney Barnsley's daughter Grace. The sitting room, with comfortable chairs set round the inglenook fireplace, fills the south end of the house, burrowing into the hill. Ernest Gimson, who was a master of many crafts, designed the steel fire dogs and the gleaming brass candle sconce on the wall, and the bookshelves forming a frieze at ceiling level are still filled with the Gimsons' books. In the main bedroom above, where the window in the gable end is only about a foot above the rising ground outside, a walnut chest of drawers was made by Sidney

Barnsley for Basil Gimson's 21st birthday. Another outstanding piece of craftsmanship is the walnut coffer standing by one of the windows, its carved decoration of wild plants, by Joseph Armitage, including a panel of oak leaves and acorns that is very like the winning entry Armitage submitted in 1935 in a competition to find a logo for the National Trust.

From every room there are glimpses of the garden, sometimes a close-up of rock, heather and bilberry, sometimes a long view to the oak and birch woodland which enfolds the cottage, with the conical slate roof of the Well House, for long the only source of drinking water for both Stoneywell and Lea Cottage, visible through the foliage. Although Sydney planted the daffodils in rough grass by the weather-boarded stables, created the tennis court, and established a walled vegetable plot, the garden as it is now owes much to Donald and Anne, who tamed it and planted the many species of rhododendrons, azaleas and magnolias that make a visit to Stoneywell in spring such a delight. Anne died in 2008 and the Trust acquired Stoneywell four years later.

BELOW Stoneywell, built of rough local stone and set into rising ground, seems rooted in the landscape of Charnwood Forest, with its rocky outcrops and drystone walls.

Stourhead

Wiltshire
At Stourton, off the B3092,
3 miles (4.8 kilometres)
north-west of Mere

This fine classical house standing high on a ridge of the Wiltshire Downs looks out over the park to distant wooded hills. One of the first Palladian houses in England, it was built in 1721–5 by Henry Hoare I, whose wealth came from the bank founded by his father, Sir Richard Hoare, in 1672. Henry had purchased the Stourton Manor estate, where the Stourton family had lived for 700 years, in 1717. Four years later he demolished the existing house and employed Colen Campbell, a leading advocate of Palladian architecture, to design this replacement on a new site. The square main block, with its temple-like portico rising the height of the building, is flanked by pavilions added in the 1790s to house a picture gallery and library. The rather severe lines of the façade are softened only by three lead statues set above the portico and by two flights of steps rising to the entrance, their end pillars supporting stone basins surmounted by the Hoare eagle. The portico was part of Campbell's design, but was added, along with the pillars, basins and eagles, in 1838–9. The statues, also proposed by Campbell, were later additions too.

Sadly, fire gutted this central block in 1902, destroying much of the original decoration, but from which most of the furniture and paintings on the ground floor were saved. More or less faithful Edwardian reconstructions of Campbell's intentions by the local architect Doran Webb and the more prestigious Sir Aston Webb who replaced him are now sandwiched between the Regency rooms in the pavilions, both of which survived virtually unscathed. The contents, a rich collection of family heirlooms with finely crafted furniture by Thomas Chippendale the Younger, reflect the interests of several generations of Hoares and the addition of pieces from Wavendon, the family's house in Buckinghamshire, in the nineteenth century.

The nucleus of paintings, sculpture and *objets d'art* acquired by Henry Hoare II to embellish his father's new house was greatly extended by his grandson Sir Richard Colt Hoare, who inherited in 1785 and added the pavilions to the house. This eminent antiquary, scholar and county historian was an omnivorous collector, amassing a magnificent library in one of his purpose-built extensions and displaying the pick of his grandfather's art collection, together with his own acquisitions of works by Italian and British contemporaries, in the other. Although some of the finest were sold in the late nineteenth century, the paintings still hang triple-banked against pea-green walls, some simple gilt frames contrasting with florid rococo creations on the end wall. Cigoli's *Adoration of the Magi* dominates the room, an expression of great tenderness lighting the face of the grizzled king in an ermine-fringed cloak who kneels at the Virgin's feet.

Similarly, although many of his books have now been dispersed, Colt Hoare's evocative green and white library is one of the most beautiful surviving Regency rooms in England, with the arch of the high barrel-vaulted ceiling echoed in the curves of the alcoves lined with books. Thomas Chippendale's rich mahogany furniture (including massive staircase-like library steps), gilded calf bindings and the deep-green and ochre carpet all contribute to a feeling of luxurious opulence, while the muted tones are lifted by flashes of colour from the painted glass in the lunettes set high up at each end of the

LEFT The entrance hall is hung with family portraits and has been decorated to give the room an Edwardian flavour.
OPPOSITE Doran Webb rebuilt the west front in a classical idiom after fire gutted the house in 1902, but the graceful flight of steps was designed by Sir Aston Webb, who replaced him.

room. Of the other treasures in the house, perhaps the most memorable is the sixteenth-century 'Pope's cabinet' designed like the façade of a Renaissance church, a framework of ebony and bronze setting off a multi-coloured inlay of marble, porphyry, jasper and other ornamental stones.

At the back of the house, handsome stone steps designed by Aston Webb fan out gently to a sweep of tree-framed grass. Beyond, hidden in the trees, the ground suddenly falls away into a steep-sided valley and the magical landscape garden created here in the second half of the eighteenth century. Sheltered and enclosed by windbreaks along the rim of the combe is a serene arcadia, with classical temples and other eye-catchers set against wooded slopes and mirrored in an artificial lake. A grotto devised on the edge of the water has sombre rock pools and a sculpture of a river god. All around are the trees, with native species such as beeches and oaks mixed with exotics, among them the Norwegian maple, tulip trees, cedars, the dawn redwood and the Japanese white pine, *Pinus parviflora*.

Although later members of the family, in particular Sir Richard Colt Hoare, enriched the planting by widening the range of species and also made some more fundamental changes, the landscape garden is primarily the creation of Henry Hoare II. Perhaps turned in on himself by the tragic loss of both his wives, the first of whom, Anne, died in 1727, the second, Sarah, in 1743, the garden was to be Henry's absorbing interest for 40 years from 1741. The only professional engaged in its creation was the architect Henry Flitcroft, who designed the classical eye-catchers: the Doric Temple of Flora,

which was the first building to be added to the garden; the domed Pantheon, with a broad flight of steps leading up to a pedimented portico; and the tall, circular Temple of Apollo, enclosed in a continuous colonnade. A gothic cottage, its prominent traceried windows and thatched roof almost buried in vegetation, was devised by Sir Richard Colt Hoare out of an existing building in 1806, and Sir Richard was also responsible for the impressive castellated gateway through which the house is approached, re-siting it from a previous position leading to the stableyard. Some 2 miles (3.2 kilometres) away, standing high on the chalk scarp overlooking Somerset, is the triangular brick eyecatcher known as Alfred's Tower, which was also designed by Flitcroft.

Stone-tiled cottages with mullioned windows in the estate village on the edge of the valley stretch down to the Palladian bridge over an arm of the lake. Built by Henry Hoare, they were originally hidden behind a screen of trees so that they would not intrude on his design, but now this row of buildings forms another attractive feature. Opposite the cottages is the medieval parish church, picturesquely crowned with fretwork parapets and filled with monuments to the Hoares and their predecessors, the Stourtons. Just beyond the churchyard, dominating the view over the lake, is the slender column of the medieval cross that Henry acquired from the City of Bristol in the 1760s, its tapering length suggesting the spire of a buried church. Statues of medieval kings standing round the base are carved stone replicas of the originals, which are on loan to the Victoria and Albert Museum.

Sudbury Hall and the National Trust Museum of Childhood

Derbyshire
6 miles (9.6 kilometres) east of Uttoxeter at the crossing point of the A50 Derby–Stoke and the A515 Lichfield–Ashbourne roads

Sudbury is one of the most important of the many great houses created during Charles II's reign, with outstanding work by some of the best craftsmen of the day. It is also home to the nationally significant Museum of Childhood, where children can engage with the challenges as well as the pastimes and playthings of childhood in the past.

The house was built by George Vernon, who set out to replace an existing Elizabethan manor shortly after inheriting the estate in 1660. The building and fitting out of his new mansion, with which he hoped to enhance his status, evolved over some forty years, during which Vernon, who acted as his own architect and supervisor, adapted his ideas to take account of changing fashions. The result is a building that bridges changes in seventeenth-century taste, marrying many old-fashioned Jacobean features with elements that reflect knowledge of up-to-the-minute fashions. The house has an outdated E-shaped plan, incorporating a great hall and long gallery, and yet is fashionably decorated, with rich plasterwork and woodcarving of the highest quality. The message of the exterior is similarly contradictory. The stone-mullioned and transomed windows were not yet old-fashioned when Sudbury was begun, but the diapered brickwork and carved stone ornaments over the ground-floor windows suggest a Jacobean house. By contrast, the hipped roof and gleaming central cupola, visible for miles around, show knowledge of more up-to-the-minute styles, such as the design of Roger Pratt's Kingston Lacy (see p.192).

Competent but uninspired early work by local men contrasts with the skills displayed by the London craftsmen Vernon employed as time went by, in particular the woodcarvers Edward Pierce and Grinling Gibbons, and the plasterers Robert Bradbury and James Pettifer. The balustrade of Pierce's virtuoso staircase, one of the finest and most elaborate of its date, is a mass of writhing foliage carved out of limewood, with baskets of fruit fashioned from elmwood set on the newel posts. Pettifer's plasterwork overhead, in which garlands of fruit and flowers

and acanthus scrolls form three-dimensional encrustations, is similarly rich. Twenty years after this work was finished, in the 1690s, Vernon added a taste of the exuberant baroque style that was then popular at court by employing Louis Laguerre to paint mythological scenes in the plasterwork panels.

Another painting by Laguerre fills a plaster wreath on the ceiling of the saloon. One of the richest of Sudbury's interiors, this room is lined with family portraits, each of which is set in a gilded ornamental panel, with swags of fruit and flowers above, below, and in some cases framing the pictures. The decorative woodwork was carved by Pierce, but the paintings were only inserted in the eighteenth century, when the wainscot was altered to accommodate them. A limewood carving by Grinling Gibbons over the fireplace in the drawing room next door, for which Gibbons was paid £40, depicts fruit, flowers, dead game and fish with lifelike realism.

The decoration of the sunny long gallery running the length of the south front has a lighter touch. At first glance, Bradbury and Pettifer's intricate plasterwork appears to repeat established motifs. But all is not what it seems. The classical busts portrayed along the frieze are humorous caricatures, while a lion, a horse, a boar and other animals leap gaily out of the swirls of foliage on the ceiling, and grasshoppers dance playfully round the sunflower rosette in the central window bay. William Wilson, a renowned master carver of stone and alabaster based in the Midlands, was responsible for the superb alabaster chimneypiece and overmantel in a room nearby, and also for the stonework on the frontispiece to the hall.

The small family rooms 'resurrected' by the Trust at the east end of the house are a contrast to all this magnificence. Lady Vernon's cosy sitting room, with its leaf-green walls and tranquil view over the lake below the south front, has a communicating door to her husband's study. It is easy to imagine them talking through it, and walking together across the passage to eat in the small dining room.

Although Sudbury has lost some of its original contents, there are family portraits in almost every room, including works by Thomas Lawrence, John Hoppner, J.M. Wright and Enoch Seaman, and several other outstanding furnishings

OPPOSITE The Museum of Childhood at Sudbury includes this evocation of a period schoolroom, complete with slates for each pupil.

On the blackboard:

Queen Victoria

Union among
friends is becoming

Lsgb. 14 : 10/2

LEFT Sudbury, built in the 1660s, is an idiosyncratic house with an old-fashioned Jacobean exterior. The interior, worked on by outstanding London craftsmen, mirrors the taste of the day.
OPPOSITE The staircase hall, with its Jacobethan staircase and array of nineteenth-century family portraits, is the heart of Sunnycroft.

remain, among them walnut dining chairs of *c.* 1735 which have been bought back for the house. In the long gallery, a seventeenth-century Flemish ebony cabinet is enchantingly decorated with scenes of the Creation by Frans Francken the Younger. The first panel shows a purple- and red-robed God hovering above an endless expanse of ocean, brooding on what he is about to unleash.

The red-brick service wing in a sympathetic neo-Jacobean style was added to the hall in the nineteenth century by George Devey, who was engaged by the 6th Lord Vernon. This part of the house, and the seventeenth-century stables with which it connects, are now devoted to the Museum of Childhood, where the extensive collection of toys and other childhood objects includes dolls' houses, mechanical toys, books and photographs and material relating to popular films and television programmes, such as *Doctor Who* and *Harry Potter*. The imaginative and involving displays put across something

of what children once experienced, from the fun of playing period games to some of the harsher aspects of childhood in the past, such as the reality of life for a chimney sweep. The plan is for Sudbury to have an increasingly child-centred approach and to act as a gateway for the young to engage with heritage and culture.

The Vernon family owned Sudbury until it was transferred to the Trust in 1967. The warm yellow of the staircase walls and most of the other paint schemes were suggested by John Fowler, who masterminded the redecoration of the house after the Trust took it over. This work is now seen as a classic example of the approach to historic buildings of the time.

Grassy terraces lead down to the lake below the south front. Neither the lake, nor the wider surroundings of the house, are owned by the Trust, but from the first floor there are memorable views of the castle-like deercote-cum-folly dating from the eighteenth century in the park to the north of the hall.

Sunnycroft

Shropshire
200 Holyhead Road, Wellington

This substantial Victorian house looking south towards the wooded humps of the Wrekin hills on the outskirts of Wellington is a rare survival of a way of life that lasted from *c.* 1850 to the Second World War. During this period, bankers, solicitors, businessmen and others from the well-to-do upper middle classes acquired mini-estates on the outskirts of the towns where they worked. Here they built houses large enough to pursue a version of the landed-gentry lifestyle to which they aspired and with enough land to keep livestock and grow produce for the table as well as to have ornamental gardens. After the Second World War, when the way of life that had supported them was no longer viable, some villas became institutions; others were demolished and their land sold for building. Largely because it was owned by the Landers from 1912 to 1997, Sunnycroft survived. The house still has many original features and contents and the grounds, 5 acres (2 hectares) in extent, are still worked, with productive areas set around and dovetailed into the ornamental parts.

Built of strident red brick, Sunnycroft is a plain, almost austere house, with large plate-glass windows, a gabled roofline and a turret over the entrance porch. A long verandah dotted with potted plants shades the main rooms and on the west side, so close to the house as to seem part of it, is an enchanting Victorian glasshouse. The earliest part, where the rooms are more modest, was built in 1880 for J.G. Wackrill, who founded the Shropshire Brewery. He sold the house to Mary Jane Slaney, the widow of a wine and spirit merchant, and in 1899 she extended Sunnycroft, adding the capacious hall, with its Jacobethan staircase, and the larger reception rooms

LEFT Sunnycroft was originally built for a brewery-owner in 1880, but the house was extended for Mary Jane Slaney, the widow of a wine and spirit merchant, in 1899, when this entrance was created.

and creating the present entrance. The first of the Landers, John Vernon Thomas, a Wellington solicitor who used to walk into work wearing a white bowler hat and a carnation from the glasshouses, bought the property in 1912. His son Offley, who was a founder-director of an ironworks at Coalbrookdale, acquired the house on J.V.T.'s death in 1943, and then, in 1973, it was inherited by Offley's daughter Joan, who left the estate to the National Trust.

The interior is an evocative period piece. There is much sombre decoration and substantial late-Victorian and Edwardian furniture, windows and archways are hung with heavy curtains, and the house still has original parquet and decorative tiled floors, ornamental gas brackets, its Victorian rooflight, filled with tinted glass, and cast-iron radiators, part of the up-to-the-minute technology installed in 1899. There are separate servants' quarters and the family's social aspirations come through in the billiard-room, equipped with a full-size table, which formed a masculine domain for the men of the house, and in the stately dining room where the Landers hosted five-course dinners and where lunch was held punctually at one. Something of the Landers themselves can be sensed in fine needlework by Joan, who trained as an embroiderer, and in the coat and leather gloves Offley wore when he drove to work in the black Daimler, number plate AW1, which still sits in the garage outside.

Sutton House

London
At the corner of Isabella Road
and Homerton High Street,
Hackney

An inner-city borough in East London is the unexpected setting for this fine red-brick Tudor house. A three-storey H-shaped building set back from the road across a paved yard, with diamond diapering marking the west wing, it sits at the west end of Homerton High Street, just where the road starts to swing north. Dating from 1534 to 1535, Sutton House was built for the high-flying courtier and statesman Sir Ralph Sadleir (1507–87) in what was then desirable countryside on the edge of Hackney village, with open fields between here and London. Right-hand man to Thomas Cromwell, Sadleir survived his patron's fall in 1540, and was one of those who tried the ill-fated Mary, Queen of Scots in 1586, when he would have been 79. His house has had a more chequered career. Remodelled in c. 1700, when the Tudor gables and mullioned windows were replaced with the present elegant sashes and roofline parapet, divided into two in c. 1750, partly faced in heavy stucco in the mid-nineteenth century and reunited in 1904, Sutton House has served as school, working men's institute and offices as well as one or more private dwellings. It was restored by the National Trust after a period of uncertainty and decline in the twentieth century.

The restoration exposed original features hidden behind later alterations and, apart from the great hall that once filled the bar of the H, the basic Tudor plan also survives, with staircases in the wings and a few cupboard-like garderobes. The parlour in the west wing is one of the finest Tudor interiors in London, with oak linenfold panelling running from floor to ceiling and a fireplace of carved Reigate stone. On the first floor, above what was the great hall, is the airy, high-ceilinged great chamber, lit by windows to both north and south. As in the parlour, the panelling here has been rearranged, and some of it is Jacobean rather than Tudor, but this is a striking room, its effect enhanced by Sadleir family portraits, an oak refectory table and a Charles II dresser.

Other features reflect later history. There is painted Jacobean strapwork imitating what richer folk would have had executed in stone or wood, a panelled Georgian parlour in a delicate mint green, Georgian barley-twist balusters on the east staircase and a Victorian study. There is also one surviving leaded and mullioned Tudor window, looking out onto the secluded, stone-flagged court at the centre of the house.

The sparse furnishings are not original but all are in keeping, including a couple of reproduction seventeenth-century harpsichords. 'Finds' on display – thimbles, bobbins, scissors, pins, the odd shoe – date from the school years, and a squatter has left a sinister red and black eye on the wall of an attic room. The Wenlock Barn closing the court, a balconied hall with an open timber roof built by Lionel Crane, son of Arts and Crafts designer Walter Crane, is now a function room and a first-floor gallery is often used to show the work of Hackney's sizeable community of artists, said to be the largest in Europe.

Art installations are also a feature of Breaker's Yard, next to the house, where what was scrubland has recently been transformed into a green oasis.

BELOW Built for a high-flying courtier in the 1530s in what was then open countryside outside London, Sutton House has a fine Tudor parlour with linenfold panelling and a fireplace of carved Reigate stone.

Tattershall Castle

Lincolnshire
On the south side of the A153,
15 miles (24 kilometres)
north-east of Sleaford, 10 miles
(16 kilometres) south-west of
Horncastle

Ralph, 3rd Baron Cromwell, was an ambitious man, reaching the climax of his career as Treasurer to Henry VI from 1433 to 1443. His sturdy brick tower, rising prominently from the Lincolnshire Fens, is one of the most striking monuments of the later Middle Ages, all that remains of the largely brick-built castle he created here. That anything survives is entirely due to Lord Curzon, who bought the building back from speculators in 1911 and who also engineered the return of chimneypieces which had been removed from the tower and were about to be shipped to America.

Tattershall looks both forwards and backwards. By 1430, when Cromwell started on extensions to the existing buildings, keeps had gone out of fashion in England, but were to be built for another century or so in France. The magnificent products of Franco-Burgundian culture, so exquisitely illustrated in the *Très Riches Heures* of the Duc de Berry, may well have inspired the young nobleman, who would have had ample opportunity to see them while serving with the English army in the Hundred Years' War. Like its French counterparts, Tattershall has an air of unreality, as if it too had stepped from a contemporary manuscript. It is essentially a status symbol, equivalent to the gatehouse towers that other men of substance were to build in the years that followed (*see*, for example, Oxburgh and Sissinghurst, pp.258 and 307).

Although outwardly defensive, girdled by two moats and with machicolated fighting galleries underneath the battlements, this is in fact a domestic country mansion masquerading as a fortress, with large and plentiful windows and several entrances. Each of the four floors above the vaulted basement is filled with one great chamber. Margaret, Lady Cromwell's bedchamber was probably at the very top of the tower, with the Treasurer's on the floor below. Stone chimneypieces carved with Cromwell's arms and his treasurer's purse and elaborate window tracery point to luxuriously fitted interiors.

Tattershall is as significant for its material as its design. Although bricks were used in the eastern counties in the thirteenth and fourteenth centuries, they were usually concealed under plaster. Tattershall is one of the earliest examples of the deliberate choice of this material, with its decorative possibilities exploited in the rows of corbels at the top of the façades. Inside, the skill of the craftsmen shows particularly in the spiral staircase with a finely moulded stone handrail set into the wall that fills one of the corner turrets, and in the brickwork of the decorative vaults.

Cromwell was a man of the world, acquiring large estates across the East Midlands and building manor houses elsewhere as well as constructing his lavishly appointed tower-house at Tattershall. He was also a creature of his age, concerned for his fate in the next world as much as his comfort in this one. Like other great men of his time, he anticipated the Last Trump by endowing a memorial college to be built close by his castle. Apart from a ruined, two-storey brick building, possibly offices and lodgings, only the beautiful collegiate church, with its armorial stained glass and mutilated brass commemorating Cromwell and his wife, survives, the attractive row of almshouses having been rebuilt in the seventeenth century (neither is owned by the Trust).

In the late Middle Ages this considerable complex of buildings, rising like an island of the civilised world from the sea of the Fens, tellingly revealed the self-importance and aspirations of the man who created them.

ABOVE A spiral staircase with a finely moulded stone handrail sunk into the wall fills one of Tattershall Castle's octagonal turrets.
OPPOSITE The keep-like brick tower which formed the core of Tattershall Castle is a medieval country house masquerading as a fortress.

Tatton Park

Cheshire
3½ miles (5.6 kilometres) north of
Knutsford, 4 miles (6.4 kilometres)
south of Altrincham, 3½ miles
(5.6 kilometres) from the M6 at
the Manchester interchange

The 4th Lord Egerton, who
inherited the Tatton estate
in 1920, was a restless and
individual man who was
intrigued by the scientific
discoveries of his day. Widely
travelled, he staked a claim in
the Yukon during the Gold Rush
of the 1890s and once lived
with a tribe in the Gobi Desert,
but he also experimented with
short-wave radio and was a
pioneer aviator. His 1900 Benz
proudly displaying the number
plate M1 was the first car to be
registered in Cheshire.

The 4th Lord's enquiring
mind seems to have been an
inherited trait. In all the plans
for the remodelling of the
existing eighteenth-century
house, on which Samuel Wyatt and his nephew Lewis were
employed between 1774 and about 1825, the library is given
particular prominence. A comfortable room filling the centre of
the garden front, it was designed to be used, not admired. Books
lie companionably on the reading chairs and stands, leather-
padded armchairs are drawn up by the fire and a library ladder
invites inspection of the topmost shelves. There is something
for everyone here, including first editions of Jane Austen's
novels, volumes of music, and illustrated works on the arts and
classical antiquities, most of them finely bound. The nucleus
of the collection is the sixteenth-century library acquired by
Thomas Egerton, founder of the family fortunes, who rose from
unpromising beginnings to become Lord Chancellor of England.

Lewis Wyatt's formal drawing room hung with cherry-
coloured silk is much grander, with a relentless coffered ceiling

ABOVE Like other great country houses, Tatton Park was largely self-sufficient,
generating its own electricity until 1961. This intriguing calorifier was used for
heating the water.
RIGHT The Neo-classical Regency south front, with the colonnaded family wing
added later in the nineteenth century to the left, overlooks a magnificent formal
Italian garden.

and with specially commissioned gilt-framed chairs and sofas carved in a sinuous rococo style by Gillows of Lancaster that would not seem out of place in a Venetian palazzo. Van Dyck's *Martyrdom of St Stephen* seems curiously appropriate in these unrelaxed surroundings, cherubs hovering overhead to receive the saint's soul. Two moody Venetian views by Canaletto are full of delightful detail, such as the little white dog with a jaunty tail that trots purposefully along the quay in the scene in front of the Doge's Palace.

Lewis Wyatt was also responsible for the inspired treatment of the staircase in the centre of the house and for a theatrical vista through a colonnade-like series of arches on the first floor. The Regency lifestyle for which Tatton was designed emerges strongly here, every bedroom except one sporting a dressing room. Each suite was originally distinguished by the colour of its textiles and the wood of the furniture, the pieces in the principal apartment being of mahogany inlaid with ebony.

The Wyatts' exterior is a pure Neo-classical design, with a giant pedimented portico dominating the south front, a low-pitched roof and almost no decoration except for the chaste swags in panels over the sash windows. Only the dining room designed by T.F. Pritchard, with its superb rococo plasterwork, remains from the earlier house, to which it was added in *c.* 1760.

The atmosphere of opulent grandeur extends into the spacious gardens with their sweeping lawns, herbaceous borders and a rich variety of trees. Grassy terraces on the south front, with shallow flights of steps descending to a fountain surrounded by an Italianate parterre, were designed by Joseph Paxton and there is an impressive range of glasshouses, including Wyatt's classical conservatory and Paxton's fernery, the roof of which has been raised to allow for the huge New Zealand tree ferns which now reach to the glass. More informal planting surrounding the artificial lake known as the Golden Brook almost conceals the Japanese garden laid out here in 1910, with stone lanterns dotting a mosaic of water and islands. Another surprise is the small beech maze hidden behind a bank of rhododendrons beside the long avenue known as the Broad Walk.

The Home Farm at Tatton Dale was once the heart of the extensive Egerton estates, with pigsties, stockyards, stables and workshops surrounding the office from which nearly 1,000 tenant properties were administered. Humphry Repton

ABOVE The servants' quarters at Tatton Park would have seen much activity in 1887 when the Prince and Princess of Wales stayed in the house and the prince planted a tree in the garden to mark his visit.

produced a Red Book for the extensive park, but most of the landscaping probably dates from William Emes's work in the mid-eighteenth century, with some early nineteenth-century modifications by John Webb. There are deer and flocks of Soay and Hebridean sheep beneath the trees, and the remains of the medieval manor house are used to introduce visitors to the realities of pre-modern life.

Theatre Royal, Bury St Edmunds

Suffolk
In Westgate Street, Bury St Edmunds, close to the A14

This delightfully intimate theatre, with seating for just 350 people, is the only surviving Regency playhouse in Great Britain that is still used for performances. Built in 1819, it dates from an era when Bury was a provincial capital, and farmers and gentry from miles around crowded into the town for the short autumn season. Comfortable plush seats have replaced the benches in the pit, but original boxes still fill the dress circle and the stalls are steeply raked towards the stage. The theatre was designed by William Wilkins the Younger, one of the leading Neo-classical architects of his day, who was later responsible for the National Gallery in London and Downing College, Cambridge. Wilkins was inspired by the ancient Greek amphitheatre at Taormina in Sicily and this is reflected in the shape of the auditorium,

the use of classical motifs, such as the winged sphinxes and griffins decorating the dress circle, and the painted ceiling, which represents the open sky.

Although the theatre continued to put on plays over the next hundred years, including the world premiere of Brandon Thomas's *Charley's Aunt* in 1892, attendances gradually declined. In 1920 it was bought by the Greene King brewery, whose huge buildings adjoin the theatre's arcaded façade on Westgate Street. Greene King closed the theatre five years later and turned it into a barrel store. It was largely forgotten until the 1960s, when a group of residents spearheaded a movement to restore it. The theatre was officially reopened in 1965 and ten years later Greene King leased it to the National Trust.

All kinds of performances have been held here since, and in 2005 a further restoration project reinstated Regency features which had been lost. In particular, the forestage that projected into the auditorium with boxes either side was reintroduced, so plays of the period can once again be staged as was intended, with the actors interacting closely with the audience. The original decorative scheme was also re-created and the theatre is thriving once again.

BELOW In the days when Bury St Edmunds was a provincial capital, farmers and gentry from miles around used to flock to the Regency Theatre Royal, where the original stage has been re-created.

LEFT The little fourteenth-century building known as the Old Post Office, built of local slate and occasional pieces of granite, has a tiny medieval hall rising to smoke-blackened rafters in the roof.

Tintagel Old Post Office

Cornwall
In the centre of the village of
Tintagel, on the main street

Among the hotels and teashops in the centre of this much-visited Cornish village is a pocket-sized late-medieval house, its walls spotted with lichen and ferns. Massive chimneystacks rise from an undulating roof. Dating in part from the fourteenth century, and a precious survival of early domestic architecture in this part of England, the Old Post Office is traditionally built of local brown slate, now weathered to a uniform grey, with the occasional piece of granite and greenstone surrounds to the windows. As the deep sills reveal, the walls are impressively thick, but even so the house is buttressed at the back to take the weight of the stone slates on the roof. Nothing is symmetrical, from the placing of the small casement windows to the off-centre porch.

Inside, a diminutive hall rises to smoke-blackened rafters in the middle of the building and a passage runs through the house to the split-level garden behind. Smaller rooms to either side have bedrooms open to the roof above them, and there is a sleeping platform above the hall reached by slate slabs set into the thickness of the wall. Coming to the Trust with no contents, apart from the table in the hall, the house has been furnished with the kind of pieces, largely of oak, that would have been found in farmhouses and cottages round about, and there is a collection of needlework samplers.

Despite its name, this picturesque building served as a post office only for a few years in the 1870s. The owner at that time, William Parnell, was a farmer who took on the role of sub-postmaster for a while. In the early nineteenth century, when Tintagel, or Trevena as it was then known, was a remote village on the wild north coast of Cornwall, letters had to be picked up from Camelford, 5 miles (8 kilometres) away. But after the Penny Post was introduced in 1840, postal traffic in the area increased and in 1844 the GPO decided to set up a letter-receiving office in the village. Various other premises also performed this function over the years, but this was how the Old Post Office was being used, as a supplement to farming, before it fell into disrepair, hence the name. One of the ground-floor rooms in the house is now fitted out to resemble a Victorian letter-receiving office and a rare letterbox of 1857 is fitted to the wall outside.

When the rest of Tintagel was being ruthlessly redeveloped in the late nineteenth century to cater for Victorian romantics in search of King Arthur, the Old Post Office was saved by a local artist, Catherine Johns, who bought the building in 1895; shortly afterwards it was sensitively restored by the Arts and Crafts architect Detmar Blow.

Townend

Cumbria
3 miles (4.8 kilometres)
south-east of Ambleside at the
south end of Troutbeck

A fine example of domestic Lake District architecture, Townend is a rare and remarkably intact survival of a house lived in by a family of yeoman farmers for centuries. An L-shaped building with limewashed stone walls, oak-mullioned windows and a slate roof topped with six round chimneys, it probably dates from the late sixteenth or early seventeenth century, but has been much altered and extended since. Just across the lane, built on a much grander scale, is the homestead's stone-and-slate galleried barn, with a ramp up to the granary floor and the date 1666 carved on one of the lintels.

The Browne family who lived here for over 400 years were sheep farmers, and they seem to have gradually risen in society through careful management of their affairs and by judicious marriages. Much of Townend's attraction derives from the fact that its contents reflect slow accretion by several generations of the Brownes. In the little library, Milton rubs shoulders with Clarke's sermons, Walton's *Compleat Angler*, a history of England and volumes of farming periodicals, the collection as a whole giving a unique insight into the interests and preoccupations of a rural middle-class family.

The preservation of the house and its contents owes much to the last George Browne (1834–1914), who was both a noted antiquary and a gifted joiner and woodcarver. The rooms are filled with ornate examples of his work, from the richly carved chairs in the firehouse, the oldest part of the building, to the little spindle-fronted cupboard in one of the bedrooms, in which no two spindles are alike. The wealth of heavy oak furniture displayed at Townend also includes the long seventeenth-century dining table in the firehouse, undoubtedly assembled *in situ*, where the Brownes would have taken meals with their farmhands and servants. From the kitchen next door, an early seventeenth-century spiral staircase made of solid blocks of oak winds steeply upwards to the simply furnished quarters for the housekeeper and maids. Charmingly naïve paintings of the family's sheep elsewhere in the house are by the local nineteenth-century artist William Taylor Longmire. Perhaps he took his models from the ancestors of the beasts that still graze the fells rising behind Townend.

The colourful little garden, with beds filled with traditional cottage-garden flowers, is a partial re-creation of George Browne's layout based on his notebooks, orders for seeds and cuttings and some surviving plans. Plums, damsons and apples grow in the orchard George established.

BELOW Some of the last George Browne's wood-carving can be seen in Townend's atmospheric stone-flagged kitchen, where he made the child's chair for his youngest daughter in 1873 and decorated the cupboards.

Treasurer's House

North Yorkshire
In Minster Yard, York, on the
north side of the Minster

Treasurer's House, bordering a narrow medieval cobbled street in the shadow of York Minster, was once attached to one of the wealthiest and most sought-after benefices in England. Successive treasurers of the cathedral lived in a mansion on this site from 1100 until the office was abolished under Henry VIII. Little remains of the building now except the name, but, intriguingly, the remains of a Roman road have been found in the cellars, suggesting a history of occupation going back 2,000 years.

The present elegant and airy town house incorporates some Elizabethan fabric but structurally it dates largely from c. 1630, when the attractive garden front with its classical central entrance bay was built and curved Dutch gables were added to the wings either side. Extensive alterations at the turn of the century and in Georgian times account for the Venetian windows on this front and for the elegant William and Mary staircase, its beautifully carved balusters possibly the work of the local carpenter-architect William Thornton, who was responsible for the magnificent woodcarving at Beningbrough Hall (see p.51).

Among the many residents of the house at this period were the writer and literary hostess Elizabeth Montagu, who was born here in 1720, and Dr Jacques Sterne, whose nephew, the novelist Laurence Sterne, satirised the inward-looking cathedral set in his *A Political Romance* (1759), his savage attack on local ecclesiastical courts provoking the banning of the book.

In the nineteenth century, the house was subdivided into at least five separate dwellings and became increasingly run down. It was rescued by the wealthy industrialist and aesthete Frank Green, who acquired it in 1897. With the help of the architect Temple Moore, Green carefully restored the house to what he thought was its original appearance, removing all nineteenth-century alterations and additions and creating a huge hall out of the two-storey central block, with a half-timbered gallery supported on classical columns. Appropriate antiques were used to form a sequence of period rooms. Furniture reflecting the craftsmanship of two centuries includes a fine oak refectory table of c. 1600, a marquetry grandfather clock of 1680 and three early eighteenth-century tester beds in the rooms where Edward VII, then Prince of Wales, Princess Alexandra of Wales and their daughter Victoria slept when visiting the house in 1900. Ornate early eighteenth-century giltwood mirrors make the airy drawing room looking over the garden, with panelling painted a brilliant peacock blue, seem even larger than it is and there is a set of walnut chairs of the same period covered in contemporary needlework. The house is further enriched by English and Flemish portraits from the sixteenth to eighteenth centuries. Frank Green composed each room carefully, using stud-marks in the floors to specify where each piece of furniture stood. The house today is largely as it was when he gave it to the National Trust in 1930.

The formal walled garden setting off the south front was established between 1897 and 1900 by Frank Green and, like the house, is mostly as he had it. A central sunken lawn is bordered on one side by a pollarded plane-tree avenue and there are raised terrace walks along the walls. Fragments of carved stonework incorporated in the walls were found in the garden, which was once the site of the mason's yard for the minster.

OPPOSITE The garden front of the Treasurer's House was given an elegant new façade in the early seventeenth century.

Tredegar House

Newport
M4 junction 28, then take A48 to
St Mellons from roundabout

Those heading west on the M4 out of Newport get a tantalising glimpse of this striking late seventeenth-century house set at the end of an avenue of oaks leading away from the motorway. Built to replace a Tudor mansion on the same site, and approached across two courts and through a gilded wrought-iron screen and gates of *c.* 1714–18, Tredegar was designed to impress. The long, symmetrical, red-brick entrance front, lit by huge stone-mullioned and transomed windows on both the principal floors and with projecting pavilions at both ends, is richly decorated with carved stone. Baroque spiral columns frame the central doorway, swags of fruit hang beneath the first-floor windows and heraldic cartouches flanked by endearingly realised lions and griffins crown all the ground-floor windows. A sizeable red-brick stable block closing one side of the outer court,

ornamented with brick pilasters topped by pineapples and an elaborate central doorway, and with an interior that includes a riding school, is almost as imposing.

The heraldry of the entrance front relates to the upwardly-mobile Morgan family, who owned land here for over 500 years. John ap Morgan's support of Henry Tudor's bid for the English throne in 1485 brought the family power and status in south-east Wales, a position which was reflected in the grey-stone Tudor house set round three sides of a courtyard which was subsequently built here in the mid-sixteenth century. One wing of the old place, with a low roofline and large stone-mullioned windows looking onto what is now an enclosed courtyard at the heart of the house, still survives, and this is where Charles I would have been entertained when he came to Tredegar in 1645. William Morgan, who greatly increased the family's wealth and landholdings by judicious marriages, remodelled Tredegar between 1666 and 1674, a few years before his death. The stables were probably added by his son. The Morgans were further enriched by the industrial development of this part of Wales in the late eighteenth and nineteenth centuries, when coal was mined on the estate and the family collected tolls from a lucrative tramroad across their land.

By the early twentieth century, when the Morgans had been elevated to the peerage and owned an estate of some 53,000 acres (21,500 hectares), Tredegar was at a high point and the family was known for their philanthropy as well as their wealth. But the extravagance of Courtenay Morgan, who inherited in 1913, and of his colourful son Evan, together with crippling death duties and the ever-increasing expense of maintaining Tredegar, led to the sale of the house in 1951.

A school for 23 years, in 1974 Tredegar was acquired and refurbished by Newport Borough Council, who bought back, or obtained on loan, many family portraits and other original furnishings. In 2012 the National Trust took a 50-year lease on the house.

ABOVE LEFT The main entrance to Tredegar is crowned by endearing carvings of the lion and griffin from the Morgan coat of arms.
LEFT The Gilt Room, the most ornate of the late seventeenth-century state rooms, was designed for candlelight.
OPPOSITE Tredegar's entrance front, lit by large stone-mullioned and transomed windows and decorated with carved stonework, was designed to impress.

Atmospheric late-seventeenth century state rooms interconnecting along the entrance front and seen by simulated candlelight are as richly decorated as the exterior, although, except in the Gilt Room, the original ornamental plaster ceilings have been lost. Oak panelling in the dining room is enriched with a wide band of carved foliage full of creatures, some of them half-animal and half-human, and each panel is crowned with a scrolled broken pediment carrying the bust of a Roman emperor. The adjoining Gilt Room filling the south-west corner of the house is even more spectacular. Here pine panelling has been painted to imitate walnut and richly gilded, the chimney piece resembles a baroque Italian altarpiece, original plasterwork on the ceiling frames an allegorical painting based on one in the Palazzo Barberini in Rome, and more inset paintings, including a version of a nude by Titian, decorate the walls. Like the work on the ceiling, these paintings, a motley collection of the Seasons and Virtues, some of which are based on sculptural decoration in Amsterdam Town Hall, were probably copied by local artists from books of engravings. A portrait of the 90-year-old Sir William Morgan, whose son built the house, is set over the fireplace, and more family portraits, including a piece by John Wootton showing the high-spending eighteenth-century Sir William with his racehorse Lamprey, are on show throughout the ground floor. Several portray Godfrey, 1st Viscount, who was one of only two officers to survive the suicidal Charge of the Light Brigade in the Crimean War, and whose likeness as an old man hangs on the seventeenth-century staircase.

Upstairs, the Best Chamber on the south-west corner of the house, lit by windows on two sides and lined with panelling painted white, is perhaps the most beautiful room in Tredegar. It has a seventeenth-century plasterwork ceiling and looks out over the formal walled gardens with wide gravel walks in the style of the early 1700s to the west of the house.

A suite of first-floor rooms on the east side of the house reflect Tredegar in the 1930s, when Evan Morgan held wild weekend parties here, during which guests of both sexes bathed in the nude, and entertained many leading artistic figures of the day, among them Augustus John, whose portrait of Evan's mother is in the house, H.G. Wells and Ivor Novello. In Evan's light and airy bedroom, with its cool grey and white colour scheme, photographs of the two women he married despite his homosexuality, the actress and wild child Lois Sturt and Princess Olga Dolgorouky, stand on the dressing table in the middle of the room and evening dress is laid out ready on the bed. A bedroom fitted out with loaned Biedermeyer furniture has been re-created with the help of Princess Olga, whose room it was.

Servants' quarters include a stone-flagged, high-ceilinged room that has been the kitchen since the house was built, the Victorian fittings here now including a gleaming copper boiler and an immensely long kitchen table.

Rooms in the 1930s suite look out towards the lake created when the park was landscaped in the late eighteenth century, its outlines now partly obscured by rhododendrons and ornamental conifers.

Trelissick

Cornwall
4 miles (6.4 kilometres) south of
Truro, off the A39, on the B3289
above the King Harry Ferry

On the south coast of Cornwall, the estuary of the Fal, one of the finest natural harbours in the world, winds far inland, with tidal creeks and inlets, like watery fingers, penetrating deep into the woods and meadows fringing it. Trelissick, surrounded on three sides by the waters of the Fal, stands high on its own peninsula jutting out from the west bank, with panoramic views south down the broad reach of Carrick Roads towards Falmouth and the sea. Below the house, wooded parkland falls steeply to the water and a beach while downriver wooded headlands fade into the distance. Boats dot the water like a flock of seagulls outside Mylor harbour and the outline of Pendennis Castle on the horizon marks the mouth of the river, with open sea beyond.

The lichen-spotted classical house rises two storeys to a roofline parapet, with generous sash windows lighting the principal rooms. A startlingly white Ionic portico dominates the south front, its six fluted columns topped by a central pediment giving the house the look of a Grecian temple when seen from the Fal. A more austere Doric portico, also white, marks the west-facing entrance front. These neo-Grecian features were added to Trelissick when an existing villa dating from *c.* 1750, and already enlarged in 1815, was substantially redesigned from 1825 for Thomas Daniell, whose father had made a fortune in tin mining. The new work, based on a design by Peter Frederick Robinson, a pupil of Henry Holland, produced a central block with single-storey wings. Further alterations, when a second storey, with a billiard room open to the rafters, was added to the wings, were made later in the nineteenth century, after Daniell's profligacy had forced him to

sell the house. But it was he who was responsible for planting the hanging woods of beech, oak and pine above the Fal and along the creek to the north of the house which give so much character to the place. Miles of carriage drives winding through the trees with views up and down the estuary and over the water to the further bank were constructed by Thomas's father.

Most recently, Trelissick was lived in for over seventy years by the Copeland family, after Mrs Ida Copeland was left the property by her stepfather, the distinguished collector and financier Leonard Cunliffe, in 1937. Ida and her husband, Ronald Copeland, who was Managing Director and later Chairman of the family business, W.T. Copeland & Sons Ltd (the Spode china factory), in Stoke-on-Trent, moved here from Staffordshire in 1948. They greatly enhanced the existing planting in the woodland garden north and east of the house, adding the rhododendrons that are now such a feature of Trelissick, and also hydrangeas, camellias and other species which flourish in Cornwall's mild climate. Ida Copeland transferred Trelissick to the National Trust in 1955, but the Copelands continued to live in the house until 2013 when Ida's grandson, William Copeland, and his wife Jenny decided it was time to downsize.

Inside, spacious, high-ceilinged family rooms lead off the entrance hall and open one into another down the south front, with a stone-floored solarium filled with tender plants at the east end. There is original plasterwork, gold silk lines the walls of the drawing room and George III mahogany furniture, such as the circular library table in the entrance hall and the Carlton House desk in the drawing room, are among pieces bought back when most of the contents were dispersed in a two-day sale in July 2013. Family portraits and photographs, including likenesses of Ronald and Ida, are on show, and there are displays of china from the Spode-Copeland factory decorated with paintings of rhododendrons grown at Trelissick. The Copelands would choose blossoms from the garden and send them to Stoke-on-Trent to be copied by designer Harold Holdway, one of whose drawings is in the house, the many species involved resulting in a colourful and varied display. Usually, the rooms are filled with the sound of music from the Broadwood grand piano in the drawing room, and always there is the view, over the terrace below the south front and the park beyond, to the waters of the Fal stretching into the distance.

ABOVE The south front looks over the terrace and the park beyond to the estuary of the Fal, stretching out to sea.
OPPOSITE The classical portico on Trelissick's south front, standing out white against the grey walls of the house, looks like a Grecian temple when seen from the Fal.

Trerice

Cornwall
3 miles (4.8 kilometres)
south-east of Newquay, via the
A392 and the A3058

This delightful Elizabethan manor house, constructed of local buff-coloured elvan stone and incorporating parts of an earlier medieval and Tudor building, was completed in 1572–3 for John Arundell V. The house is not grand but, despite being hidden away in the depths of Cornwall, it is built with an awareness of the latest fashions of the day. It is also largely unchanged, perhaps escaping alteration in the eighteenth and nineteenth centuries, when Cornish prosperity, based on mining, was at its height, because its owners chose to live elsewhere. Belonging to the Arundells, one of the wealthiest and most prominent families of Cornwall, for over 400 years, in 1802 the estate passed to the Aclands, whose principal properties were in Devon and Somerset (see Killerton, p.190).

The nature of the house is heralded in an approach down a narrow winding lane, with hedges high on either side, and in the unpretentious gateway that leads into the small walled garden setting off the entrance front. This E-shaped façade has a central porch and scrolled gables in the newly fashionable Dutch style. Among the earliest such features in Britain, these sophisticated gables are particularly unusual in Cornwall. Two granite Arundell lions guard the path to the front door and the bay to the left of the porch is entirely filled by the two-storey window lighting the great hall. An intricate lattice of mullions and transoms supports 576 panes, many of them still with their original sixteenth- and seventeenth-century glass. Although the stone of this part of the house is now all pleasingly weathered, the north wing to the right of the porch was partly demolished in the 1860s, after storm damage was thought to have made it unsafe, and was not rebuilt until the 1950s. Fortunately, the carved stonework of the scrolled gables had been preserved and could be incorporated in the new work.

The interior of the house fulfils the promise of the exterior. The sunny, south-facing great chamber on the first floor is richly decorated with bold Elizabethan plasterwork over the fireplace and on the splendid barrel ceiling, which is one of the best of the period in the West Country. Apart from the long table in the hall, made for the house in the nineteenth century, none of the furniture is original, but there are some good oak and walnut pieces among the furnishings introduced by the Trust, including a longcase clock by Thomas Tompion and a Queen Anne escritoire, and also some fine Chinese and English eighteenth-century porcelain and glass. Paintings by John Opie, who was born at Trevallas, only 15 miles (24 kilometres) away, add an appropriately Cornish flavour, among them portraits of his two wives, Mary and Amelia. There are also many reminders of the Arundells' devotion to the royal cause in the seventeenth century. The hall is filled with Stuart portraits and a haunting picture of Charles I by Henry Stone hangs in the court chamber upstairs. The face is careworn, the eyes withdrawn and watchful. Also in the house is an enchanting Jacobean embroidery panel, believed to depict Charles and his queen, in which Henrietta is shown giving the king a bunch of flowers, while a large snail crawls between them and a long-eared rabbit looks on.

Across the cobbled courtyard behind the house lies a magnificent great barn of a size and age – it probably dates from the fifteenth century – rarely seen in Cornwall. A ramp from the flat lawn above, where the Home Guard drilled in the Second World War, leads to the loft of the former stable.

No traces remain of the geometric Elizabethan garden that would once have set off the entrance front, but steps from the grassy court in front of the house lead up onto what was a Tudor bowling-green, from where there is a roof-level view of the gables on the east front. To the south, what was the lowest of a suite of Elizabethan terraces stepping down the hill has been planted as a formal knot garden as a nod to the ornamental Tudor layout that was once here. An early fifteenth-century chapel has also disappeared, although its site lives on in the field name 'Chapel Close'.

OPPOSITE Despite being hidden away in rural Cornwall, this unspoilt Elizabethan manor, built in c. 1570, has scrolled gables in the newly fashionable Dutch style.

Tyntesfield

Somerset
Off the B3128, 3 miles
(4.8 kilometres) east of Nailsea

This romantic High Victorian mansion is set on steeply rising ground, with woods behind and a panoramic view south over parkland and the valley of the Yeo to the distant ridge of the Mendips. Still all of a piece, with its original furnishings and decorative schemes and the accumulated possessions of the family that lived here for four generations, this memorable place is an unspoilt and largely unaltered example of a gothic revival country house. Windows are stone-mullioned and traceried, there are pepper-pot turrets, huge chimneystacks and fanciful gothic dormers, and window bays and rooflines are finished off with carved friezes, pierced parapets, finials and finely carved creatures, such as a badger and a goat. Rising over the house is the steeply pitched roof of a sizeable chapel, with finialled buttresses between the gothic windows and a west-end stair turret.

Together with almost 540 acres (218 hectares) of gardens, park and estate, Tyntesfield was acquired by the National Trust in 2002 after a whirlwind campaign to save the property from being sold on the open market, which required the Trust to raise over £20 million in 50 days. This was only made possible by a huge public response, and a measure of the brinkmanship involved is that the contents had already been ticketed and sorted for sale by auction. Much-needed conservation and restoration has been going on ever since.

Tyntesfield is predominantly the creation of the entrepreneurial William Gibbs (1790–1875). Involved in the family firm, which had business interests in Spain and Latin America, from a young age, by 1842, when he was in his early 50s, William was in charge. In the same year, the firm's South American agent concluded the deal that was to make him a fortune, giving Gibbs and Sons a virtual monopoly in the shipment of Peruvian guano, then a fertiliser of prime importance, the extraction of which involved labourers working in conditions which resembled slavery. A growing family may have encouraged William and his wife Blanche, 28 years his junior, to look for a place out of London, and in 1843 William bought what was then a Georgian country house with some decorative gothic touches. Twenty years later he commissioned the architect John Norton, who had learned his trade from a pupil and friend of Augustus Welby Pugin and so had direct links with the most influential figure of the gothic revival, to remodel Tyntesfield.

The house is built of golden Bath stone, with roofs covered partly in tiles, partly in heavy stone slabs quarried in Wiltshire. Carved stone decoration enlivening every façade includes some finely detailed, three-dimensional work by a certain Mr Beates, who realised the plants and creatures of the gardens and estate in stone. There are primroses, cobnuts and strawberries carved on corbels in the porch, and a capital carries a dormouse, bees and a lizard. As throughout the house, the craftsmanship is of the highest quality.

William's son Antony (1841–1907), an art collector and highly skilled amateur craftsman rather than a businessman, moved into Tyntesfield in 1890 after the death of his mother. He embarked on alterations, but his chosen architect, Henry Woodyer, who had already added on a substantial verandah for Blanche in 1883, also worked in the gothic revival style and his changes were all in keeping with the earlier work. By the next generation, a shift in taste was reflected in changes made by George Gibbs, 1st Lord Wraxall (1873–1931), who was a prominent politician and socialiser and invited members of the government down for country-house weekends. Again, though, with the exception of the drawing room, the essential character of the place was retained.

The 2nd Lord Wraxall (1928–2001) succeeded to the title when he was only three, and his mother Ursula, Lady Wraxall ran Tyntesfield for many years. At the end of his life, Lord Wraxall was living at Tyntesfield alone and many of the main rooms were shut up, but he maintained a keen interest in the gardens and estate and cared for the fabric of the place. Most importantly, although he sold some items, he did not follow the reaction against High Victorian art that led to other houses

ABOVE LEFT The vaulted roof of Tyntesfield's cloister-like entrance hall.
OPPOSITE The beautiful library, with its soaring oak roof and comfortable chairs, was a favourite family sitting room where theatricals were sometimes staged.

being stripped of their contents, and he added pictures and other objects to the collection.

The interior is of a piece, combining original decorative schemes with much surviving Victorian furniture, some of it, such as a richly ornamented rolltop desk, by the Warwickshire cabinetmakers Collier and Plucknett, who supplied the family with various items in the later nineteenth century. Wood and stone have been used profligately: there are open timber roofs, decorative panelling and parquet floors; monumental fireplaces, stone arches and doorways and pillars of polished marble. The main rooms are arranged around the top-lit staircase hall, with clerestory windows beneath an open roof of English oak. Paintings hung thickly on the walls include a portrait of William, with white hair and side-whiskers, by his close friend Sir William Boxall, and a seascape by Sir Augustus Wall Callcott, all steely sky and blue-grey sea. The chenille stair carpet, in ribbons when the Trust acquired Tyntesfield, has been rewoven in wool, to the original design, for which 27 colours were required.

William's spirit is strong in the spacious library which

ABOVE Tyntesfield's chapel is fitted out with ornate metalwork, stained glass from one of the best designers of the day, and a mosaic floor of exceptional richness, incorporating pieces of Mexican onyx and Derbyshire bluejohn.
OPPOSITE The Regency house acquired by William Gibbs in 1843 was transformed in a gothic idiom, complete with stone-mullioned windows, towering chimney stacks and pepperpot turrets, in the 1860s.

fills one of the wings on the entrance front. A comfortable, welcoming room rising to an open oak roof, it has the original carpet, in deep reds and blues, by the fashionable decorators J.G. Crace and Son and this company also provided the deep-buttoned armchairs and sofa. William's seven children staged theatricals here, and the bookcases round the walls, carefully numbered in Latin numerals, are stuffed with the gilded bindings of his library. William's religious sympathies lay with the Oxford Movement, which was launched in the 1830s to return ceremony and ritual, and thus elements of beauty and mystery, to the Church of England. The main texts of the movement are here, and so too are key works on the gothic revival, with which it went hand in hand, including the writings of Pugin and Ruskin. Above the bookcases at the west end of the room is a striking display of Imari porcelain – blue and white, green and red.

The dining room, entered through a flamboyant carved stone doorway and lined with wallpaper imitating Spanish leather, is Antony's. But the drawing room, with a Renaissance-style fireplace and an original Crace carpet that has been dyed to match the crimson damask on the walls, was altered and refurnished by Antony's son George, 1st Lord Wraxall, and his first wife Via. Much more relaxed in spirit is the capacious billiard-room, with an array of antlered heads on the walls, skins thrown casually over ageing sofas, and a centrally heated table with an electric scoreboard.

Upstairs, a run of bedrooms along the south and east fronts includes the room used by Via, who died at the tragically early age of 39. The peach-coloured carpet was installed for her and the room is furnished with Italian and Dutch marquetry pieces that she brought with her to the house. Because of the slope of the hill, the family could walk from these first-floor rooms straight into the chapel which William commissioned from Arthur Blomfield and which was only just finished when William died in 1875. Provided with a chancel and ornate screen and richly fitted out with gleaming mosaics, stained glass and an inlaid floor, it proclaims William's commitment to High Church principles. A silver communion set designed by William Butterfield in 1876 was commissioned by Blanche in memory of her husband.

The layout of the garden is still very much as it was when William died. Close to the house, billowing hollies lap the marble urns set along the lower terrace, and bright displays of bedding plants reflect the taste of the 2nd Lord Wraxall. Luxuriant magnolias and camellias outside the billiard-room mark the site of John Norton's huge conservatory, with an onion dome and gilded cupola, which was demolished after the dome collapsed in a storm in March 1916. A formal walk lined by mushroom domes of holly stretches away from the west front, past the former rose garden, and another long walk, marked by clipped Irish yews, echoes the line of the terraces, with views over the sadly waterless lake. Architectural stone gothic seats punctuate the ends of the walks.

Everywhere in the landscaped grounds are huge specimen trees and a ha-ha allows uninterrupted views across the park and the valley beyond. Hidden from the house are the walled kitchen gardens, with greenhouses that are still very much in use, and a splendid classical orangery, of brick and stone. Cut flowers and fresh vegetables are still supplied to the house from these gardens as they always have been.

Uppark House and Garden

West Sussex
5 miles (8 kilometres) south-east of Petersfield on the B2146, 1½ miles (2.4 kilometres) south of South Harting

This serene two-storey house stands high on a crest of the South Downs. Built in about 1690 for Ford, Lord Grey, Earl of Tankerville, it replaces an earlier house, of which little is known, dating from c. 1585. The amoral and duplicitous Lord Grey, who, because he turned king's evidence and bribed influential courtiers, emerged remarkably unscathed from his involvement in the Duke of Monmouth's rebellion against James II in 1685, is one of many colourful characters connected with the estate. His new house, whose architect is uncertain, was in the latest Dutch style. Standing four-square like a giant doll's house, it is built of red brick with weathered, lichen-tinted stone dressings and dormer windows in a hipped roof. A pediment crowns the south front and detached mid-eighteenth-century service blocks balance the composition on either side.

The rich interior is mostly the work of Sir Matthew Fetherstonhaugh, who bought Uppark in 1747. This cultivated man, heir to the vast fortune of a distant relative, redecorated most of the principal rooms and enriched the house with a magnificent collection of carpets, furniture and works of art, much of it, such as portraits by Batoni and four harbour and coastal scenes by Claude-Joseph Vernet, purchased on a Grand Tour with his wife Sarah in 1749–51. The couple were responsible for the hauntingly beautiful saloon, with its delicate plaster ceiling and ivory silk brocade curtains framing the long south-facing windows, and with paintings set into fixed plasterwork frames in the Adam style. Fireplaces inlaid with Sienese marble warm both ends of the room, one of them carved with the Sienese wolf suckling Romulus and Remus. Sarah also introduced the doll's house of c. 1740, with three floors of rooms behind a pedimented façade. The interior is realised in fine detail. Diminutive landscape paintings hang on the walls, hallmarked silver and glass gleam on the dining-room table and there are fire irons of silver and brass. Meticulously dressed dolls people the mansion, those representing the family identifiable by their wax faces, the lower orders depicted in wood.

Matthew's only son Harry inherited his parents' good taste and enriched their collection. But in other respects he was a prodigal young man, with a love of hunting and the turf which is echoed in his sporting pictures and silver-gilt cups. His close friend the Prince Regent was a guest at the lavish house parties staged at Uppark, with superb meals produced by Moget, Harry's French chef. It was on one of these occasions that the 15-year-old Emma Hart, the future Lady Hamilton, is said to have been forced to dance naked on the dining-room table. Sir Harry's liaison with Emma, whom he had discovered in London, was only brief and the letters she wrote to him after she had been sent away, six months pregnant, went unanswered. Decades later, Sir Harry caused another stir when, in his 70th year, he married young Mary Ann Bullock, his head dairymaid.

LEFT In the staircase hall, an eighteenth-century French clock sits on an ornate side table that was probably commissioned by Sir Matthew for the saloon.
OPPOSITE With its symmetrical brick façades, Uppark looks like a giant dolls' house perched on the crest of the South Downs.

Largely because of Mary Ann and her sister Frances, who joined the household, Uppark was to survive the nineteenth century little changed.

In the basement is an extensive range of service rooms. There is an authentically laid out butler's pantry, and the sunny room where H.G. Wells's mother presided as housekeeper from 1880 to 1893 has easy chairs drawn up by the fire and tea laid on a tray. Long whitewashed tunnels, where the young Wells had his first kiss and which inspired his science-fiction fantasy *The Time Machine*, lead to the eighteenth-century pavilions flanking the house. One was a stable block, the other a laundry and greenhouse where, in *c.* 1815, Sir Harry installed a new kitchen. During most of the nineteenth century the present kitchen, with a long scrubbed table and gleaming pots and pans, was probably a still room, used for making cakes and drinks and for giving final touches to the dishes for upstairs after their long journey through the tunnel.

Much of Uppark's charm derives from its setting, with a great stretch of downland turf sweeping away from the house and leading the eye across a rolling landscape to the sea. Humphry Repton, who added the pillared portico to the north front, was probably also responsible for Mary Ann's elegant dairy, its white tiles decorated with a blue and green frieze of clematis.

One of the more traumatic events in the National Trust's history was the fire at Uppark in 1989, from which most of the furniture and paintings were rescued but which destroyed much of their eighteenth-century setting. Restoration took five-and-a-half years, and required the relearning of traditional skills. Plasterwork was re-created, intricate mouldings and architraves recarved, new curtains woven and wallpaper printed. From the outset, the Trust aimed to maintain the air of faded elegance that makes the house so attractive. New was carefully matched to old, even to the extent of imitating picture-protected patches of wallpaper and time-darkened white paint, but almost every room has also been left with scorched floorboards and chimneypieces and other reminders of the fire, or with unfinished, newly created detail, such as an ornamental cherub that has not been gilded. Wherever possible, fire-mangled and shattered fittings were put back together: lanterns and chandeliers that had been reduced to twisted metal shapes and fragments of glass were painstakingly reconstructed and a scagliola table-top was pieced together, bit by bit. The house itself seems unchanged. As before, the most enduring memory is of mellow pink brick and lichened stone against a life-enhancing view. And the martins came back to nest under the eaves.

Upton House

Warwickshire

1 mile (1.6 kilometres) south of Edge Hill, 7 miles (11.2 kilometres) north-west of Banbury, on the west side of the Stratford-upon-Avon road (A422)

Walter Samuel, 2nd Viscount Bearsted, was lucky enough to inherit a fortune from his father, who had profited greatly from the expansion of trade with the Far East in the late nineteenth century and, together with his brother, had developed the Shell Transport and Trading company, building it up into an international corporation. One of the twentieth century's most generous philanthropists, the 2nd Viscount used his inheritance to benefit a long list of charities, hospitals and schools. At the same time, it also enabled him to pursue his great passion for painting and the decorative arts, and to acquire one of the finest art collections of his time.

Lord Bearsted bought Upton in 1927, shortly after the death of his father, as somewhere to display his collection. At the heart of the house, making up the central seven bays of the long, sash-windowed entrance front, is the mansion built in 1695 for Sir Rushout Cullen, but this was altered substantially in the eighteenth century, when the entrance bay acquired its baroque broken pediment, and in 1927–9 the architect Percy Morley Horder reworked the place for Lord Bearsted, giving the building a strong horizontal emphasis. Morley Horder's interiors, which include a 100-foot (30-metre) long gallery on the south-facing garden front, were among the most luxurious of the period, but were deliberately bland and restrained in order to create a suitable setting for the collection. Only the first-floor suite created for Lady Bearsted, which includes a Chinese bedroom looking out over the garden and a striking Art Deco bathroom decorated in silver, red and black, has a strong character of its own.

Lord Bearsted's collection included tapestries, furniture, silver, miniatures and many other fine things, but the rooms at Upton are now largely devoted to displaying his paintings, including some inherited from his father, and his eighteenth-century soft-paste French and English porcelain, some of which was also inherited. In both areas he had an eye for the unusual

LEFT The central seven bays of the entrance front are part of the original house built of local sandstone in 1695. The broken pediment was a later addition.

ABOVE To imitate silver-leaf, which would have tarnished, Morley Horder covered the walls and vaulted ceiling of the Art Deco bathroom at Upton House with aluminium-leaf.

and outstanding. Among a number of works by fifteenth- and sixteenth-century masters is El Greco's *El Espolio* (Flagellation of Christ), the spears of the soldiers grouped behind Our Lord suggesting a crown of thorns. In another strongly atmospheric work, Brueghel's *Dormition of the Virgin*, Our Lady is shown receiving a lighted taper from St Peter in a dimly lit room. The use of grey and black alone gives the picture a ghostly quality. Serene Dutch interiors and landscapes with diminutive figures set against immense skies include Saenredam's cool study of St Catherine's Church, Utrecht, in which beetle-like clerics and two men inscribing a stone set into the floor are dwarfed by the soaring arches of the nave.

Sporting pictures feature in the dining room. Here, too, hang Stubbs's scenes from rural life, *Haymakers, Reapers* and *Labourers*, the weariness evident in the horses about to take

away a laden cart as real as the chill conjured up in Hogarth's portrayal of an early winter morning in front of St Paul's, Covent Garden, one of the paintings for his engraved series, *The Four Times of Day*, which are hung in the picture gallery.

The porcelain collection is similarly wide-ranging. Here, again, perhaps reflecting Lord Bearsted's essential humanitarianism, figures feature prominently, among the most memorable being two Chelsea pieces in the long gallery depicting a wet nurse suckling a swaddled baby and a shepherd teaching his shepherdess how to play the flute, holding the instrument for her as she blows.

Embroidery on some eighteenth-century-style walnut chairs in the dining room is the work of the 3rd Lord Bearsted, who started doing it as therapy after he was badly injured in the Second World War. The war, and the years leading up to it, had also seen the 2nd Lord embrace new concerns. As a Jew himself, he was particularly troubled by the treatment of Jews in Nazi Germany in the 1930s. He helped many to emigrate and had a hand in the Kindertransport that brought 10,000 Jewish children to Britain in the final months before hostilities started. During the war, Lord Bearsted was a Colonel in the Intelligence Corps. He and Lady Bearsted moved into the Dorchester Hotel, allowing Upton to be used as the offices of M. Samuel & Co. bank. The long gallery, with paintings still on the walls, became the typing pool and guest bedrooms were turned into staff dormitories.

Bank staff working at Upton would have been able to look out on the tranquil gardens stretching away from the south front. On the other side of a broad double terrace and cedar-framed lawn, there is a sudden steep descent to a chain of ponds in the valley below. An Italianate balustraded stairway added in the 1930s leads into the depths of the combe, its lichen-stained steps overhung with wisteria. The mellow brick wall of the old kitchen garden on the slopes of the valley still carries espaliered fruit trees as it did in the seventeenth century and a 1930s flavour to the planting of the ornamental terraces, with drifts of colour, re-creates the style of the garden designer Kitty Lloyd-Jones, who was involved at Upton for many years. Kitty was responsible for devising the enchanting bog garden in a natural amphitheatre to the west of the house, where the red brick of a late seventeenth-century banqueting house is a perfect foil for trees, grass and water.

The Vyne

Hampshire
4 miles (6.4 kilometres) north of
Basingstoke, between Bramley
and Sherborne St John

This long red-brick house with diaperwork lacing the façades looks north over a peaceful, tree-fringed lake to the wooded park beyond. A pedimented portico on this front and mid-seventeenth-century sash windows replacing the original mullions help to disguise the fact that The Vyne was originally part of a much larger Tudor courtyard house, dating from between 1500 and the early 1520s, that was created for William, 1st Lord Sandys out of some existing medieval buildings. A major player at court, Sandys was closely involved in the meeting of Henry VIII and Francis I at the Field of Cloth of Gold in 1520 and a long career in the service of the king culminated in his appointment to the office of Lord Chamberlain in 1526.

Although some two-thirds of the Tudor buildings were demolished in the seventeenth century, the magnificent chapel that Sandys incorporated in his mansion still juts out conspicuously at the east end of the house. One of the most perfect private oratories in England, this lofty room rising the height of the house is still largely as it was built in 1518–27. Intricately carved canopied stalls face across the chapel and the stained glass painted in jewel-like colours in the windows of the east end, seen at its best in morning sunlight, is matched in quality and importance only by that in the chapel of King's College, Cambridge commissioned by Henry VIII. In the lower lights, below scenes of Christ's passion, crucifixion and resurrection, are depictions of Henry VIII and, in another window, of his first queen, Catherine of Aragon, who is accompanied by a little dog. Henry and Catherine visited The Vyne in 1510 and the king came again in 1531 and 1535, on the second occasion accompanied by his new queen, Anne Boleyn, but the royal visitors would not have seen these windows. Despite the fact it appears to fit the chapel so well, the glass seems to have been introduced in the early seventeenth century

and to have come from a chantry chapel in Basingstoke which Sandys built in 1524. Early sixteenth-century Flemish tiles richly glazed in blue, yellow, orange and green that fringe the stalls and the altar step are decorated with an intriguing mix of motifs, among them a delightful tortoise and a profile head with a prominent hooked nose.

The Oak Gallery stretching the length of the west wing on the first floor – and the Stone Gallery beneath, which was used as stabling when Henry VIII visited The Vyne – also survive from the Tudor house. The Oak Gallery, lined with delicate linenfold panelling carved with Tudor badges and devices, is one of the finest examples of its date in Britain. Most of the motifs on the panelling, such as the Tudor rose, Catherine of Aragon's pomegranate and Wolsey's cardinal's hat, are relatively mainstream. More unusual is the inclusion of the curious portcullis-like hemp bray that was used in the separation of flax fibres and which appears on the panelling

LEFT One of the Tudor stained-glass windows in the chapel at The Vyne shows Henry VIII, a deep blue cloak over his gilt-plated armour, kneeling in prayer beside his patron saint, Henry II of Bavaria.
BELOW The chapel at the Vyne, built between 1518 and 1527, is a largely unaltered Tudor interior.

because it was the crest of Sir Reginald Bray, uncle of Lord Sandys's wife, Margary. The white marble of a seventeenth-century classical fireplace is picked up in a series of portrait busts set down the room, a mixed company in which portrayals of Shakespeare, Milton and Mary, Queen of Scots rub shoulders with a typically arrogant Nero and a world-weary Seneca.

Lord Sandys's service to Henry VIII was rewarded at the Dissolution of the Monasteries with the gift of Mottisfont Abbey (*see* p.228) and it was here that the family retired when they were forced to sell The Vyne in 1653 after being impoverished by the Civil War, in which they supported the king. The new owner was another successful and astute politician, Chaloner Chute, shortly to be Speaker in Richard Cromwell's parliament, who reduced the size of the house and created the present north front, building a tower and the west range to balance the earlier Tudor work and adding the dramatic classical portico designed by John Webb, which is thought to be the earliest on a domestic building. A number of Chute family portraits in the house include an enchanting likeness of the six-year-old Chrysogona Baker, painted in 1579. Chaloner Chute's grandson Edward acquired the Queen Anne furniture and Soho tapestries on display and Edward's son John, who inherited The Vyne in 1754, was responsible for introducing the exquisite early seventeenth-century *pietra dura* casket, which he bought in Florence while on his Grand Tour, the semi-precious stones with which it is encrusted portraying fruit and flowers and even a blue-winged butterfly.

John, who was a friend of Horace Walpole, also made some significant alterations to the house. He created the theatrical classical staircase, with busts of Roman emperors on the newel posts, ornate fluted columns fringing a first-floor gallery and a moulded ceiling in pale blue and white, introduced some illusionistic gothic vaulting, as suggested by Walpole, in the chapel, and added the tomb chamber on the south side, which he built to honour his great-grandfather. Here the Speaker lies immortalised in Carrara marble on the top of a box-like monument loosely disguised as a Greek temple. His lifelike effigy rests on an unyielding plaited straw mattress, his head supported on his right arm, one finger extended along the curve of his brow.

An ambitious project to conserve the roof of The Vyne, which involved rebuilding all the chimneys, was completed in 2018.

RIGHT A dramatic portico designed by John Webb was added to the north front of The Vyne in the mid-seventeenth century by its new owner, the lawyer and politician Chaloner Chute.

Waddesdon Manor

Buckinghamshire
6 miles (9.6 kilometres)
north-west of Aylesbury, on the
A41, 11 miles (17.6 kilometres)
south-east of Bicester

The great châteaux of the Loire made such an impression on the young Ferdinand and future Baron de Rothschild, grandson of the founder of the Austrian branch of this Jewish banking family (*see* Ascott, p.26), that he was determined to model any house he might build on what he had seen in France. This magnificent palace designed by Gabriel Hippolyte Destailleur and built in 1874–9, when the baron was in his late 40s, fulfilled the youthful Ferdinand's dreams, its pinnacles, mansard roofs, dormer windows, massive chimneys and staircase towers reproducing the characteristic features of Maintenon, Blois and other French Renaissance châteaux. The hill on which Waddesdon is set was purchased from the Duke of Marlborough, a platform was carved out for the mansion and the slopes were planted with semi-mature trees. Building materials were brought up by tramway, while the timber was hauled laboriously up the hill by teams of horses.

This pastiche chateau has similarly extravagant, French-inspired interiors, with a procession of high-ceilinged reception rooms recreating the elegance and splendour of the pre-Revolutionary regime. Profiting from the flood of elaborately carved woodwork which came onto the Parisian market in the late nineteenth century, Ferdinand and Destailleur were able to install fittings from great eighteenth-century town houses in many of the rooms. Tapestries designed by Boucher hang in the dining room, where a table set for eighteen is seen in simulated candlelight; and there are Savonnerie carpets decorated with the royal fleur-de-lis from the Parisian factory that supplied Louis XIV. Eleven pieces of furniture were made for the French royal family by the great Jean-Henri Riesener, the leading cabinetmaker of his day, including a marquetry writing-table created for Marie Antoinette and a drop-front secretaire ordered by the queen for Louis XVI. Elegant little tables with delicate gazelle-like legs contrast with the baron's massive cylinder-top desk that once belonged to the dramatist Beaumarchais and a monumental black and gold secretaire surmounted by a clock and crowned by a huge bronze eagle. Tear-drop chandeliers are reflected in mirrors with ornate gilt frames and every surface is crammed

with clocks, Sèvres and Meissen porcelain and *objets d'art*, among them three Sèvres pot-pourri vases in the shape of ships, complete with portholes, of which only ten survive worldwide. Paintings by Watteau, Lancret, Boucher and Greuze help to create a sense of pre-Revolutionary France.

These French pieces are harmoniously combined with a fine collection of eighteenth-century English portraits by Gainsborough, Reynolds and Romney, and with a number of seventeenth-century Dutch paintings, such as Jan van der Heyden's tranquil view of an Amsterdam canal, with stepped red-brick gables reflected in the still waters, and a garden scene by de Hooch. One of the two galleries leading from the main entrance is dominated by two huge canvases of Venice by Francesco Guardi, one a view to Santa Maria della Salute and San Giorgio Maggiore, gilded and canopied gondolas gliding across the water between them, the other looking towards the Doge's Palace from across the lagoon.

On the first floor, the flavour is more varied, with displays of precious things acquired by other members of the family and, in recent years, by the Rothschild Foundation, which manages Waddesdon for the Trust, as well as pieces from Ferdinand's collection. There are cabinets of Sèvres porcelain, a room hung with panels commissioned by the late James de Rothschild from the stage designer Leon Bakst, who incorporated portraits of the family and their friends in paintings illustrating the story of Sleeping Beauty, and a corridor lined with arms and armour largely acquired by Ferdinand's sister Alice. The White Drawing Room, from where there are spectacular views south over the Vale of Aylesbury towards the Chilterns, is devoted to displaying the recently acquired silver dinner service made in Paris for George III and some pieces of contemporary art on this floor include a striking chandelier made of broken porcelain by Ingo Maurer. Ferdinand's sixteenth-century portraits, two of them by Nicholas Hilliard, hang in the bachelor's wing at the east end of the house, where there were ten bedrooms for single male guests, and here, too, is a billiard room lined with sixteenth-century panelling of exceptional delicacy.

On the floor above, in a space no bigger than a box room, is the newly formed Treasury, where brightly lit cabinets hold a glittering array of small and precious things: ancient Roman jewellery, carved jade from China, silver and glass, gold coins and enamels, and an array of snuff boxes. Ferdinand himself

can be sensed in the sitting room of what was his private apartment, which has been returned to how he had it, his favourite eighteenth-century portraits on the walls, family photographs adorning a screen and a comfortable sofa and chairs round the fire.

The house is set off by an exceptional Victorian garden. Steps from the south front lead down to the great parterre designed by the Baron. The wooded park beyond, with rich plantings of specimen trees and some contemporary sculpture, is part of the extensive grounds designed by the French landscape gardener Lainé, while artificial rockwork by Pulham

ABOVE Waddesdon Manor, built on a hill above the Vale of Aylesbury in 1874–9 for Ferdinand de Rothschild, was designed to look like a Renaissance French château and given pinnacles, mansard roofs, staircase towers and massive chimneys.

and Sons bordering the approach north of the house shelters an aviary in eighteenth-century style, its presence heralded by chirruping from the exotic inhabitants, many of which are bred here. The aviary is the heart of the west garden as Baron Ferdinand conceived it, with flamboyant beds and hedges giving way to tranquil glades.

Wallington

Northumberland
12 miles (19.2 kilometres) west of
Morpeth on the B6343, 6 miles
(9.6 kilometres) north-west of
Belsay on the A696

Many country houses are hidden behind walls or screens of trees, but there is nothing secluded about Wallington. The pedimented south front of this square stone building crowns a long slope of rough grass, in full view of the public road through the park. Nor is there a lodge or an imposing gateway. The pinnacled triumphal arch built for the house was found to be too narrow for coaches and now languishes in a field.

Wallington is largely the creation of Sir Walter Calverley Blackett, 2nd Baronet, who commissioned the Northumbrian architect Daniel Garrett in *c.* 1738 to remodel his grandfather's uncomfortable house. Garrett's cool, Palladian exteriors are no preparation for Pietro Lafranchini's magnificent rococo plasterwork in the saloon, where delicate compositions in blue and white, with winged sphinxes perched on curling foliage, garlands of flowers and cornucopias overflowing with fruit, suggest an elaborate wedding cake.

Oriental porcelain in the alcoves on either side of the fireplace is part of a large and varied collection, much of it the dowry of Maria Wilson, who married into the family in 1791 just a few years after Wallington had passed to Sir Walter's nephew, Sir John Trevelyan. A bizarre Meissen tea-set in the parlour features paintings of life-size insects nestling in the

ABOVE A portrait of the 2nd Baronet by Reynolds surveys the saloon at Wallington, which is decorated with exceptional rococo plasterwork by the Italian Pietro Lafranchini.
OPPOSITE The Northumbrian architect Daniel Garrett, who remodelled Wallington in the mid-eighteenth century, made the south front more imposing by adding a pediment and deepening the entablature.

bottom of each cup. Even more extraordinary is Wallington's Cabinet of Curiosities, which Maria also introduced, its strange exhibits ranging from a piece of Edward IV's coffin to stuffed birds set against painted habitats and a spiky red porcupine fish like an animated pin cushion.

The hall rising through two storeys in the middle of the house reflects another era. Created in 1853–4 out of what was an internal courtyard, this individual room was the inspiration of the talented Pauline Trevelyan, whose vivid personality attracted a stream of artists and writers, John Ruskin, Algernon Swinburne and Dante Gabriel Rossetti among them. Under her influence, Rossetti's friend William Bell Scott was commissioned to produce the eight epic scenes

from Northumbrian history which decorate the walls, the subjects portrayed including the death of the Venerable Bede and Grace Darling in her open boat rescuing the men of the *Forfarshire*. In the canvas showing the landing of the Vikings, savage heads on the prows of the fleet emerge out of the gloom over the sea like an invasion of prehistoric monsters. Ruskin and Pauline herself, among others, painted the delicate wild flowers – purple foxgloves, brilliant-red poppies and yellow columbine – on the pillars between the pictures. The family's later connection with the Macaulays brought associations with scientists and politicians as well as artists and writers, and Lord Macaulay wrote his monumental history of England here.

Sir Walter Calverley Blackett's spirit lives on in the extensive estate, which embraces several parishes. This he transformed, laying out roads, enclosing fields, building cottages, planting woods and devising follies. His formal pleasure grounds were later converted into a naturalistic landscape park, possibly with the advice of the young 'Capability' Brown, who was born nearby and went to school on the estate and who, in about 1765, was employed to design the setting for the ornamental lake at Rothley. But Sir Walter himself was responsible for damming the River Wansbeck and for James Paine's imposing three-arched bridge below the house.

Sir Walter also laid out the walled garden that lies in a sheltered dell half a mile (0.8 kilometre) east of the house. Once a vegetable garden, it is now an unexpected delight of lawns and mixed herbaceous beds following the lines of the valley, with a little stream running out of a pond in a stone niche that was created in 1938. To one side a raised terrace walk carries a little brick pavilion, surmounted with the owl of the Calverley crest, and Sir George Otto Trevelyan's 1908 conservatory. A hedged nuttery on the slopes below marks the site of the former vegetable patch, while across the valley is a broad, sloping mixed border. Although this must be one of the National Trust's coldest gardens, roses, honeysuckles, clematis and sun-loving plants thrive against the south-facing walls.

BELOW Wallington's vast central hall was created out of what was a courtyard in 1853–4 and is painted with murals by William Bell Scott illustrating scenes from Northumbrian history.

575 Wandsworth Road

London
Close to Wandsworth Road station, about ½ a mile (0.8 kilometre) north of Clapham Common

On the south side of Wandsworth Road, screened by a leafy front garden, is a small and unobtrusive brick-built early nineteenth-century terraced house, with two floors over a semi-basement and a steep flight of steps up to the front door. This unexceptional frontage conceals rich and elaborate interiors created by the Kenyan novelist and poet Khadambi Asalache (c. 1935–2006), who bought No. 575 in 1981 and over a period of 20 years, from 1986, turned his home into a work of art. Almost every surface, from walls and ceilings to shelves, doors and kitchen drawers, is embellished with fretwork patterns and motifs, which Khadambi carved by hand from pine floorboards and door-panels rescued from skips and from wine crates. The designs are mostly abstract, but included within them is an abundance of realistic detail, often small enough to need searching out: here a tiny frieze of jazz musicians, or a *corps de ballet*, caught in a moment from *Swan Lake*, there a couple of moon-shaped masks peering from a corner, or a gaggle of geese. In places, such as where Khadambi added fragile shelving to the walls, the texture becomes many-layered and overlapping. Like anything that is created by hand, no two motifs are ever exactly the same. There is delicate painted decoration too, such as a frieze of meadow flowers in the basement bathroom and another, of giraffes, hippos and elephants in the African bush, in the spare bedroom. In some places Khadambi even added painted shadows to bring out the three-dimensional quality of the fretwork.

Furnishings and ornaments contribute to the striking effect. In the double sitting room that runs across the raised ground floor, cushions in deep reds and purples are flung across a low sofa, there are richly coloured kelims on the floor and pierced Moorish lampshades, an array of pressed and moulded glass inkwells on a low table, and shelves of pink lustreware, much of it purchased from street markets, reflect and diffuse the light. Coarsely woven hangings from Senegal on the walls are painted with naïve depictions of African birds and animals that could have inspired Picasso, and there is a collection of silver Coptic crosses from Ethiopia, and of antique glasses with twisted stems. These disparate things are arranged with

ABOVE The richly-decorated staircase has a window looking onto the garden which Khadambi stocked with his favourite plants.

the eye of an artist, to create a sense of harmony and balance, and Khadambi also had a keen awareness of the importance of sight lines and the play of light: the sitting room door was always open to give a vista out to the hall and staircase, while the patterning of the ornate ceiling in the main bedroom was devised to be enjoyed while lying in bed. Other vistas take the eye out into the greenery of the back garden, stocked with Khadambi's favourite plants.

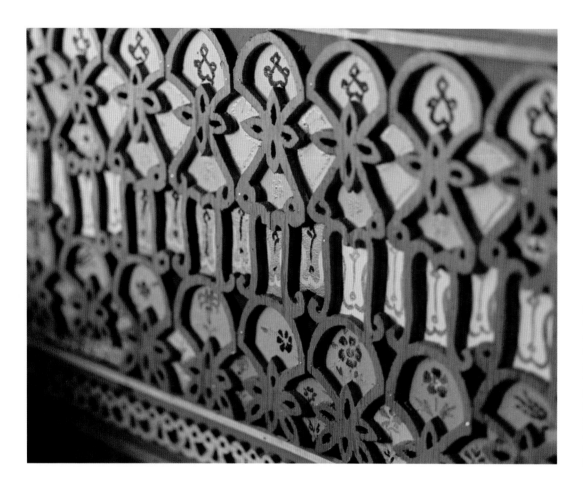

LEFT The fretwork decoration embellishing walls, ceilings and doors was all painstakingly carved by hand from pieces of pine that Khadambi rescued from skips and old wine crates. OPPOSITE The ancestors of George Washington, the first president of the United States, lived in the medieval house that forms the basis of Washington Old Hall.

Although No. 575 is an entirely individual creation, Khadambi's rich artistic imagination was influenced by Moorish architecture, in particular the wooden, waterside houses, or *yali*, which line the shores of the Bosphorus in Istanbul and which often carry elaborate carvings on the frontages overlooking the water, and by the filigree woodwork found in the Alhambra in Granada. The Africa of his childhood, where traditional houses in Mombasa and on the island of Lamu were characterised by carved niches filled with Chinese porcelain, was another important influence. Intriguingly, though, Khadambi started ornamenting the house for practical rather than artistic reasons. Unhappy with the look of some old floorboards that he had used to conceal persistent patches of damp in the basement, he came up with the idea of disguising them with fretwork. It was this inspired solution to a particular problem that led to his unique creation.

Khadambi trained as an architect in Nairobi and studied fine art in Europe. When he came to London, in 1960, he combined teaching and working for the BBC with writing, publishing his important novel, *A Calabash of Life*, in 1967. He then worked as a civil servant in the Treasury, creating his exquisite interiors in his spare time. Particularly memorable is the intricate carved screen across one of the bedroom windows on which Khadambi intertwined the initials K and S, for himself and his partner, Susie Thomson. A little scene of Thomson gazelles in an African setting on the skirting at the top of the stairs was painted for Susie's Tibetan spaniel, so the dog had something to look at as she made her way to her kennel beside the bed in the front bedroom. Made by Khadambi, the kennel doubles up as a bedside table.

Khadambi left No. 575 to the National Trust, and it was Susie's tireless advocacy that helped ensure the survival of the house as it was when Khadambi lived here.

Washington Old Hall

Tyne & Wear
5 miles (8 kilometres) west
of Sunderland, 2 miles
(3.2 kilometres) east of the A1,
south of the Tyne tunnel

Two nineteenth-century watercolours on the staircase show Washington Old Hall as it once was: an unassuming house on the edge of Washington village, close by the church on its wooded hill and with cornfields stretching away behind. The village has now been swallowed up by Washington New Town, but there is still a little green valley below the house with a view across it to the red-brick mansion which was the home of the Bell family, connected by marriage to the Trevelyans of Wallington (*see* p.362).

Washington Old Hall is a modest Jacobean manor with small mullioned windows and rough sandstone walls that was built in *c.* 1613 on the foundations of a twelfth-century house. The interior was conventionally designed on an H-plan, with a great hall occupying the centre of the building. Two arches from the original house lead from the hall into the kitchen.

The medieval building that forms the basis of the present hall was the ancestral home of George Washington, who was elected first President of the United States in 1789; his direct ancestors lived here for five generations and the property remained in the family until 1613. Mementoes of the Washington connection and the American struggle for independence are on display. A portrait of George Washington executed on drum parchment while he was on campaign as leader of the rebel forces hangs alongside a letter from Percy, 2nd Duke of Northumberland, who served with the British troops. A lottery ticket signed by Washington and a uniform of the Washington Greys are displayed on the stairs.

Although none of the furniture is original, it is all in tune with the house and includes some interesting pieces, such as the seventeenth-century baby-walker in the bedroom and the beautifully embroidered stumpwork cabinet in the parlour.

Washington Old Hall was divided into tenements in the mid-nineteenth century and continued to be lived in by several families, each of whom occupied one or two rooms, until 1933. Displays in a room that was home to William and Annie Bone and their children conjure up life here in the 1930s. By this time the hall had become seriously dilapidated and only a concerted campaign, instigated by the tireless Frederick Hill, saved the building from demolition. Restoration was made possible by generous gifts from across the Atlantic and the people of the United States continue to offer much-needed help, many of them visiting the Old Hall every year. A print of Mount Vernon, given by President Jimmy Carter when he visited the house in 1977, symbolises the importance of this connection.

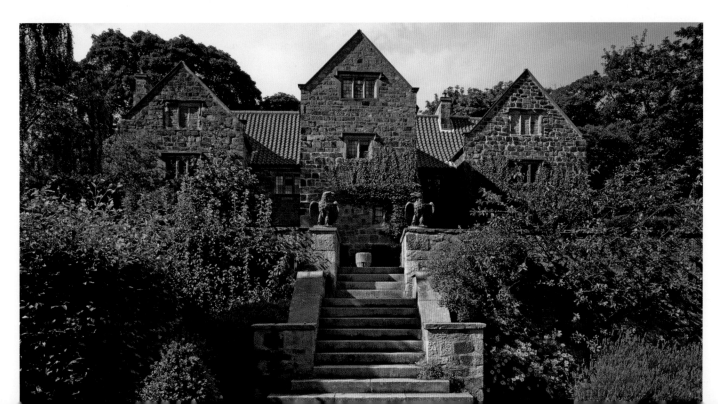

West Wycombe Park and Village

Buckinghamshire
2 miles (3.2 kilometres) west of
High Wycombe, on the A40

Everything about West Wycombe bears the stamp of the man who created it, the mercurial eighteenth-century dilettante Sir Francis Dashwood. Armed with the fortune his father had made trading with Africa, India and the East, Sir Francis interleaved several visits to Italy with tours as far afield as Russia and Turkey. Months of foreign travel not only gave him a taste for high living but also an appreciation of art and a depth of learning that led him, in 1732, to be a founder member of the Dilettanti Society. Formed to champion classical art and architecture, this group was to have an important influence on English taste. Sir Francis is now remembered chiefly for his connection with the notorious Hellfire Club, a mock religious order which met in caves burrowed into the hill rising steeply to the north of West Wycombe, but the more serious side of his character comes across in his successful political career. Although disastrous as Chancellor of the Exchequer in 1762, he proved himself a more than able joint Paymaster General in the years that followed.

Between 1735 and Sir Francis's death in 1781, the square, red-brick Queen Anne building he inherited was transformed into a classical mansion and filled with paintings and furniture acquired on his Grand Tours. The architect John Donowell supervised the remodelling until 1764, but it is not clear who was responsible for designing the house. Sir Francis undoubtedly had strong ideas of his own, but he may also have had expert advice from Giovanni Servandoni, Roger Morris and Isaac Ware, and Nicholas Revett was involved in the later stages of the work. In his remodelling, Sir Francis was no more than a man of his time; but the architecture and decoration with which he enriched West Wycombe give the house its highly individual and theatrical character. An unusual double colonnade rising to roof height stretches almost the full width of the long south front, rivalling the huge porticoes decorated with frescoes, one of which was designed by Revett in imitation of a Greek temple, that dominate the east and west façades. The richly decorated interior, with gilded mirrors reflecting glittering vistas through the house, mixes illusion with fine craftsmanship.

Sensual baroque painted ceilings by the Italian Giuseppe Mattias Borgnis, who was brought to England specially for this commission, adorn some of the principal rooms, his *Triumph of Bacchus and Ariadne* in the Blue Drawing Room a riot of overweight cherubs, heavily muscled bodies and flowing drapery. Paint was also used to imitate marble, fine plasterwork and joinery of burr walnut and satinwood and Sir Francis's Neo-classical hall and dining room, with illusionistic coffered ceilings by Giuseppe's son Giovanni, marbled walls and elaborate stone floors, were intended to evoke the houses of Roman antiquity. The hall was even fitted with hypocaust heating.

Some delicate rococo plasterwork is the real thing, and elaborate marble chimneypieces in many of the rooms include at least two by Sir Henry Cheere, who carved doves, and an owl devouring a small bird, on the one in the music room and was probably also responsible for the plaque showing cherubs warming themselves by a fire in the study, and for the grand columned doorcase of the saloon. The mahogany staircase inlaid with satinwood and ebony is similarly fine and one of very few examples of work of this kind (*see also* Claydon, p.95).

Hardly altered since Sir Francis's death, the house still displays his catholic collection of lesser Italian masters, family portraits stretching back to the seventeenth century, and views of the house painted in the 1750s by William Hannan. But much of Sir Francis's fine eighteenth-century furniture, including a state bed embellished with carved pineapples, was sold in 1922 by the 10th Baronet. Although the 11th Baronet, who inherited in 1963, was able to buy back some of these pieces, many of the present furnishings, all of which seem totally in keeping, are not original.

The house is set off by Sir Francis's serene landscape garden, which he created by remodelling his own earlier, more formal layout. A composition in grass, trees and water, it is focused on an islanded lake and richly embellished with ornamental buildings, many of which are as individual as the house. John Donowell was probably responsible for the gigantic grey arch of flint and stone known as the Temple of Apollo that stands next to the house, and for the octagonal tower carried on flintwork arches. Later eye-catchers designed by Nicholas Revett between 1770 and 1781 include a Doric temple on the largest island in the lake, a cottage disguised as a church and a colonnaded circular dovecote with a pyramidal roof known as the Round Temple. The 11th Baronet added new features to the garden, such as the huge fibreglass equestrian

ABOVE The staircase is decorated with frescoes by Giuseppe Borgnis illustrating mythological and biblical scenes. These become increasingly erotic as they reach the bedroom floor.
OPPOSITE The Palladian north front of West Wycombe Park is less theatrical than the other sides of the house and looks over the eighteenth-century landscape created by Sir Francis Dashwood.

statue on the crest of the hill above the house, and restored others that had been lost, among them the Temple of Venus on a grassy mound in the woods to the west of the lake.

From the north front of the house the ground falls away into a wooded valley, rising again to an extraordinary hexagonal mausoleum and the church remodelled by Sir Francis on the top of the hill opposite. Hidden in the valley is West Wycombe village, which was acquired by the Dashwood family, as part of the estate, in 1698. This is an exceptional place, owing much of its character to the fact that, before the building of the M40, it lay on the main route from London to Oxford, the Midlands

and Wales. Timber-framed, flint and brick cottages, many of them dating from the sixteenth century or earlier, line the long main street. One of the oldest buildings, the fifteenth-century Church Loft, was originally a rest house for pilgrims, and there are three former coaching inns.

ABOVE The huge portico on the west front of West Wycombe was designed as a replica of a Greek temple dedicated to Bacchus and has a large statue of the deity standing in the middle of the façade.
OPPOSITE Wightwick Manor, with its rich and intricate timberwork, carved and fretted gables and soaring Tudor-style brick chimneys, was designed to look as picturesque as possible.

Wightwick Manor

West Midlands
3 miles (4.8 kilometres) west of Wolverhampton, up Wightwick Bank, beside the Mermaid Inn, just north of the A454 Bridgnorth road

In 1848, seven young men barely out of their teens, including William Holman Hunt, John Everett Millais and Dante Gabriel Rossetti, founded the Pre-Raphaelite Brotherhood, a revolt against the artistic establishment and what they perceived as the emptiness and artificiality of contemporary art. The group was short-lived, but its ideals were enormously influential, feeding into the reaction against mass production and the return to pre-industrial techniques that became identified with William Morris and the Arts and Crafts Movement. Rossetti, Ford Madox Brown and Edward Burne-Jones were among the founders of Morris's design and furnishing company, which started life as an artist's co-operative in 1861 (*see* Red House, p.287).

Wightwick Manor is one of the best surviving examples of a house built and furnished under the influence of the Arts and Crafts Movement, the ideals of which were imparted to the builder of the house, the industrialist Theodore Mander, a paint and varnish manufacturer, through Oscar Wilde's lectures on *The House Beautiful*, one of which Mander attended, assiduously recording what he heard in a notebook. Morris wallpapers, textiles and carpets, William de Morgan tiles and Benson metalwork supplied by his company set off paintings and drawings by Ford Madox Brown, Holman Hunt, Millais, Burne-Jones and Ruskin. The Jacobean furniture,

the heart of the house is a great parlour in the form of a feudal hall, with an open timber roof painted by the talented Charles Kempe. A minstrels' gallery across one end, a deeply recessed fireplace alcove and extensive use of panelling add to the period atmosphere. Kempe was also responsible for the glowing colours in the painted windows and the deep plaster frieze telling the story of Orpheus and Eurydice that may well have been inspired by that in the High Great Chamber at Hardwick (*see* p.169). Orpheus sits with his harp in a forest, enticing a whole menagerie of beasts with his music, from a trumpeting elephant and a kangaroo to a peacock with a golden tail. Morris's last woven fabric design, featuring white and pink blossom on a deep-blue background, like a meadow full of spring flowers, hangs below the frieze. Wightwick also has a copy of Morris's last major artistic project, an edition of the works of Chaucer, published by Morris's Kelmscott Press in 1896. Burne-Jones, who was responsible for the book's intricate illustrations, is represented as well by his fine late work, *Love Among the Ruins*, which dominates the gallery end of the hall, the tendrils of briar rose in which he has entangled the young couple recalling those in his cycle of paintings at Buscot Park (*see* p.66). A drawing of Scarborough by J.M.W. Turner that was recently found in the house and once belonged to Ruskin is also on display.

The attractive 17-acre (7-hectare) garden slopes away from the house into a little valley with a stream and two pools and is shielded by trees and tall hedges from the suburbia around. First laid out on the advice of the watercolourist Alfred Parsons, it was largely redesigned by the Edwardian landscape architect Thomas Mawson, who married strongly architectural formal gardens round the house, marked out with terraces, walls, clipped yew hedges and topiary, with an increasingly informal and natural approach to the layout and planting of the valley, which has orchards and paddocks and winding mown paths. Wisteria and other climbers flower on the house and there is a show of rhododendrons and azaleas round the two pools in the valley. A wooden bridge over the road up to the house was inspired by the Mathematical Bridge over the River Cam at Queens' College, Cambridge.

A new gallery in the Old Malthouse, created in partnership with the de Morgan Foundation, shows drawings, paintings and ceramics by Evelyn and William de Morgan.

oriental porcelain and Persian rugs with which the house is also furnished complement rather than compete with the nineteenth-century work, demonstrating how well Morris's products blend with good craftsmanship from other periods. There is a particularly pleasing juxtaposition of antique and Victorian in the drawing room, where rich green tiles by William de Morgan featuring a bestiary of mischievous creatures are inset into an Italian Renaissance chimneypiece.

Built in two stages in 1887 and 1893, Wightwick was commissioned from the Liverpool architect Edward Ould, and was designed in a traditional, half-timbered idiom. The later, eastern half is more richly decorated and is clearly inspired by the Tudor buildings of the Welsh Marches. Decorative black-and-white timbering, in stripes, swirls and quatrefoils, rises from a plinth of local stone, with banks of spiral Tudor-style chimneys crowning the gabled roofline.

In keeping with the late medieval character of the exterior,

ABOVE Burne-Jones's *Love Among the Ruins*, painted in 1894, only four years before he died, hangs below the minstrels' gallery in the great parlour.
OPPOSITE Wightwick's period furnishings include a fine collection of richly coloured decorative tiles, many of them by William de Morgan.

2 Willow Road

London
Near the junction of Willow Road and Downshire Hill, Hampstead

Next to some assertive Victorian villas on the western edge of Hampstead Heath is an unobtrusive three-storey, brick and concrete rectangle with a flat roof and an uninterrupted expanse of glass lighting the first floor. Compact and all of a piece, what appears to be one house is in fact a terrace of three, with a hidden basement giving onto gardens behind.

This piece of pre-war modernism was the work of the anglophile Austro-Hungarian architect Ernö Goldfinger, who designed the central house for his artist wife Ursula Blackwell and their children and lived here from 1939 until his death in 1987. The first example of modernist architecture to be acquired by the National Trust, 2 Willow Road still has its original fixtures and fittings, including some of Ernö's prototype furniture, and the Goldfingers' important collection of contemporary art, reflecting their close links with the avant-garde. The couple met in Paris, where he had trained with Auguste Perret, known for his innovative use of reinforced concrete, and she was a student of the painter Amédée Ozenfant, who reacted to Cubism by advocating a return to a minimalist representational art, in which forms are reduced to 'pure' outline. The Goldfingers came to London in 1934, but in these pre-war years Ernö's designs, apart from some work for the toy firm Abbatt, were largely unexecuted. After the war, he was responsible for some of London's now controversial developments, notably the large office complex, now converted to housing, at Elephant and Castle and high-rise housing in North Kensington and Poplar.

Willow Road probably sees Ernö at his best. No.2 is by no means large, but there is a sense of both space and light, with the glass walls of the main rooms drawing the eye out over the heath in front and onto the south-facing balcony and gardens behind. Ernö's hand is in every detail. A spiral staircase is the backbone and main artery of the house, carrying the concrete frame. Wrapped round it on the first floor is a versatile space, with movable partitions and a change in floor level indicating dining room, studio and living room. Above is the nursery and bedroom floor, with compact internal bathrooms lit through the flat roof. Built-in wardrobes are flush with the wall, study bookshelves are recessed into a room partition and the studio has a tall cupboard for Ursula's canvases. The furniture too is functional, with upturned Anglepoises either side of the low double bed in the master bedroom, a lino-topped dining-table on a lathe base, and dining-chairs made out of tubular metal and plywood.

But this is not an austere house. On the walls are some of Ursula's drawings, including a surreal vision of two huge disembodied ears, abstract and figurative works by Amédée Ozenfant and Robert Delaunay, Max Ernst and Bridget Riley, a watercolour study of standing figures by Henry Moore, and a strong photographic portrait of Ursula by the Goldfingers' close friend Man Ray. Masks brought back from holidays in the Far East, one a grinning face surmounted by a writhing mass of cobras, provide colourful contrast and the artworks include two cars in typewriter script by Ernö's grandson Dominic. The living-room area has a parquet floor and oak-veneer panelling, and there are scarlet doors and areas of deep crimson paint. It is clear, too, that Goldfinger had a particular lifestyle in mind. The basement was designed with accommodation for two servants, and his house is the only one in the terrace to be provided with two garages, one of which has an inspection pit.

ABOVE LEFT Goldfinger's study, with his important collection of architectural books filling the shelves and filing cabinets holding his slides and photographs.
OPPOSITE The spiral staircase, its coils suggesting the shell of an ammonite, has concrete steps supported from the wall, a brass handrail and a balustrade that is largely made out of rope.

Wimpole Estate

Cambridgeshire
8 miles (12.8 kilometres) south-
west of Cambridge, 6 miles
(9.6 kilometres) north of Royston

When Rudyard Kipling visited his daughter Elsie here, a few months after she and her husband Captain George Bambridge took up residence at the house in 1933, he was moved to remark that he hoped she had not bitten off more than she could chew.

The Bambridges were faced with the restoration and refurnishing of the largest house in Cambridgeshire, whose red-brick and stone façades, three and four storeys high in the central block, stretch over 250 feet (76 metres) from end to end. A double staircase leads up to the pedimented entrance bay on the south front, which is ornamented with a Venetian window over the front door and a carved coat of arms in the pediment above. From here, an immense avenue lined with young limes runs over 2 miles (3.2 kilometres) into the distance. Immediately in front of the house, urns and busts on pedestals flank the courtyard like guards standing rigidly to attention.

The remodelling of the original mid-seventeenth-century house by James Gibbs and, later, Henry Flitcroft, in the first half of the eighteenth century marks Wimpole's golden age. From 1713 to 1740 the house was the property of Edward Harley, 2nd Earl of Oxford, who entertained a brilliant circle of writers, scholars and artists here, Swift and Pope among them, and whose household included a Master of the Horse, a Groom of the Chamber and a Master of Music. Perhaps it was for the latter and his orchestra that Lord Harley commissioned James Gibbs's baroque chapel, Bavarian in its opulence, which is such a striking feature of the house. In Sir James Thornhill's *trompe-l'oeil* decoration, statues of Saints Gregory, Ambrose, Augustine and Jerome stand in niches between pairs of classical columns, their shadows etched sharply on the stone behind. Gregory leans eagerly forward with a book in his hand, as if about to escape his perch, while half-naked St Jerome displays a splendidly muscled physique. The east wall is filled with Thornhill's *Adoration of the Magi*, in which the three kings are accompanied by a sizeable retinue of armed men and Mary herself sits amid a romantic classical ruin, her ruddy-faced, bearded husband watching quietly in the background.

Gibbs also designed the long library to house Harley's exceptional collection of books and manuscripts, the largest and most important ever assembled by a private individual in England and later to form the nucleus of the British Library. An oak and walnut pulpit on castors gives access to the upper shelves and a brown, pink and beige carpet picks up the subdued tones of the plaster ceiling. This room is reached through a gallery that was created by Henry Flitcroft in 1742 for Wimpole's next owner, Philip Yorke, 1st Earl of Hardwicke, as a setting for his finest paintings. Now used to display pictures particularly associated with the house, such as *The Stag Hunt* by John Wootton, who frequently visited Wimpole in Lord Harley's time, the room's long sash windows framed by red curtains and the grey-green walls help to create an atmosphere that is both restful and warm.

Wimpole's most individual interior, John Soane's Yellow Drawing Room, was added 50 years later, in the early 1790s, for Philip Yorke's great-nephew, the 3rd Earl. Running from the north front into the centre of the house, the room opens out into a domed oval at the inner end that is lit from a lantern in the roof above. Yellow rayon on the walls sets off blue upholstery on the gilt chairs and on the long settees curved round two semicircular apses on the inner wall, with a large painting of cherubs at play above the chimneypiece that divides them. The overall effect is of a chapel transformed into a room of exceptional elegance and grace.

Soane's indulgent bath house, with a grand double staircase sweeping down to a tiled pool which holds over 2,000 gallons (9,000 litres) of water, is a delightful reminder of another side of eighteenth-century life.

When the Bambridges moved to Wimpole, they were faced with refurnishing a largely empty house, the contents of which had been gradually dispersed. Aided by royalties from the Kipling estate, which Mrs Bambridge inherited in 1936, they bought treasures for the house on their travels abroad and at auction, and Mrs Bambridge continued to buy after her husband's death in 1943. While he was responsible for two Tissots and a portrait by Tilly Kettle, she acquired portraits connected with the house and paintings by Mercier, Hudson and Romney. Porcelain figures on show are from her

OPPOSITE The magnificent library at Wimpole was specifically designed to take Lord Harley's vast collection of books, pamphlets and manuscripts.

collection, and she also added notable books to the library, including some rare editions of Kipling's work.

Wimpole's extensive wooded park fully matches the grandeur of the house and reflects the influence of some of the most famous names in the history of landscape gardening. The great avenue running to the south, now planted with limes but originally with elms, its unyielding lines striking through a patchwork of fields like a grassy motorway, was created by Charles Bridgeman, who was employed by Lord Harley in the 1720s to extend an elaborate formal layout which already included the east and west avenues to either side of the house.

Remarkably, these remains of what was once an extensive scheme of axial avenues, canalised ponds, ha-has and bastions

survived the attentions of Lancelot 'Capability' Brown and his disciple William Emes later in the century, both of whom set about 'naturalising' the park. The view from the north front, artfully framed by the clumps of trees with which Brown replaced a felled avenue, looks over his serpentine ornamental lake to a hillock crowned with a three-towered gothick ruin. Built in 1774, this eye-catcher was based on designs by Sanderson Miller made 25 years before. Brown's belts of trees defining and sheltering the park were thickened and extended by Humphry Repton, who produced a Red Book for the 3rd Earl in 1801, but Repton also reintroduced a touch of formality, creating the small flower garden enclosed by iron railings on the north side of the house.

Sir John Soane's home farm to the north of the house, built in a pleasing mixture of brick, wood, tile and thatch, was also commissioned by the 3rd Earl, who was passionately interested in farming and agricultural improvement. The thatched barn that forms a central focus is surrounded by the paddocks and pens of Wimpole's rare breeds farm.

A short distance south-east of the house is the parish church. Substantially rebuilt to Flitcroft's design in 1749, it is all that remains of the village that was swept away to create the park. In the north chapel, the only part of the medieval building not demolished in the mid-eighteenth century, the recumbent effigy of the 3rd Earl with his coronet at his feet dominates a number of grandiose monuments to successive

ABOVE A decorative dome carrying a lantern lights the inner end of the extraordinary T-shaped yellow drawing room.
ABOVE LEFT Wimpole's north front, with the wing housing the library on the right, looks out over a formal garden where the parterre is planted with tulips in the spring.

owners of this palatial place, sleeping peacefully in the midst of all they once enjoyed. Banks and ditches in the grass to the south mark the house plots of medieval villagers who tilled the land centuries ago, the ridge and furrow they created still visible on a slope of old pasture.

Woolsthorpe Manor

Lincolnshire
At Woolsthorpe, 7 miles
(11.2 kilometres) south of
Grantham, ½ mile (0.8 kilometre)
north-west of Colsterworth,
west of the A1

The premature and sickly boy born in this modest limestone house on Christmas Day 1642 came into a world that still believed that the Earth was the centre of the Universe. He grew up to be the leading scientist of his day, whose work was to lay the foundations of modern scientific thought and to demonstrate that our planet is merely a satellite of the Sun. The boy was Sir Isaac Newton, the offspring of a prosperous Lincolnshire farmer who died two months before his son's birth. While his mother raised a second family nearby, Isaac spent an isolated and introverted childhood at Woolsthorpe, cared for by his grandmother. Although he left to pursue his studies in Cambridge in 1661, he returned to Woolsthorpe again in 1665 when the university was closed by the plague. During this 18-month period, 355 years ago,

Newton's self-styled 'year of wonders', he changed how we think of the world, coming up with his revolutionary work on gravity, light and mathematics.

With its mullioned windows and simple T-shaped plan, Woolsthorpe is a typical early seventeenth-century manor house, and was bought by Isaac's grandfather, Robert Newton, in 1623. Reflecting the inventory of Newton's mother's possessions and illustrating how simply even a moderately wealthy yeoman family would have lived at this date, its plain rooms are sparsely furnished. The young Newton is evoked in some scribbled drawings on the kitchen wall, among them a sketch of a post windmill and a rough outline of a church that may be a building he knew in Grantham, where he went to school. Upstairs is the room Isaac used when he came back from Cambridge to see his mother, now hung with a portrait of the great man by Thornhill and prints of other famous scientists of the day, many of whom fell out with their brilliant but difficult contemporary. Also here is a copy of the third edition of Newton's major work, the *Principia Mathematica*.

The apple tree which is said to have inspired Newton's theory of gravity blew down in about 1820, but the old trunk has resprouted and the new growth continues to produce apples. Newton's work is brought to life in hands-on activities in the Science Centre.

ABOVE LEFT An Elizabethan table stands in the middle of Woolsthorpe's kitchen, where the young Newton is said to have covered the walls with his drawings.
LEFT Woolsthorpe Manor, where the scientist Isaac Newton was born on Christmas Day 1642, is a small seventeenth-century manor house built of local limestone with original stone-mullioned windows.

Wordsworth House and Garden

Cumbria
Off the A66, on Main Street
in Cockermouth

Three men born in the early 1770s and known as the Lake Poets – Samuel Taylor Coleridge, Robert Southey and William Wordsworth – did much to change contemporary views of landscape, their appreciation of the wild beauty of nature suggesting new ideals for people seeking an escape from the realities of the Industrial Revolution. Of the three, William Wordsworth was the most innovative and his best work permanently enlarged the range and subject matter of English poetry. Wordsworth's love of the Lakes shows above all in the fact that he chose to live here all his life.

Although the adult Wordsworth is mainly connected with the central Lakes (*see* Allan Bank, p.388), his formative years were spent in the north, in the prosperous little market town on the River Derwent where his father was agent to Sir James Lowther.

The elegant late seventeenth-century house where he was born on 7 April 1770, almost two years before his sister Dorothy, stands at the west end of Cockermouth's main street, its garden stretching down to the river. Close by is the ruined castle from which William derived so much inspiration. The years he spent here, up to the age of 13, when his father died, left him with a deep love of Cumbria and also saw the forging of the intense bond with Dorothy that was so important to the poet in later life.

On the death of his father, Wordsworth and his siblings lost their home and the contents of the house were dispersed. The interior has been returned to how it might have been when the Wordsworths lived here. The rooms are elegant but not showy, with carved overmantels and one ornamental plaster ceiling. Period colour schemes have been re-created based on paint samples taken from the house, and the best rooms have been fitted out with mid- to late eighteenth-century furniture, including some pieces associated with the poet. A desk that belonged to Wordsworth's father, its surface strewn with copies of his letters and documents, dominates the panelled room by the front door that may have been his office. Upstairs, a panelled olive-green drawing room at the front of the house is graced by a set of walnut chairs that once belonged to Southey and a bureau-bookcase that was Wordsworth's; a longcase clock

that belonged to the poet is also in the house. Other interiors, such as Mr Wordsworth's bedroom or the re-created Georgian kitchen, are furnished with high-quality reproductions.

Luckily, the floods which swept through Cockermouth in November 2009 and December 2015 did not do serious damage to the house, but the garden was devastated on both occasions. It has been re-created in an authentic eighteenth-century style, as it might have been in William and Dorothy's day.

Wordsworth's ideas about the appreciation of nature and the wild beauty of landscape were to inspire the founders of the National Trust and were a vital step in the creation of today's global conservation movement. A programme of rolling exhibitions linked to nature and language reflects William's passions.

BELOW The recreated kitchen, with its cast-iron range and period pans and utensils, conjures up the room where Mrs Wordsworth and her maid would have prepared meals.

The Workhouse, Southwell

Nottinghamshire
8 miles (12.8 kilometres) from
Newark on the A617 and A612

On the eastern edge of Southwell, sitting well back from the road at the top of a gentle grassy slope, is a striking, early nineteenth-century building of mellow red brick. Three storeys tall with rows of regularly spaced iron-framed windows, massive chimneystacks and a grey slate roof, it is solid and functional, typical of the many institutional buildings of the period. It was built as a workhouse in 1824 as part of a pioneering approach to poor relief instigated by the Rev. J.T. Becher, a local magistrate. By the early nineteenth century, the existing system, based on the 1601 Poor Law that made each parish responsible for its destitute, with the accent on helping the poor live in their own homes, was breaking down, partly because the scale of the problem had escalated, partly because there was no incentive for the poor to work. It was also becoming too expensive.

In Southwell, the Rev. Becher came up with a new approach that was designed to deter as well as provide relief. He tried it out first in a small workhouse just for Southwell parish, and then, in 1823, proposed a much larger institution to serve a group of neighbouring parishes. The workhouse was built on what were then open fields outside the town, with a plan that reflected the Rev. Becher's ideas on how denizens should be treated. Housing both the able-bodied and the aged and infirm, men, women and children, it was designed so each group would be segregated, day and night. Wives were separated from husbands, children from their parents. Inmates were made to wear a uniform and were fed a nutritious but very plain diet. The able-bodied were expected to undertake hours of hard and monotonous work: breaking stones, unpicking old rope, or

ABOVE This peeling wall shows the condition the workhouse was in when the Trust took it over.
RIGHT The food given to the inmates was laid down in dietary tables which specified what they were to have on each day of the week.

endlessly cleaning the interiors and repainting the walls. Above all, they were strictly supervised. It was a narrow and cheerless existence. All this is reflected in the plan of the workhouse, which has separate day rooms for each group on the ground floor, with segregated dormitories above. Inmates passed from one to the other by separate staircases, set side by side, and each day room gives onto a brickwalled exercise yard with an open privy, just a hole in the ground, set behind a wall in the corner. From the yard, nothing can be seen of the outside world apart from the tops of the trees in the workhouse orchard.

The interior is a succession of comfortless rooms with painted and whitewashed brick walls and stone-flagged or lime-ash floors. Each room has a small fireplace, but there was little else to lift the spirits. Rows of narrow beds with mattresses and bolsters stuffed with straw in the former dormitories and clothes hanging from pegs conjure up the conditions in which the inmates lived. In the middle of the main range, marked by a projecting bay with a grand pedimented entrance, are the quarters for the master and the administration of

the workhouse. Here the walls are plastered and there is a hierarchy of other refinements, which peaks with picture rails, skirting boards and a wooden floor in the master's office. There are cupboards, and the airy board room where the workhouse guardians met, and where families could see each other briefly on Sundays, has a mantelpiece and a fender in front of the fire. From his rooms, the master could look down on the exercise yards, but there were some corners out of his sight, one of which has what may well be a gaming board scratched into the brickwork. The workhouse laundry, drying room and bakery are ranged round the inner courtyards.

The system used at Southwell influenced poor relief across the country. Hundreds of workhouses were built, 15–20 miles (24–32 kilometres) apart, each serving a group of parishes. As the years passed, the focus shifted away from deterrence towards helping those who needed shelter and nursing. In 1871, an infirmary was added to the workhouse complex. A sizeable red-brick building with a pedimented centrepiece that stands outside the main compound, Firbank Infirmary catered for the sick and took in patients from the local community,

as well as paupers from the workhouse. After a five-year restoration project, this, too, can now be visited. Visitors can see the recreation of a ward of the 1870s and how a ward would have looked a hundred years later.

The introduction of pensions in 1908 and national insurance in 1911 did much to alleviate the poverty of the old and unemployed and the numbers needing relief declined; children were moved to separate homes. Despite all this, the workhouse continued to function into the 1980s, being used, in its latter years, as temporary accommodation for the homeless. On show is a room fitted out as a 1970s bedsit that would have housed an entire family. The infirmary building also continued to be used. In the latter part of the twentieth century it became a residential unit for older women and visitors can see where the last occupants, who lived here in the 1980s, were accommodated. A new visitor hub and exhibition spaces tell the story of both workhouse and infirmary.

Wray Castle

Cumbria
In Low Wray, 2 miles
(3.2 kilometres) south of
Ambleside

On the western shore of Lake Windermere, the battlements and turrets of a Victorian castle rise boldly above the trees. Complete with arrow slits, spiral staircases, coats of arms carved in stone and a portcullis, this theatrical residence was built in the 1840s for Dr James Dawson, a retired Liverpool surgeon, and his wife Margaret to designs by the little-known Liverpool architect John Jackson Lightfoot. Dr Dawson started acquiring land here from 1834, soon after his wife inherited a fortune from her father, building up a sizeable estate. In contrast to the classical villas which by then lined the eastern side of the lake, Wray, the only building of any size on the western shore, was designed in a gothic-revival idiom. Impressive and eye-catching, the castle was intended to make a statement and to be a focal point in views across the lake, where it is seen against the backdrop of the Langdale Pikes.

The massive walls are largely constructed of slate rubble, with slate ashlar facings on some façades and limestone dressings. All features are exaggerated, as if built for a family of giants, and drainpipes are hidden within the walls so as not to detract from the castle's impact.

Inside, spacious living rooms are gathered round a central hall which rises dramatically into the lantern tower that dominates the castle. Original panelling, a very early Minton encaustic tile floor, and intricate skirtings and mouldings point to the grandeur of the castle's heyday.

Estate buildings were designed to match the castle, among them a castellated lodge on the back road from Hawkshead to Ambleside, a double boathouse by the jetty on the lake, and the church of St Margaret of Antioch, up a short drive from the lodge, that served as the castle chapel. The home farm was remodelled at the same time and the park was landscaped and planted with specimen trees, many of which survive.

In the 1880s Wray was the setting for a meeting between two of the most significant people in the history of the Lake District and the National Trust. In 1878, Hardwicke Rawnsley, one of the future founders of the Trust, moved to Cumbria to be vicar of Wray at the invitation of his cousin, Edward Preston Rawnsley, who had inherited the estate a few years earlier. Edward Rawnsley rarely came to the castle, preferring to live

ABOVE LEFT The central hall rises dramatically through the building into the tower that dominates the castle.
LEFT With its turrets and battlements, the castle looks like a fortress but the interior was designed with spacious living rooms. This is where the young Beatrix Potter was introduced to the Lake District on a family holiday in 1882.

on an estate in Lincolnshire which he had also inherited, and the property was let. This is where the Potter family came for their first Lake District holiday in the summer of 1882, a holiday that introduced their lonely 16-year-old daughter Beatrix to the lakes and fells amongst which she would spend most of her adult life, and which, like Rawnsley, she would do so much to defend. The Potters invited Hardwicke Rawnsley to the castle and he and Beatrix became lifelong friends. He took an interest in her drawing and painting and her love of nature, and encouraged her to publish her first book, *The Tale of Peter Rabbit*.

Wray came to the Trust in 1929 after a period of neglect, during which much of the estate was sold off and some fittings taken out. Years of institutional use followed. The interior is shown unfurnished, but a watercolour of the castle library painted by Beatrix and her father's photographs of the castle help to conjure up how it would have looked in the nineteenth century. And those who are at Wray at the end of the day can watch the portcullis being lowered.

BELOW The castle rises out of woodland on the western shore of Lake Windermere, with the Langdale Pikes forming a backdrop behind.

Other Buildings

Aberconwy House

Conwy

At the junction of Castle Street and High Street in Conwy

When Edward I built his great castle at Conwy in 1283, he invited English settlers to colonise the little walled town established at its feet. This medieval house dating from the thirteenth century occupies what would have been a prime site in the new settlement, at the junction of High Street and Castle Street, the two principal thoroughfares, and close to the gate through which most of the town's trade passed down to the quay on the river. Now the oldest building in Conwy after the castle and the church, it is probably typical of the prosperous burgess houses that once formed the body of the town, with two lower floors of stone supporting a half-timbered upper storey jettied out over the street. Furnished rooms illustrate life from different periods of the building's history.

Acorn Bank (right)

Cumbria

1 mile (1.6 kilometres) north of Temple Sowerby, 6 miles (9.6 kilometres) east of Penrith on the A66

A long drive through the park leads to this substantial old house set on a little bluff above the fast-flowing Crowdundle Beck in the idyllic Eden valley. Ranges of tawny-red local sandstone enclose three sides of a spacious courtyard, a roundel of grass in the middle. The three-storey main block, lit by a regular array of sash windows, looks over the court and the ha-ha bounding the park to fields sloping down to the River Eden and the distant fells of the Lake District beyond, while the Pennine moors lie only a few miles to the north. Stair turrets project from the back of the house and there is a small north wing too.

Once owned by the Knights Templar, who gave their name to the nearby village of Temple Sowerby, Acorn Bank was acquired by Thomas Dalston at the Dissolution and his descendants lived here until c. 1930. Although there may be some remnants of a sixteenth-century house in the present building, the oldest parts of Acorn Bank, the hall and the west and north wings, are probably Jacobean. John Dalston, who had a large family, substantially remodelled the house in the seventeenth century, extending it eastwards to introduce a

panelled drawing room with a parlour above. He subsequently added the top floor to the main block and gave the east front the striking façade of rusticated ashlar which now overlooks the garden. Further improvements in the mid-eighteenth century, by another John Dalston, account for the sash windows and the stylish staircase in one of the turrets that is lit by a Venetian window and ornamented with a decorative plaster ceiling, possibly executed by Joseph Rose the Elder.

The Boazmans, who inherited the house in 1808, started gypsum mining on the estate, but generally preferred to live elsewhere, leaving Acorn Bank little altered. Then, in c. 1930, the estate was sold to the wealthy travel writer, folk historian and art collector Dorothy Una Ratcliffe and her second husband Captain Noel McGrigor Phillips. DUR, as she liked to be known, renovated the house in an antiquarian manner and renamed it Temple Sowerby Manor. She and her husband also revitalised the walled garden dating from the seventeenth century which is now such a major attraction of the property, and established a wildflower and bird reserve on the bank above the burn.

In 1950, DUR gave the house and 186 acres (75 hectares) of the park to the National Trust, but none of the contents. For some forty years the house was tenanted. The Trust has now taken it over again and it is being slowly brought back to life. There are holiday apartments on the upper floors, but visitors can wander through the atmospheric, unfurnished ground-floor rooms.

Behind the house, a leat off the Crowdundle Beck leads to an early nineteenth-century water mill which has been returned to working order. Primarily a corn mill, it once also provided power to the gypsum mines on the estate.

Allan Bank (below)

Cumbria

Above Grasmere village to the north-west, 3 miles (5 kilometres) north-west of Ambleside

This large, stuccoed nineteenth-century villa set high above Grasmere has one of the most glorious positions in the Lake District. Behind it, fells rise steeply to the craggy ridge of Silver Howe and the park falls away to the lake below. Like other villas built in the Lake District at this time, Allan Bank was sited to take full advantage of the landscape, the drama of which had begun to be appreciated from *c.* 1770 onwards by those in pursuit of the Picturesque. From the windows of the house, and from viewpoints in the grounds, there are panoramic vistas south over the lake and its small wooded island and east over the pastoral Grasmere valley to the slopes of Rydal Fell.

Built as a rural retreat in 1805 for the Liverpool timber merchant and attorney John Gregory Crump, Allan Bank was remodelled and extended from *c.* 1834 to 1851, and the estate enlarged by Thomas Dawson, another Liverpool merchant and former barrister, who bought the place when he was only 22. Fretwork barge-boards and other Picturesque details added

by Dawson have been lost, but his detached billiard-room in the garden survives and he was responsible for the dramatic pleasure grounds embracing rocky outcrops to the north and west of the house.

As well as its fine position, Allan Bank is also notable for its connection with two of the Lake District's most significant figures. Although John Crump had built the house as a holiday home, in 1808 he rented it to William and Mary Wordsworth, who moved here from Dove Cottage in the village, together with William's sister Dorothy and his sister-in-law Sara Hutchinson. Both Sara and Dorothy loved the view over the lake and Wordsworth wrote his *Guide to the Lakes* here, but this was not an idyllic time. The chimneys smoked and increasing tensions with the opium-dependent Samuel Taylor Coleridge, who had come to live with them, escalated into a major rift. Coleridge departed for London and in 1811 the Wordsworths moved to the parsonage in Grasmere.

Allan Bank was also the last home of Canon Rawnsley, one of the three founders of the National Trust, who bought the estate in 1915 and bequeathed it to the Trust. Left semi-derelict after a serious fire in 2011, the house has been only partly restored and redecorated and has no historic contents. It is a place to relax, to enjoy musical and other events and, above all, to savour the views and landscapes which both Wordsworth and Rawnsley loved so passionately.

Ashleworth Tithe Barn

Gloucestershire

6 miles (9.6 kilometres) north of Gloucester, 1 mile (1.5 kilometres) east of Hartpury (on the A417), on the west bank of the River Severn, south-east of Ashleworth

Ashleworth barn stands in a group of picturesque buildings on the banks of the River Severn, close to a riverside inn and a fine medieval house and just west of the largely fifteenth-century parish church. Although smaller than Great Coxwell or Middle Littleton (*see* pp.405 and 414), this substantial limestone building, with two projecting wagon porches, is still impressive. An immense stone-tiled roof is supported on timber trusses that stretch the width of the barn. It was built in about 1500, probably by the Canons of St Augustine's, Bristol, who were lords of the manor here.

Bembridge Windmill and Fort (right)

Isle of Wight

Just south of Bembridge on the B3395

Set on a hill about a mile (1.6 kilometres) from the easternmost point of the Isle of Wight, this weathered four-storey stone mill with its great 30-foot (9-metre) sails is a familiar landmark and has inspired generations of artists, J.M.W. Turner among them. A fine example of an eighteenth-century tower mill, Bembridge was built in about 1700 and still contains original wooden machinery. The turning gear, which rotated the wooden cap to bring the sweeps into the wind, is still visible on the outside of the mill; the miller would originally have operated it by walking round the building hauling on a chain. For some 200 years until the outbreak of the First World War, the mill ground flour, meal and cattle feed for the village and surrounding countryside. Derelict by the 1950s, it has now been partly restored and is the only surviving windmill on the Isle of Wight.

On the downs to the south, what looks like a large earthwork is the remains of a fort built in the 1860s as part of Lord Palmerston's drive to strengthen the defences of the south coast.

Blaise Hamlet

Bristol

4 miles (6.4 kilometres) north of central Bristol, west of Henbury village, just north of the B4057

These nine rustic cottages set self-consciously around a green were designed by John Nash, who was once heard to say that no place had ever given him as much pleasure as Blaise Hamlet. His tiny settlement is certainly individual. Built in 1810–11 for the Quaker banker and philanthropist John Harford, who had bought the Blaise Castle estate in 1789, it was one of the first Picturesque estate villages and a reflection of the growing appreciation of traditional vernacular architecture. In this vision of an idealised village, each building is different. Some are thatched, some tiled, and all have varied rooflines, with gables and dormers at different levels. Porches, verandahs, sheds and lean-tos ensure no profile is repeated and contribute to the deliberate asymmetry. Even the pump on the green is defiantly off-centre. But everything in the hamlet is to the

same scale and all the cottages have soaring brick Tudoresque chimneys, now seen against a backdrop of mature trees as Nash intended. And the aged retainers whom Harford housed here were all provided with a small garden and an outside seat where they could doze on summer afternoons.

Boarstall Tower and Duck Decoy

Buckinghamshire

Midway between Bicester and Thame, 2 miles (3.2 kilometres) west of Brill

This enchanting three-storey tower, with hexagonal turrets rising from each corner of the battlemented roofline, is all that remains of the fortified moated house built here in the early fourteenth century by John de Handlo. The only entrance to his carefully guarded property was through this gatehouse, its massive limestone walls, almost 3 feet (1 metre) thick, falling sheer to the waters of the moat and surviving arrow slits suggesting the formidable prospect it must once have presented.

Today Boarstall seems charmingly domestic. An array of Tudor and Jacobean windows surveys the world, octagonal chimneystacks rise almost to the height of the turrets, and a two-arched brick and cobble bridge leads over the moat. A beautiful room running 40 feet (12 metres) across the length of the third floor, now occasionally used for chamber concerts, was probably once a dormitory for the men of the establishment.

Romantic and informal gardens at the back of the tower were laid out in the twentieth century. Over the fields, about half a mile (0.8 kilometre) to the north, but reached by a separate entrance off the Boarstall road, a tree-fringed lake marks Boarstall Duck Decoy. This tranquil place is one of the few surviving working examples of a once-common feature of the English countryside, introduced from Holland by Charles II. Ducks enticed into netted-over channels leading off the lake were once an important source of winter food but are now ringed for scientific purposes.

Bodysgallen Hall Hotel
Conwy
Off the A470 south of Llandudno

This tall, many-gabled stone house with stone-mullioned windows and massive chimneys stands high on a hill above Llandudno, with spectacular views of Snowdonia. The date 1620 on one of the gables flags the seventeenth-century south front, but the house also incorporates a five-storey tower which may date from the late thirteenth century, the kitchen wing was added in 1730, and in *c.* 1900 Lady Augusta Mostyn, whose family had been connected with the place since the sixteenth century, restored and enlarged it for her second son Henry. Of the seventeenth-century interiors, the large entrance hall and the equally capacious chamber above, now the drawing room, survive. Bodysgallen is set off by romantic walled gardens and surrounded by 230 acres (93 hectares) of parkland. A hotel since the early 1980s, when it was acquired and restored by Historic House Hotels Ltd, the house and company were generously given to the National Trust in 2008, together with Middlethorpe Hall (*see* p.415), and all the company's interests in Hartwell House (*see* p.407). Bodysgallen is still run as a hotel.

Bourne Mill (above)
Essex
1 mile (1.6 kilometre) south of the centre of Colchester, in Bourne Road, off the Mersea road (B1025)

This unusual little building with dormer windows in its steeply pitched roof and fanciful pinnacled Dutch-style gables was built by Sir Thomas Lucas as a banqueting house in 1591. Constructed of rubble and brick from the ruins of the Abbey of St John in Colchester, which had been dissolved some half a century before, the walls incorporate Roman remains and various medieval moulded stones, and the lake-like millpond may have been the monks' stewpond. A weather-boarded projecting sack hoist and the surviving machinery, including an 18-foot (5.5-metre) overshot water-wheel with 64 buckets, date from the mid-nineteenth century, when the mill was first used to grind corn. For the previous 200 years it had played a part in the East Anglian cloth industry and was used to spin yarn and for fulling woven cloth. Golden-yellow butterworts and other water-loving plants along the mill-stream and borders filled with herbs and medicinal plants contribute to the special appeal of this property.

Bradenham Village

Buckinghamshire
4 miles (6 kilometres) north-west of High Wycombe, off the A4010

This pretty village, with flint and tile-hung cottages set loosely round a large sloping green, lies in a fold of the Chilterns backed by beech woods on the hill above. Most of the cottages date from the sixteenth or seventeenth century and are timber-framed behind their later facings. At the top of the green, surveying all, is a fine late seventeenth-century red-brick manor house with long sash windows and a hipped roof. Beside it, dwarfed by its neighbour, is a little flint church with elaborate Norman carving round the south door. The manor is now offices, but once it was the home of the writer Isaac D'Israeli, whose oldest son, the Victorian prime minister Benjamin Disraeli, bought the Hughenden estate just over the hill (*see* p.181).

Bradley

Devon
On the outskirts of Newton Abbot, on the A381 Totnes road

From the top of Wolborough Hill just outside Newton Abbot there is a panoramic view over rolling countryside to the windswept heights of Dartmoor. Deep in the valley below, half hidden by a thick blanket of oak and beech, is this L-shaped medieval manor house, with glimpses of gables and tall chimneys through the trees. A long, low building, home of the Yarde family for over 300 years, it is built of roughcast local limestone limewashed white, with granite doorways and fireplaces and a slate roof. Despite some intrusive nineteenth-century castellations, the striking east façade is almost entirely fifteenth century, from the projecting chapel with a magnificent perpendicular window at one end to the original cusped gothic lights in the gables.

The interior is medieval in plan, with a screened passage running across the house and a Great Hall open to the rafters. The rooms are mostly low-ceilinged and rough-walled, with a massive granite fireplace in the old kitchen. Only the Great Hall is spacious. Here there is a brightly painted Tudor coat of arms high on an end wall and a carved oak screen in the arch leading to the chapel. In a panelled upstairs room, lifelike

depictions of roses, tulips, primroses, acorns and beech husks in the seventeenth-century plasterwork echo the flowers and trees in the woods around the house. Good collections of Pre-Raphaelite paintings and Arts and Crafts furniture are in tune with the medieval setting.

Braithwaite Hall

North Yorkshire
1½ miles (2.4 kilometres) south-west of Middleham, 2 miles (3.2 kilometres) west of East Witton

This remote seventeenth-century stone farmhouse is the centre of a hill farm in Coverdale on the eastern edge of the Pennines. Massive chimneystacks frame the gabled principal façade with mullioned windows looking north to Wensleydale. Original interior features include seventeenth-century fireplaces, oak panelling in the drawing room and the exceptional oak staircase with turned balusters which rises from the stone-flagged hall.

Branscombe (below)

Devon
Off the A3052, between Sidmouth and Seaton

Among the picturesque stone and cob cottages straggling along a lush green valley towards the sea which make up Branscombe are three examples of the kind of working buildings that were once found in every village. Below the church, at the bottom of the hill leading down into the village,

are a working smithy and, in an orchard on the other side of the road, the old bakery (now a tea-room), both of them in thatched premises over 200 years old. Further down the valley is the stone-walled, slate-roofed manorial water-mill, which is now restored to working order.

Bredon Barn
Worcestershire
3 miles (4.8 kilometres) north-east of Tewkesbury, just north of the B4080

This cathedral-like building on the banks of the River Avon was built in 1350 for the Bishops of Worcester, lords of the manor here for about 600 years, and is beautifully constructed of local Cotswold stone, with stone tiles on the steeply pitched roof. It is the only aisled barn in Worcestershire: 18 great posts like the columns of a nave march down the interior, some blackened timbers being a salutary reminder of the fire that badly damaged the building in 1980.

External stone steps lead up to a room over one of the two porches on the east side, comfortably equipped with a fireplace and a garderobe. From here the bishop's reeve could look down into the barn to check on the corn being brought in and the threshers at work.

Bridge House
Cumbria
In the middle of Ambleside

This tiny, two-storey building poised precariously on a bridge over Stock Ghyll in the middle of Ambleside has been immortalised by numerous artists, including Ruskin, and is one of the most photographed buildings in the Lake District. With rough stone walls and a slate roof, it dates from the seventeenth century and has just two rooms, one above the other. Built as an apple store for the Braithwaites of Ambleside Hall up the hill, it has also served as a cobbler's shop, a tea-room and a National Trust information centre.

Bruton Dovecote (above)
Somerset
½ mile (0.8 kilometre) south of Bruton across the railway, just west of the B3081

Nothing remains of the Augustinian abbey that once dominated the little town of Bruton except a section of wall and this unusual dovecote, standing alone on a hillock in what was the abbey's deer park. Adapted by the monks from a gabled Tudor tower with mullioned windows, it is now roofless.

Buckingham Chantry Chapel
Buckinghamshire
On Market Hill, Buckingham

The fine Norman arch over the south door, probably brought here from elsewhere and originally intended for somewhere grander, is the most memorable feature of this tiny, 38-foot (11.5-metre), rubble-built fifteenth-century chapel, the oldest building in Buckingham. It was used as a school from the Reformation until 1907 and was substantially restored by Sir George Gilbert Scott in 1875. It is now a coffee shop and second-hand bookshop.

Buscot Old Parsonage (below)
Oxfordshire
On A417 between Lechlade and Faringdon

On the banks of the Thames a mile (1.6 kilometres) or so below Lechlade is this beautiful three-storey house of Cotswold stone, built in 1703 to a symmetrical design. A central flight of steps gives access to the raised ground floor and some of the rooms have original painted panelling. Close by is the thirteenth-century church of St Mary, with Pre-Raphaelite stained-glass windows by Burne-Jones, whose friend William Morris lived at Kelmscott Manor across the river.

Cartmel Priory Gatehouse
Cumbria
Cavendish Street, Cartmel

Although both the turret and battlements that once crowned this picturesque stone gatehouse-tower straddling Cavendish Street have been removed, it still rises imposingly above the roofs of the surrounding houses, a reminder of the need for protection against attacks by the Scots in the troubled border country of the Middle Ages. Apart from the church of St Mary, it is all that remains of the Augustinian monastery founded here in 1189–90; the strengthening of the priory's defences with the construction of the gatehouse in 1330–40 may have been prompted by Robert the Bruce's devastating raids in the neighbourhood a few years earlier. Despite the insertion of later windows and the slate roof, this former stronghold has a substantially medieval appearance and is the only secular pre-Reformation building in Cartmel. The large room over the archway was once used for manorial courts and from 1624 to 1790 as a school.

Chiddingstone Village (above)

Kent

4 miles (6.4 kilometres) east of Edenbridge

This leafy single-street village is one of the most attractive of
the Kentish Weald. Opposite the largely seventeenth-century
church of St Mary stands a perfect group of sixteenth-
and seventeenth-century timber-framed buildings with
overhanging upper storeys, barge-boarded gables and lichen-
stained, red-tiled roofs. What is now the village shop and post
office is mentioned in a deed of 1453, and most of the houses
probably incorporate earlier material. Built at a time when the
Wealden iron industry was at its height, Chiddingstone was
originally part of a much larger settlement, but much of this
was destroyed when Chiddingstone Castle park was created.
The sandstone block known as the Chiding Stone, by which
local men are supposed to have chided their nagging wives,
and from which Chiddingstone is said to take its name, lies
in the small park also owned by the National Trust on the
southern side of the village.

Chipping Campden Market Hall

Gloucestershire

Opposite the police station, Chipping Campden

This little gabled and pinnacled Jacobean building stands
prominently in the centre of Chipping Campden, on one side
of the broad high street. Like the medieval houses of wool

merchants with which it is surrounded, the market hall is
built of golden Cotswold stone and roofed with stone slabs.
Open arcades on all four sides give access to the cobbled floor
where farmers and traders gathered to sell and buy cheese,
butter and poultry.

As the coat of arms in a gable at one end signifies,
the market hall was built by Sir Baptist Hicks in 1627,
only two years before his death. A financier who helped
support the extravagances of the court of James I, Baptist
Hicks was raised to the peerage at the end of his life and is
commemorated by a restrained classical monument in the
south chapel of the wool church down the street.

The Church House

Devon

Widecombe in the Moor, in the centre of Dartmoor, north of
Ashburton, west of Bovey Tracey

The medieval church in this popular Dartmoor village boasts
a magnificent early sixteenth-century pinnacled tower, paid
for by prosperous tin miners. The two-storey granite building
known as the Church House in the tiny square by the lych-gate
is of much the same period, dating from 1537. One of the finest
such houses in Devon, it is substantial and well proportioned,
with round-headed two-light granite windows and a verandah
supported on octagonal granite pillars running the length of
the entrance front. Each pillar rests on a roughly hewn boulder.
Originally a brew-house, it later became a school and is now
partly leased as the village hall and partly used as a National
Trust information centre and shop.

Cilgerran Castle

Pembrokeshire

Set high above the left bank of the Teifi, 3 miles (4.8 kilometres)
south of Cardigan, 1½ miles (2.4 kilometres) east of the A478

Like the great fortress at Durham, Cilgerran is so superbly
sited that it seems a natural part of the landscape. Round
towers linked by massive walls over 3 feet (1 metre) wide in
places stand on a rocky bluff above wooded slopes plunging
precipitously to the gorge of the Teifi River and its tributary
the Plysgog. Only a few miles from the sea, Cilgerran could

be supplied by water and it also controlled the crossing point at the tidal limit of the Teifi. Once a formidable stronghold, the castle on its leafy height has for long been a romantic and picturesque ruin and has inspired a number of artists, Turner, Richard Wilson and Pieter de Wint among them.

Built by William Marshal, Earl of Pembroke, in about 1223 on the site of an earlier stronghold captured from the Welsh in the Norman conquest of Wales, Cilgerran was constructed only a few years after Skenfrith (*see* p.422), but already castle design had moved on. In place of a central keep, the defensive strength of the place is concentrated in the two round towers projecting from the curtain wall that encloses the tip of the promontory. The remains of a third, rectangular tower probably date from the late fourteenth century, when Edward III ordered the reinforcement of a number of Welsh castles against the threat of a French invasion. In the event, it was the south coast of England that suffered, with raids from Rye to Plymouth. A wide ditch, once crossed by a drawbridge leading to the gatehouse, separates this inner ward from the outer court; the grooves for two portcullises still mark the walls of the gatehouse. A second great ditch added further protection beyond the outer ward, where little of the original defences survives. Possibly ruined at the time of Owain Glyndwr's revolt in 1405, when the castle was briefly held by the Welsh, Cilgerran seems never to have been subsequently repaired. Although owned by the National Trust, it is in the guardianship of Cadw.

Claife Viewing Station (right)
Cumbria
On the western shore of Windermere opposite Bowness, about 1 mile (1.6 kilometres) east of Far Sawrey

On the wooded western shore of Windermere, set high above the jetty for the ferry to Bowness, is an octagonal two-storey gothic ruin. An open staircase leads to the upper floor, where huge windows, now largely glassless, look out over the lake. In the 1790s, when the Lake District was becoming a fashionable destination for tourists and its landscapes, once thought wild and forbidding, were increasingly admired, this unusual building was constructed as the first 'viewing station', a place where people, often with sketchbook in hand, would come to enjoy the panoramic vistas up and down the lake and across to the opposite shore. The fashion was for visitors to turn their backs on the view and observe the scene with the aid of a Claudian glass, which softened and framed a reflected image. Coloured glass in the windows gave the illusion of different seasons and times of day – dark blue, for example, producing the effect of moonlight and orange the impression of autumn. As part of their restoration of the viewing station, the National Trust has inserted some panels of coloured glass in the windows to show how they might have appeared. In the 1830s and 40s parties and dances were held here, with Chinese lanterns lighting up walks round about.

Many other viewing points were established in the Lake District in addition to Claife. Seven have been recorded around Windermere and a station at Brackenthwaite Hows, from where Turner painted a watercolour of the view over Crummock Water, was acquired by the National Trust in 2019.

Cobham Wood and Mausoleum
Kent
At the east end of Cobham village

Overlooking Cobham Hall (not National Trust), and set amongst open woodland where some of the mature trees pre-date Humphry Repton's landscaping of the park in the early nineteenth century, is an arresting stone building, with a pyramidal roof rising from columned façades. Designed by James Wyatt and built in the mid-1780s for John Bligh, 3rd Earl of Darnley, it was intended as a mausoleum for the earl and his descendants. A bridge over a dry moat leads to the chapel filling the interior; beneath it is a vaulted crypt with shelves, known as loculi, to hold the coffins. Long neglected and vandalised in the twentieth century, the mausoleum has now been restored after a 50-year struggle to secure its future. For reasons unknown, it was never consecrated and the earl and his descendants are buried in Cobham parish church nearby.

Coggeshall Grange Barn (below)
Essex
½ mile (0.8 kilometre) south of Coggeshall, on the B1024

This majestic building, with a sweeping tiled roof above weather-boarded walls, is one of the oldest timber-framed barns in Britain. Constructed for the Savigniac monks of Coggeshall Abbey, it dates from the thirteenth century.

Although the barn was extensively rebuilt in the late fourteenth century, original posts still support the roof.

A small collection of farm carts and wagons is housed in the barn and the byre contains the Bryan Saunders collection of rare carpentry tools and examples of his work. A thirteenth-century chapel not far away once stood outside the abbey gate, and some other monastic buildings are now part of a nearby farm.

Coleridge Cottage
Somerset
At the west end of Nether Stowey, on the south side of the A39, 8 miles (12.8 kilometres) west of Bridgwater

The Ancient Mariner pub at the end of Lime Street flags the cottage across the road where the young Samuel Taylor Coleridge lived for three years from 1797 with his wife Sara and infant son Hartley. Once a low, thatched building, it was substantially altered at the end of the nineteenth century when it became an inn and only the four front rooms are relatively unchanged. Coleridge's time here was a period of great creativity, when he wrote some of his best-known poems, among them 'This Lime Tree Bower My Prison', 'Frost at Midnight', the first part of 'Christabel', 'The Nightingale' and 'The Rime of the Ancient Mariner', with its many references to places in the neighbourhood. The last two were included in *Lyrical Ballads*, on which Coleridge collaborated with Wordsworth, who was living at Alfoxden nearby, and which had a huge influence on the development of English Romantic poetry. During his time here, too, on a walk west across Exmoor, Coleridge rested at a remote farmhouse between Porlock and Lynton and, in an opium-induced reverie, set down 'Kubla Khan'.

The rooms Coleridge would have known are presented as they might have been in his time, with period furnishings and low light levels. Original features include a large inglenook fireplace, and there is a smoky open fire in the parlour, as Coleridge himself recorded. Mementoes of the poet in the Victorian rooms include his boulle inkstand, locks of his hair and letters in his distinctive hand. There are pictures of the Devon village where he was born, the room in London at No. 3 The Grove, Highgate, where he died, and also of friends and acquaintances. The little garden at the back of the house is where Coleridge went to escape the hubbub of family life.

Conwy Suspension Bridge

Conwy

330 feet (100 metres) from Conwy town centre, adjacent to Conwy Castle

In the late eighteenth and early nineteenth centuries trade with Ireland was increasing, but goods had to be carried to and from Holyhead along the appalling roads of North Wales and ferried across the wide estuary of the Conwy and the tide-race of the Menai Strait. The only alternative was a journey of about 15 miles (24 kilometres) upriver to the first bridge over the Conwy at Llanrwst. In 1811 the great engineer Thomas Telford, by then 54 years old and much in demand, was asked to survey a road to Holyhead. The route he devised through Snowdonia is a triumph. Now followed by the A5, it never exceeds the gradient of 1 in 50 which allowed a stagecoach to make a steady 10 miles (16 kilometres) an hour.

Six years later, when Telford designed a bridge to carry the road across the Menai Strait, he opted for a suspension bridge, producing only the third such structure to be built in the British Isles. His scheme for Conwy came shortly afterwards, his early plan for conventional arches soon abandoned in favour of another suspension bridge. The site of the crossing is magnificent. On the wooded left bank of the river the bridge seems to spring from the rocky crag crowned with medieval Conwy Castle. The turrets supporting the road, with their battlements and machicolations, look like extensions of the ancient fortifications. Between them stretches the 327-foot (100-metre) span of the bridge, suspended from the graceful curve of the original chains.

The bridge was opened in 1826, the same year that the Menai Bridge was badly damaged in a storm, convincing the old engineer that a span of 600 feet (183 metres) was the limit for a suspension bridge (although young Brunel's design for the Clifton Bridge over the Avon was to exceed this length in Telford's lifetime). The bridge and toll-house have been restored to their nineteenth-century glory and the road surface reconstructed to a contemporary specification.

The Crown Bar (left)

Belfast

Great Victoria Street, Belfast

The Crown Bar glitters and gleams. Coloured glass in bright blues, oranges and reds sparkles behind the bar, mirrors reflect tiles and polished wood, and the shiny finish on the moulded ceiling is a kaleidoscope of changing patterns set up by the lively clientele below. Originally the Ulster Railway Tavern, designed to serve thirsty travellers disgorged from the terminus of the Great Northern railway across the street, the Crown was renamed in 1885 and remodelled in 1898 to produce this High Victorian fantasy, one of the greatest late nineteenth-century public houses in the British Isles.

Classical pilasters, a parapet topped with urns and a portico crowned with finials and supported by cast-iron columns add theatrical touches to the exterior, suggesting an affinity with Frank 'Matchless' Matcham's opera house close by. Inside, drinkers can be convivial or sit in secluded intimacy. A long bar runs down one side of the room, its inward curve designed for

the comfort of those perched on stools along its length. Facing the bar is a row of snugs enclosed by screens of wood and coloured glass, guarded by crouching heraldic beasts and fitted out with upholstered benches and tables. With the door shut, the snugs become private drinking compartments. Mellow gaslight, bar staff in waistcoats and bow ties and a menu board offering Irish broth and oysters in season all contribute to the individual atmosphere.

Cushendun (above)
Co. Antrim
Off the A2 coast road between Cushendall and Ballycastle,
23 miles (37 kilometres) north of Ballymena

This picturesque village on the east coast of Northern Ireland, with panoramic views towards the Mull of Kintyre, lies at the mouth of the River Dun, which runs down to the sea through one of the loveliest of the nine glens that drain the basalt heights of the plateau of Antrim. The village, much of which is owned by the National Trust, is clustered around the bridge over the mouth of the Dun, with most of it on the north side, above the little harbour. Delightful white-washed, slate-hung cottages in a Cornish idiom were designed by Clough Williams-Ellis, who was engaged here by Ronald McNeill, Baron Cushendun, and his Cornish wife Maud, who came to the village in 1910. The architectural style of the buildings was to please Maud, who loved the vernacular architecture she had

grown up with. Two-storeyed terraces surround the square built by Clough Williams-Ellis in 1912, with arches linking the corners and massive gate piers at the entrance, while round the corner, facing the sea, is the terrace built in 1925 in memory of Maud. Williams-Ellis also designed Glenmona House in a Georgian idiom for the baron after the IRA burned down the existing 'big house' in 1922.

Cwmdu
Carmarthenshire
7 miles (11.2 kilometres) north of Llandeilo, off the B4302

Deep in the heart of Wales, in a countryside of green hills, steep narrow lanes and scattered farms, is the small hamlet of Cwmdu. The National Trust owns the little late Georgian terrace standing beside the River Dulais in the centre of the hamlet. Built of rough stone and slate in the Welsh vernacular tradition, and washed a rich warm yellow, the terrace consists of two tiny one-up, one-downs, which originally housed agricultural workers, a village shop and a small inn that was once a farmhouse. A lean-to at the end of the farmhouse used to be a stable. The terrace looks across the street onto a riverside garden bounded by a neat clipped hedge. The National Trust also owns the eighteenth-century chapel set back from the road at one end of the terrace and what was the parish vestry at the other. Both the pub and the shop are going concerns, run by the community.

Cwmmau Farmhouse
Herefordshire
Near Brilley Mountain, 4 miles (6.4 kilometres) south-west of Kington between the A4111 and the A438

Winding lanes lead to this half-timbered black-and-white house set in a slight hollow in the hillside in one of the most beautiful and remote areas of the Welsh borders. Although for many years a farmhouse, as the eighteenth-century barns and other outbuildings grouped round a yard to one side confirm, this attractive and substantial place was built in the 1620s as a hunting lodge for Philip Holman, who had bought the estate in 1621 and became High Sheriff of Herefordshire a few years later.

The wattle and daub which originally infilled the timber framing was replaced with brick in the early nineteenth century. At that time the farm employed a sizeable workforce, but after a sale in 1918, when the estate which then owned it was broken up, Cwmmau was increasingly neglected and derelict and some original features, including oak panelling, the huge oak front door (the frame for which can still be seen), the staircase and doors to the rooms upstairs, were sold to America. The house was rescued by George Menges, a Lloyds underwriter, who bought it in 1934 and, together with his wife Ianthe and sister-in-law Phyllis Jerrold, meticulously restored it and added panelling to the south-facing parlour. Phyllis enriched the house with her paintings and needlework, examples of her work here now include a coverlet embroidered with flowers in one of the bedrooms, a honeysuckle painted on panelling in the hall, and a wax crayon mural of the story of Genesis in the little room over the porch, to which George and Ianthe contributed the decorative borders.

Cwmmau came to the National Trust on George's death in 1964 and is now fitted out as holiday accommodation.

Dalton Castle
Cumbria
At the top of the high street in Dalton-in-Furness

Overlooking the market place in the middle of Dalton-in-Furness is this arresting rectangular tower, built of limestone rubble with sandstone dressings. With walls 5 feet (1.5 metres) thick and a roofline parapet pierced with arrow loops corbelled out from the walls, the tower looks defensive but, although dating from the fourteenth century, when this part of the world was much troubled by Scottish raids, it was built as a manorial courthouse for Furness Abbey. Originally it included a guardroom and a dungeon (the pit for which can still be seen) as well as the abbot's courtroom. There is some medieval stonework in the traceried windows and weathered sandstone figures at each corner of the parapet are carvings of fourteenth-century men-at-arms; a grinning head is the only survivor of the ten gargoyles that once marked the base of the parapet. The abbey was dissolved in 1537, and drastic remodelling in 1856 by the 5th Duke of Buccleuch, whose family had acquired the place in 1767, resulted in two of the three upper floors being removed and a new staircase built to supplement the original stone spiral stair in the thickness of the west wall. A collection of sixteenth- and seventeenth-century armour was introduced at about this time.

Manorial courts continued to be held here until 1923. Today, there is a small museum of local history on the ground floor.

Dapdune Wharf (below)
Surrey
On Wharf Road, Guildford, ½ mile (0.8 kilometre) from the town centre via the towpath

Running for some 20 miles (32 kilometres) through the heart of Surrey, from Godalming north to the Thames at Weybridge, is the green and tranquil corridor of the part-canalised River Wey. Pleasure boats now navigate the locks and walkers tramp the towpaths, but from 1653, when the Weybridge to Guildford stretch was opened, until the 1960s, working barges used

the waterway. These flat-bottomed wooden boats were made and repaired at Dapdune Wharf. Here, too, cargoes were discharged and loaded, among them Wealden timber for the rebuilding of London after the Great Fire in 1666, corn for mills along the Wey, and chalk to feed riverside lime kilns. A picturesque group of brick and weatherboarded buildings set along the grassy east bank of the navigation, together with some larger iron sheds, are reminders of the wharf's industrial past. The cottage-like gunpowder store dates from the mid-seventeenth century, but most reflect a nineteenth-century heyday when the Stevens family presided over the wharf. A stable and smithy stand close to a shed built over a creek off the Wey, where boats would be moored for repairs above the waterline, capstans hauled boats out of the water and a huge barge-building shed sits at the north end of the site. *Reliance*, an original barge fitted out here in 1931–2, is now beached on the grass, allowing visitors to experience the claustrophobic cargo hold and cramped quarters for the crew for themselves.

Derrymore House
Co. Armagh
On the A25, off the Newry–Camlough road at Bessbrook,
1½ miles (2.4 kilometres) north-west of Newry

Set on a natural terrace with fine views over Newry, and to the Mourne Mountains beyond, is this delightful example of the kind of artfully rustic buildings that were added to many Irish estates in the late eighteenth century. Often these *cottages ornés* were just designed to be garden ornaments or eye-catchers in the park, but a few, Derrymore among them, were intended to be lived in.

Single-storey ranges like diminutive cottages, each separately thatched, enclose three sides of an oblong courtyard. Plentiful windows, including a huge bay looking out over the park, reflect the up-to-the-minute design, intended to dissolve the boundaries between inside and outside, and bring the garden and surrounding landscape into the house. The interior is plainly decorated with simple ornamental mouldings.

Originally, Derrymore House was set in an idyllic miniature farmed landscape of small hedged fields designed by John Sutherland, who may also be the architect of the place, but it is now a charming eye-catcher in the landscape park that surrounds the Victorian mansion with which it was replaced. It was built for the politician Isaac Corry, who represented Newry in the Irish Parliament for 30 years and rose to be Chancellor of the Exchequer in 1799.

Derwent Island House (below)
Cumbria
In Derwentwater, Keswick

This intriguing house, reachable only by boat, is set on the largest of the four wooded islands that dot the length of Derwentwater. It dates from the late eighteenth century, when the wealthy Joseph Pocklington, who had inherited a fortune from his banker father, built a pedimented villa here, and it was then extended in an Italianate style in the 1840s by Anthony Salvin, who fitted out the interiors with restrained classical decoration. Salvin was working for Henry Cowper Marshall, whose father had founded the Leeds flax-spinning industry, and Marshalls continued to live here until the house came to the National Trust in 1951. Some of the original furnishings are still here, among them the 1850s mahogany and carved oak pieces supplied by the Leeds cabinetmakers John Kendell & Co. in the dining room and the English and Dutch paintings, including works by Charles Eastlake, Edwin Landseer, Jacob Storck and Jan Steen, which hang in Salvin's capacious staircase hall. Henry Marshall was also responsible for the landscaped grounds and fine trees that set off the house.

Most evocative is Pocklington's first-floor drawing room, which was designed to have views across the lake in three directions. From here, and from the terrace added by Salvin at one end of the room, there are panoramic vistas north to Skiddaw, west to the ridge of Catbells and south down the water to the fells at the heart of the Lake District, showing how this magical scenery, for so long unappreciated, was beginning to be admired in the late eighteenth century.

Tenants now live in the house. On the few days a year it is open, visitors reach the island by pre-booked canoes, which they paddle themselves.

Duffield Castle
Derbyshire
On the northern edge of Duffield village

A defensible spur between the River Derwent and its tributary the Ecclesbourne at the north end of Duffield village was once crowned by the stone keep of a formidable Norman castle. Built by William Ferrers in 1177–90 to replace earlier work in timber, the great keep, with walls up to 15 feet (4.6 metres) thick, was razed to the ground during the Montfortian rebellion of the 1260s. The castle mound, built on a prominent knoll overlooking the Derwent and reached up a long and steep flight of steps, is impressive still and gives spectacular views across the river valley, but there are no visible remains of the keep, some stones on the top of the mound outlining the foundations probably having been put in place in the nineteenth century. Two ditches which defined the bailey to the west have now been engulfed by housing, but a small fragment of ditch still survives in the grounds of Castlehill House to the south.

Dunstanburgh Castle (right)
Northumberland
9 miles (14.4 kilometres) north-east of Alnwick

No roads lead to Dunstanburgh. This magnificent ruin stands lonely and isolated on the Northumbrian coast and can be reached only by walking along a grassy track beside the sea from Craster to the south or Embleton to the north. Built where the Great Whin Sill reaches the sea in a bold outcrop of basalt, the castle occupies a natural defensive site. To the north, soaring cliffs fall sheer to the waves breaking on the rocks below; to the west the ground drops almost as precipitously to the patchwork of fields stretching away to the Cheviots; and on the east the sea is again a natural barrier, although the shore slopes gently here. The castle was most vulnerable to the south, where it now overlooks land that is marshy and cut off from the sea but where once there was a deep inlet that was used as a harbour.

Dunstanburgh's might is concentrated in massive towers set along the walls enclosing the castle's outer ward. An impressive gatehouse-keep with two D-shaped towers bulging out round the entrance passage guards the castle's south-west corner and further towers project from the curtain wall running east along the southern side of the site. To the north the long finger of the Lilburn Tower stands silhouetted against the sky on the highest point of the bluff.

Dunstanburgh was built between 1313 and 1316 for Thomas, 2nd Earl of Lancaster and grandson of Henry III. But the earl had little time to enjoy his castle: following his defeat by his cousin Edward II at the Battle of Boroughbridge, he was executed in 1322. Strengthened by John of Gaunt in the late fourteenth century as a stronghold against the Scots, Dunstanburgh's defences were put to the test in the Wars of the Roses, when the Yorkists besieged Lancastrian forces here in 1462 and 1464. Severely damaged in these engagements, the castle was barely repaired; too remote to be useful, it was left to gradually decay. It is now a hauntingly beautiful place, the restless murmur of the sea and the plaintive cries of seabirds wheeling overhead adding to its enchantment.

Although owned by the National Trust, the castle is managed by English Heritage.

Eastbury Manor House
London
In Eastbury Square, Barking, ¼ mile (0.4 kilometre) south of Upney station

This fine H-shaped Elizabethan gentry house, with a tiny paved courtyard embraced by the wings to the south, is now surrounded by interwar housing but once looked out over rich hay meadows and marshland to the Thames and the hills of Kent beyond. Red-brick façades rise three storeys to a gabled roofline with soaring Elizabethan chimneystacks. The crowning finials have been lost, but one of the original stair turrets remains, with rough oak treads leading up to a rooftop prospect chamber, from where, in the sixteenth century, London would have been a distant smudge on the horizon. There are traces of decorative diaperwork on the north-facing entrance front and the brickwork round the casement windows has been covered in lime rendering to imitate stone dressings.

Built by Clement Sysley and his third wife Anne Argall, and finished by *c.* 1573, Eastbury suffered a long period of neglect and decline in the seventeenth century. By the 1850s the manor was a farmhouse and partly ruinous, with stables and a hayloft occupying the east wing. Although the plan of the house is little altered, few original interior features survive. The long gallery that runs the length of the third floor rises to an open timber roof and the former Withdrawing Chamber has two

substantial fragments of painted decoration dating from *c.* 1600, one a view over an island-dotted sea with a ship in full sail, the other a prospect of a garden, with trees framing fish-ponds and a steepled town in the distance.

Apples, pears and cherries in the surviving Tudor walled garden on the east side of the house recall the orchards that once led down to the River Mayesbrook. Eastbury is managed by the London Borough of Barking and Dagenham, who run community activities and family events here.

Elizabethan House Museum
Norfolk
4 South Quay, Great Yarmouth

The elegant early nineteenth-century brick frontage of this three-storey house, with a classical portico sheltering the front door and ironwork balconies decorating the sash windows on the first floor, is only a façade. Behind lies an Elizabethan building dating from 1596 in which many original features, such as oak panelling, carved chimneypieces and moulded plaster ceilings, survive. The house is now a museum of domestic life run by Norfolk Museums Service.

Fen Cottage and Workshop (above right)
Cambridgeshire
Wicken Fen, south of the A1123, 4 miles (6.4 kilometres) east of Stretham, 3 miles (4.8 kilometres) west of Soham

The great expanse of fenland which once covered much of East Anglia with a watery landscape of open meres and waterways, vast sedge and reed beds, and patches of willow and alder woodland, has largely disappeared, its rich peaty soils now drained and intensively farmed. Wicken Fen is a unique remnant of what has been lost, long supporting a local population that made a living from exploiting and managing the resources of the fen, harvesting sedge and reed, digging peat, catching eels, cutting willow and wildfowling, moving across it along the man-made channels know as lodes.

Fen Cottage, set back from the lane leading to Wicken Fen behind a little front garden, is one of the last surviving buildings of a hamlet whose inhabitants lived and worked on the fen. Originally divided into two, as the different roof levels

industry. Three thundering wheels driving huge hammers, a grindstone, metal-cutting shears and a sharpening stone once powered one of the South West's most successful edge tool factories which, at its peak, produced around 400 tools a day. In business from 1814 to 1960, the foundry was always a Finch family affair, and there was much ad hoc patching-up of machinery and buildings. Demonstrations are given regularly.

A thatched, circular summer-house in the garden behind belonged to Tom Pearse, who had a serge mill in Sticklepath and was immortalised in the folksong 'Widecombe Fair'.

Flatford (below)
Suffolk
On the north bank of the River Stour, ½ mile (0.8 kilometre) south of East Bergholt

This gentle countryside on the banks of the lower Stour, with its meadows, ponds and pollarded willows and a cluster of half-timbered houses and cottages, is where the artist John Constable spent his boyhood and where he painted some of his most evocative work. The National Trust's holding of some 495 acres (200 hectares) includes the eighteenth-century water-mill which was owned by Constable's father and which the artist painted, and also the substantial Suffolk farmhouse known as Willy Lott's House, which appears

suggest, one end of the cottage is reed-thatched, the other tiled. Inside, small, low-ceilinged, sparsely furnished rooms with plank doors and brick floors lead one into another. Originally, both cottages had sleeping lofts in the roof, reached up a ladder, but only one is now accessible. There is an outside privy, but water had to be fetched from a well down the road or from the lode nearby. Built of materials from the fen – sedge and reed, with clay for daub, and dried peat blocks – the cottages date from the late eighteenth century and were joined together in 1925. Four generations of the Butcher family lived here, the last of them, Alice Butcher and her son Reggie, continuing to occupy the cottage until Alice's death in 1972. Also here is a recreated 1930s fenman's workshop.

Finch Foundry
Devon
At Sticklepath, 4 miles (6.4 kilometres) east of Okehampton, off the A30

Now bypassed by the busy A30, Sticklepath stands on the old route from London to Cornwall, where the youthful River Taw has carved a deep valley into the northern flank of the Dartmoor massif. The nineteenth-century Finch Foundry, housed in rugged buildings of granite and cob, is the only survivor of the village's once flourishing water-powered

in *The Hay Wain*. These and other buildings are let to the Field Studies Council and are not open, but there is a small exhibition on John Constable and his links to Flatford in the information centre, and visitors to the area can experience Constable's viewpoints for themselves. There are gentle walks along the valley towards Dedham through the meadows fringing the Stour.

The Fleece Inn
Worcestershire
In Bretforton, 4 miles (6.4 kilometres) east of Evesham, on the B4035

The delightfully irregular, black-and-white half-timbered façades of this little village pub with a partly tiled, partly thatched roof date back to *c.* 1400, when the inn started life as a one-storey long house, sheltering a farmer and his stock under the same roof. Owned by the same family from the Middle Ages until it was bequeathed to the National Trust in 1978, the building is crammed with furniture, crockery and farming implements handed down through the generations. It has been an inn since 1848, when Henry Byrd Taplin decided to become a publican rather than a farmer, and what was once the byre for the animals is now the beer cellar at the south end of the building. Beer was still being brewed for sale in the back kitchen well into the twentieth century.

Grange Arch
Dorset
At Creech, 3 miles (4.8 kilometres) west of Corfe Castle, 4 miles (6.4 kilometres) east of Worbarrow Bay

This simple early eighteenth-century folly, a pierced wall of lichen-stained grey Portland stone, stands on a crest of the Purbeck Hills, with magnificent views south to the sea and north over the unspoilt wooded Dorset countryside. A central round-headed arch is flanked by smaller rectangular openings on either side and the stepped profile is crowned with battlements and obelisks. Also known as Bond's Folly after its creator Denis Bond, the arch was specifically designed to be silhouetted against the skyline as seen from Creech Grange, the Bond family house nestling in the woods below.

Grantham House
Lincolnshire
In the centre of Grantham, immediately east of St Wulfram's church

The earliest part of this attractive town house, one of the oldest buildings in Grantham, dates from the same period as the fourteenth-century parish church across the road, with its soaring tower and spire. But, apart from the central hall, built in *c.* 1380, most of the building is Elizabethan or Georgian. Sixteenth-century mullioned windows in the entrance front were the result of alterations by the Halls, a family of wealthy wool merchants, while the long garden façade facing the River Witham, with its elegant sash windows and central pedimented doorway, was largely the result of remodelling by Anne, Lady Cust soon after 1734, when her husband, Sir Richard, bought the house for her. She was probably also responsible for panelling the drawing room and introducing the three large still-lifes by Jean-Baptiste Monnoyer in the hall, thought to have come from Belton House just to the north of Grantham, which she subsequently inherited (*see* p.49). A walled garden runs down to the river.

Gray's Monument (above)
Buckinghamshire
Church Lane, Stoke Poges, east of the churchyard

James Wyatt's massive monument, a classical sarcophagus on a plinth inset with inscribed panels, stands on the edge of a field just east of the churchyard which Thomas Gray immortalised in his 'Elegy' and where he chose to be laid to rest with his mother. It was erected in 1799, 28 years after the poet's death in Cambridge from 'severe internal gout', and was commissioned by John Penn, who owned the Stoke Park estate.

Gray's Printing Press

Co. Tyrone

49 Main Street, Strabane

The words 'GRAY PRINTER' set above an early nineteenth-century shop front in the main street of this little border town advertise the only survivor of the printing concerns that flourished here when Strabane was an important publishing centre in the late eighteenth century. At one time there were no fewer than ten printing businesses here: Strabane had both the *Strabane Journal* and the *Strabane Newsletter* before Londonderry, its larger neighbour about 15 miles (24 kilometres) to the north, began producing its own newspaper.

The works were housed on the upper floor of the long, whitewashed building across a yard at the back of the shop. John Dunlap, who printed the American Declaration of Independence in 1776 and started the first daily newspaper in the United States, is said to have served his apprenticeship at one of the printing presses in the town. He was one of the many who learnt their trade in Strabane before emigrating to America and the colonies to set up successful printing and publishing businesses. The former works is now used to display nineteenth-century printing machinery and a fine collection of wood and metal type.

Great Coxwell Barn

Oxfordshire

2 miles (3.2 kilometres) south-west of Faringdon between the A420 and the B4019

On the edge of Great Coxwell village is a magnificent thirteenth-century monastic barn which once belonged to the Cistercian abbey of Beaulieu and was described by William Morris as 'the finest piece of architecture in England'. Built of Cotswold stone and oak and 152 feet (46 metres) long, it has buttressed walls and a soaring stone-tiled roof that more than doubles the height of the building. Inside, stone piers some 7 feet (2 metres) high carry the slender oak posts that support the roof timbers. Projecting porches either side of the barn, one graced with a dovecote, house the original doors, those at each end of the building being insertions of the eighteenth century designed to accommodate the larger wagons of the day.

Greyfriars House and Garden (below)

Worcestershire

Friar Street, Worcester

Thomas Grene, a wealthy Worcester brewer, built himself this fine town house on a site next to a Franciscan monastery in 1480, recording his initials on the jetties either side of the entrance. Although one of the two ranges running back from the street is Elizabethan, the present casement windows were probably inserted in the early seventeenth century and there were some later additions, Greyfriars is nonetheless a very good example of the medieval timber-framed buildings that must once have housed Worcester's wealthier citizens, the upper floor jettied out over the lower and the timbers on the long street façade set expensively close together. A double gateway large enough to take a coach gives access to a cobbled passage leading to a little courtyard.

None of the original furnishings has survived, the appearance of the house today being the work of Mr Matley Moore and his sister Elsie, who took on the derelict building from the Worcester Archaeological Society in 1943 and gradually restored it. Seventeenth-century furniture and sixteenth-century tapestries in the great hall contrast with the rare Georgian hunting wallpaper in the dining room. Upstairs, a fine frieze of carved dragons is a reminder that this is Welsh borders country.

The Moores were also responsible for demolishing a row of Victorian blind-back houses at the rear of Greyfriars and creating the Italianate garden, with its summer-house and gazebo.

Hadrian's Wall and Housesteads Fort (below)
Northumberland
6 miles (9.6 kilometres) north-east of Haltwhistle

In about AD122, 80 years after the Roman conquest of Britain, the Emperor Hadrian ordered the construction of a wall from Tynemouth to the Solway Firth to mark the northern limit of the empire. Some 73 miles (117 kilometres) long, the Wall was built for much of its length on the Whin Sill, a doleritic outcrop with a steep and craggy northern face, and runs along a succession of cliffs and ridges in a wild and beautiful landscape of vast distances and panoramic views.

Over 6 miles (10 kilometres) of the most dramatic section, where the Wall rises over Hotbank Crags and Peel Crags, are in National Trust ownership, and so too is the best-preserved Roman fort in Britain (maintained and managed for the Trust by English Heritage). One of what were only sixteen permanent bases along the Wall, Housesteads conjures up an evocative picture of Roman life on this northern frontier. There are considerable remains of the commanding officer's house and of barracks for the ranks, and a forest of stone pillars once supported the floor of a granary.

Hadrian's Wall faded quietly away. By the mid-fourth century troops were being withdrawn from Britain to defend Rome and 50 years later, in AD410, the Emperor Honorius unceremoniously instructed the Britons to fend for themselves. Like the trappings of Roman civilisation, the Wall, now a UNESCO World Heritage Site, gradually decayed, its stone plundered for building material and some stretches ploughed out or built over, melting into history.

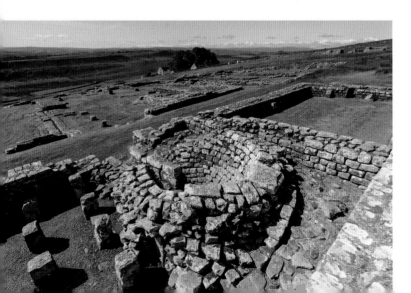

Hailes Abbey
Gloucestershire
2 miles (3.2 kilometres) north-east of Winchcombe, 1 mile (1.6 kilometres) east of the B4632 Broadway road

Set beneath the wooded western edge of the Cotswolds are the scant remains of one of the last Cistercian houses to be established in England. Apart from seventeen cloister arches and parts of the chapter house, the extensive and elaborate buildings of this once great abbey are now no more than outlines in the grass. But at one time pilgrims from all over Europe flocked to this now-secluded spot to worship at the shrine of the Holy Blood, built to house a relic given to the community in 1270 by Edward of Cornwall, whose father Richard had founded the abbey in 1246. The foundations of the five radiating chapels which once enclosed the ambulatory where the phial of Christ's blood was displayed can be seen outlined in the turf at the east end of the church, and in the little museum are floor tiles displaying the arms of the community's rich patrons and intricately carved bosses, an indication of how splendid the monastery once was. A deep stone-lined channel still carries the stream which provided the monks with water.

Pilgrim donations helped to pay for fine fifteenth-century cloisters, but years of prosperity were brought to an abrupt end in the autumn of 1538, when Henry VIII's commissioners visited Hailes and removed the phial of Holy Blood, subsequently declaring it to be 'honey clarified and coloured with saffron'.

The abbey is managed and maintained by English Heritage.

Hardy Monument
Dorset
6 miles (9.6 kilometres) south-west of Dorchester, on the Martinstown–Portesham road

This arresting stone obelisk set high on the South Dorset Downs, where it forms a prominent local landmark, is a monument to Vice-Admiral Sir Thomas Masterman Hardy, Flag Captain of HMS *Victory* at Trafalgar, who was immortalised by Nelson's dying words. Designed by A.D. Troyte and erected by public subscription in 1846, it stands boldly on the crest of Black Down, from where there are glorious views over Weymouth Bay.

Hartwell House Hotel (above)
Buckinghamshire
2 miles (3.2 kilometres) west of Aylesbury on the A418

A sweeping drive leads to this dignified and attractive house set in a hollow in the Vale of Aylesbury and surrounded by 90 acres (36 hectares) of parkland. Regular sash-windowed façades in a warm, honey-coloured stone were created by James Gibbs, who remodelled an H-shaped Jacobean house in the mid-eighteenth century for Sir Thomas Lee. Pediments are used sparingly over some of the windows and ground-floor openings in the central bay of the long south front are set within round-headed arches framed by colonnettes. The north-facing, grey-stone entrance front, with a splendid, semicircular oriel window over the central doorway, is a survival of the Jacobean house, although the original gables were removed in the eighteenth century and replaced with a parapet and cornice.

Inside, Gibbs designed the great hall of *c.* 1740, with its fine plasterwork ceiling, but the morning room and drawing room, with their rococo plasterwork, were created by Henry Keene in the 1750s for Sir William Lee and Keene was also responsible for the library, where the bookcases still have their original gilt-bronze wirework encasing the shelves. The most striking feature of the house is the grand staircase, which has 24 carved wooden figures, each just under 2½ feet (76cm) high, arranged along the newel posts, and balusters carved as caryatids. This piece of showmanship may be Jacobean, but may also be an eighteenth-century pastiche. Likenesses of Winston Churchill, complete with a cigar, and, bizarrely, G.K. Chesterton, are modern replacements for two of the balusters.

A thousand years ago Hartwell was a royal manor, and royalty returned briefly in the nineteenth century when the exiled Louis XVIII of France took refuge here, with his queen, Marie Joséphine, and some of his court, in 1809–14. After a sale of the contents in 1938, Hartwell was bought by the reclusive Ernest Cook with the aid of the fortune he had inherited from his grandfather, the entrepreneurial Thomas Cook, and the freehold of the house is now vested in a Trust bearing Ernest Cook's name. A school from 1956 to 1983, Hartwell was then acquired by Historic House Hotels Ltd who, with the help of the architect Eric Throssell, have restored both the house and the surrounding landscape park, with its eye-catchers. In 2008 the company donated all its interests in Hartwell to the National Trust. The house continues to be a hotel.

Hawford Dovecote
Worcestershire
3 miles (4.8 kilometres) north of Worcester, ½ mile (0.8 kilometre) east of the A449

Like Kinwarton 15 miles (24 kilometres) or so to the east (*see* p.411), Hawford was once a monastic grange belonging to the Abbey of Evesham. The dovecote, a three-storey, half-timbered square building standing on a sandstone plinth, with four gables pierced by mullioned windows, probably dates back to the sixteenth century. Unusually large doors on the ground floor gave access to a storage area, the birds being accommodated in the two upper storeys, where only a few of the wooden nesting boxes have survived.

Hawker's Hut (above)
Cornwall
On the coast 6 miles (9.6 kilometres) north of Bude, ½ a mile
(0.8 kilometres) from Rectory Farm and the church

Just inland from some of the most dramatic cliffs in Cornwall,
where the coast runs north into Devon, is the parish of
Morwenstow, a scatter of hamlets served by the ancient church
of St Morwenna and John the Baptist. Dating back to Norman
times, the church shelters in a little valley running down to
the sea. Out on the cliffs, across a couple of fields from here,
slate steps lead down to the hut built high above the waves
in about 1844 by the eccentric Robert Stephen Hawker, vicar
of Morwenstow from 1834 to 1875. A poet and writer as well
as a parson, the Reverend Hawker drew inspiration from the
ocean and from the wildness of the coast in what was then one
of the most isolated and thinly populated parts of the country.
His hut, set into the face of the cliffs, is built of driftwood
washed up from wrecks along the coast. There is a timber seat,
a stable door secured with wooden latches, a slate floor and
a roof covered in turf. Here, usually dressed in a fisherman's
jersey and sea boots, Hawker came for solitude, the verse he
composed often fuelled with opium, and here he would come
with his first wife, Charlotte, at the end of the day to read letters
and watch the sunset. His renown brought many visitors,
among them Tennyson and Charles Kingsley.

Hawkshead Courthouse
Cumbria
At the junction of Ambleside and Coniston roads, ½ mile
(0.8 kilometre) north of Hawkshead on the B5285

This modest two-storey gatehouse, set back from the road just
outside Hawkshead, is all that remains of the medieval grange
from which the monks of Furness Abbey, some 20 miles (32
kilometres) to the south, once administered their extensive
estates between Windermere and Coniston Water. For the most
part dating from the fifteenth century, Hawkshead Courthouse
is a plain rectangular building of rough slate rubble. Carved
sandstone forms the central archway, the large traceried
window in the south gable and the trefoil-headed windows on
the east façade. An exterior flight of slate steps at the north end
of the building leads to a large upper room where manorial
courts are said to have been held.

Holnicote Estate (below)
Somerset
Astride the A39, between Minehead and Porlock

The vast 12,000-acre (4,856-hectare) Holnicote estate runs
for 4 miles (6.4 kilometres) along the Somerset coast, from
Porlock Bay up onto the heights of Exmoor, and inland over a
succession of picturesque villages where houses, cottages and
farm buildings seem rooted in the landscape. At first glance,

the thatched, cream-washed stone cottages of Selworthy, set in a
steep wooded valley on the northern fringes of the moor, seem
all of a piece with the vernacular architecture of this part of the
West Country but, unlike the neighbouring villages, Selworthy
was largely rebuilt in 1828 by Sir Thomas Acland of Killerton
(*see* p.190), who designed a group of cottages in a local idiom
set loosely round a long green. A philanthropist who wished to
provide housing for the pensioners on his Holnicote estate, Sir
Thomas was probably inspired by his friend John Harford, who
had commissioned Nash to design Blaise Hamlet for his aged
retainers 20 years earlier (*see* p.389).

Both settlements are examples of the cult of the Picturesque,
but they could hardly be more different. Whereas Nash's
cottages are self-consciously flamboyant and exaggerated,
those at Selworthy are gentle variations on the vernacular,
with tall chimneys, deep thatched eaves, eyebrow dormers
and projecting ovens. At the top of the village is the fifteenth-
century church of All Saints, from where there is a view over
a patchwork of thatched roofs and neat cottage gardens to the
heather- and bracken-covered heights of Dunkery Beacon, the
highest point on the moor.

Horsey Windpump (above right)
Norfolk
15 miles (24 kilometres) north of Great Yarmouth on Horsey
Road, 4 miles (6.4 kilometres) north-east of Martham

Horsey Mere lies on the eastern edge of the Norfolk Broads,
little more than a mile (1.6 kilometres) from the sea, amid a
broadland landscape of marshes and reed beds which is of
international importance for its wildlife and waterfowl. The
impressive red-brick drainage mill, five storeys high and with
panoramic views from the top, stands at the south-eastern edge
of the mere. Built in 1912 on the foundations of an older mill, it
was used for pumping water rather than for grinding corn and
was the centre of an intricate and extensive system of drainage
dykes in this part of England. Via the dykes, water was drawn
from the low-lying marshes and pumped into Horsey Mere
and the river system. As much of the area lies below sea level,
drainage is still needed, but it is now done by electric pumps.
Intriguingly, although the coast is so close, the water runs by a
tortuous route 23 miles (37 kilometres) south to Great Yarmouth.

Horton Court
South Gloucestershire
3 miles (4.8 kilometres) north-east of Chipping Sodbury, ¾ mile
(1.2 kilometres) north of Horton, 1 mile (1.6 kilometres) west of
the A46 Bath–Stroud road

This picturesque stone-built manor with mullioned and
transomed windows stands on the western fringes of
the Cotswolds adjacent to the church of St James, whose
incumbents lived here. It was built in *c.* 1521 for the high-flying
Dr William Knight who, in his capacity as private secretary to
Henry VIII, visited Pope Clement VII in 1527 in an attempt to
negotiate the king's divorce from Catherine of Aragon. This
exposure to Italian Renaissance culture probably inspired the
Italianate loggia decorated with roundels of Roman emperors
which stands in the garden, the decorative surround to the front
door, with its carvings of helmets, weapons and foliage, and,
inside the house, where most original features have been lost,
the Tudor chimneypiece featuring Knight's arms and fluted
classical pilasters. Attached to one end of the entrance façade
is a remarkable Norman hall of *c.* 1185, a survival of the house
built here by Robert de Bellafago, who was given the manor
of Horton by William the Conqueror as a reward for his part
in the Conquest. Romanesque carvings of exceptional quality
ornament the two doorways, and there are Norman windows set
high in the walls and a roof that dates from the late thirteenth
century with timbers blackened by smoke from a central hearth.
This is probably the oldest roof owned by the Trust.

Houghton Mill

Cambridgeshire

In the village of Houghton, signposted off the A1123

One of a handful of surviving mills along the River Great Ouse, this unusually large four-storey brick and timber building rises from an artificial island 2 miles (3.2 kilometres) downstream of Huntingdon, the tarred weather-boarding of the upper storeys standing high above the flat water-meadows bordering the river. There has been a corn-mill on this site, once a property of Ramsey Abbey 10 miles (16 kilometres) to the north, for at least a thousand years, although the present building dates mainly from the eighteenth century. Three breastshot wheels powered the ten impressive pairs of millstones on the first floor and the hoists in the projecting gables, or lucams, which raised sacks of grain for storage at the top of the building. The wheels were removed when the mill ceased working in the 1930s, but the north water-wheel has now been reinstated and once again turns a pair of millstones, which are used to grind corn.

Keld Chapel

Cumbria

1 mile (1.6 kilometres) south-west of Shap village, by the River Lowther

The little hamlet of Keld, on the eastern edge of the Cumbrian fells, was once part of the estates of Shap Abbey, now an isolated ruin about a mile (1.6 kilometres) away, and this modest stone and slate building by the River Lowther was probably built by the abbey in the late fifteenth or early sixteenth century for the people of the village. Occasional services are once again held in the chapel, which was long used for other purposes.

King John's Hunting Lodge

Somerset

In the Square at Axbridge, on the corner of High Street

Like contemporary towns in East Anglia (*see* Paycocke's, p.262), Axbridge, Trowbridge, Bradford on Avon and other centres of the medieval wool trade in the West Country were once filled with prosperous merchants' houses such as this misleadingly named example of *c*. 1500. A three-storey timber-framed building on the corner of Axbridge's market place, it is jettied out over the street in a double overhang. A small museum of local history and archaeology run by the Axbridge and District Museum Trust is now housed here.

King's Head

Buckinghamshire

At the north-west corner of Market Square in Aylesbury

A narrow passage from Aylesbury's busy market square leads to this lovely old coaching inn dating back to 1455. A large, cobbled stableyard has its original mounting block, there is a priest's hole, and the large mullioned and transomed window which lights the bar, once the hall of a medieval house, has fragments of fifteenth-century glass.

Kinver Edge and the Rock Houses (below)

Staffordshire and Worcestershire

On edge of Kinver village, 4 miles (6.4 kilometres) west of Stourbridge

The National Trust owns some 579 acres (234 hectares) of this prominent red sandstone escarpment. A mosaic of woodland and wildlife-rich heath, with wide views to the Clent Hills and Wenlock Edge, the escarpment is notable for the unusual rock dwellings that honeycomb the soft, crumbly sandstone. Cave houses at Holy Austin Rock to the north of the Edge, occupied into the 1960s, have been restored and furnished as they would have been in the early 1900s. There is also a terrace of gabled cottages built into the cliff at the top of the escarpment.

Kinwarton Dovecote

Warwickshire
1½ miles (2.4 kilometres) north-east of Alcester, just south of the B4089

This substantial fourteenth-century circular dovecote sitting proudly in a field at the end of a muddy lane probably once belonged to the Abbey of Evesham some 12 miles (19.2 kilometres) away to the south, and is the only survivor of a former monastic grange. Some 580 nesting holes are built into the limestone walls and there is an ingenious manoeuvrable ladder supported on a pivoting central post to give access to them all. Apart from this rare survival, the dovecote is also notable for its fine ogee doorway.

Knowles Mill

Worcestershire
Next to Dowles Brook in the centre of Wyre Forest, Bewdley

Rutted tracks lead to this isolated mill in a clearing surrounded by oak trees in the depths of Wyre Forest. Built of sandstone rubble with brick dressings in the late eighteenth century and last worked, for grinding corn, in 1897–8, the mill still has much of its machinery, but this is no longer in working order and only the frame of the overshot water-wheel that was powered by a leat from the Dowles Brook survives.

A late eighteenth-century cottage with casement windows and a piggery sit beside the mill, forming a group of buildings of great charm.

The Kymin (left)

Monmouthshire
1½ miles (2.4 kilometres) east of Monmouth, signposted from the A4136

The prominent hill known as The Kymin is renowned for its wide-ranging views, said to embrace nine counties, over the Wye and Monnow valleys. The National Trust owns a piece of the high ground and the two structures that crown it. In the late eighteenth century members of a local dining club formed the habit of meeting here on summer evenings for a cold supper and, in 1794, built the round battlemented banqueting house on the brow of the hill for use in bad weather, each of its windows placed so as to give a spectacular view.

Nelson's victory over the French in the Battle of the Nile four years later inspired the construction of the little temple in honour of the Royal Navy that stands nearby, its pyramidal stepped roof suggesting an Egyptian summer-house. A prominent statue of Britannia crowns the structure and medallions record the names and principal achievements of sixteen great eighteenth-century admirals. When Nelson himself visited this spot in 1802, he thought it was one of the most beautiful places he had ever seen. History does not record the feelings of Emma Hamilton and her husband Sir William, who were accompanying Nelson on his journey down the Wye.

Lawrence House

Cornwall
9 Castle Street, Launceston

This modest Georgian brick house in the shadow of the remains of Launceston's great Norman castle was built in 1753 by the wealthy local lawyer Humphrey Lawrence and is typical of houses of the period seen in small country towns throughout England. Once the home of Caroline Pearse, a prolific Victorian author, it is now leased to the Town Council as a local museum.

Leith Hill Tower (above)
Surrey
1 mile (1.6 kilometres) south-west of Coldharbour, off the A29
and B2126

This gothic prospect tower, with a polygonal staircase turret jutting out from one corner, stands on the highest point in south-east England. As well as being an eye-catcher, it was also always intended as somewhere from which to survey the countryside around; there are magnificent views from here looking over the wooded landscape of the Weald to the South Downs, with glimpses of the English Channel beyond, and north to the skyline of London. First built by Richard Hull of Leith Hill Place in 1765, the tower was subsequently heightened and now rises to 1,029 feet (313.7 metres) above sea level. The room half way up the tower was originally furnished, so the view could be enjoyed in comfort, but the best vistas are from the roof, where telescopes are provided for visitors. Leith Hill Place (*see* p.207) lies on the wooded southern slopes of the hill.

Letocetum Roman Baths and Museum
Staffordshire
In the village of Wall on the north side of the A5

The little Romano-British town of Letocetum grew up round a posting station on Watling Street, the main imperial route to Chester and North Wales. Of the remains visible at Wall, the communal bathhouse is the most complete example of its kind in Britain, the extensive facilities on offer including the Roman equivalents of a Turkish bath and a sauna, cold baths, an undressing room and an exercise hall. A courtyard building nearby, destroyed by fire in AD160–170, was probably an inn. Finds from excavations here and from another Roman site at Shenstone, a short distance to the south-east, are exhibited in a small museum. Both remains and museum are in the guardianship of English Heritage.

Little Clarendon
Wiltshire
In Dinton, ½ mile (0.8 kilometre) east of the church, close to the post office

This old stone house, with a projecting porch, mullioned windows and a stone-tiled roof, dates back to the late fifteenth century, when it was built for a family of some local importance. There were alterations in the seventeenth century and then, in the late nineteenth century, it was divided into two, probably to house local farm labourers. In a state of decay, and with many of its original features obscured, the house was rescued by the Rev. George Engleheart and his wife Mary, who bought the property in 1901 and set about reopening blocked fireplaces, taking down room partitions, re-exposing beamed ceilings and generally restoring it. A brick-built cart shed close by was converted into a little Roman Catholic chapel and George Engleheart, who was fascinated by daffodils, experimented with new strains of narcissi here, raising them in greenhouses and long numbered beds separated by grassy walks. The three rooms on show – hall, dining room and parlour – are crammed with the Englehearts' collection of oak furniture, in particular a fine array of corner cupboards. The greenhouses and daffodil field have gone, but in spring the pretty triangle of grass behind the house, viewable from the footpath beside the garden wall, is covered with the

Rev. Engleheart's narcissi hybrids, and more of his daffodils flower along the woodland walk to the north.

Little Clarendon is open only a few days a year.

Lizard Wireless Station (below)
Cornwall
At Bass Point, near the southernmost tip of the Lizard, about ½ mile (0.8 kilometres) from Lizard village, or 1 mile (1.6 kilometres) along the coast path from Lizard Point to the east

A small wooden hut on one of the most southerly headlands in Britain is the oldest surviving wireless station in the world. This unassuming place, set on rabbit-cropped turf just yards from the edge of the cliffs, was where the visionary inventor Guglielmo Marconi conducted ground-breaking experiments in wireless transmission in 1900, work which paved the way for the instant worldwide communication we have today. Wireless itself was not new, but Marconi was the first to develop the technology that enabled signals to be sent over long distances. In January 1901, he received a transmission from the Isle of Wight, over 180 miles (290 kilometres) away, thus proving radio waves could travel beyond the horizon.

Marconi realised the commercial potential of his work and Lizard Wireless Station, together with about a dozen other coastal stations around the country, handled messages from ships for a fee. On 18 April 1910 the first SOS from a ship was received here when the steamship *Minnehaha* ran aground off the Isles of Scilly.

The hut has been restored to how it would have looked in Marconi's day. A second hut that was part of the wireless station is now a holiday cottage.

Long Crendon Courthouse
Buckinghamshire
2 miles (3.2 kilometres) north of Thame, via the B4011, close to the church

Long Crendon Courthouse lies in one of the most attractive and unspoilt villages in Buckinghamshire. Its long timber-framed façade with a jettied upper storey blends perfectly with the sixteenth- and seventeenth-century thatched cottages that line the street winding down to St Mary's church. Red handmade tiles form a warm streak of colour above the whitewashed walls. Steep wooden stairs lead directly from the street to the large room, open to the roof and floored with undulating oak boards, which runs most of the length of the upper storey.

Dating from the early fifteenth century, or even the end of the fourteenth, the courthouse seems originally to have been built for the cloth trade, to store wool from Oxfordshire destined for the weavers of East Anglia. The first floor was being used to hold manorial courts in the first half of the fifteenth century and manorial business continued to be conducted here into Victorian times, while the ground floor was frequently used to accommodate the village poor.

Loughwood Meeting House
Devon
4 miles (6.4 kilometres) west of Axminster via the A35, 1 mile (1.6 kilometres) south of Dalwood, 1 mile (1.6 kilometres) north-west of Kilmington

In the seventeenth century people walked miles to attend Baptist meetings in this little flint and sandstone building dug into the hillside, risking imprisonment, transportation or even death before the Toleration Act of 1688 legalised nonconformist forms of worship. Built in 1653 by Baptists from the nearby village of Kilmington, who needed a safe refuge where they could practise their faith, Loughwood was originally buried in dense woodland and approached only along narrow footpaths. Sited in a deeply rural part of Devon, it seems remote even today.

A homely thatched roof and round-headed clear-glass windows give this unassuming chapel the appearance of a cottage rather than a church, despite the surrounding burial ground and the buttressed walls. Inside, it is cheerful and

airy, dominated by the preacher's raised pulpit set above the baptismal pool. Unvarnished pine box pews fill the body of the chapel and the whitewashed walls and barrel roof are undecorated. Those who came from a long way away passed the time between services on Sundays in the retiring rooms underneath the musicians' gallery at the back of the building; those lucky enough to have horses quartered them in the detached stone and cob stable.

Maister House
Humberside
160 High Street, Hull

Until the building of the first commercial dock on the River Humber in 1770 led to its gradual decline, Hull's old harbour was the focus of the town's considerable trade, with grand merchants' houses lining the narrow, winding thoroughfares along the river. This fine Palladian house on the High Street is one of the few surviving from this era. Rebuilt for the merchant Henry Maister after a fire in 1743, and substantially unaltered, it is a plain, three-storey classical building fronted by railings and with a stone parapet concealing the roof. The only sign of ostentation is the pedimented doorcase framed with Ionic pilasters in the centre of the façade.

This restrained and dignified exterior and the sober pine-panelled counting house on the ground floor act as a foil for the staircase, richly decorated with plasterwork by Joseph Page, leading to what would have been the Maister family apartments. A statue of Ceres by John Cheere in a niche above the first flight surveys swags of drapery suspended from lion masks,

festoons of shells and acanthus-leaf medallions and scrolls. The coved ceiling above the gallery on the second floor is similarly richly stuccoed and there is a fine ironwork balustrade that was supplied by Robert Bakewell. The work of a highly competent architect, the design of Maister House was probably influenced by Lord Burlington, who knew Henry Maister and whose Yorkshire home was 25 miles (40 kilometres) away.

Market House
Derbyshire
In the main street of Winster, about 4 miles (6.4 kilometres) west of Matlock, on the south side of the B5057

This ruggedly attractive two-storey building is one of the few clues to Winster's former importance as a market town. Thought to date as a structure from the sixteenth century, the Market House is a pleasing mixture of brick and stone, with thick stone slates covering the steeply pitched roof and mullioned and transomed windows lighting the first floor.

As was traditional with such buildings, the ground floor was originally open, but its five pointed arches are now filled in. Still the dominant feature of Winster's long main street, the Market House was bought by the Trust in 1906. It was the Trust's first acquisition in the Peak District and is now a National Trust and community information point.

Middle Littleton Tithe Barn (above left)
Worcestershire
3 miles (4.8 kilometres) north-east of Evesham, east of the B4085

Produce from the fertile Vale of Evesham once filled this barn of coursed Lias limestone in market-gardening country on the banks of the River Avon. Some 315 feet (96 metres) long and buttressed like a church, it is both one of the largest and one of the finest barns in the country, although not all its wagon porches have survived.

Inside, oak framing forms an aisled bay at either end and eight base-cruck trusses divide the nine intermediate bays. The barn was built by the Benedictine monks of Evesham Abbey and may date from *c*. 1300 or even earlier. Like Ashleworth (*see* p.388), it is part of a picturesque group of buildings which includes an Elizabethan manor.

Middlethorpe Hall Hotel
North Yorkshire
Bishopthorpe Road, York

This charming William and Mary house close to York racecourse is all of a piece. Built of mellow red brick with limestone dressings, and with an array of sash windows standing out white against the brickwork, the house rises three storeys to a gently sloping hipped roof. Designed by an unknown architect, Middlethorpe was built in *c.* 1699–1701 for the aspiring Thomas Barlow, master cutler, who had bought the estate in 1698 and wanted a house that would help him establish himself as a country gentleman. The bustard of the Barlow family crest surmounts both north and south façades.

In the mid-eighteenth century Francis Barlow, High Sheriff of Yorkshire, added the one-storey wings ornamented with pilasters and a roofline balustrade which flank the front looking onto the gardens; a pedimented porch on the entrance front was added in the nineteenth century and the railings and gates enclosing a forecourt on this side of the house are recent embellishments. Original features inside the house include a splendid carved oak staircase; fine panelling, that in the dining room, ornamented with Ionic pilasters, being particularly noteworthy; and the ballroom that fills one of the two wings.

Once the home of the eighteenth-century socialite and wit Lady Mary Wortley Montagu, known for her entertaining and erudite letters, Middlethorpe was a girls' school for thirty years in the second half of the nineteenth century and subsequently lived in by the Wilkinson family, who owned the estate. The extensive grounds around the hall may well have inspired the young Fanny Rollo Wilkinson, who went on to become a landscape gardener and designed many of London's public gardens. More recently a nightclub, Middlethorpe was acquired in the later twentieth century by Historic House Hotels Ltd, who have furnished it sympathetically and restored the gardens and parkland, creating a ha-ha and lake and repairing a seventeenth-century dovecote. The house and company were generously given to the National Trust, together with Bodysgallen Hall and all the company's interests in Hartwell House (*see* pp.390 and 407), in 2008. Middlethorpe continues to be a hotel.

Morville Hall
Shropshire
3 miles (4.8 kilometres) west of Bridgnorth, off the A458

The eighteenth-century sash windows, giant pilasters and pedimented Doric porch on the entrance front of this beautiful three-storey stone house standing next to the Norman church of St Gregory disguise an originally Elizabethan, E-shaped building. There are still polygonal sixteenth-century staircase turrets in the angles of the façade and the pilasters, created by the architect William Baker when he remodelled Morville in the 1740s, disguise Elizabethan buttresses on the ends of the two projecting wings. Baker was also responsible for designing the delightful cupola-topped pavilions that are joined to the main house by curving screen walls, but the porch was added in the 1770s and alterations at this time also account for the addition of the top floor. An elaborate plasterwork ceiling dating from the 1580s in what is now the kitchen may be by the same craftsmen who worked at Wilderhope Manor nearby (*see* p.427), and there is some fine oak panelling.

Nether Alderley Mill (below)
Cheshire
1½ miles (2.4 kilometres) south of Alderley Edge, on the east side of the A34

Nether Alderley is a most unusual water-mill. On one side, a sweeping stone-tiled roof reaches almost to the ground, giving just a glimpse of warm sandstone walls. On the other, the mill is wedged right up against a wooded bank, the dam of the little reservoir that provides the water to turn the wheels. The stream on which the mill was sited was too small and irregular

to power the machinery effectively and this ingenious solution, with the later addition of three more reservoirs, was devised when Nether Alderley was first built, in the sixteenth century. The mill is noteworthy, too, for having a pair of water-wheels set one below the other, with a short trough leading from the first to the second. Both are 12 feet (3.5 metres) in diameter and, like all the mill machinery, date from the nineteenth century.

Four dormer windows in the sloping roof light the interior, the most remarkable feature of which is the Elizabethan oak woodwork that supports the roof. Wooden pins hold the structure together and the numbers used by the carpenters when assembling the frame can still be seen on some of the timbers. A floor of finely perforated tiles is the remains of a kiln for drying wet grain, a feature more usually seen in Scottish mills.

Nether Alderley was operating until 1939, almost 650 years after the earliest mention of a mill here in 1290. The machinery and the culvert from the reservoir have been restored and there are demonstrations of flour-grinding.

Newtown Old Town Hall (above right)
Isle of Wight
Midway between Cowes and Yarmouth, 1 mile (1.6 kilometres) north of the A3054

Despite being called Newtown, this shadow of a place on an arm of the Newtown estuary dates back over 700 years. Founded by the Bishop of Winchester in 1256 and laid out to a grid plan, much like a French bastide, it was at its height in the mid-fourteenth century when a community of some 300 prospered on the revenues from oyster beds and salt works and from the ships using the magnificent natural harbour of the estuary, regarded as the best in the Isle of Wight. Now there is just a scatter of buildings here, with grassy lanes marking the lines of the town's former streets and cattle grazing on what were medieval house plots, their outlines still visible in the turf. It seems Newtown never recovered from a disastrous French raid in 1377, gradually losing its trade and importance to Newport.

Surrounded by fields, oddly isolated from the rest of the village, is the little brick Town Hall of 1699, a relic of the days when Newtown elected two Members of Parliament despite its tiny population, the franchise granted in 1584 perhaps an attempt to stem the community's decline. Lit by four long,

round-headed windows down each side and crowned by a steeply pitched hipped roof, this simple building on an earlier stone basement was dignified by the addition of a classical portico in the late eighteenth century. By this time, elections were increasingly controlled by two families and Newtown's political life came to an end with the Reform Act of 1832, under which it was declared a 'rotten borough' and disenfranchised.

One of the National Trust's properties initially rescued from dereliction by Ferguson's Gang (*see* p.419), the building is used to display an exhibition about this anonymous group, whose exploits benefited the Trust in the 1920s and '30s. Not far away is Noah's Ark, a stone house of *c.* 1700 that was once an inn and is now the oldest building in the village, most of the others having been rebuilt in the nineteenth century.

Oakhurst Cottage
Surrey
In the village of Hambledon, 5 miles (8 kilometres) south of Godalming

This picturesque little timber-framed building in a leafy village on the fringes of London's affluent commuter belt dates from the sixteenth century. A rare survival that has escaped modernisation, it is furnished as a labourer's cottage of the mid-nineteenth century and illustrates a now vanished way of life. The front door opens straight into the main room, a quarry-tiled kitchen. There is a substantial dresser with shelves of willow-pattern china, samplers decorate the walls and a huge pot hangs over the hearth. A steep staircase leads directly up to one of the bedrooms in the roof, both of which are lit by dormer windows. In the little back kitchen, where clothes were once washed and ironed, a low bench known as a hog-form is where the hair was scraped from the family pig after it had been slaughtered, a prelude to the annual pork feast enjoyed by wealthier cottagers and so vividly described by Flora Thompson in *Lark Rise to Candleford*.

The Old Coastguard Station (below)
North Yorkshire
In Robin Hood's Bay, on the slipway of the old village

On the edge of the sea, at the bottom of the steep and cobbled main street leading down to the beach, is a small, two-storey sandstone house with a pantiled roof and a rendered and whitewashed frontage. This apparently typical piece of vernacular architecture was in fact built in the late 1990s to replicate a building which had stood here until the 1960s, when Leeds University replaced it with a modern marine research laboratory. The coastguard service was set up in the original building in 1829 in a bid to combat the smuggling for which the inhabitants of Robin Hood's Bay were notorious, and coastguards continued to operate from here until the early 1900s. A century earlier, the station had been a public house and it was divided into three tenements when the coastguards took it over. It is now a visitor and education centre.

The Old Manor, Norbury
Derbyshire
4 miles (6.4 kilometres) south-west of Ashbourne

Behind the Carolean red-brick manor house in this leafy village on the River Dove is a low medieval building with rough buttressed stone walls dating from *c*. 1250. Above an undercroft and cellars is an airy first-floor hall. Original gothic two-light windows with stone window seats survive in the west wall and a rare king-post roof spanning the room may have been installed here in the seventeenth century, when the Tudor manor was demolished. From the little knot garden, there is a good view of the tower of the fine fourteenth-century church, which is filled with monuments to the Fitzherbert family who held the manor of Norbury for over 650 years; the earliest is a stone effigy of Sir Henry Fitzherbert, who enlarged the hall house in the early fourteenth century.

Old Soar Manor
Kent
2 miles (3.2 kilometres) south of Borough Green on the A25; approached via the A227 and Plaxtol

The rectangular solar block attached to a red-brick early Georgian farmhouse is all that remains of the manor house of *c*. 1290 which stood here until the eighteenth century. The solar over the barrel-vaulted undercroft was once the apartment of a medieval knight, a private retreat away from the noise and company in the great hall. Rough walls of Kentish ragstone rise to an open timber roof, there is a bare brick floor and openings at the corners of the room lead to two projecting chambers, a chapel and a garderobe.

Orford Ness
Suffolk
On the coast between Aldeburgh and Shingle Street

Stretching 10 miles (16 kilometres) south of Aldeburgh, with a gentle curve westwards opposite Orford, this long shingle spit, and the mosaic of coastal marshland it shelters, is one of the most desolate and lonely places along an often wild and inhospitable coastline. Separated from the mainland by the

River Ore, which it forces ever further south, the bank is fluid and impermanent, changing shape in the winter storms that sweep in from the North Sea.

In 1993 the National Trust purchased 5 miles (8 kilometres), or some 1,550 acres (627 hectares), of the northern end of the spit, and a further 326 acres (132 hectares) running for 5 miles (8 kilometres) at the southern tip is leased from Natural England. Apart from its great interest as an internationally important nature reserve, this stretch of shingle bank includes the remains of a top-secret military research station and airfield that was in use for some 80 years from 1913. During the First World War, the techniques and equipment used in aerial warfare were tried out here. In the interwar years, as well as being used to test aeroplanes, ballistics and aerial combat techniques, the Ness is where, in a timber hut, Robert Watson-Watt and his team did pioneering work on the development of radar in 1935–6. A few years later, radar would play a key role in the Battle of Britain. The station continued to be used up until the 1990s, the wide-ranging research conducted here including the testing of technology for the British atomic bomb.

Eerily futuristic concrete pagodas and other laboratory structures were built from 1955 to simulate the environmental

stresses nuclear weapons would be subject to and absorb the blast from conventional explosives used in trials. Some structures have now been demolished, others are gently decaying and being reclaimed by the natural world around them.

Patterson's Spade Mill
Co. Antrim
On the A6, 2 miles (3.2 kilometres) south-east of Templepatrick

This unusual relic of Ireland's agricultural past is the last water-driven spade mill in the country. Founded in 1919 to produce a range of implements, from light tools for flower beds to heavy-duty spades for cutting turf, Patterson's Mill was run as a family business for over 70 years. It was acquired by the National Trust with all machinery and fittings intact and spades are once again being made here.

Penshaw Monument (left)
Tyne & Wear
Halfway between Sunderland and Chester-le-Street, close to the A183

Conspicuously sited on a hilltop, this roofless classical temple is visible for miles around, the honey-coloured sandstone of which it was built now blackened and sombre. Some 100 feet (30 metres) long and 50 feet (15 metres) wide, this impressive eye-catcher was the work of local architects John and Benjamin Green and was erected in 1844 to commemorate the radical statesman John George Lambton, 1st Earl of Durham, one-time Governor General of Canada, who had died four years earlier.

Pitstone Windmill
Buckinghamshire
½ mile (0.8 kilometre) south of Ivinghoe, 3 miles (4.8 kilometres) north-east of Tring, just west of the B488

This fascinating little building, bearing the date 1627, is Britain's oldest post mill, an example of the earliest form of windmill that was developed in the Middle Ages. Unlike later mills, such as that at Bembridge (see p.389), the sails are brought into the wind by turning the building as a whole, rather than by simply revolving the cap on the top of the mill.

Pitstone's two-storey timber body, reached by a ladder, is perched some 8 feet (2.5 metres) above the ground on a massive wooden post, the lower half of which is enclosed in a brick roundhouse. The building projects alarmingly on either side of its support, as if it might topple over at any moment. The tail pole sweeping down to the ground – a long beam with a wheel on the end – acted as a lever for turning the mill.

Two pairs of grinding stones, one pair used for producing coarse meal, the other for fine white flour, are now in working order, but the mill cannot at present be turned into the wind.

Priest's House, Easton on the Hill
Northamptonshire
In Easton on the Hill, 2 miles (3.2 kilometres) south-west of Stamford, off the A43

This little two-storey stone building, with fireplaces to warm the chambers on both floors, pre-dates the Reformation of the mid-sixteenth century which turned the Church upside down. Originally intended for celibate clergy, it would have been lived in by married priests after the Reformation and was superseded by the handsome Georgian rectory standing nearby. A small museum illustrating past village life is housed on the upper floor.

Priest's House, Muchelney (above right)
Somerset
In Muchelney, 1½ miles (2.4 kilometres) south of Langport

The hamlet of Muchelney, once on an island in the Sedgemoor marshes, has an exceptional clutch of medieval buildings at its heart. On one side of the fine fifteenth-century church are the remains of the Benedictine abbey of Muchelney, which may have been founded as early as the seventh century (in Somerset, only Glastonbury is older). On the other side, facing the church across a small green, is this thatched stone cottage, built by monks of the abbey to house the vicar of the parish and already here by 1308, when it was recorded. Substantially rebuilt towards the end of the fourteenth century, with a plan resembling that of Alfriston (see p.14), and modernised in the early sixteenth, when the massive fireplace with a Ham stone lintel was inserted, this was quite a grand house for the vicar of a tiny parish in the marshes. Although the interior

is much altered and the hall that once rose to the roof in the centre of the house was floored over in the early seventeenth century, the cottage still has its original gothic doorway, with a massive key to open the front door, mullioned windows and the magnificent two-tiered window to the hall, with trefoil heads to the upper lights. Internal plank doors, ingenious corner cupboards, the staircase to the first floor and other Arts and Crafts touches, all in keeping with the spirit of the house, were the work of the architect Ernest Barnsley, who restored the cottage after the National Trust purchased it in 1911.

Priory Cottages
Oxfordshire
1 Mill Street, Steventon, 4 miles (6.4 kilometres) south of Abingdon

These timber-framed medieval buildings set round a little courtyard are the remains of a small Benedictine priory. Essentially no more than a house of the period that was lived in by two monks, the buildings are now divided into two cottages, one of which contains the priory's great hall.

The cottages were the last property given to the Trust by Ferguson's Gang, who raised money for the Trust anonymously in the 1920s and '30s.

Ramsey Abbey Gatehouse
Cambridgeshire
Abbey College, at the south-east edge of Ramsey, at the point where the Chatteris road leaves the B1096, 10 miles (16 kilometres) south-east of Peterborough

In 969 St Oswald, Archbishop of York, and Ailwyn, foster brother of King Edgar, founded a Benedictine abbey on a remote island in the Fens. This surviving fragment, an ornate late fifteenth-century gatehouse with a richly carved oriel window above the entrance doorway, suggests how sumptuous the abbey buildings must once have been. A small room to the right of the gateway is filled with an impressive mid-thirteenth-century marble tomb, with a frost-damaged effigy clutching a huge key in its right hand. An intriguing mystery surrounds the identity of the figure, which was once taken to represent Ailwyn.

Rosedene (below)
Worcestershire
Victoria Road, Dodford, near Bromsgrove

The mid-nineteenth-century working-class movement known as Chartism, which led to petitions for political equality and social justice being presented to Parliament, also spawned some practical experiments in land reform. Fergus O'Connor's land plan, developed in the 1840s, aimed to settle working-class families on smallholdings that would allow them to be self-supporting. From 1845 the Chartist Co-operative Land Society, later the National Land Company, began to acquire

land, the money for which was obtained by selling shares to would-be smallholders. The estates were parcelled up into 4-acre (1.6-hectare) plots, with narrow lanes to give access, and a one-storey brick cottage was built at the head of each plot. The smallholdings were initially allocated by ballot, but a more inequitable system involving the payment of entry bonuses was introduced after a time.

Dodford, where Rosedene was built, was the last of the National Land Company's five settlements. The estate was purchased in 1848 and the first tenants moved in a year later, when this little cottage was first occupied. The smallholders, who grew strawberries and early vegetables for sale in Birmingham, only 13 miles (20.8 kilometres) away, were the most successful of the Chartist settlers and enjoyed an Indian summer during the First World War, when the strawberry crop was used to make jam for the army. Generally, though, the plots were found to be too small for self-sufficiency and for keeping an essential cow, for milk and manure, and most families had to supplement their income as best they could. Largely unaltered since it was built, Rosedene shows the kind of conditions in which the early Chartists lived, its period features including a working range, water pump and earth closet. There is a restored vegetable garden and orchard on the plot.

St George's Guildhall
Norfolk
In King's Lynn, on the west side of King Street, close to the Tuesday Market Place

Medieval King's Lynn was a market town and port of considerable importance, trading in wool and agricultural produce across the North Sea and to Scandinavia. The Guild of St George was one of the largest of the 60 or so that flourished here in late medieval times, and this substantial building by Tuesday Market, the biggest surviving medieval guildhall in England, is a graphic illustration of the wealth and status of the fraternity.

Although the 107-foot (32.5-metre) great hall on the first floor is now a theatre, many original fifteenth-century features survive, such as the five massive buttresses against the north wall and the open timber roof. There are also traces of the Georgian theatre constructed here in 1766.

St John's Jerusalem (above)
Kent
3 miles (4.8 kilometres) south of Dartford at Sutton-at-Hone, on the east side of the A225

After the noise and traffic of Dartford, this charming place, set amongst undulating lawns, shaded by magnificent trees and moated by the River Darent, appears as an oasis of peace and serenity. A huge cedar of Lebanon, probably planted by Abraham Hill in the late seventeenth century at the same time as he made alterations to St John's, frames the first view of the house, a pleasant two-storey stuccoed building with dormers in the steeply pitched roof. The sash windows and interior plasterwork were later additions by Edward Hasted, the eminent local historian, who lived here from 1755 to 1767.

The oldest part of St John's, and all that is open to visitors, is the medieval chapel joined onto the east end of the house. With buttressed flint walls and tall lancet windows, it is all that remains of the former Commandery of the Knights Hospitallers of the Order of Saint John of Jerusalem that was established here in 1199. Dissolved at the Reformation, the order lives on in the name of this delightful property.

Segontium
Gwynedd
On the A4085 on the south-east outskirts of Caernarfon

Edward I's great castle at Caernarfon was partly built of dressed stone plundered from the Roman fort of Segontium on the top of a hill about half a mile (0.8 kilometre) to the east. One of over 30 forts built to control the rebellious tribes in the valleys west of the Rivers Severn and Dee, Segontium was sited in a commanding position above the Menai Strait and on a route inland to the much larger garrison at Chester. Founded in AD78, it was held until about 390, longer than any other Roman fort in Wales, which probably reflects its strategic importance. Over the years, the clay rampart flanked by a ditch that originally marked the perimeter was gradually replaced in stone, to strengthen the defences.

The 5½-acre (2.2 hectare) site is crossed by the Caernarfon to Beddgelert road and only the ground plan of part of the northern half is excavated. The fort was of the usual playing-card shape and laid out to a standard design, with barracks for the men in tidy rows either side of the commander's house and the headquarters building in the middle of the compound, the latter displaying the remains of an underfloor heating system. Nothing can be seen of the two large granaries which housed a year's supply of corn for the garrison (up to 1,000 strong), but a rather basic bath suite added in the late third or early fourth century shows facilities here were less lavish than at Letocetum (*see* p.412). The fort is in the guardianship of Cadw and the site museum is not National Trust.

Shalford Mill
Surrey
1½ miles (2.4 kilometres) south of Guildford, east of the A281

This large eighteenth-century water-mill sits confidently astride the Tillingbourne, a tributary of the River Wey. Two timber-framed upper storeys attractively hung with warm red tiles are built on a brick ground floor, with three brick arches on the upstream side channelling the water of the river through the mill. A prominent projecting gable at third-floor level housed the hoist, which once raised sacks of grain for storage in the large bins running the length of the attic.

All the principal machinery is still intact, but the mill can no longer be worked as only the top half of the 14-foot (4.5 metre) breastshot water-wheel remains. A vertical shaft made from a single pine trunk transmitted power from the wheel to three pairs of millstones, one of which is still complete, and to the hoist in the attic and winnowing and grading machinery on the second floor.

Shalford Mill is one of the properties that was presented to the National Trust by the anonymous band of conservationists known as Ferguson's Gang, who used to meet here in the 1930s. Part of the building is now converted into a house and is privately let.

Skenfrith Castle
Monmouthshire
6 miles (9.6 kilometres) north-west of Monmouth, 12 miles (19.2 kilometres) north-east of Abergavenny, on the north side of the B4521 Ross road

The remains of some 80 castles scattered across South Wales are echoes of the drawn-out conflict between the Welsh and the English following the Norman Conquest. The little early thirteenth-century fortress of Skenfrith, set on low ground by the River Monnow, is one of the more important survivals; together with White Castle to the south and Grosmont to the north, it protected a natural routeway into Wales. Washed by the river on one side, the castle is protected by a wide moat, now a dry ditch, on the other three. Above these defences rise the remains of the massive curtain wall, best preserved along the river, which encloses a trapezoid-shaped area: ruined circular towers, from which attackers could be subjected to deadly raking fire, project boldly from each of the corners. In the centre of the castle is a large round keep, in the style of those being built by the French king at this period, the mound on which it is built probably a survival from a more primitive fortress established here in the decades after the Conquest.

Skenfrith is the work of Hubert de Burgh, Earl of Kent, who was granted the 'Three Castles' by King John and may have been influenced in his design by what he had seen while imprisoned in France. Like the builder of Bodiam away to the east (see p.61) two centuries later, the Earl of Kent was concerned with acquiring a nobleman's residence as

well as a fortress and his castle includes a great hall range, the foundations and lower walls of which can still be seen against the west curtain wall. Little changed since it was built, Skenfrith is a splendid example of the castles that foreshadowed the formidable symmetry of Edward I's great fortresses. The castle is in the guardianship of Cadw.

Souter Lighthouse (below)
Tyne and Wear
2½ miles (4 kilometres) south of South Shields, on the A183

Just south of the Tyne estuary, overlooking a stretch of unspoilt limestone coastline owned by the National Trust, is a prominent cliff-top lighthouse, its 76-foot (23-metre) tower painted in bold red and white stripes. Built in 1870, it was the first lighthouse to be powered by an alternating electric current and could be seen from some 19 miles (30.4 kilometres) out to sea. A focal point on a stretch of open grassy cliff-top, the lighthouse dominates a row of nineteenth-century coastguard cottages and other ancillary buildings. A nearby array of lime kilns is a reminder of former quarrying along these cliffs, and there was once a colliery village here too.

South Foreland Lighthouse

Kent

3 miles (4.8 kilometres) east of Dover, between St Margaret's at Cliffe and Langdon Cliffs

This lighthouse set on chalk downland high above the sea is a conspicuous landmark on the White Cliffs of Dover. Sited to guide mariners past the shifting shoals and banks of the notorious Goodwin Sands, the lighthouse, which is 69 feet (21 metres) tall, dates from 1843, when the light was an oil lamp. In 1858 it became the first lighthouse in the world to be lit by electricity. Subsequently, Marconi used the grounds of the lighthouse for his first successful trials in radio navigation, making contact with the East Goodwin lightship, 10 miles (16 kilometres) away, on Christmas Eve 1898. There are views over Dover docks and the Channel from the balcony round the light.

About half a mile (0.8 kilometres) away from the lighthouse, just off the coast path, 125 steps lead steeply down to Fan Bay Deep Shelter, a network of tunnels 70 feet (21 metres) underground. Only recently excavated, the tunnels were built in 1940–1 as accommodation for those operating a gun battery on the cliffs above, and are now all that remains of these defences. Dish-like shapes cut into the chalk and lined with concrete near the entrance to the tunnels are the remains of two sound mirrors, one of which dates from 1917. One of the first early warning systems, these mirrors were designed to focus the sound of an aircraft, so a plane could be heard before it was seen.

Sticklebarn Tavern (above right)

Cumbria

On the B5343 in Great Langdale, north of Skelwith Bridge, 7 miles (11.2 kilometres) north-west of Ambleside

Now a pub much patronised by those walking the fells, this sizeable, rugged stone building set at the foot of the Langdale Pikes in some of the most beautiful upland scenery in England was built as a two-storey bank barn, with an upper floor accessed from the higher ground against which it is placed (the double doors by which the first floor was entered are still in place). Like the dry-stone walls criss-crossing the valley floor, the barn was constructed of surface-gathered material. The slate-covered pentice roof which shelters weary walkers sitting at the

tables at the front of the tavern once protected the openings to the stables and byres of the lower floor. Just 50 feet (15 metres) behind the barn are the remains of a fifteenth-century fulling mill, which was powered by a leat off the Stickle Ghyll.

Stoke-sub-Hamdon Priory

Somerset

2 miles (3.2 kilometres) west of Montacute between Yeovil and Ilminster

This picturesque group of buildings set round a grassy farmyard is reached through an archway from the road. On one side of the yard is a buttressed, two-storey house with a projecting porch and stone-mullioned windows. Farm buildings closing the other sides and set round a second yard behind include a magnificent great barn, the ruins of a cart shed, granary and cattle shed, and a splendid circular dovecote, now roofless, fitted out with 500 nesting boxes. This enchanting complex, mostly of mellow Ham Hill stone, dates from the early fourteenth century, when the five chaplains of an Augustinian chantry founded by the Beauchamp family in 1304 were housed here and supported by income from the farm. A medieval hall open to the rafters which forms one wing of the house dates from this period, but most of the house is of the fifteenth century or later. When the chantry was dissolved, in 1548, the complex continued as a farm.

Templetown Mausoleum
Co. Antrim
In Castle Upton graveyard, Templepatrick

This perfect Neo-classical temple, erected by Sarah Upton in 1789 in memory of the Hon. Arthur Upton, who had died 20 years earlier, dominates the quiet graveyard at Castle Upton. Urns in niches flank a rusticated arch on the dignified entrance façade and three more stand on the parapet above the simple inscription. Coade stone plaques commemorate other members of the Upton family. One of the finest monuments ever designed by Robert Adam, the mausoleum is also one of the few examples of the architect's work in Ireland. Adam was commissioned to give a new look to Castle Upton (not owned by the National Trust), but the house was subsequently remodelled and only his castellated stables near the graveyard have survived.

Totternhoe Knolls
Bedfordshire
2 miles (3.2 kilometres) west of Dunstable off the B489

A dramatic grassy spur running north from the Chiltern ridge above the village of Totternhoe is crowned with the well-preserved remains of a substantial Norman motte and bailey castle. A conical mound encircled by a ditch rises conspicuously from the highest point, and ridges and hollows in the turf mark the three baileys with which the motte was surrounded. Built in the years after the Conquest, probably by one Walter de Wahull, the castle was constructed to command the Ouzel valley and the countryside around.

Scars, the humps of former spoil heaps and in-filled pits on the hillside below, some now hidden in woodland, mark medieval stone quarries, where the hard chalk known as Totternhoe Clunch was extracted. Much in demand for carving and dressing, the stone was used in churches round about and also in some high-status buildings, such as Westminster Abbey. A flight of medieval cultivation terraces stepping down a steep-sided combe on the southern slope of the ridge may have been used for growing vines or hops, or to enhance the setting of the castle and impress visitors.

Town Walls Tower
Shropshire
Close to the centre of Shrewsbury and St Chad's church

Despite Edward I's conquest of Wales in the late thirteenth century, towns in the Welsh borders still needed to be defended against possible attack by rebels from the west. This fourteenth-century four-storey tower which once overlooked a great loop of the Severn – the view is now obscured by buildings and trees – is one of the few remaining fragments of the fortified walls, then studded with twelve watch-towers, which once protected the town.

Treasurer's House, Martock
Somerset
Opposite the church in the middle of Martock village;
1 mile (1.6 kilometres) north-west of the A303 between Ilminster and Ilchester

Of the clutch of late medieval priests' houses owned by the National Trust, this comfortable building of mellow Ham stone, marked by a traceried two-light window and set back from the street through an archway, is perhaps the grandest. Flagstones across a grassy court lead to the late thirteenth-century great hall, open to an arch-braced timber roof dating from the fifteenth century and with windows of c. 1350. A screens passage divides the hall from the earlier solar block to the south, in fact a hall house of c. 1260 with a first-floor hall above what was originally an undercroft. In what would have been a private chamber is a wall painting of the crucifixion. A paved internal courtyard, now a peaceful garden, gives access to the kitchen set at right angles to the main house in the fifteenth century, with a massive block of Ham stone forming the fireplace at one end.

This substantial medieval survival has been linked to the village church since at least the thirteenth century, when the treasurer of Wells Cathedral lived here and acted as Martock's rector and patron. In later years the house and associated farmland were tenanted, but a succession of treasurers continued in the same roles until 1840.

Tudor Merchant's House
Pembrokeshire
Quay Hill, Tenby

This narrow, late fifteenth-century three-storey building looking down Bridge Street just above the harbour is typical of the prosperous medieval dwellings that would have crowded the lanes of this little town when it was a thriving port in the fourteenth and fifteenth centuries.

Sturdily built of roughly coursed rubblestone, the house still boasts a garderobe turret rising the height of the building, its original jointed roof trusses, and a circular chimneystack characteristic of this part of Wales. The interior has been much altered. A trailing flower pattern painted in red, black and yellow that emerged from beneath no fewer than 23 coats of whitewash on a partition is thought to have been executed in the late eighteenth or early nineteenth century.

A re-created merchant's shop on the ground floor and specially commissioned reproduction furniture show how the house might have looked in 1500.

Ty Mawr Wybrnant (above right)
Gwynedd
At the head of the little Wybrnant Valley, 3½ miles (5.6 kilometres) south-west of Betws-y-Coed via the A470, 2 miles (3.2 kilometres) west of Penmachno

This little sixteenth-century farmhouse hidden away on the eastern edge of the Snowdon massif, with its rough granite walls, slate roof, massive chimneys and small, deep-set windows, is typical of Wales's scattered upland dwellings. Today it is remote, but at one time drovers taking animals from

the fertile Llŷn peninsula to the markets of the Welsh borders would have regularly passed down the valley.

This tranquil spot was the birthplace of Bishop William Morgan, whose translation of the Bible into Welsh is still in use today. In 1563, realising that the Welsh had no alternative to the Latin service, Elizabeth I ordered the four Welsh bishops and the Bishop of Hereford to produce a translation of the Prayer Book and the Bible within three years. The New Testament published in 1567 was a stilted, pedantic text, bearing no comparison to William Morgan's triumphantly fluid masterpiece produced in Armada year (1588), with a dedication to his queen. Alas, although the bishop was born and grew up in this remote valley, the farmhouse almost certainly post-dates him, although fragments of an earlier, cruck-framed hall house are embedded within the structure. A re-created Tudor garden is stocked with herbs, fruit, vegetables and flowers of the period.

Wellbrook Beetling Mill
Co. Tyrone
4 miles (6.4 kilometres) west of Cookstown, ½ mile (0.8 kilometre) off the A505 Cookstown–Omagh road

Like the wool industry in medieval England, linen manufacture was of major importance in eighteenth-century Ireland, particularly in the north, where new landowners from England and Scotland were anxious to maximise the return from their estates. Official encouragement included the setting up of a Linen Board in 1711, the removal of duty on Irish linen imported

into England, and a body to fund development. Although some spinning and weaving continued to be done in the home, the industry was increasingly mechanised, with many mills established on the rivers around Belfast. Beetling was the last stage in the process, in which the cloth was pounded with heavy hammers for up to two weeks to give it a gleaming sheen.

This functional isolated building in a remote valley west of Cookstown is the only surviving part of the once-extensive Wellbrook linen works. Built in 1765 and modified in the nineteenth century, it continued operating until 1965, although the main bleaching mill closed about a hundred years earlier. Seven beetling engines, their hammers resembling rows of organ pipes, were powered by a large breastshot water-wheel, 16 feet (5 metres) in diameter, set against the eastern gable of the long two-storey mill. Water for the wheel was brought from a weir on the Ballinderry River a short distance away, with an impressive wooden aqueduct on brick piers to transport it the last 50 feet (15 metres) or so. After beetling, the cloth was hung to dry on the upper floor, where the airing racks and louvred windows still survive. The linen was then folded on a special table for dispatch.

Now restored to working order, the mill once again reverberates to the heavy pounding of the beetling hammers.

Wellington Monument
Somerset
2 miles (3.2 kilometres) south of Wellington on the A38, just west of the Wellington–Hemyock road

Anyone travelling south-west along the M5 or by train from Taunton to Exeter will recognise this stark stone obelisk, which rises prominently from the Blackdown Hills on the Devon–Somerset border. Designed in 1817 by Thomas Lee, the architect of Arlington Court (see p.23), and some 175 feet (53 metres) high, it was commissioned by a group of local gentry to commemorate the achievements of the Duke of Wellington, who had defeated Napoleon at the Battle of Waterloo two years before. The Iron Duke would probably have appreciated the military advantages of such a splendid position, with breathtaking views in all directions. At present, visitors cannot climb the spiral staircase to the top, but funds are being raised for a project to make the monument fully accessible again.

Westwood Manor (above)
Wiltshire
1½ miles (2.4 kilometres) south-west of Bradford on Avon, in Westwood village

The sixteenth century was a golden age for the west of England, when men amassed considerable fortunes in the woollen cloth trade with Antwerp and built the many fine but unpretentious houses that are such a feature of towns and villages in this part of the country. One of these men was Thomas Horton, who acquired a little fifteenth-century house built by a prosperous farmer and transformed it into a residence more fitting for someone of his position. Fluid plasterwork now found in many of the rooms of the manor, and some fine panelling, are the result of further embellishment by John Farewell in the early seventeenth century. Becoming a farmhouse again in the eighteenth and nineteenth centuries, when part of the manor was demolished and other alterations made, Westwood was rescued by Edgar Lister, who acquired the property in 1911, restored it with great sensitivity, and left the house and his collection of furniture to the Trust.

Westwood is both dignified and welcoming and is still a home. A modest L-shaped building of warm local stone, its low ranges frame a grassy court crossed by flagged paths and there is a great medieval barn close by the house. One of the most satisfying rooms is Farewell's Great Parlour over the hall, with its unusual interior porches, an elaborate plaster ceiling and early keyboard instruments introduced by Lister. The long, low window giving onto the courtyard from this room has a beautiful view of the village church and over the valley of the River Frome beyond.

Wichenford Dovecote

Worcestershire

5½ miles (8.8 kilometres) north-west of Worcester, north of the B4204

Perhaps built at the same time as the adjoining farmhouse was given its elegant late seventeenth-century façades, this tall, timber-framed black-and-white dovecote strikes a similarly domestic note, with mown grass surrounding the sandstone plinth on which it stands. A lantern crowning the steeply pitched roof admitted birds to some 550 nesting boxes stacked on short brick piers.

Wilderhope Manor (below)

Shropshire

7 miles (11.2 kilometres) south-west of Much Wenlock, 7 miles (11.2 kilometres) east of Church Stretton, ½ mile (0.8 kilometre) south of the B4371

This tall, gabled Elizabethan manor stands on the southern slope of Wenlock Edge, deep in the remote wooded Shropshire landscape evoked so vividly in the work of the local novelist Mary Webb, who used Wilderhope Manor as her model for Undern Hall in *Gone to Earth* (1917).

Built of local grey limestone with tall brick chimneys and a stone-tiled roof, this is a delightfully asymmetrical house, with an off-centre entrance, marked by a curious detached pediment, on the south-east front and projecting bays of varying widths. Large mullioned and transomed windows on this side of the building look out over the pastoral valley below.

Apart from the notable circular wooden staircase capped by a conical roof which ascends right through the house, the main feature of the interior is its unexpected plasterwork ceilings, executed with such skill that they were once thought to be the work of Italian craftsmen rather than of a provincial team. The initials of Francis and Ellen Smallman, who built Wilderhope in about 1586, recur frequently in the moulds punctuating the plaster ribs, alternating with standard motifs such as the Tudor rose, the fleur-de-lis and the portcullis. Of the original contents, only a bow rack survives.

The spot known as the 'Major's Leap' on Wenlock Edge nearby commemorates Francis and Ellen's descendant, Thomas Smallman, a supporter of the Royalist cause in the Civil War, who was imprisoned at Wilderhope. Escaping into the garden, probably by means of an old garderobe flue, he evaded his pursuers by riding his horse over Wenlock Edge. Although his unfortunate mount was killed, the major's fall is said to have been broken by a crab-apple tree.

The manor is now a youth hostel and is managed by the YHA. Shropshire's largest colony of swifts returns to nest in the roof every year.

Winchester City Mill (below)

Hampshire

At the foot of Winchester's High Street, beside Soke Bridge

This attractive brick corn-mill with tile-hung gables and a delightful island garden was built over the River Itchen by Soke Bridge in 1743 on a site that has been occupied by a succession of mills since at least Saxon times. The fast-flowing river, which emerges in a spectacular mill-race, once powered several medieval mills in the city, a reflection of Winchester's early importance as capital of England and as a market for grain and wool. Already in decline by the late fourteenth century as a result of the ravages of the Black Death and the removal of the English wool staple to Calais, the town never recovered its former prosperity.

One of a number of Winchester mills recorded in Domesday Book as being connected to the Church, the mill at Soke Bridge was then a property of the Benedictine nunnery of Wherwell a few miles north of the city, passing to the Crown when the monastery was dissolved in 1538–9. Some years later, in 1554, it was given to the city by Mary I in partial recompense for the expense of her marriage to Philip of Spain in Winchester Cathedral. The current mill, with its undershot water-wheel, dates from the fourteenth and fifteenth centuries, but the walls were rebuilt in Flemish brick in 1744. It was restored to working order in 2005.

Willington Dovecote and Stables (above)

Bedfordshire

In Willington, 4 miles (6.4 kilometres) east of Bedford, just north of the A603

The serrated roofline of this imposing sixteenth-century dovecote built by Sir John Gostwick, Cardinal Wolsey's Master of the Horse, can be seen for miles across the flat Bedfordshire countryside. Built on a scale commensurate with the large mansion to which it was once attached, the dovecote's kidney-shaped nesting boxes set into the thickness of the stone walls could accommodate some 1,500 birds. Showy, crow-stepped gables are supported on thirteenth-century corbels that were probably recycled from local priories at the Dissolution of the Monasteries. Across the road is a contemporary barn-like building with similarly ornate gables and late gothic windows. The young John Bunyan, born at Elstow only 5 miles (8 kilometres) to the west in 1628, is alleged to have stayed here, leaving his signature and the date, 1650, etched on a stone fireplace.

The architecture of both dovecote and stables is exceptionally flamboyant for their apparent purposes, and it is likely that they were built by Sir John for a visit by Henry VIII in 1541 and that the stables were originally designed as a banqueting house.

ABOVE Montacute House,
Somerset (*see* p.224).

Maps

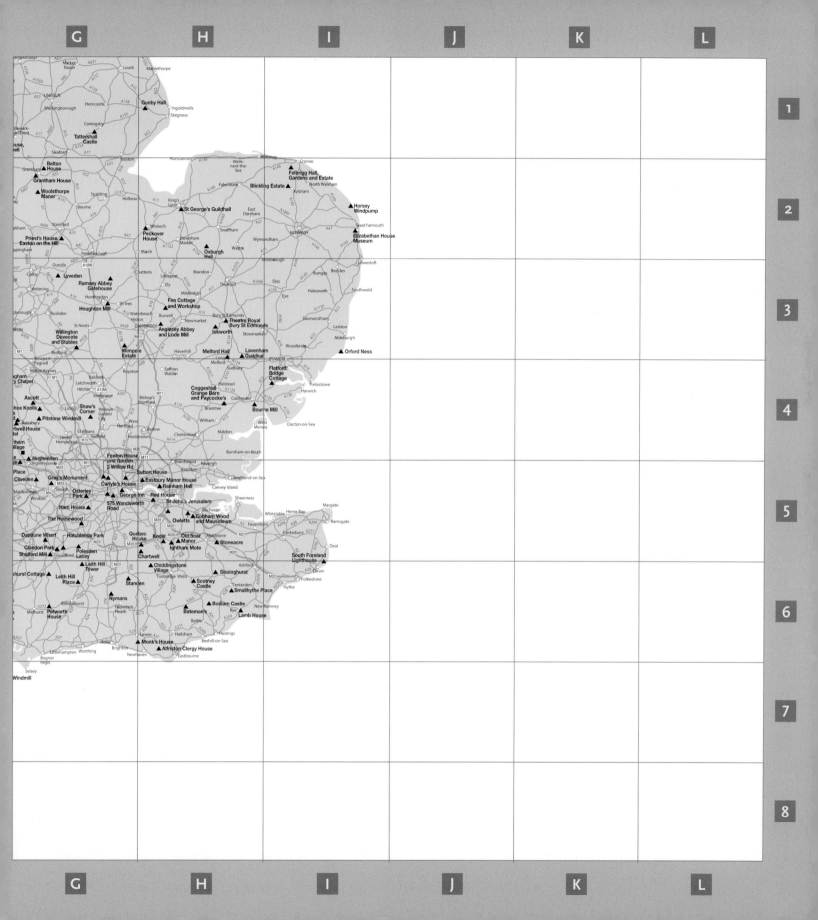

Grid labels (top and bottom): A B C D E F
Grid labels (left): 1 2 3 4 5 6 7 8

Rathlin Island

Portrush
Ballycastle
Downhill Demesne and Hezlett House ▲
Coleraine
Cushendun ▲
Cushendall
Limavady
A2
Ballymoney
A26
LONDONDERRY
A5
A6
Dungiven
A42
Larne
Gray's ▲ Printing Press
Strabane
Ballymena
A44
Whitehead
Islandmagee
Newtownstewart
Maghera
M2
A36
Templetown Mausoleum
Castlederg
Magherafelt
Randalstown
Ballyclare
Carrickfergus
Patterson's Spade Mill ▲
Moneymore
M22
Ballynure
Newtownabbey
Wellbrook Beeting Mill ▲
Springhill ▲
Cookstown
Antrim
M2
Bangor
Omagh
A47
Coalisland
Crumlin
Holywood
BELFAST
The Crown Bar ▲
A5
Dungannon
Lisburn
Comber
Newtownards
Mount Stewart ▲
The Argory ▲
M1
A26
Lurgan
Carryduff
Ardress House ▲
Craigavon
Enniskillen
Portadown
Dromore
Ballynahinch
Castle Coole ▲
A28
Tandragee
Castle Ward ▲
Lisnaskea
Armagh
A51
Banbridge
Downpatrick
Florence Court ▲
A3
Keady
A25
Castlewellan
Rathfriland
Newcastle
Derrymore House ▲
Newry
Crossmaglen
Warrenpoint
Rostrevor
Kilkeel

(England / Cumbria region, right side)
Hadrian's Wall - Housesteads F ▲
Longtown
Haltwhistle
Brampton
Carlisle
A69
Wigton
Maryport
A66
Penrith
Acorn B ▲
Workington
Wordsworth House and Garden ▲
Bassenthwaite Lake
Applet
Westm
Whitehaven
Keswick
Derwent Island House ▲
Crummock Water
Derwentwater
Egremont
Haweswater
Keld Chapel ▲
Allan Bank ▲
Bridge House, Ambleside ▲
Sticklebarn Tavern ▲
Wray Castle ▲
Townend ▲
Beatrix Potter Gallery ▲
Hawkshead ▲
Claife Viewing Station ▲
Courthouse ▲
Hill Top ▲
Coniston Water
Kendal
Cartmel Priory Gatehouse ▲
Sizergh ▲
Sedbe
Millom
Grange-over-Sands
Ulverston
Dalton Castle ▲
Barrow-in-Furness
Morecambe
Lancaster
M6
Fleetwood
Garstang
Clithero
Blackpool
Kirkham
M55
Preston
Gawthorp ▲
Lytham St Anne's
Warton
Blackburn
Leyland
Chorley
Rufford Old Hall ▲
Southport
Ormskirk
Standish
Wigan
Bolto
Skelmersdale
M61
Crosby
Kirkby
M58
Bootle
St Helens
M62
LIVERPOOL
Dunham Massey ▲
The Hardmans' House (Mr Hardman's Photographic Studio) ▲
The Beatles' Childhood Homes ▲
Warrington
Widnes
M56
Speke Hall ▲
Runcorn
M53
Tatton Park ▲
Nether Ald
North

(Wales, bottom)
Bodysgallen Hall Hotel
Conwy Suspension Bridge
Llandudno
Amlwch
A5025
Aberconwy House ▲
Conwy
Colwyn Bay
Prestatyn
Rhyl
Holyhead
Beaumaris
Abergele
Holywell
Llangefni
Bangor
St Asaph
Flint
Plas Newydd ▲
Penrhyn Castle ▲
Caernarfon
Denbigh
Mold
Chester
Winsford
Llanberis
Ruthin
A55
A51
Crewe
Ty Mawr Wybrnant ▲
Betws-y-coed
A5
Nantwich
Blaenau Ffestiniog
Wrexham
Erddig ▲
Ffestiniog
Llangollen
Whitchurch
Pwllheli
Criccieth
Porthmadog
Bala
Chirk Castle ▲
Ellesmere
Market Drayton
Plas yn Rhiw ▲
Abersoch
Wem
Barmouth
Dolgellau
A470
Welshpool
Attingham Park ▲
Tywyn
Mallwyd
Shrewsbury
Town Walls Tower ▲
Su ▲
Aberdyfi
Machynlleth
Benthall Hall ▲
Powis Castle ▲
Montgomery
Morville Hall ▲
Wilderhope Manor ▲
Dudmasto
Newtown
Bishop's Castle
Aberystwyth
Llanidloes
Kinver Edge and the Rock H ▲
Llangurig

Map references

Aberconwy House 430 C1

Acorn Bank 432 F3

A la Ronde 430 D7

Alfriston Clergy House 431 H6

Allan Bank 432 F4

Anglesey Abbey and Lode Mill 431 H3

Antony 430 C7

Ardress House 432 B4

The Argory 432 B4

Arlington Court 430 C6

Ascott 431 G4

Ashdown House 430 F5

Ashleworth Tithe Barn 430 E4

Attingham Park 430 D2

Avebury 430 E5

Baddesley Clinton 430 E3

Barrington Court 430 D6

Basildon Park 430 F5

Bateman's 431 H6

Bath Assembly Rooms 430 E5

The Beatles' Childhood Homes 432 F6

Beatrix Potter Gallery 432 F4

Belton House 431 G2

Bembridge Windmill and Fort 430 F7

Beningbrough Hall, Gallery and
Gardens 433 H5

Benthall Hall 432 F8

Berrington Hall 430 D3

Birmingham Back to Backs 430 E3

Blaise Hamlet 430 D5

Blickling Estate 431 I2

Boarstall Duck Decoy and Tower
430 F4

Bodiam Castle 431 H6

Bodysgallen Hall Hotel 432 E6

Bourne Mill 431 H4

Bradenham Village 430 F4

Bradley 430 C7

Braithwaite Hall 433 G4

Branscombe: The Old Bakery, Garden
and Estate 430 D7

Bredon Barn 430 E4

Bridge House 432 F4

Brockhampton Estate 430 E3

Bruton Dovecote 430 E6

Buckingham Chantry Chapel 430 F4

Buckland Abbey 430 C7

Buscot Old Parsonage 430 E4

Buscot Park 430 E4

Calke Abbey 430 F2

Canons Ashby 430 F3

Carlyle's House 431 G5

Cartmel Priory Gatehouse 432 F4

Castle Coole 432 A4

Castle Drogo 430 C7

Castle Ward 432 C4

Charlcote Park 430 E3

Chartwell 431 H5

Chastleton House 430 E4

Chedworth Roman Villa 430 E4

Cherryburn 433 G3

Chiddingstone Village 431 H6

Chipping Campden Market Hall
430 E4

Chirk Castle 430 D2

The Church House 430 C7

Cilgerran Castle 430 B4

Clandon Park 431 G5

Claydon 430 F4

Claife Viewing Station 432 F4

Clevedon Court 430 D5

Cliveden 431 G5

Clouds Hill 430 E7

Clumber Park 430 F1

Cobham Wood and Mausoleum 431 H5

Coggeshall Grange Barn 431 H4

Coleridge Cottage 430 D6

Coleton Fishacre 430 C7

Compton Castle 430 C7

Conwy Suspension Bridge 432 E6

Corfe Castle 430 E7

Cornish Mines and Engines 430 A8

Cotehele 430 C7

Coughton Court 430 E3

Cragside 433 G2

Croft Castle and Parkland 430 D3

Croome 430 E3

The Crown Bar 432 C3

Cushendun 432 C2

Cwmdu 430 C4

Cwmmau Farmhouse 430 D3

Dalton Castle 432 F5

Dapdune Wharf 431 G5

Derrymore House 432 B4

Derwent Island House 432 F4

Dinefwr 430 C4

Downhill Demesne and Hezlett House
432 B2

Duffield Castle 430 F1

Dudmaston 430 E3

Dunham Massey 433 G6

Dunstanburgh Castle 433 G2

Dunster Castle 430 C6

Dyffryn Gardens 430 D5

Dyrham Park 430 E5

Eastbury Manor House 431 H5

East Riddlesden Hall 433 G5

Elizabethan House Museum 431 I2

Erddig 430 D1

Farnborough Hall 430 F3

Felbrigg Hall, Gardens and Estate
431 I2

Fen Cottage and Workshop 431 H3

Fenton House and Garden 431 G5

Finch Foundry 430 C7

The Firs – Birthplace of Edward Elgar
430 E3

Flatford: Bridge Cottage 431 I4

The Fleece Inn 430 E4

Florence Court 432 A4

Fountains Abbey and Studley Royal
433 G5

Gawthorpe Hall 433 G5

George Inn 431 G5

Gibside 433 G3

Goddards 433 H5

Godolphin 430 A8

Grange Arch 430 E7

Grantham House 431 G2

Gray's Monument 431 G5

Gray's Printing Press 432 A3

Great Chalfield Manor 430 E5

Great Coxwell Barn 430 E5

Greenway 430 C7

The Greyfriars 430 E3

Greys Court 430 F5

Gunby Hall 430 H1

Hadrian's Wall and Housesteads Fort
433 G3

Hailes Abbey 430 E4

Ham House 431 G5

Hanbury Hall 430 E3

Hardman's House (Mr Hardman's
Photographic Studio) 432 F6

Hardwick 430 F1

Hardy Cottage 430 E7

Hardy Monument 430 D7

Hartwell House Hotel 430 F4

Hatchlands Park 431 G5

Hawford Dovecote 430 E3

Hawker's Hut 430 B6

Hawkshead Courthouse 432 F4

Hill Top 432 F4

Hinton Ampner 430 F6

Holnicote Estate 430 C5

The Homewood 431 G5

Horsey Windpump 431 I2

Horton Court 430 E5

Houghton Mill 431 G3

Hughenden 431 G4

Ickworth 431 H3

Ightham Mote 431 H5

Kedleston Hall 430 F2

Keld Chapel 432 F4

Killerton 430 C6

King John's Hunting Lodge 430 D5

King's Head 430 F4

Kingston Lacy 430 E6

Kinver Edge and the Rock Houses
430 E3

Kinwarton Dovecote 430 E3

Knightshayes 430 C6

Knole 431 H5

Knowles Mill 430 E3

The Kymin 430 D4

Lacock Abbey, Fox Talbot Museum and
Village 430 E5

Lamb House 431 H6

Lanhydrock 430 B7

Lavenham Guildhall 431 H3

Lawrence House 430 B7

Leith Hill Place 431 G6

Leith Hill Tower 431 G6

Letocetum Roman Baths and Museum
430 E2

Lindisfarne Castle 433 G1

Little Clarendon 430 E6

Little Moreton Hall 430 E1

Lizard Wireless Station 430 B8

Llanerchaeron 430 C3

Lodge Park 430 E4

Long Crendon Courthouse 430 F4

Loughwood Meeting House 430 D6

Lyme 433 G6

Lytes Cary Manor 430 D6

Lyveden 431 G3

Maister House 433 I5

Market House 430 E1

Melford Hall 431 H3

Middle Littleton Tithe Barn 430 E3

Middlethorpe Hall Hotel 433 H5

Mompesson House 430 E6

Monk's House 431 G6

Montacute House 430 D6

Morville Hall 430 E3

Moseley Old Hall 430 E2

Mottisfont 430 F6

Mount Grace Priory 433 H4

Mount Stewart 432 C3

Mr Straw's House 430 F1

Needles Old and New Batteries 430 F7

Nether Alderley Mill 433 G7

Newark Park 430 E5

Newtown Old Town Hall 430 F7

Nostell 433 H6

Nuffield Place 430 F5

Nunnington Hall 433 H4

Nymans 431 G6

Oakhurst Cottage 431 G6

The Old Coastguard Station 433 H4

The Old Manor, Norbury 430 E2

Old Soar Manor 431 H5

Orford Ness 431 I3

Ormesby Hall 433 H4

Osterley Park 431 G5

Overbeck's 430 C8

Owletts 431 H5

Oxburgh Hall 431 H2

Packwood House 430 E3

Patterson's Spade Mill 432 C3

Paycocke's 431 H4

Peckover House 431 H2

Penrhyn Castle 430 C1

Penshaw Monument 433 H3

Petworth House 431 G6

Pitstone Windmill 431 G4

Plas Newydd 430 C1

Plas yn Rhiw 430 B2

Polesden Lacey 431 G5

Powis Castle 430 D2

Priest's House, Easton on the Hill
431 G2

Priest's House, Muchelney 430 D6

Priory Cottages 430 F5

Quarry Bank 430 E1

Quebec House 431 H5

Rainham Hall 431 H5

Ramsey Abbey Gatehouse 431 G3

Red House 431 H5

Rosedene 430 E3

Rufford Old Hall 432 F6

St George's Guildhall 431 H2

St John's Jerusalem 431 H5

St Michael's Mount 430 A8

Saltram 430 C7

Sandham Memorial Chapel 430 F5

Scotney Castle 431 H6

Seaton Delaval Hall 433 G2

Shalford Mill 431 G5

Shaw's Corner 431 G4

Picture credits

2, 179, 180 left, 180 right: ©National Trust Images/Stuart Cox; 6, 13, 33, 34, 39, 40, 53, 86, 87, 94, 101, 120, 126, 128, 175, 178, 192, 193, 195 top, 195 bottom, 196–197, 210, 211, 214–215, 221, 227, 245, 253, 265, 278, 285, 300, 301, 321, 323, 332, 339, 343, 345, 352, 380 bottom, 395, 405, 426: ©National Trust Images/James Dobson; 12, 24, 25, 26, 35, 70, 91, 100, 113, 139 top, 140, 161, 162, 163, 164, 165 left, 165 right, 181 top, 200, 202, 241, 246, 247, 273, 276, 287, 294, 295, 297 right, 305, 307, 325, 334, 397: ©National Trust Images/John Hammond; 14, 158, 308: ©National Trust Images/Marianne Majerus; 15, 19, 38, 43, 50, 64, 92, 96, 99, 102, 106, 117, 123 top, 132, 135, 147 bottom, 148, 150, 154 top, 156 bottom, 185, 187, 191, 203, 207, 232–233, 239, 251, 279, 284, 288, 303, 309, 315, 330, 342 top, 370, 378: ©National Trust Images/Andrew Butler; 16–17, 46 bottom, 47, 69, 90, 104, 252 bottom, 286, 312, 314, 324, 331, 337, 374: ©National Trust Images/Dennis Gilbert; 18 top, 366, 407: ©National Trust Images/Cristian Barnett; 9, 18 bottom, 32, 41, 42, 44, 45, 49, 52, 68, 71, 81, 82, 95, 98, 116, 118, 133, 138 right, 146, 159, 167, 168, 169, 170, 181 bottom, 190, 198, 199, 204, 209 top, 222, 228, 229, 234, 244, 258, 260, 267, 269, 270, 272, 281, 290, 310 top, 316, 317 bottom, 318 bottom, 327, 336, 338, 342 bottom, 349, 350, 356, 357 bottom, 363, 377, 379: ©National Trust Images/Andreas von Einsiedel; 20, 46 top, 76, 268, 291, 317 top, 333, 375, 382 top, 382 bottom, 384 bottom, 425: ©National Trust Images/Arnhel de Serra; 21, 30–31, 61 top, 80, 144, 188, 252 top, 262, 362: ©National Trust Images/Matthew Antrobus; 22, 79, 111, 137, 138 left, 174 top, 177, 208, 224 bottom, 271, 311, 358–359, 390, 393, 396, 403 top, 403 bottom, 429: ©National Trust Images/John Miller; 23, 36, 37, 62, 93, 112, 125, 127, 141 top, 141 bottom, 142, 149, 171, 172, 173, 174 bottom, 256, 282, 340, 354, 361, 383, 383, 384 top, 385, 389, 398, 406, 408 top: ©National Trust Images/Chris Lacey; 11, 27, 78, 83, 103, 147 top, 205, 206, 209 bottom, 216, 329, 351, 400, 411, 412, 415, 418: ©National Trust Images/John Millar; 28, 357 top: ©National Trust Images/Derrick E. Witty; 29: ©National Trust Images/Rachael Warren; 48: ©National Trust Images/Alex Black; 54, 88, 97 top, 134, 143, 194, 220, 296, 348: ©National Trust Images/Rupert Truman; 55, 58–59, 73, 119, 129, 136, 156 top, 212, 289, 318 top, 381: ©National Trust Images/Nadia Mackenzie; 56, 63, 74, 115, 124, 186, 189, 230, 248–249, 275, 328, 371, 420: ©National Trust Images/Robert Morris; 57: ©National Trust Images/Samantha Burgess; 60, 259: ©National Trust Images/Justin Minns; 61 bottom: ©National Trust Images/Gesine Garz; 65: ©National Trust Images/George Wright; 66, 306: ©National Trust Images/David Dixon; 72, 84, 319: ©National Trust Images/Chris Jonas; 75: ©National Trust Images/Andreas von Einsiedel (reproduced by kind permission of Lord Belmore); 77, 264 top, 264 bottom, 364, 410: ©National Trust Images; 85: ©National Trust Images/Ciaran McCrickard; 89: ©National Trust Images/Ian Shaw; 97 bottom: ©National Trust Images/Paul Mogford; 105, 151 top, 151 bottom, 201: ©National Trust Images/Mark Bolton; 107: ©National Trust Images/Simon Tranter; 108–109: ©National Trust Images/Don Bishop; 114, 277, 353: ©National Trust Images/Gary Cosham; 121: ©National Trust Images/John Hubble; 122, 423: ©National Trust Images/Paul Harris; 123 bottom, 293: ©National Trust Images/David Noton; 130: National Trust Images/James Aitken; 139 bottom, 298, 299, 394, 413, 414, 421: ©National Trust Images/David Sellman; 145, 386: ©National Trust Images/Trevor Ray Hart; 152, 231: ©National Trust Images/Mark Sunderland; 154 bottom, 155: ©National Trust Images/Aerial-Cam; 157, 219 left, 219 right: ©National Trust Images/Nick Guttridge; 166: ©National Trust Images/Brian && Nina Chapple; 176: ©National Trust Images/Val Corbett; 182–183, 404: ©National Trust Images/Hugh Mothersole; 213, 217, 274, 408 bottom: ©National Trust Images/Nick Meers; 218, 261, 428: ©National Trust Images/Mike Selby; 223: ©National Trust Images/Caroline Arber; 224 top: ©National Trust Images/Neil Campbell-Sharp; 225: ©National Trust Images/W H Rendell; 226, 399: ©National Trust Images/Derek Croucher; 236: ©National Trust Images/Elaine Hill; 237: National Trust Images/Geoffrey Frosh; 238, 313, 392: ©National Trust Images/Andy Williams; 240 left, 240 right, 344, 347: ©National Trust Images/Hilary Daniel; 242–243: ©National Trust Images/Freya Raby; 250: ©National Trust Images/Clive Nichols; 254, 380 top: ©National Trust Images/Bill Batten; 257: ©National Trust Images/Nick Dougan; 263: ©National Trust Images/David Levenson; 266: ©National Trust Images/Gwenno Parry; 280: ©National Trust Images/Erik Pelham; 283: ©National Trust Images/Derek Hatton; 297 left: ©National Trust Images/A C Cooper; 302: ©National Trust Images/Linda Goudie; 304: ©National Trust Images/John Blake; 310 bottom: ©National Trust Images/McCoy Wynne; 320: National Trust Images/John Bethell; 335: ©National Trust Images/Joe Wainwright; 365: ©National Trust Images/Robin Forster; 367, 401, 417: ©National Trust Images/Joe Cornish; 368: ©National Trust Images/Martin Hailey; 369: ©National Trust Images/Tim Imrie; 372, 373: ©National Trust Images/Paul Raeside; 387: ©National Trust Images/Clive Boursnell; 388: ©National Trust Images/Steven Barber; 391: ©National Trust Images/Eric Macdonald; 409: ©National Trust Images/Rob Coleman; 416: ©National Trust Images/Scott King; 419: ©National Trust Images/Tamsin Holmes; 422: ©National Trust Images/Dougie Holden; 427: ©National Trust Images/PJ Howsam; 428 bottom: ©National Trust Images/Phil Ripley.

Index

The National Trust

Whether you're interested in gardens, castles, wildlife, places linked to famous events and people, looking for a new coastal path to walk or just somewhere peaceful to relax and enjoy a cup of tea, National Trust membership gives you a wide variety of things to do, as often as you like.

Join today and you can explore over 500 special places. What's more, you'll be helping to care for them forever, for everyone. As a member you'll enjoy free entry to hundreds of places, park free at most of our car parks and receive an informative handbook full of places to discover.

Visit www.nationaltrust.org.uk or phone 0344 800 1895 for more details.